THE ART OF EMBROIDERY

in the 90's

by

COLEMAN SCHNEIDER

Coleman Schneider, Publisher
20 Stony Brook Rd.,
P.O. Box 625
Tenafly, NJ 07670, USA

Library of Congress catalog Card Number: 91-91165
International Standard Book Number: 0-9601662-4-6

To My Wife and Friend

Yvonne

Who Allows Me The
Freedom To Create
All Things.

FORWARD

Lace and embroidery are as old as recorded history. Excavations, drawings and tombs all contain references to wearing apparel adorned with embroideries. There is evidence that ancient Chinese, Egyptian, Greek, Persian and Roman emperors, as well as court people, wore clothing with ornamental stitching (embroidery). Fine ornamental needlework was reserved for those who could afford it and different areas produced embroideries that were native to their culture and art.

Lace, by the end of the 16th century, had become an important part of costume; and indeed, was the ultimate status symbol. Again, technique varied from country to country.

Despite its long and colorful history, little has been written about this fascinating art and history and how what was available only to royalty is now available to all. In 1968, after exhaustive research, Coleman Schneider set out to rectify this situation and wrote his definitive book, "Machine Made Embroidery", which was very well received.

In 1978, he updated and expanded it to include the innovations in creating beautiful laces and embroideries and entitled it "Embroidery: Schiffli and Multi-head." Now, some dozen years later, he is again updating this important reference book.

We, in the Embroidery & Lace Industry, are delighted that he is doing so, for there is much to learn about this unique industry. His is an easy to read style and his book provides added insight in what goes into making the lovely things that adorn their homes or enhance their apparel.

To Mr. Schneider goes our heartfelt thanks.

I. Leonard Seiler
Executive Director
Schiffli Lace & Embroidery Mfrs. Assoc., Inc.
North Bergen, NJ, USA

INTRODUCTION

The fascinating art of embroidery, which was once reserved for the wealthy, was in such demand in the 1800's that great inventive minds sought ways of fulfilling the demands created by its popularity. Hand work was employing thousands upon thousands who labored tediously with needle and thread to complete the orders received. Then, during the industrial revolution, new principles and machines were devised to emulate the hand work. These new machines copied the hand crafts and produced them economically enough so the majority of the population could afford fashionable and stylish embroidered clothing.

The industry exists, based on the fashions of the times, in all advanced cultures. It has seen great days, it has seen bad days. During all this time, embroiderers with machines have continuously tried to improve production, quality, and create new uses for embroidery. In all cases they have succeeded.

This is a study of the manufacture of embroidery by machine, how it developed, what has happened since its inception more than 100 years ago, where it is now and where it is going. In short, its evolution.

It is a fascinating trade. There is constant developing, experimenting, designing. For as sure as one season ends, styles change, another evolves, and the cycle goes its full course to return at a later date with greater demand.

This study might seem technical. However, complete books could be written about some of the subjects discussed. It is constructed to enlighten the fashion industry and users of embroidery of the possibilities of creative style and design without expecting them to become experts.

Many of the terms in everyday embroidery jargon come from the country which became the heart of the machine embroidery industry, Switzerland. A wheel is a radeli; lace is aetz; a thread cam is a fadenleiter. I have used and written the familiar words as embroiderers do, phonetically. It will be impossible to find some words in a standard dictionary, but you will find them in the Glossary. There are terms, machines, and processes which exist in almost no other industry.

There is little reference material; nothing to go on except the everyday experience within the trade. Knowledge came from working with others who learned by doing and from family members who were willing to divulge closely held secrets.

It is fascinating; it is a business one can love; it creates a continuous challenge; it's always changing. It's a traditional art; it's creation; it's mechanical; it's electronic; it's difficult and at the same time it's easy. It's working with your hands, your head and your heart. It can offer the greatest satisfaction.

I have enlarged upon the 1978 edition, "Embroidery: Schiffli and Multi-head". The advances in the industry from the beginning of the embroidery machine age in the early 1800's until 1978 have doubled in the last 12 years. The industry is more diversified, not held to one geographical area, not held to the production by one type machine. Design is not as traditional, but enhanced by new generations of better educated, and dedicated people. The issuing in of the electronic age created possibilities that no one could imagine 20 years ago. That also opens the door for the next 20 years and beyond, and by no means can we see the end of this expansion of knowledge as it applies to the embroiderer and his equipment.

Just writing this new book and researching the new equipment, methods and possibilities for embroidery, leaves one overwhelmed by where we are and where we can go.

本書為首次介紹九十年代有關刺繡最詳盡完整之著作，內容豐富，涵蓋大型刺繡機，各種機型之多頭電腦刺繡機，週邊設備；及其所繡圖案設計等之圖解亦均作深入淺出之說明。

葉德昭謹誌

ACKNOWLEDGEMENTS

The accumulation of information herein and in previous embroidery books can be credited to hundreds of people in and out of the industry. No guides existed for the business of embroidery, manufacturing or the design and pattern making of embroidery before my publication of "Machine Made Embroidery" in 1968.

Publishers shied away from publishing anything about the embroidery industry; now after two successful books about embroidery in 1968 and 1978 (which sold out completely) and many new books on the horizon by other well informed authors you would think an updated essay in a field that has expanded more than 1000% would be a publisher's delight. Not so. This volume was also refused by the largest scholastic publisher in the world. Therefore, once again this book is being written, published and marketed by the author with three times as many copies as his previous books on embroidery.

Some information from the two previous books has been included; the sources were once again checked.

Information has been freely offered by all segments of the industry. Once again I have to thank the major embroidery manufacturers around the world that provide the beautiful embroidery we all use and wear: the talented Swiss, Austrian, Japanese and American, industries where embroidery production flourishes; the German engineering that improved the existing mechanical ideas; the many in America where the first automat was developed and where the electronic age was born.

Special thanks from the beginning of this book goes to Leonard Seiler, Executive Director of the American Schiffli Industry. All of the machinery manufacturers have been only too happy to send in information on their existing machinery and answered numerous requests for additional information. Visits to most of the companies have helped me to understand their equipment better.

Thanks also to Leon Hotz, Oscar Thalparpan, Hans Wallimann and Otmar Stillhard of the Saurer Company who helped greatly with information on their new equipment; Erik Schoenenberger, Al Dimant, and Thomas Albiez who offered much help with new computer techniques; Herb Petermann of Schlesinger Industries who was there again to dig up some long lost photos and whose explanations of some machines were essential to complete parts of this work; Dominic and Ken Golia who gave much support and insight into the possibilities of Multi-head machines at a time when all electronic knowledge was exploding; Minoru Goda, President of the Japan Embroidery Association, whose ideas have changed the face of embroidery world-wide, and who translated my last book into Japanese; Bruce Anton with yarns, Geoffrey Macpherson and his son Neal for information about world markets and the Barudan machines; and Paul Levine of Hirsch. The author's mentor in punching was Jimmy Habeeb and in designing, Paul Schuler; this information is strictly from experience. Design credits go to Robert Schlaepfer, whose innovation, style and quality have enhanced the garments of the best couturiers in the world.

In 45 years of business experience the author has had the pleasure of a working partnership with Al Stahnke in punching, with Joe Brody in emblem manufacturing, and Ben Amoruso merchandising and negotiating, with Sid Hauser in marketing, and Bob Bucher in licensing.

The assistance of Bob Nietert at U.S. Customs and James Bucher with copyrights and trademarks were invaluable.

Special thanks go to Meryl Schneider, the author's daughter who was willing to edit and put this work in an easily readable form. Thanks also to Paul Radziunas, Walter Floriani, and Deborah Jones.

Credits to Bill Childs and Marty DeSantis for work, assistance and encouragement in developing the first embroidery computer punch system. Also to Ron Ball and the Advertising Specialty Institute with assistance for the cover and Alphonse the photographer.

Needless to say, there are many more whose names have not specifically been mentioned, but to all the author's sincerest thanks and appreciation.

CONTENTS

CHAPTER I
SCHIFFLI EMBROIDERY

CHAPTER II
SCHIFFLI MACHINES

CHAPTER III
MULTI-HEAD MACHINES

CHAPTER IV
THE MULTI-HEAD MACHINE MANUFACTURERS

CHAPTER V
DESIGNING & PATTERN MAKING

CHAPTER VI
PUNCHING

CHAPTER VII
EMBLEMS & DIRECT EMBROIDERY

CHAPTER VIII
COSTING

CHAPTER IX
THE BUSINESS OF EMBROIDERY

CHAPTER X
THE LEGALITIES OF EMBROIDERY

CHAPTER XI
THE POLITICS OF EMBROIDERY

APPENDIX

SEE SUPPLEMENT
PAGE 445

CHAPTER I

A BRIEF HISTORY OF EMBROIDERY

Embroidery is a true art form. The painter has his pallet, the sculptor his clay, the engraver his metals and the woodcarver his wood. Embroidery is as much an expression of man's aesthetic talents as painting, sculpture, engraving, or carving. But the embroiderer has hundreds of combinations with which to work. He starts with his basic fabric, which alone can be a work of art, with its constructions of knitted and woven textures. Anything that a needle and thread can penetrate, even plastic and leather, can be embroidered.

What is embroidery? It is the addition of art and design by use of needle and thread to an existing fabric.

The embroiderer can use threads of cotton, wool, silk, leather or man made fibers in a multitude of colors, textures and thicknesses to form designs or to attach decorations such as appliques, mirrors, pearls, beads, or glass. He can copy art forms already established in other media, modern, ancient and between. He has three dimensional color and texture and with use of all the above mentioned forms of art, he has an unlimited mode of expression. While making any fabric more beautiful, embroidery adorns wearing apparel with art and tells a story.

The idea of embroidery is 'painting' with needle and thread, revealing a story on fabric. The basic element is the stitch. Like painting, embroidery reflects intellectual, psychological, traditional and national trends.

There are many good studies of ancient embroidery, its history and development. They are listed in the bibliography. I will not dwell on information contained in these earlier volumes. But as basis for this book, let us take a short look at embroidery from its origins to the introduction of the machine.

No one can trace the origin of embroidery. Suffice it to say that it began in the East perhaps along with the development of languages which began in the same areas. Cloth was made, threads were known, art was an expression of affluence and therefore, someone adorned a garment with a different color of thread or design to make it distinctive. The beginnings of recorded history told of embroidery in China and India. These traditions are carried on to this day. It has retained its primitive roots and cultural eminence even while improving and innovating designs and methods.

Western cultures were introduced to this art form through trading. Egypt records many forms of embroidery in its sculpture and crypts, and actual samples exist in mummy cloths. In Greece, Homer mentions garments embroidered with networks of gold.

The main use and expression of embroidery was in the Near East, through which it reached its peak during the Byzantine empire.

The Jews learned the art while captives in Egypt. Many descriptions appear in the book of Exodus and throughout the Bible. Greeks and Romans returned from their conquests with robes of rich embroidery never before seen in their empires.

The early Christian church was to become the main promoter of the art of embroidery in the West. It unfolded religious mysteries to the unlettered masses, in beauty, form and texture. It enriched ecclesiastical furniture and apparel.

In the 7th century Mohammedanism breathed new life into fabrics at a time when the Byzantine influence was waning. Nomadic Arabs delighted in embroidered tents, saddles, boots and scabbards. However, from the 9th to the 16th centuries the majority of embroidery was devoted to ecclesiastical purposes.

It was during the 12th century that the Crusaders, who found many examples of embroidery in the Holy Land, used embroidery to depict heraldic devices, which greatly helped its development in the west. As its range and technique developed, embroidery became widely used for apparel.

When England became a leader in embroidery in the 12th century, guilds were developed to oversee instruction and the quality of the work being done.

French embroidery expanded during the reign of Louis XI, a patron of the arts. During the Renaissance, Francis I commissioned Raphael (1483-1520) to design an embroidery, now on view in the Cluny Museum. Louis XIV, another patron, used it lavishly at the royal court at Versailles. It dazzled Europe in its grandiose style. Men and women were equally adorned and style demanded the extensive use of lace and embroidery.

The Germans were individualistic in style, using wool embroideries following religious themes of the times. They became design conscious, and in the 19th century established a school of needlework in Krefeld.

Germany was famous for its Dresden lace, made exclusively on cambric, drawn stitching pulling cotton goods together or completely covering the goods.

Swiss linens became popular in the 13th century. They were famous for their classic white on white motifs.

The Italian trade started in Palermo in the 10th century, and it soon gained an international reputation for its silks, brocades and velvets. By the 16th century it had become the design and supply center of Europe. Peasant blouses of cross stitch were popular in many variations. Embroiderers of Abruzzi worked their stitches in red cotton on coarse linens.

Spain's embroidery was influenced by the Romans, the Moors, and later the Incas. They used a high degree of art, introduced by the Moors, who most likely developed black and white embroidery. Gold rings and spangles were used to a great degree. Spain soon surpassed Italy as the center of embroidery.

Portugal was influenced by embroidery of the east because of its seafaring explorations.

Flanders also became a rival of the Italians, influenced by the artists of the Flemish and Dutch schools. Some of the most magnificent embroideries of the period were made there.

Eastern Europe developed in the same manner, each region evolving a particular style using base cloths, colors and yarns obtained locally. Art was individualistic, but the occasions on which embroidery was used were always special. Ceremonies always demanded the finest linens and apparel. Weddings, funerals and the church were the greatest influences on design. Embroidery became part of a woman's dowry and was passed on from generation to generation. The Czechs introduced a wide diversity of stitch forms. The Hungarians used leather. The Nordics used geometric forms in abstract, which had a great influence on Rumanian embroideries. All of these created a historical chronicle of events and showed a love of color and design.

Norway had a reverence for craftsmanship, using cross stitches and flat stitches in mostly blues from local dyes. Russian embroidery, in the north, emulated the Finns with gold and silver, while in the south the influence was Eastern. The Danish specialized in white embroidery, while the Icelandic embroidered the northern lights, midnight sun, mountains and animals. Brides in Iceland wore black with gold and silver embroidered sleeves and collars.

Swedish embroidery was characterized by designs for furnishings as well as ceremonial occasions in folk art. The southern part of Sweden was influenced by Europe, the northern part by the East because of its trade. Cushions embroidered with pewter were popular.

America has added to the art by the introduction of crewel-type embroideries borrowed from England and made with home spun yarns. Children were taught embroidery by sewing alphabets, scenes and map drawing by hand. America was the home of the "sampler". Much embroidery was done on burlap depicting folk lore and contemporary life. It was a mode of relaxation.

Quilting parties or 'bees' were a means of meeting.

Candlewick embroidery was popular, with such motifs as the tree of life, star of Texas and the hour glass. Patches and crazy quilts were made with much decorative stitching. Bethlehem, Pennsylvania was the American center of much of the skillful needlework of the 1700 and 1800s. Many religious buildings were beautified with hanging embroideries. In Central and South America, before the arrival of the Europeans, the Mayas, Aztecs and Incas used embroidery lavishly. Some of this embroidery has never been rivaled.

Embroidery was always a tedious craft, extremely time consuming and expensive, and therefore exclusively available to the rich. It was time for the introduction, during the industrial revolution, of some method to stitch embroidery economically and make it available to the masses.

LACES

Laces are plain or ornamental net work consisting of interwoven threads, plaited, looped or twisted so as to form a beautiful textured design. "Lace" or "net" are sometimes used synonymously, although "net" is usually employed for plain, unpatterned mesh. Lacey effects existed in various forms of embroidery. A true lace is one in which only the thread construction remains.

Laces as we know them today were unknown before the 15th century. Their greatest development was in Burano Italy, near Venice, which became the largest center in the world. Embroidery was made on parchment, which was later removed leaving an open work of threads. The name "guipure" comes from France, where laces were made by twisting silk around another thread or a core, made on a pillow or frame. In many cases, a ground work of nets forming a filet were made and designs added. Nets formed designs of squares or diamonds. It was an offspring of embroidery where laces were used to imitate cut works, but later developed into an art of its own.

Many well known lace centers developed in Europe, making characteristically regional designs. In each instance, the laces are different enough to be categorized by the name of the district in which they were made. As the popularity of laces increased, so did the cost. Lace became so expensive that it was relegated almost exclusively to the rich and the church.

In the French courts, laces were used for cuffs and cravats along with embroidery decorating the pants and jackets. Workers were enticed to migrate from Venice to France to build the lace industry there. Labor shortages were so acute at times that departing workers were sometimes threatened and their families imprisoned.

Hand made laces can be duplicated by various lace and embroidery machines, and as well by knitted and woven form.

THE DEVELOPMENT OF LACE AND EMBROIDERY MACHINES

Machines were sought to meet the demand for embroidery. A net machine was developed by an Englishman, Robert Brown. The ideas were improved upon by Robert Heathcoat and in 1809 a patent was issued for a bobbin net machine which became the basis for the first true lace machine. The principles of John Levers allowed, in 1813, a design to be made at the same time the net was produced. Thus we had the first machine to imitate and reproduce this art form.

As early as 1768, attempts were made by Carl Weisenthal in Germany to produce embroideries by mechanical means. In 1828, Josua Heilman produced the first hand loom embroidery machine, built by Koechlin of Mulhouse. It was sold to Houldsworth in Manchester, England, in 1829, with the patent rights. The first machine in Switzerland was purchased by Francois Mange in 1829, for his factory in St. Gallen. He retired in 1839, leaving the machine to his son-in-law, Bartholame Rittmeyer, who gave it to his son Franz Rittmeyer, who made many changes with the aid of Antoine Volgar.

A pantograph was attached to the frame holding the goods, and by tracing the design with the pantograph and moving it while the needles were out of the goods, then making one stitch, etc., the hand motions of embroidery were copied. They had reversed the motion of the hand where the needle moved to form the design; here the needles were fixed and the goods moved to form the design.

The spread of machine made embroidery until this time was very small. The machines were shown at the Paris exposition of 1834, where they were awarded the gold medal of the legion of honor. These machines were fascinating to watch and always drew crowds. They produced mostly ribbons, which were then in demand, but the market was well covered by hand embroiderers and not much came of their production.

Rittmeyer and Volger made many changes but kept the French zoll measurement for the spacing of the needle repeats. They changed the enlargement size from four to six times, which gave more accuracy to the finished work. They also enlarged the frames, allowing more space to stitch larger embroideries. These and other improvements were such a success that Franz Rittmeyer is considered the inventor of the first practical embroidery machine. He and Volger enjoyed a monopoly until 1880. The handloom machines were operated completely by hand.

The firm of Schnoor and Steinhouser in Plauen, Saxony (Germany) began to develop a similar machine, but did not complete it until the 1870's.

Rittmeyer's machine utilized 180 needles that were pointed on both ends with a hole in the center for a length of thread. The goods were spanned on an upright frame which was moved by a pantograph to form the design as the needles were pushed through on a fixed track. The needle duplicated the motions of the hand embroiderer. The needles were threaded by hand, driven through the goods and held by a clipper. On the reverse side another clipper grabbed the needle and drew it through the goods, thus tightening the thread. The frame was moved by the pantograph, the needle once again was driven through the goods to its starting point. The process was repeated, mechanically forming the design. The motion of the fabric rather than that of the needle duplicated the embroideries that were then made by hand.

Handloom Machine

The machine was an immediate success. An auxiliary machine was developed by Victor Kobler in 1884 to thread the needles automatically. The number of colors required in a design were not important because the embroidered design was stitched with lengths of thread which continuously required rethreading. It was just as simple to replace a thread with a different color. The hand loom machine was extremely productive in comparison with other production methods and placed Switzerland in the forefront of embroidery production.

Handloom machine manufacture grew in Germany, from the two machines imported by Schnook and Steinhauser in 1860 to 42 units by 1862, and 2325 by 1882.

It is possible that some handloom machines are still in production 140 years after their introduction. They would still be hand powered. They have not been built since the early 1900's and may exist only for certain specialties.

THE DEVELOPMENT AND HISTORY OF THE SCHIFFLI MACHINE

The Schiffli machine is also known as a shuttle machine. The word "Schiffli" derives from the shape of the shuttle, which looks like a small boat. The word Schiffli in the Swiss-German vernacular means "small boat".

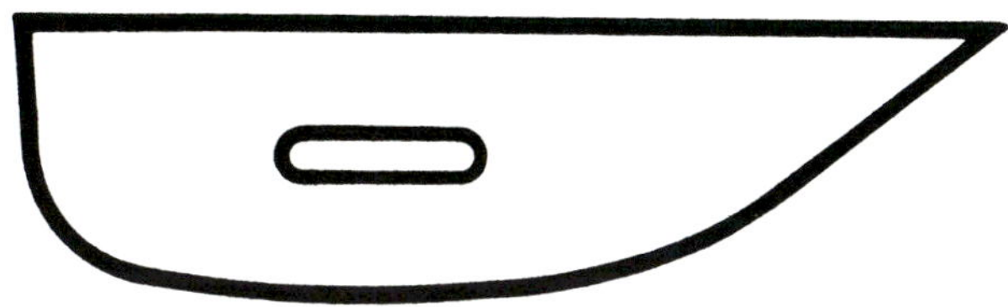

The Schiffli Shuttle

Isaak Groebli (1822-1917) of Oberuzwyl, Switzerland, is considered the inventor of the Schiffli machine. He was trained as a weaver, starting his career at the age of 11. He was schooled in Lyon in the art of jacquard weaving and soon became a master. Intrigued by the sight of the handloom embroidery machine, he saw vast possibilities for improvement. The punched patterns that direct the Schiffli frame are based on the jacquard principal used in weaving. This was the first machine to use perforated cards for design reproduction.

Basile Bouchon, a Frenchman, was the first in 1725, with the use of his new design, a series of punched wooden slats that controlled the movements of bunches of looped string, that formed the design in weaving. M. Falcon made additional improvements in 1728, but Jacquard perfected the system in 1801. This proved so successful that in 1803 it was made state property. By 1812 there were 11,000 jacquard looms operating in France. More refinements were made by Jacques de Vaucaison whose basic idea still prevails.

As the jacquard weaving industry slowed around 1860, Groebli became more interested in the handloom business, which was flourishing. Sewing machines were becoming popular at the same time, and he immediately saw the possibility of combining the two operations in a single machine. The first task was to develop a machine that could use a continuous thread from a spool, since one of the disadvantages of the handloom machine was the constant rethreading of short lengths of thread. This would greatly improve production.

Handloom had duplicated hand stitching by moving one thread back and forth through the goods. The sewing machine used two threads, a front yarn and a bobbin. The front yarn was on a spool, the bobbin yarn a small spool of thread encased in a shuttle. By using the two interlocking threads instead of one, Groebli revolutionized the manufacture of embroidery.

The goods to be embroidered would have to be spanned on a frame and held firm to stitch. A needle bar was loaded, set to embroider simultaneously with bobbins on the other side of the goods, like a row of sewing machines turned on their ends. A pantograph guided the frame to form the pattern as with the handloom machine. Speed was not essential since many needles were working at one time thus cutting costs tremendously. The idea was great but far from reaching its potential.

To prove the idea, Groebli proceeded to build a one needle model, inserting the needle in the goods and having a helper pull it through on the other side, passing a bobbin through the loop that was formed thus making a lock stitch. Stitch by stitch, he formed an embroidered design which he used to find financial backing.

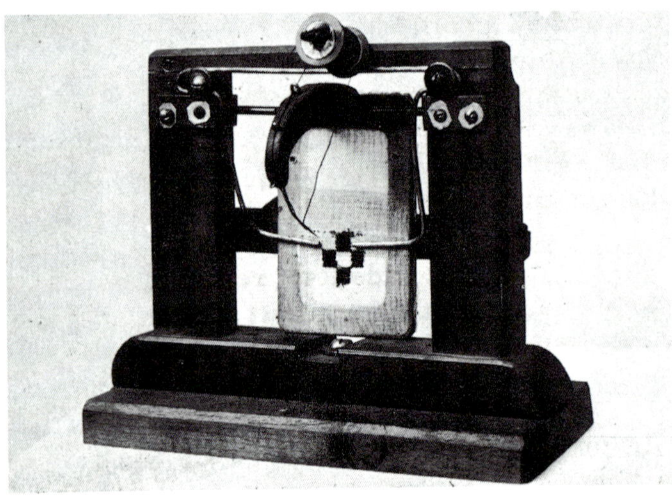

Groebli's Demonstration Model

The first to show interest in his design was Mr. M. Wehrli, who offered space within his factory for the first experimental machine of 24 needles, 1½ yards long. A wooden frame, pantograph, a bar of needles and mechanical cams were put together in a few months. By 1864 he had one needle working properly; the balance were duplicated one after the other. At this time, because of financial problems, the project was taken over by Mr. Reiter, a machine manufacturer from Winterthur, who had become interested in it.

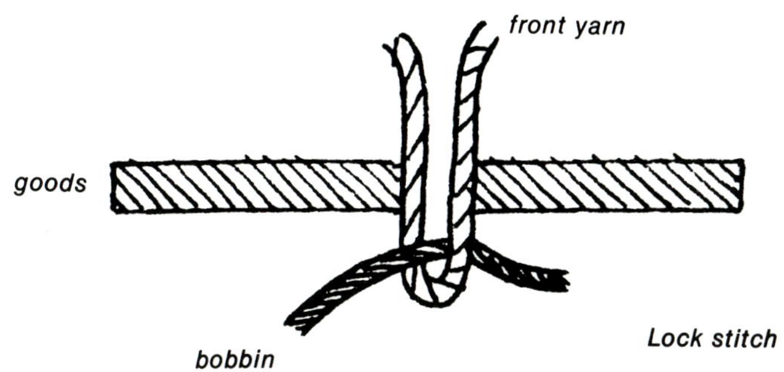

Lock Stitch Formation

The greatest task was developing a workable shuttle. The sewing machine had used a round spool with thread inside the case, but this was difficult to adapt. The Schiffli shuttle case had two spindles on which the thread was wound, and a spring was added to control the tension, or flow of the yarn. The spool unwound as the thread was drawn out.

The more thread the bobbin could hold the less down time required for rewinding new bobbins, so it was imperative to make the bobbin as large as possible. To produce the most embroidery on a piece of goods demanded that the needles be close together. This in turn required a smaller bobbin with sufficient thread. Small spools of thread would not work. Finally, a shuttle was developed that would unwind within itself and the spinning bobbin was eliminated. No spindles were required leaving more space for yarn. This modified shuttle ran horizontally on a slide between the needles. The stroke had to be small due to limited space.

They could stitch the most intricate designs with this machine and continued to improve quality and eliminate problems. A major problem had been stitching blatt stitches, which are long satin type stitches, because of the shuttle motion. They redesigned the shuttle with points on either end which worked by catching the loop each time, eliminating dropped stitches.

The shuttles were further developed, redesigned with one pointed end and the shuttle holding box tilted upward, holding the shuttle at an angle. The shuttle could then be enlarged allowing more thread to be loaded.

1865 saw the advent of the standard model Reiter (Schiffli) machine of 4 ½ yards in length. They continued to produce embroidery, adding eyelets by hand to make boring type work. The speed was 28 revolutions per minute. Stocks began to pile up while orders were scarce, and once again consideration was given to abandoning the project. Mr. Steigermeyer, a merchandiser, bought all the goods and gave them direction in design.

At the Paris world exhibition of 1867, the first products of the Schiffli machine were shown and were awarded the "Medal of Recognition". At the time the market for embroidery was again depressed, so the machines were again moved to a factory of Mr. Wehrli's in St. Gallen, while experimentation continued. As fashions changed again, all machines began to run full production and, as more machines were required, they moved to a new factory in Winterthur. The company of Wulflingen was formed, and a total of 20 machines were soon in production. Once again fashions changed and business slowed, giving Groebli's group a chance for more experimentation with different fabrics and types of yarns.

1873 saw another award for progress at the Vienna world exhibition.

Alphonse H. Kursheedt

Isaac Groebli

J. Arnold Groebli

The firm of Gibson Brothers & Co., in Glasgow, Scotland, placed the first order, for 14 machines, followed in 1875 by the Kursheedt Company of New York. Steiger & Cie, of Paris and Ikle Freres bought 18 each. The company manufacturing the machines was known as Reiter & Cie, of Winterthur. It was apparent that the machines were much more readily accepted by foreigners than by the Swiss themselves.

By 1877 the machine had been extended to 5 yards and stitched at 40 rpm. In the late 1870s, tulle embroideries became fashionable and the demand for machines grew. Saurer and Sons of Arbon, Switzerland, began building Schiffli machines of 4 ½ yard length and 32 rpm in 1878, as the demand for tulle embroideries soared. Adolph Saurer Company had contributed much to the handloom machine's development since 1867. They introduced a continuous thread machine in 1868, handkerchief frames in 1879 and a braiding machine in 1884.

In Zurich in 1883 three types of Schiffli machines were exhibited: Reiter of Winterthur, Saurer of Arbon, and Martini and Tanner of Frauenfeld, Switzerland. Both Saurer and Martini and Tanner were well known companies for their manufacture of handloom machines.

Saurer Cam Disc Schiffli Machine

As production grew, prices for embroidery decreased. The Swiss formed an Embroidery Association of Manufacturers to control to some degree the prices of embroidery, compensate labor and unemployment, and to exact penalties from manufacturers who did not adhere to the prices. As business slowed again, this was abandoned and many of the machines were scrapped. Mr. Groebli developed the festoon attachment to reinforce scallops, but due to the business slow down little attention was paid to this achievement.

1882 saw Franz Rittmeyer develop another festoon attachment for scallops, and Mr. Oettli a boring device.

Tulle embroideries, which imitated lace, were still very popular. These designs were embroidered on a net fabric, which was a simple operation at this time for the Schiffli machines. Another embroidery made by hand, which was difficult to imitate by sewing machines or handloom machines, was petit point. Schiffli filled the gap with an extreme sharpness of design.

The Vogtlandischer Machine Works AGE (known as Vomag) had begun building Schiffli machines in Plauen, Saxony, by 1880. They added many improvements. First was the oblique movement of the shuttle, which allowed more thread to be wound in the shuttle case and increased the speed of the stitching process. Boring and festoon devices were added. They changed the name of the machine to 'schnellaufer' meaning high speed, since their speed surpassed that of the Swiss machines.

Herman Dietrich was the developer of the 'aetzing' process in 1887, which imitated hand lace. Designs were embroidered on a fragile fabric which could be eliminated after embroidering, by heat or an acid wash, leaving only the stitched thread, as in true lace.

The Saxon company, Vomag, soon became the leader of Schiffli machine manufacturers, forcing the others to improve their machinery designs. Many Plauen machines were being sold in Switzerland until Saurer's 1878 introduction of the 6¾ yard machine, 50% longer and therefore, 50% more productive. This then became the standard length for cotton goods.

Even though the principles of the Schiffli machine grew from the knowledge and experimentation with the sewing machine, it was still some 20 years before the sewing machine could stitch embroidery successfully.

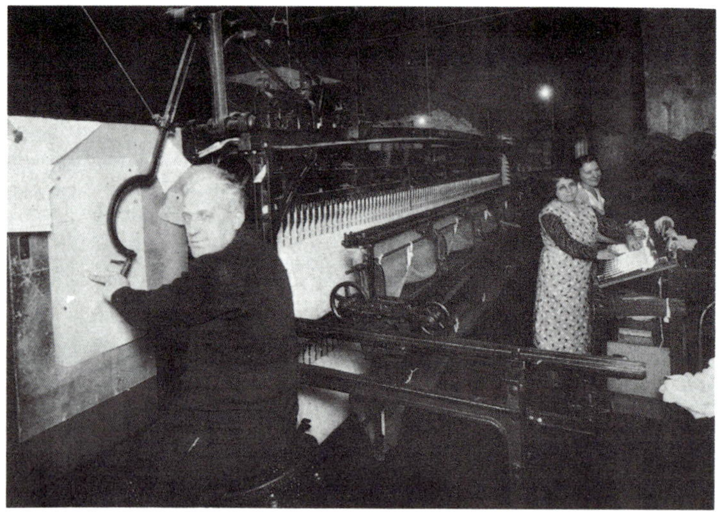

Framing and Stitching on the Handloom Machine

The first patents for the Schiffli machine had been issued in Germany in 1869. This took place before the first patents applied for by Mr. Groebli, since Switzerland only began issuing patents in 1888, his patent was dated June 29, 1889.

Mr. Kursheedt of New York traveled to Switzerland where he first saw the handloom machines. He became so fascinated with them that he immediately ordered 12 from the St. Georgen machine works. They were delivered in 1873, accompanied by Jacob Klaus as machinist. A subsequent visit to Switzerland in 1875 acquainted Kursheedt with Schiffli machines, and he immediately ordered them from the Reiter company. He also bought the patent rights for the U.S.A., which he held until 1904. Arnold Groebli, Isaak's son, was sent along as machinist and he and Jacob Klaus remained in the United States to develop the first Schiffli automat attached to an embroidery machine.

Some of the costs of the development of the Schiffli automat attached to this machine were borne by the Kursheedt Company itself.

The action for boring, starting and stopping of the stitching (needle roller in and out) and frame suspension were designed and built in New York. These are the basic forms of the Schiffli machines as we know them today.

The American company of Loeb and Schoenfeld was operating 40 machines in Rorschach, Switzerland in 1882; all were 6/4 Saurer pantographs. 1887 saw the first 4/4 machine, introduced by the Vogtlandischer Machine Works in Plauen, Germany. This is now the world standard repeat for Schiffli machines. The machines at this time operated at 85 stitches per minute and included a boring device.

The first mechanical automat was operating in New York in 1890, but it took another 6 years to develop a punching system for this mechanical device. The automat 'read' a paper tape patterned after the jacquard device where punched holes allowed certain measured frame movements, thus replacing the stitcher.

The Groebli Automat

Later, Jacob Klaus left the Kursheedt Company to form his own company, building handloom machines in the U.S.A.

Other pantograph machines were developed and built as competition grew. Kappel in Chemnitz, Germany, introduced a machine stitching 85 rpm in 1893 and by 1895 the speed was at 90 rpm with bore and stupfel devices which were now available from all machine manufacturers. In the late 1890's the introduction of Groebli's automat opened a new era of production.

Production of the Groebli automats for the Reiter type Schiffli machine was begun by the Dietrich Company in Germany. It is strange that the Swiss inventor, Groebli, had his automats constructed by a German company. The Groebli automats were attached to 10 yard Vomag machines in 1907.

Mr. Robert Zahn, the chief engineer of the Vogtlandischer Machine Works (Vomag) in Plauen, Germany, studied the Groebli automat and from it devel-

Inventor, Robert Zahn

oped an entirely new mechanical automat for reading tapes and directing the frame. So superior was the new Zahn automat that it immediately replaced the existing Groebli automat in all new machine production and is considered by some as the forerunner of mechanical computers.

New Groebli automats, patented in New York in 1898, were ready in 1903. Continuous updating resulted in the increased length and speed of the machines. In 1905, both Saurer and Plauen machines were standard at 10 yard length with stitch heights of 55-60 cm (21-23 inches).

Plauen Pantograph 1910

Groebli continued to build automats until 1912. Plauen introduced the 15 yard machine in 1910.

Schiffli stitching machines with their automats were far in advance of anything then in use in the textile industry. The next major advance in the Schiffli industry was the introduction of hydraulics in the 1950's followed by the introduction of electronics in the 1970's.

Those companies that did not keep up with the times soon disappeared. Most of the pantograph machine manufacturers stopped building in the 1920's.

A 3 deck Vomag Schiffli machine was built in the 1910's with a reinforced Groebli automat. It was delivered to the Glenham Embroidery Co., in Beacon N.Y. in the U.S.A.; however, it was never erected because of a change in fashion. It was abandoned and scrapped in the early 1920's. The machine could have stitched 30 yards of fabric at one time on a 10 yard machine.

The Zahn automat attached to the Plauen machines early in 1910 eventually made the Groebli obsolete. There are, of course, some Groeblis still operating. However, not more than a handful exist in worldwide production today.

R. Freitag established a factory in Jersey City in 1877 with 29 handloom machines. Others included J. Sturzenegger and Emil Kuenzler both of whom opened factories in the Bronx, N.Y. John Bodenmann did the same, but soon relocated his plant to Chicago to form the Chicago Embroidery Works, still in existence today. Herman Aukam Company was organized with 243 Saurer handloom machines in South River, N.J. which became a center for handkerchief embroidery. Frederick Brunner opened a plant in New York becoming the first to manufacture laces with the Schiffli machine in the U.S.

The Schiffli machines had utilized only full length and full width goods. Therefore, the production of embroidery on cut pieces required special frames. In addition to those of Saurer in 1879, frames for handkerchiefs were built almost simultaneously in 1884 by Hirzler and Tobler of Thal, St. Gallen, Switzerland, and Fridolin Schnelli of West Hoboken, N.J. Frame work has changed as the sizes and styles to be embroidered have changed, and it has become an integral part of the total embroidery industry in the United States. However, this has changed in the last 10 years, with the shift from the Schiffli machine to the Multi-head machine.

Production of frame embroideries on Schiffli machines required low speeds and the machines best suited for this delicate work were the Groebli's, that is why they lasted as long as they did.

The first Groebli punch system was working in New York where it was developed, but the first in Switzerland was purchased by Stickeri Feldmuhle in Rorschach in 1897.

The years from 1890 to 1906 saw a tremendous growth in the Schiffli industry in America with the establishment of 143 factories containing 616 machines in the U.S. and 4 in Canada. Saurer was represented by 259 machines, Vomag by 361.

By 1908 Switzerland had the greatest concentration of Schiffli machines with 6000, along with 16,000 handloom machines, all located in close proximity to St. Gallen. Most of the large factories were owned by Americans. Machine manufacturers and other service industries such as yarn, fabrics, bleaching, design, cutting and pattern services were located close by. The Swiss industry enjoyed one of the highest standards of living in Europe and employed 87,000 workers. At least half of its production at this time was for the American market. The Schiffli industry in the United States was growing near the New York area because it was the center of the American garment industry and could offer faster deliveries.

Handloom machines in Switzerland were usually in the homes of farmers, where they existed on the overflow business of the larger factories. Their 4½ yard length was standard for the production at the time. Production prices varied with the demand, so in order to stitch on a steady basis, one sometimes had to work at starvation wages.

The factories were using machines of 6¾ and 10 yards, until Vomag introduced the 13 ½ yard machine which helped reduce the cost of embroidery even more, since production was doubled with no additional labor cost.

The years 1904 to 1907 were very prosperous ones for the Swiss industry. Any cancellation of an order for customers outside the United States only allowed them to export more goods to the U.S. where the demand was greater than the supply.

The U.S. had a Treasury Department agent stationed in St. Gallen to oversee the classifications of embroideries being exported. Duties were set at 60%. Machines were being erected as fast as they were built. Saurer had orders for 550 machines with deliveries of 90 per month, going mainly to Switzerland and the Vorarlberg of Austria., There were not enough machines being produced in Switzerland, so many were ordered from Vomag in Germany.

Embroideries were used in a very limited market at the time, so when a change of style took place it was a disaster. In the U.S. such a change came about coupled with an election year and a financial crisis, so there were numerous cancellations.

Swiss farmers bought machines through jobbers and the manufacturers who supplied the work. They installed them in their homes or barns, forming a cottage industry, and worked years to pay off their debts. During the winter months the family supplied the labor and in the spring and summer they became farmers again. When business slowed down, which happened often, they were the first to lose the orders.

Swiss goods could always be distinguished from American goods because of the exceptionally soft water used in aetzing and bleaching. Some American manufacturers, trying to duplicate Swiss goods exactly, even went so far as to import water from Switzerland. However, it was also the knowledge and experience of several generations of Swiss that resulted in superior embroidered products.

The industry in England was centered around Nottingham, which was already an established lace center. The first to set up handloom machines was John Hewetson in 1898, with 4 machines he purchased from a St. Gallen manufacturer. In 1905 he imported his first Schiffli machines. Hewetson is still a viable company today and still operates handloom and Schiffli machines, probably the same ones purchased in 1898 and 1905.

It is not difficult to switch from handloom to Schiffli design for the embroidery pattern maker. Many of the design principles are the same.

The first designer in the U.S.A. was Mr. Wehril, an experienced Swiss designer. An organization of designers was formed in 1903, to be known as the "Zeichner Ferein, New York", which existed under different names until the demise of the designers association in the 1970's.

The company of Robert Reiner was formed in Weehawken, N.J. in 1903, as an American agent for the German Vomag machines in the U.S. Reiner had developed many financial plans for prospective customers so that the machines could be bought on installment. Under these conditions, many of the hand-

John Hewetson, left, with Schiffli Pantograph in 1905

loom embroiderers switched to the more productive Schiffli machines, which were installed in small factories attached to their homes. Competition from this home type industry, with low overhead and family labor, began forcing the larger companies out of business. Hudson County, N.J., was the center of America's industry, across the river from New York's fashion center. All of the support services were in close proximity: cutting, bleaching and aetzing, yarn manufacture, design and punching, as well as inexpensive labor, since it was here that many immigrants entered the U.S.

Other centers of embroidery were being established. In Riga, Latvia, 500 Schiffli pantograph machine were in use until World War I. In Kalish, Poland, one factory had 500 machines; in the area there were more than 5000 handloom machines and 1000 Schiffli machines. This too disappeared as a center after World War I.

An official American census of embroidery machines revealed the following count in 1906; handloom: 280 factories, 1086 machines in 13 states; Schiffli: 143 factories, 616 machines in 8 states.

The Schubert and Salzer company was another manufacturer of pantograph Schiffli machines, 10 yards in length. Many of these were sold in the U.S. and throughout Europe. Hilscher and Kappel machines were built in Chemnitz, Germany, and there were other manufacturers supplying machines with pantographs. All these were well constructed machines serving a similar need. Having had the opportunity to be employed as a watcher on the Schubert and Salzer and the Kappel pantograph machines, the author knew them as good stitching machines.

Kappel had developed an automat and tape (punching) machine with its own code, and two of them were operating in Long Island, N.Y., until the early 1970's when they were scrapped. Some still operate in England. Schubert and Salzer also was supposed to have built an automat, the first of which was lost in a fire. They discontinued further manufacture.

The Kappel Schiffli with automat

Robert Reiner company in the U.S., had, by 1911, more than 500 Vomag machines operating, while 4000 were operating in Switzerland. An American census at the time, conducted by the Embroidery Information Bureau showed 241 factories with 1013 Schiffli machines, 872 of which were in the New York area. The industry employed 5900 people. There were 1159 handloom machines, with 2500 employees in 248 factories.

Postcards with complete scenes stitched in many colors were a popular handloom product of the early 1900's.

Embroidered emblems were manufactured for the first time by Schiffli machines during World War I.

Embroidered styles were in fashion during this period, reaching a peak in 1919. The best prices ever paid to Schiffli embroidery contractors in the 20th Century were paid during this period.

Machine lengths varied from 2½ yards to 13½ yards in the U.S. A 1914 survey showed 1311 Vomag machines in the United States while 8090 Schiffli machines of various types were in use in Switzerland. The Swiss had 4953 Saurer machines, 3028 Vomag machines, 65 Kappel, 39 Hilscher and 5 Reiter. 1792 were automatic and 6298 were pantographs. In other parts of Europe the Vomag company also sold 116 of the newer size 15 yard machines.

Robert Reiner, under license from the Vomag company, began building Zahn automats in the U.S. The machines were known as Reiner machines and were aggressively sold to convert the pantographs to automats. The number of handloom machines soon dwindled.

Kellner's Official Statistics listed the Glenham Embroidery Co. in Beacon, N.Y. as the largest company in the U.S., with 82 10 yard and 3 13.5 yard Groebli Schiffli machines. The Kursheedt Mfg. Co., had 2 4.5 yard Reiter, 14 14.5 yard Saurer, and 35 Vomag 10 yard, all 51 machines with Groebli automats. The 1815 Schiffli machines existing at this time included: Hilscher 35, Kappel 55, Saurer 259, Schubert & Salzer 98, and Vomag 863. 605 were automatic, while 1310 were pantographs. Meanwhile, another 1429 handloom embroidery machines were in use.

The main reason machine builders discontinued further development and stopped production in the early 1920's was due to changes in style, to prints, plain fabric or trims, causing a general down turn in embroidery demand. Machine sales dried up.

During the 1920's, some of the most difficult embroidery ever attempted on Schiffli machines was produced. "Spanish shawls" were stitched on all types of machines, small and large but nothing was large enough to produce the designs required. The shawl would measure up to 39″ (1 meter) square with the design differing over the whole area. Repeats constantly changed along with yarns and could be a puncher's nightmare. The shawl was used as a decorative piece draped over the then popular upright pianos. The drawings, enlarged six times, measured up to 18 x 18 feet (6 meters) square; of course it was punched in parts. Tapes were cut on punch machines or stitched on pantographs where the board size would be from 2.5 x 5 foot (7.5 x 1.5 meter). The author learned punching on a Groebli punch machine where some of these designs were punched. They were masterpieces of patience, the cartoons had to be constantly folded and moved without any punch sample reference. It's a wonder they were produced at all.

The introduction of Multi-head machines in the late 1920's solved the problem of running small orders on cut goods.

The embroidery industry was in full production until 1929 when fashions once again changed, resulting in another decline in the use of embroidery and a financial upset for many manufacturers.

Vomag had built 14,500 machines by 1924, another 1000 after that were shipped mainly to Japan. During the recurrent decline within the industry, the machines would became more valuable as scrap than for embroidery production. In these slow times, machines were scrapped by the thousands.

The Hand Machine Embroidery Association of America Inc. in 1934, listed 600 machines in 300 factories concentrated around South River, N.J., Passaic, N.J. and Lindenhurst, N.Y. 60% of the industry became a cottage industry, run by the family at home in a small attached factory. News of the industry was distributed in English, Russian, Polish and German since it was made up at that time of a variety of experienced immigrants.

A code of fair competition was established to try to control prices for labor in 1933, limiting work to 8 hours per day, 5 days a week, with no overtime permitted and no free family labor. Another national law for the same purpose was the National Recovery Act, which was declared unconstitutional. There was no policing of the codes and none of the rules were followed. The industry had good times and bad, but there was little any organization could do to prevent style changes. At those times chaotic conditions prevailed. In the slow times during the 30's the tinkerers went to work inventing new uses for their machines, devising chenille embroidery, cut pile, imitation persian lamb, stitched hosiery, all made by Schiffli. Attempts were made to use the machine for purposes other than embroidery, but that ended in failure.

Embroidery manufacture was generally depressed during the 1930's, with slight recovery followed by lack of work. The recession lasted until 1942. With the advent of World War II, military work in the form of embroidered emblems and a price fixing law on finished embroideries saw the industry flourish again.

It was impossible and impractical to fix prices on embroidery because of the multitude of designs and small orders. There were about 1200 Schiffli machines then in the U.S. and importation of additional machines was impossible. The industry enjoyed one of its most profitable periods, and machines appreciated more than 500%. Half the industry was working for the government stitching patches for the armed forces. 90% of all emblems used by the armed services were made on Schiffli machines. The handloom industry did not participate in the boom. New Schiffli designs for the fashion trades were not necessary, since anything could be sold and old designs were revitalized, so designers had little or no work and many left the industry never to return.

When the war ended, so did the embroidery boom. As prices and orders receded, the price of machines dropped to their prewar levels. Younger men with younger ideas returned from the war to the American industry, and with them they brought the end, for the time being, of a boom and bust mentality, and developed a year-round business. New lines were made, new fields explored and new uses of embroidery developed. Business was good again and exports were realized by the American embroiderer. The machines were growing old, money was available and the market required additional production.

Machines were sought from other parts of the world, used machines were imported from Austria, Japan or wherever available. Europe was rebuilding, so the world markets were more open to American manufacturers. For the first time, the industry was on a 12 month production basis.

In the U.S.A., the average embroidery shop was really a sweat shop. Working conditions were poor, hours were long, wages were low and benefits were non-existent. The author recalls a employee complaining about her wage as a watcher in 1942 when she earned 19 cents per hour. When the author entered the industry in 1946, $1.50 per hour was paid for an experienced watcher.

In the middle 1950's the Textile Workers of America tried and succeeded in organizing the embroidery factories. In addition to federal laws, the unions did much for the average employee, initiating a health plan, pension and grievance committees and a promotional fund; someone at last represented the worker. By the beginning of the 1970's they lost much of their representation, because many factories closed or were sold to family members who could not be organized. From the height of union representation at 80% in the 1950's, it fell to less than 50% by 1980.

In the late 1950's, Nigeria, in Africa, became a huge customer for Austria, Switzerland and the United States. The national trend in fashions were all Schiffli embroidered, they had earned large revenues from oil and placed many, many orders. Unfortunately, letters of credit were not honored and unscrupulous buyers promised payments they could not or would not make. Financially, many embroiderers were hurt. Nigeria then began to purchase Schiffli machines and built an industry that numbered upwards of 500 machines. Because of changes in styles, many of those have today been scrapped, abandoned, or exported to other countries.

In the U.S.A. in the 1950's, embroidery plants began to move to the south, into states that offered 'right to work laws', i.e., you could not be forced to join a union but could still enjoy the benefits. Naturally, this was tough on the unions when they could not organize the votes to unionize factories. At the same time land was cheap, life was more economical than in the cities, and plentiful labor was available. One of the first companies to move away from the prewar area was Conrad Embroidery (AB Emblem) who relocated to Ashville, N.C. Organizing the company, teaching new help and building all the services he required was almost enough to change his mind. He considered it, but held out and it all worked in his favor. Now with 40 Vomag machines with some the latest models built with color change, Conrad Embroidery is still an important name in the emblem industry in the U.S. By adding many Multi-head machines, it is one of the few to keep up with the times.

Soon thereafter, in the 1960's, Kaufman and Kreiger, with many 15 yard 2S55 Saurer machines, joined the move and relocated in Travelers Rest, S.C. They were followed by Schwartz and Sneiderman to the vicinity of Atlanta, in the 1970's by Stuki, Grazone, August, and in the 80's by Carol Lace and Ace Schiffli. Now the center of embroidery is nowhere, unless you want to call its center the cottage industry, mainly one and two machine shops, which remain in northern Hudson County, N.J. All of the large embroidery manufacturers have left the New Jersey center. Except for EMB-TEX and Kreiger, there are no two out of town factories in close proximity to one another. Each must provide the full services they need within their own environment.

The handloom machines that have survived are exclusively on frames. Their total in the U.S. are very few.

Automatic color change was the next natural step required to make the Schiffli machine more productive. Embroidered emblems always required color changes and the method used on the Schiffli machine was to run one color down a span, hand change by cutting off the previous color, twisting on the new yarn and rethreading each needle. This set up the machine for color #2. Stitch up the frame, change again by hand to color #3 and stitch down the frame. You can see how color registration would be a problem and the damage rate would go up with each color added. At one time, the author was involved in running a 14 color change on a 10 yard machine for a U.S. Navy contract.

Since the machines were fitted with spindles for 4/4 work and change work was never done in repeats of less than 8/4, you could always fit enough spools for 2 colors when stitching 8/4; 3 colors for 12/4; 4 colors for 16/4 etc. When the colors exceeded the number of spindles, the watcher would have to remove and replace a set of spools while the machine was running. Just picture this problem with a 14 color order.

By running up and down the Schiffli machine to change colors, you could stitch a 3″ emblem, which would run 7 times (with a 24″ machine) down the goods before each color change was required. This would amount to 1596 emblems being worked upon on one span.

Color change was tried and demonstrated by various people but the most practical system was developed in the late 1960's by the Haggar Bros. with their 15 yard Zangs machines in Paterson, N.J. They added a pneumatic system on their machines. The author's company supplied the punching of their patterns and to him it was a nightmare to remember all the needle movements on a sampler that had fixed needles. However, they punched hundreds of patterns and the company was very successful. Zangs finally developed an easier system, as did Saurer. The system most in use today, built and sold by Saurer, was aided by the purchase of the Zangs company in the 1980's.

The introduction of the electric watcher in 1952, invented by a young, enterprising Lenny LaVeghetta in his own factory, was another advancement for Schiffli. Instead of the watcher continuously walking the length of the machine on two levels, looking for broken needles, loose shuttles or broken threads, a simple electric device through which the yarn was threaded, timed to the slack of the thread would cause an electrical contact to show a light or ring a bell. The watcher would then have a specified area to check for the cause of the problem and could rethread the needle while the machine was stitching. The damage was located quickly; therefore, the damages were greatly reduced. LaVeghetta did not market the device, but his ideas were improved upon and are now sold throughout the world by the Alge Co., of Austria.

Another improvement in watcher devices was made in 1988 by Stefan Markel of St. Gallen Switzerland. The unique difference of his system is that it can detect the thread breakage of 8 threads of a color change system with a simple turn of a knob for each color. Prior systems could only detect one set of threads or all those threaded into the system at one time.

In 1950, a survey in N.J. showed 468 factories with 1067 Schiffli machines, mostly automatic. That would average 2.28 machines per factory. It was still a cottage industry. There was no count taken of the handloom machines; they had almost entirely disappeared.

Robert Reiner, Inc., the largest importer of machines before the WW II, realized that new machines would be required. For the first time in the United States a company began the construction of the complete Schiffli machine. 13 mechanical and 20 newly designed pneumatics were built and sold by 1952. The costs of construction were very high and machines could be built at a lesser cost in Germany, therefore, Robert Reiner licensed the designs to the Zangs Co., of Krefeld, Germany, and once again Reiner became an importer of Schiffli machines. At the same time, the Swiss, Italians and Japanese began construction programs to supply the new demand for Schiffli machines.

The embroidery designers association in the U.S. tried to fix prices in the early 1940's. A list was prepared and each designer would charge the same price. As a design was completed, he would sneak a look at the price list and inform the customer. Naturally, there was a lot of complaining about price fixing in the industry.

Suit was brought for price fixing and it ended. The author solved the problem by drawing up his own price list and posting it for all to see. The young upstart, as he was known at the time, solved the problem of price fixing. His list was known as Schneider's list and the others just copied or changed it as they chose. Likewise, a list was created for punching, but that was generally a uniform price per 100 stitches used by all punchers.

Hitatchi Seiki produced a Plauen type machine in Japan but it is no longer manufactured; Metal Meccanica produced a Plauen type machine in Italy from 1954 until 1975 and stopped production; Zangs of Germany also built a Plauen type machine. Well known as a weaving machinery manufacturer, they had financial problems in their weaving division after a long and prosperous tenure. In the mid-1980's, after filing for bankruptcy, they were purchased by Saurer of Switzerland.

One company that remained was Comerio Ercole of Italy, a long established textile machinery manufacturer, which built a copy of the Plauen machine. Interestingly, they brought most of their employees from the Plauen area in Germany, who were all experienced Schiffli machines builders. The Hiraoka Company of Japan also built a Plauen type machine. The Saurer Company, the oldest of the Schiffli machine builders, well versed and experienced, did much redesign work, including increasing speed and quality, to build the 2S55, one of the finest Schiffli machines of that era. You will see 2S55's stitching for many years to come.

The Vomag plant in Plauen, Germany had been destroyed during the war and politically joined to the east. Many of the experienced employees emigrated to the western machine builders.

When the American Embroidery Designers Association celebrated their 50th anniversary in 1953, they had 60 members, all of whom were from the Saxony area of Germany or Switzerland. The span in years between the majority of the membership in 1953 and the author, the youngest member at the time, was 20 years, which testifies to the fact that designers had been in a long depression.

Joe Baurer planned to modernize his old Saurer machines in 1958. He rebuilt the vertical frames to the size of the newer Saurers by building new end walls, thereby enlarging the stitching area. This added greatly to production. He also took two old 10 yard machines and joined them together end to end to form one 20 yard machine. Joe Salacan assisted with the engineering, and the machine did produce embroidery for a few years, but was eventually scrapped.

The business of converting older machines to pull larger repeats and larger spans was accomplished by other machinists in the trade. The cost was less than that of a new machine and the foundations and electrical work were already in place. At the same time the machines were overhauled and fitted with light weight aluminum rails and frames to increase speed.

You must remember that these machines could run for years. Parts could wear out, but an overhaul with replacement of cams, shuttles and any worn parts, and upgrading of the heavier parts with aluminum could make a machine as good as new, increase its speed and revitalize it for many future years of production.

The South American markets began to close to the United States manufacturers in the late 1950's as these countries built their own Schiffli industries. Politically, the governments wanted to build their own industries and avoid importing.

Unlike the industries of the U.S. and Europe, which were concentrated and drew the suppliers and service industries the embroiderers needed, the new Schiffli manufacturers in these countries usually had individual, isolated factories. Since a concentration of factories was required in order for independent service industries to be viable, these embroiderers could not attract the service groups. Therefore, all of the services required had to be incorporated in the Schiffli plant itself. They had to twist the yarns, spool the thread, dye the colors, make the bobbins, bleach and dye the goods, aetz, maintain the spare parts and a machine shop, employ the mechanics, the designers, the punchers, the cutters, the heat sealing equipment, and depend on their own sales people besides. Most of these functions and services are those which are provided to the stitcher by service industries when there are many embroidery manufacturers in one area.

Experienced people were expensive and usually had to be enticed financially to teach and move to new locations in other countries. Special formed machine foundations required experienced masons. The same was true with machine erectors. The problems were in some cases insurmountable. One factory the author visited in Columbia, South America required 6 watchers per machine and 42 apprentice menders for 3 machines. They did not survive.

A good market in the U.S. existed for embroidered products in 1958 and 1959. At the same time, a large influx of new machines was taking place, with deliveries of Plauen type machines from Zangs in Germany, Saurer with the

Saurer 2S-55 15 yd. Machines

new 2S55 10 and 15 yard machines from Switzerland, Plauen type machines from Metal Meccanica and Comerio Ercole of Italy and Plauen type machines from Hitatchi of Japan. The market for machinery was soon satisfied and the production equaled demand. Approximately 1000 old and new machines were imported during this same period.

Sales of new machines slowed after 1963, with the exception of the Saurer 2S55 which enjoyed a reputation for the best quality and production.

A friend of the author bought 2 Plauen machines from Austria, sight unseen, and had them imported into the U.S. When the cases were opened he found he had bought Plauen machines with Groebli automats attached. This was in the 1950's when Groebli automats were almost extinct (Groebli as well as the newer Zahn automats were attached to Plauen machines). It was like buying a car, sight unseen, anticipating a Mercedes and finding, when the box was opened, that you had purchased a Yugo. The value, of course, was less than half of a machine with a Zahn automat, but it was a Plauen machine!

Business was successful once again. By 1968 it was on a steady 12 month a year schedule, as the industry leaders became more market and research oriented. New machines were once again in demand in the local market. Some of the older machines had been sold back to Austria and other countries where the industry was thriving. More than 50 machines were exported in 1967.

Saurer developed a new model, 1040, which was supplied as 10, 15 and 21 yard machines, an asset to production and the customer's cutting table. Strangely, embroidery manufacturers agree that production of a 21 yarn machine is almost double that of a 15 yard machine. Saurer, the leading developer of Schiffli machines, really built a winner in the 1040. The 21 yard stitches with a maximum of 1416 needles at 150 to 170 rpm, producing 40 yards at a time.

The revitalized Metal Meccanica, Comerio Ercole and Hiraoka manufacturers showed photos of machines like the 21 yard machines, but the Metal Meccanica Company soon folded. The other companies are still viable builders of Schiffli machines, including 21 yd. machines.

Mr. R. Reiter had worked with Mr. Brettschneider and others to solve the problem of continuous length embroidery. The first production machine was developed from his plans by the Barfuss Company. Many of the problems could not be solved and this was abandoned.

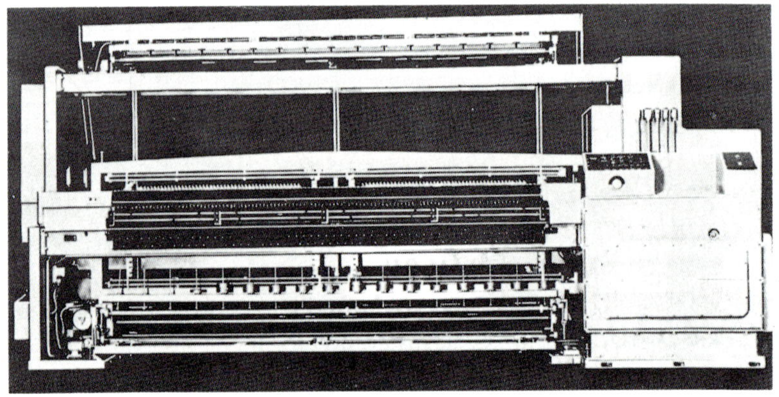

Barfuss Machine

It was the first Schiffli machine to be controlled electronically and directed by a 25mm tape. The idea was eventually revised, the machine was sold to the Pfaff Company and redesigned. Pfaff successfully built 4 machines in the middle 1970's. Two went into production in Italy and still produce embroidery on endless rolls, and 2 were never sold.

A world wide list of the machines in use in 1991 was supplied by Adolph Saurer.

Pfaff Embroidery Machine

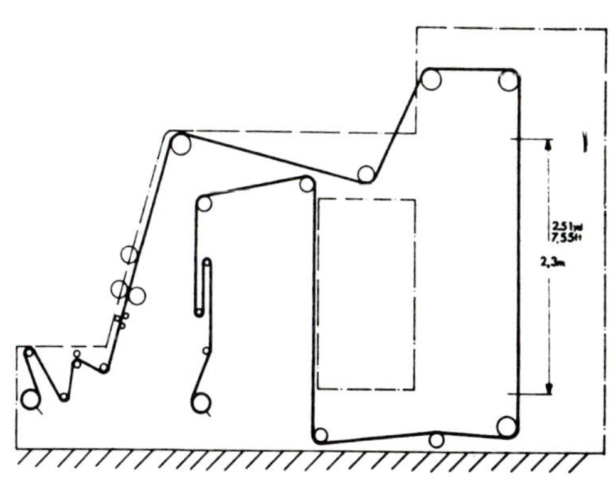

Flow Chart, Pfaff Embroidery Machine

Total machines in the U.S.A.

U.S.A.	N.J.	Size
825	(488)	10 Yard
454	(178)	15 Yard
36	(3)	21 Yard
1315	(669)	

		U.S.A.	N.J.
Factories with	1 - 5 machines	238	(204)
	6 - 10 machines	33	(12)
	11 or more machines	26	(6)
		297	(222)

Age of machines:		
	Before 1950	897 machines
	1950-1970	327 machines
	1970-1990	91 machines

Breakdown of age of machines:

Before 1950		
Saurer NV/(S)/1S/2S	155 machines	
Plauen	742 machines	897
1950 - 1970		
Saurer 2S-55	182 machines	
Zangs	48 machines	
M/M and Comerio Ercole	76 machines	
R. Reiner	13 machines	
Hitatchi	8 machines	327
1970 - 1990		
Saurer 1040	39 machines	
Saurer 2S-55	24 machines	
Zangs	18 machines	
Comerio Ercole	10 machines	91
	total	1315

Approximate world wide list of all types of Schiffli machines in 1990, prepared by Saurer:

North America	1300
South America	300
France	800
Germany	2000
Austria	1100
Italy	600
Switzerland	700
Europe	5500
Africa	800
Japan/Taiwan	1400
Asia (other)	700
Total	10000

The Saurer machine is known by only that name, but sometimes it is referred to as the "left hand machine" since the threading requires the hook to be held in the left hand.

The Plauen machine is known by many names. It was first designed by the Vogtlandischer Maschinenfabrik Co., in Plauen, Germany. Thereafter, it took the name of importers and other manufacturers who copied and modified the original design. The Plauen machine requires the hook to be held in the right hand for threading.

Plauen machine built by Vogtlandischer Maschinenfabrik, Plauen, Germany:	Vomag
Plauen machine with Groebli automat:	Groebli
Plauen machine with Zahn automat:	Zahn
Plauen machine built in U.S.A. by R. Reiner	Reiner
Plauen machine built by Comerio Ercole:	Comerio
Plauen machine built by Hiraoka, Japan:	Hiraoka
Plauen machine built by Zangs, Germany:	Zangs
Plauen machine built by Metal Meccanica:	Metal Meccanica
Plauen machine built by Hitatchi, Japan:	Hitatchi

HOW THE SCHIFFLI MACHINE WORKS

The Schiffli machine is a variation on the sewing machine. It has a front yarn and a bobbin (yarn in the back of the cloth) which forms a lock stitch, similar to that of a sewing machine. The front yarn is threaded in a needle which passes through the goods to a predetermined point. It is then retracted slightly, and the friction of the goods holds the thread, forcing a loop to be formed. A shuttle, containing the yarn which is attached to the previous stitch in the back of the goods, is driven through this loop, and the needle is driven again, slightly further into the fabric, to allow enough thread for the shuttle to pass through the loop. The needle is retracted while the shuttle is at its highest point, and the shuttle returns to the bottom of the box.

As the needle retracts, tensions are applied as the fadenleiters tighten the stitch thus formed. The loop has been closed with the bobbin thread locked inside.

The combination of these two actions, needle and shuttle, form the lock stitch. Each stitch forms in the same manner. Between each of these stitches the frame is moved, stopped for the stitch and moved again, thus forming the embroidered design.

In the American industry we count each movement or revolution as a half stitch, while most of the world counts each movement as one full stitch.

The descriptive names of parts and actions of the machine are German in origin and sometimes have no counterpart in English. Therefore, the author has taken the liberty of spelling them phonetically.

The spool of yarn used for the Schiffli machine is unique because it is in the form of a spool with two headers mounted on a shaft to hold a large quantity of yarn. The spool is placed on an angular spindle, the yarn is drawn off its side. This works out much better than a cone because the yarns are used for short periods and are easier to store and the ends are easily located without upsetting the flow of yarn.

Cones are sometimes used for heavier yarns, when the spool would not hold enough yarn for a long run without constant changing. In such cases the yarn is drawn from the top end of the cone, which might be standing on the floor.

THE FLOW OF YARN ON A SCHIFFLI MACHINE

The Schiffli spool "A" is placed on the spool rack "B". The thread is drawn from the left side of the spool in all cases to help standardize the flow of yarn. It is drawn to the emery roller "C". The roller is usually covered with an emery paper so that the yarn is gripped and pulled from the spool. The roller is driven mechanically. At times, the roller is covered with corduroy or a softer material so it does not fray the yarn (such as rayon). The yarn is wrapped from bottom to top 3 or 4 times to the right. In this manner the yarn has a firm hold on the roller and will not slide. The turning of the roller is governed by the 'sperrzeug', which acts as a brake on the thread roller, thus allowing a controlled amount of yarn to feed uniformly from each spool.

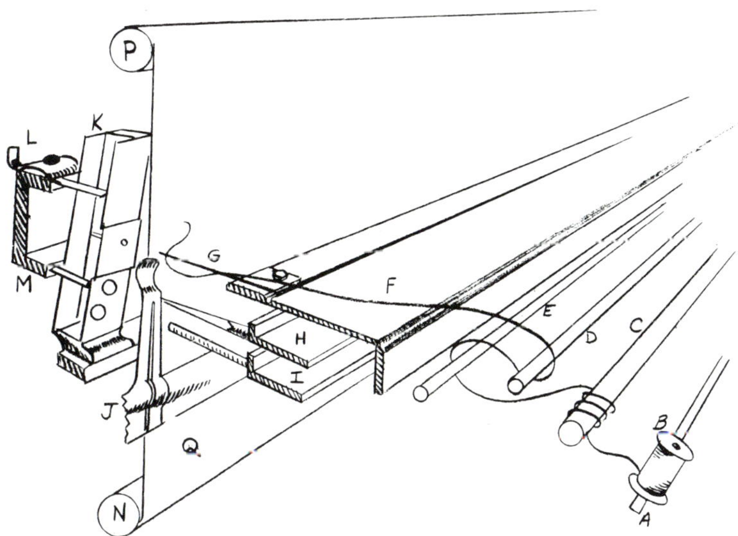

Next, the thread is placed under the small "fadenleiter" bar "E", then over and around the long "fadenleiter" bar "D". These fadenleiter bars pull the yarn from the emery rollers, and are governed by cams to assist in the feed and tensioning to form the correct stitches. The thread from "C" to "E" usually has a jumping motion, and this is where the electrical thread watcher is mounted. A slack thread (caused by a broken thread or needle or a loose bobbin) at a fixed time in the stitch cycle will cause a break in electrical contact that causes a bell or light to be activated. Next the thread is placed directly into the needle "G" mounted on the needle bar "F". The threading of one needle is complete. Every needle is done in the same manner; therefore, a 21 yard machine with 1416 needles in 4/4 (actually 40 yards of needles) does require some time for threading.

The bore rack "H" has a borer fit for each needle in the same repeat as the needles. Borers can be clipped or screwed into a bar or set to match various needle settings. Complete replacements of spare bore racks are sometimes made, for example where a change from 4/4 to 12/4 would prove much easier. The borers are like pointed knives that puncture the goods in preparation for eyelets. Some systems do exist that automatically change borers as needles are automatically changed for color change work.

The stupfel rack "I" is a separate set of round cutters below the borer rack. These are adjustable in like fashion to the borers. The stupfel is used to clean all the loose threads that might be left from the boring cutters. The stupfel is not used frequently in production, and many factories have removed them completely. This rack also serves as a place for another set of borers that might be required in a different repeat. The rollers "P" and "N" are attached to the frame which will move according to the punch tape to form the embroidered design. There are two sets of rollers per machine, upper and lower, i.e., a 10 yard machine can be spanned with 20 yards of goods. Goods can be sewn lengthwise, according to the weight and type of embroidery, to span up to a total of 600 yards on a 15 yard machine at one time, thus saving much reloading time.

The fabric to be stitched is spanned on roller "P" by hand, the salvage of the fabric is hooked onto a bar with pins similar to a curtain stretcher which will hold the goods. The goods is then rolled completely onto roller "P" until the bottom end of the goods is within reach so it can be attached to the pinned stripe of the bottom roller "N". Newer machines have motor driven rollers. The goods is now rolled onto the "N" roller until the top edge of the goods appears on the "P" roller, which is where we will start the embroidery stitching.

A suitable tension will hold the goods firm for stitching. This is accomplished by turning the rollers against one another, a ratchet holding one roller while the other is turned and stretched with the use of a ratchet bar or weller hook.

The presser bar "J" moves in rhythm with the needle bar "F", to hold the fabric while the needle is penetrating the goods and long enough for the needle to form the stitch and retract. The presser holds the goods against the shuttle box so the needle can pull itself free of the goods. It then releases the goods so the frame can move to its next position. There should be no movement of the frame while the needle penetrates the goods. Movement only takes place while the needle is out of the goods.

The shuttle box "K" is fixed on the shuttle bar. The box contains the shuttle which is driven up by pin "M". The motion is timed with the needle to thrust the shuttle through the loop formed by the motion of the needle "G". The slide "L" eliminates the problem of the shuttle being thrown out of the shuttle box by the action of stitching. It also serves as a slide to open the box for reloading.

Each of the parts named, from the spool to the needle, is mechanically controlled and adjustable through the use of cams. There are many different types of tensions that can be effected. Different embroidery designs, yarns and fabrics require adjustments in order to produce the proper stitched effects.

Herein lies the greatest skill of the foreman or stitchmaster, since well designed and punched embroidered effects will not look correct without the machine tensions being properly set.

THE SCHIFFLI MECHANICAL AUTOMAT

The automat is a mechanical system of cams and levers used to direct the embroidery frame in forming the design. It also controls other functions of the machine such as the needle and borer operation, speed, stopping and special attachments.

The frame, which can weigh up to one ton, is carefully balanced and suspended. It requires a minimum of pressure to move it vertically or horizontally or in combination. The automat "reads" the tape, thus transferring the movements to the frame to form the embroidered design.

The punching is read by a set of wire fingers known as Platines which are preset at zero. The punched pattern is moved against the Platines, which remain in place. If they penetrate an empty place, a hole, they take the value of that pin. When they hit the solid unpunched tape, they are pushed back and are not read. Therefore, the holes that we read, such as 4mm right and 14mm up have caused

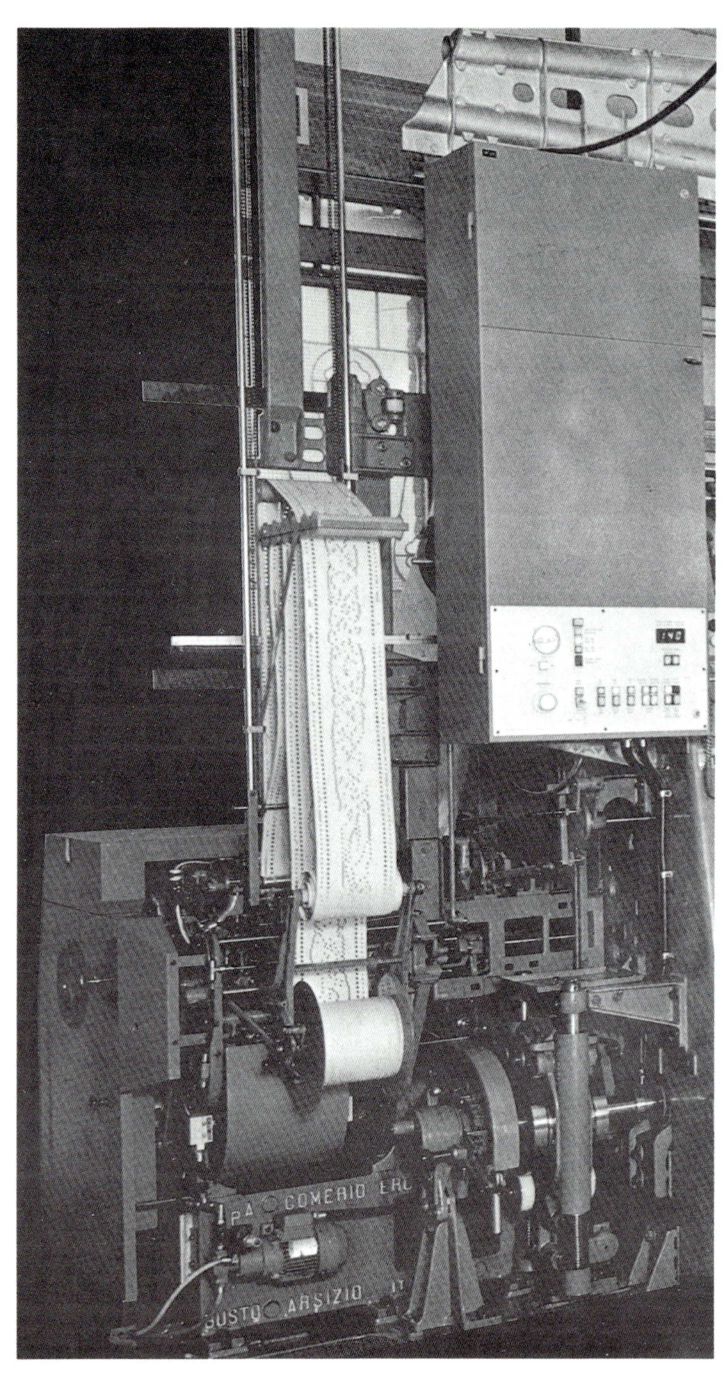

Plauen Mechanical Automat

Saurer Cam Driven Automat

the Platines to be set. The mechanical automat is connected with a system of gear racks known as "Sheabers" which cause the required movements of the frame. This duplicates the function of the stitcher on the pantograph machine.

The Platines are a group of metal wires in three parts. Those penetrating the jacquard card are the needle Platines, the second group is connected to the whole Platines which in turn is connected to the "L" Platine. This group is used exclusively to direct the frame. They activate a definite amount of X or Y and plus or minus movements of the frame according to the value of the Platines. Another group of Platines, reading the function part of the tape, only acts upon the machine functions, i.e., connects and disconnects the needle rack, borers, stupfels, speed, or any special functions. The system described is basic to the Plauen mechanical type automat, while the Saurer and mechanical Multi-head machines use cams instead of racks to move the frame.

One revolution of the automat activates the complete cycle of the machine and all of its hundreds of moving parts, forming one half stitch or one movement.

THE SCHIFFLI ELECTRONIC AUTOMAT

The introduction of electronic reading devices in the middle 60's was the first improvement in the translation of the punched jacquard tapes since the

mechanical Groebli, Saurer and Zahn automats were developed at the turn of the century. The automat had been a major stumbling block to increasing the stitching speed of the complete machine.

The combination of electronic readers and electrohydraulic drives and stepping motors has allowed the machine speed to increase with greater accuracy.

The first machine to use these principles was the now defunct Zangs Model 117, which, with proven efficiency, could successfully operate at 200 rpm. The photo electric reader scans without touching the paper card, thus there is no wear to the punching. By changing the scanning format, the reader can scan cards of any other Schiffli formats. Therefore, the manufacturer with a mixture of Saurer and Plauen embroidery machines is able to use the existing tapes punched for other equipment with any machine.

For the 1990's this advancement has become complete. The electronic readers are now being attached to older machines, but the electronic automats are replacing the mechanical automats. The machine's pattern now can be executed via a 3.5 inch disc, and with computer assistance the pattern can be read, edited, reduced or enlarged, and sing a much softer tune with the elimination of the mechanical automat.

Comerio Ercole Computerized Futura

These readers transmit the information on direction and function to the electronic control, which in turn converts it into electric impulses for the hydraulic servo motors. These motors drive the frame by hydraulic intensifiers and corresponding racks and gears. The horizontal and vertical frame movements are synchronized on both ends of the frame by servo gears. The complete hydraulic system is served by pumps to maintain oil pressure for the servo drives.

The basic operation has been simplified by the computer for ultimate control. Machine functions are shown visibly on the control panel. Repairs are simpler with the use of interchangeable printed circuit boards. Computer assisted tension regulators offer greater control of embroidered effects.

These new techniques have led to the renewed use of all existing design libraries, those very fine and irreplaceable works of art in punched tape form. Already, within the last 2 years, computer developments have allowed computer assisted devices to read and edit old tapes and convert them to the desired reading device. Here on a screen you can follow the stitching of previous masters, alter stitches, reduce, enlarge, twist, rotate, reduce widths without changing lengths and vice versa. At these stations, you can add to or take away from existing designs. Costly reproductions are saved and art is maintained.

Saurer and Plauen machines started with different tapes, nontransferable. Today with a computerized converter the Schiffli machine can read any tape converted and programmed into disc form.

There is no question that all future machines will be built without mechanical automats, and will read simplified discs. There is fear of the unknown to the average Schiffli manufacturer who knows his mechanical automat and can help himself with minor repairs, but is at a loss to understand electronics. The next generation of embroiderers will wonder how the old timers ever put up with the mechanical monsters. Repairs become simple once the cause is discovered. A simple program board is replaced and in minutes production is resumed. This also helps to reduce storage space. Older established embroiderers have thousands of square feet devoted to pattern storage, this new conversion to 3.5″ discs reduces that space by almost 99%.

CHAPTER II

SCHIFFLI MACHINES

COMERIO ERCOLE S.p.A.

Comerio Ercole S.p.A. was founded in 1885. It was the first Italian company, in 1955, to build a Plauen type Schiffli embroidery machine. The first machines were well received, leading to the development of a 15 yard machine. Then, in 1982, the first 21 yard machines were built. In 1984 they began planning the "Futura" series, which is driven by servo motors with a completely computerized electronic automat.

Comerio Ercole has developed and constructed many different machines for the textile industry world-wide and was an ideal company to build embroidery machines. They have constructed more than 950 Schiffli machines which are in use in almost every country in the world.

In their history, they went beyond machine construction. During the Second World War they became a haven for the depressed and hunted enemies of the Third Reich. A Jewish friend of the author spent his early youth during these troubling times as a resident in their factory.

Today they also manufacture advanced machinery for the textile, plastics and rubber industries.

Comerio Ercole Futura

Servo Hydraulic System

3.5-inch disc
The New Punching

Comerio Ercole Color Change

The author had the pleasure in November 1990 of examining the first Comerio Ercole 21 yard with color change operated by a Futura drive system in Kalish, Poland. The management of this 44 machine factory expressed great pleasure in the change work device with which they have never had a problem. Likewise, the 21 yard machines and the service rendered them by the Comerio Ercole Company were highly praised.

Mechanical automats and Futura available

TYPE	LENGTH	WIDTH	SAFE SPEED	NEEDLES	MIN REPEAT	SIDE MOVEMENT	SHUTTLES
CE 5/75R	5 YD	75cm	155	340	4/4	108/4	4-6
CE 10/75R	10 YD	75cm	155	690	4/4	108/4	4-6
CE 10/108	10 YD	110cm	155	690	4/4	108/4	4-6
CE 15/75R	15 YD	75cm	155	1030	4/4	108/4	4-6
CE 15/108	15 YD	110cm	155	1030	4/4	108/4	4-6
CE 21/108	21 YD	110cm	155	1418	4/4	108/4	4-6

Width = frame vertical movement in centimeters
Speeds can be as high as 200 to 220 rpm on certain types of stitches.

HIRAOKA KOGYO CO., LTD

Hiraoka Kogyo is one of the leading manufacturers of Schiffli (Plauen type) embroidery machines in the world. Many of the machines you will find in the Far East are manufactured by them. The Oriental Embroidery Company in Tainan, Taiwan, alone has 48 15 yard machines with large frames of 47″ (1200mm) vertical movement, and is contemplating additional equipment. Hiraoka has kept abreast of all new developments in electronics and computerization and has incorporated these advances into their new models.

Hiraoka SNC (Super Needle Control) system allows the embroidery manufacturer to program any needle combination, working or nonworking positions. This offers endless possibilities for variety and versatility in design. This system applies to borers and tension rollers as well. This system can be programmed at the main station of the computer controlled automat.

In order to speed spanning and tensioning time, Hiraoka has a completely automatic electronic drive for winding up and down the span as well as tensioning the fabric properly.

Standard Mechanical 15 yard

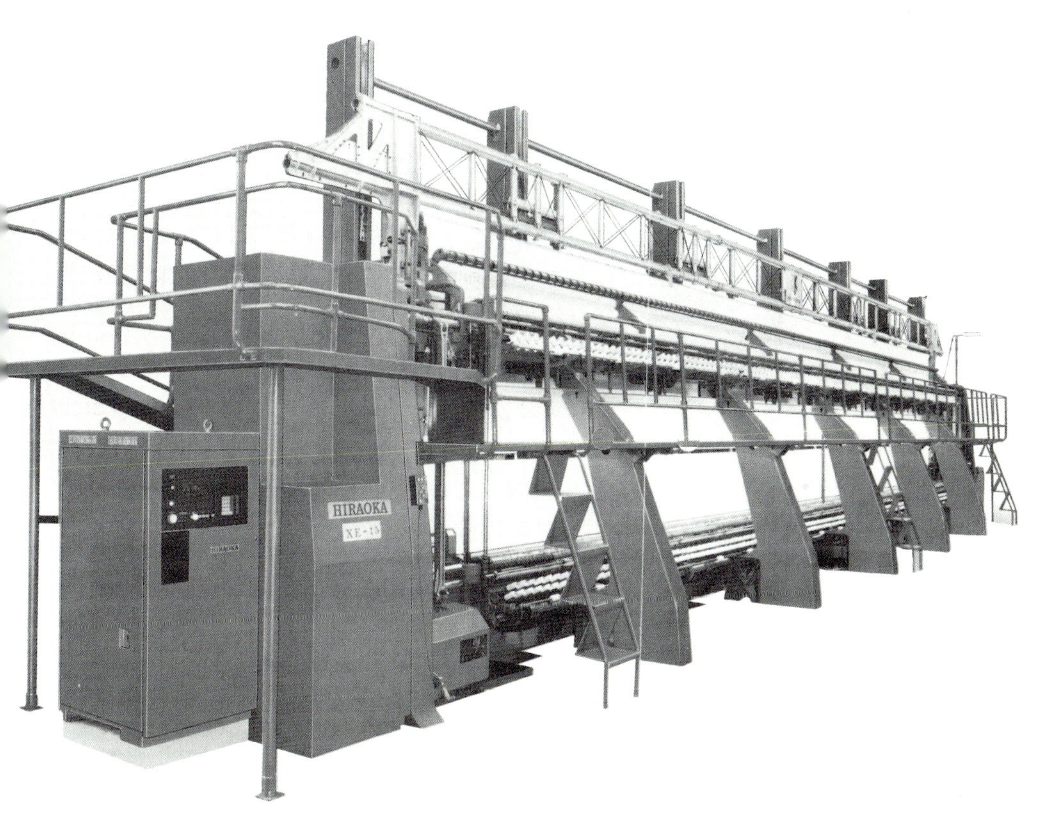

Computerized, Electronic 15 yard

MODEL	LENGTH	NEEDLES	HORIZONTAL MOVEMENT	VERTICAL MOVEMENT	SPEED
SHUTTLE					
SG-15 F6	15.4 YD	1040	540 mm	1200mm	130/160
XE-15 F12	15.4 YD	1040	540 mm	1150mm	180/200
VE-5 SNC F6/F12	5.1 YD	174	704 mm	1200mm	230rpm
VE-15 SNC F6/F12	15.4 YD	1044	704 mm	1200mm	180/210
VE-21 SNC F6/F12	20.6 YD	1392	704 mm	1200mm	150/180

F12 shuttles hold double the amount of bobbin thread than the normal F6. Basic frame repeats are 4/4

Hiraoka Sample Machine

LÄSSER AG

Stickmaschinen

Franz Laesser began his business in 1954 making changes and rebuilding older Plauen and Saurer type machines, adding aluminum shuttle rails, frame parts, and needle bars. His workmanship has always been in demand because of his expertise and innovative work. He stands 100% behind his work and had come to understand enough about Schiffli embroidery machines to start, in 1980, to design and build a completely new machine.

The machines offered are not from a single plan, but are individually built to order in any 2½ yard length. Samplers are supplied as well as 10, 15, 15.4 and 20 yard machines. The 15.4 length is built to match an existing machine.

Laesser 10 yard

We have read about new machines, such as the Saurer 1040 in 1975 and the additions of electronic readers and servo drives, tape converters for reading other machine types, and 21 yard machines.

There is really only one 'new' machine available today, the one designed by Franz Laesser. It is not a Saurer nor a Plauen, but it is a Schiffli machine which can be right hand or left hand. Some parts are from existing machines and have been modified, while others are original improved parts. The company is small enough to cater to any customer's whims. The pattern system reads Saurer and Plauen all electronically with the use of 3.5 inch discs. Machine adjustments are automatically controlled by the computer (no more hand or mechanical tool hand settings), with 15 speed adjustments for stitch size as well as pattern repeats and editing. The color change Pentomat (by Saurer) is available, as well as a sequin apparatus of their own design. The frame is driven by servo motors. Optical and acoustical thread break detectors are standard equipment.

The new Laesser machines have been delivered to Switzerland, Taiwan, and Japan, and many orders exist for other countries. With only 40 employees, they build to order in size and attachments. Recommended speed is 205 rpm, since all mechanical moving parts have been replaced by electronic components.

Recently, a long time friend of the author's was interested in finding some used Zangs 15 yard color change machines with 1 meter frames. He found them, but the customer was so impressed with Laesser's recent rebuilding of some of his old Metal Meccanicas that he phoned and said he decided to buy 2 new Laesser machines instead.

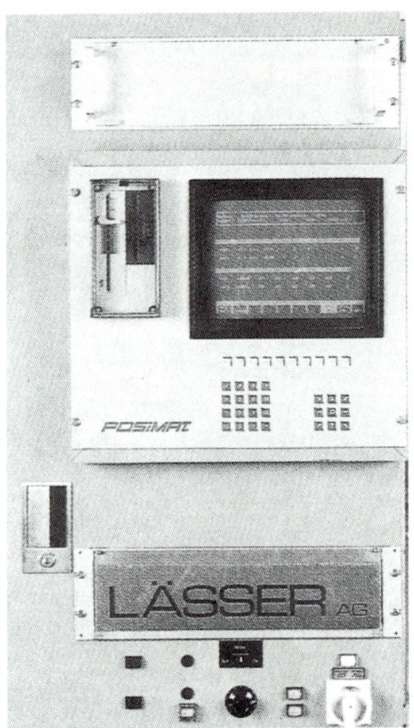

Laesser Control Center

Technical Data:

Embroidery length	**5 yd.**	**10 yd.**	**15.4 yd.**	**20 yd.**
Vertical frame movement		82cm or 108cm		
Horizontal frame movement		61cm or 88 cm		
Speed	250rpm	220rpm	205rpm	185rpm
Data Carrier		3.5 inch disc		
Number of needles	352	688	1024	1360
Stitch length		1mm to 17.1mm		
Type of Shuttles		Saurer or Plauen		
		S8 to 12		P7 to 12

Bore depth, 12 steps with 4 fine adjustments
Large thread guide, in 12 steps
Special size machines on request.

Laesser 15 yard

SAURER

The Saurer Company was established in 1853 as a supplier of parts and services to embroiderers. Soon thereafter, they began construction of their own originally designed machines. Saurer built their first handloom machine in 1869. In the early 1870s, many were set up in the New York area, thus helping to establish the embroidery industry in the United States.

The Saurer factory is located in the heart of the embroidery industry near the small town of St. Gallen in eastern Switzerland. This is where it all started, the development of the handloom machines, and many still exist in the Appenzell area nearby. This is also where Groebli first invented and improved his new Schiffli machine, and many prestigious embroidery manufacturers are still in operation here.

After the invention of the Schiffli machine by Isaac Groebli, Saurer also began building a similar machine in about 1875. The original machines were 4½ yards long operating at 30 spm. Cam disc design machines followed, then the VM machine, and finally in 1916 the 1S in 10 and 15 yard lengths. These were outstanding machines and many are still stitching in daily production.

The next development was the 2S in 1931. By this date, Saurer has sold 10,000 handloom and 10,000 Schiffli machines worldwide.

Despite the many ups and downs of the embroidery industry, when many machines were scrapped, there are still hundreds of these machines in use today. The quality of these machines can be retained by parts replacements and updating. The 2S55, introduced in 1955, became the finest machine on the market, and was surpassed only by the 1040, introduced in 1977.

Since 1988, Saurer has gone through many changes. Management has changed, and computers became part of their total package offered to the embroidery trade.

Through the leadership of Dr. Tito Tettamanti, Chairman of the Board, many new companies were acquired and Saurer has greatly consolidated its position in the embroidery industry.

Saurer 1040

The newer 1040's are now known as 2040's, with the integration of the following:

1. The Pentamat; an electronic color change device with 40 to 90 needle combinations in memory.
2. The Datamat; which will read any Schiffli tape, Saurer or Plauen and feed the information to the mechanical automat by computer, or, 8 channel tape.

Datamat

3. The Positronic; frame positioning, servo drive, without a mechanical automat, completely electronic.

Speeds have increased to 200 rpm for the 10 yard and slightly less for the 15 and 21 yard machines.

Saurer 2040

SAURER 2040

LENGTH	REPEAT	SPEED	NEEDLES	HORIZONTAL MOVEMENT	VERTICAL MOVEMENT
5 YD	4/4	210/230	340	96/4	75/104/110 cm
10 YD	4/4	200/220	680	96/4	75/104/110 cm
15.5 YD	4/4	190/210	1048	96/4	75/104/110 cm
21 YD	4/4	160/180	1416	96/4	75/104/110 cm

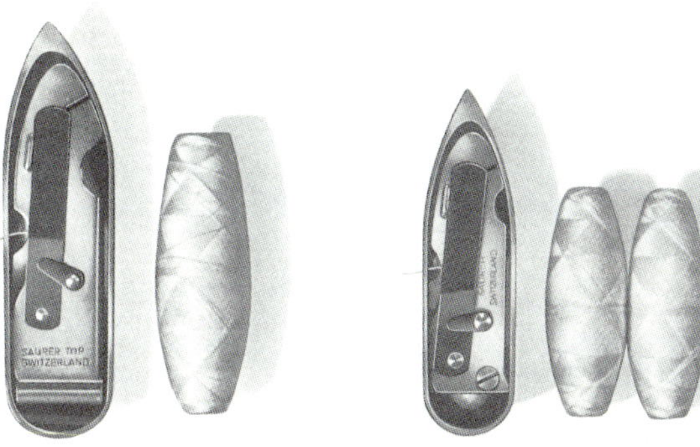

New Saurer Top, older S8

Shuttles can be standard sizes or the new Saurer Top which are twice the size and hold twice the volume. Frames are driven by servo motors for the greatest accuracy. Optional spanning equipment includes an automatic spanning system.

Original Zangs Color Change System

Saurer has been active in purchasing companies in the embroidery industry. The first was Saurer-Horeschy GmbH in Austria, which built and stocked parts for all embroidery machines of all ages. Then the Robert Reiner Company in Weehawken, N.J. and the Saurer agent and supply company known as Saentis, Inc., in Union City, N.J. were acquired.

The bankruptcy of Zangs of Krefeld, Germany a leading manufacturer of Plauen type embroidery machines and a major competitor, led to Sauer's acquisition of that company, through which they gained customers and a color change system which readily augmented the Saurer system then in use. It is unfortunate that they did not buy Zangs' Multi-head division, which has become ZSK, an independent company. Oehler, another Swiss company, which was a large supplier of parts and services to the Schiffli trade as well as a manufacturer of high speed quilting machines, was also acquired by Saurer. The latest acquisition is the Melco company, builder of multi-head embroidery machines and punch systems. There were also purchases of many other companies that were not embroidery oriented.

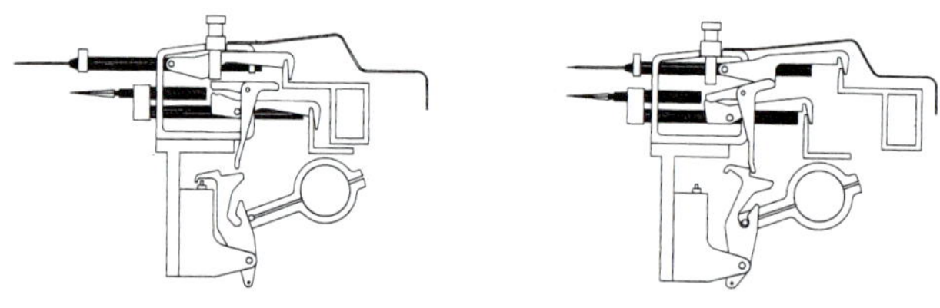

Connect & Disconnect System

Melco will face significant changes, since Saurer's punch system IV, to be introduced at the ITMA Show in September 1991, is far superior to the existing Melco. Also, some changes will surely arise with the Melco machines using Tajima color change heads, because a company like Saurer has the resources to build the heads themselves.

Saurer has sold off some assets to better concentrate on embroidery. Their bus and truck division was sold to Mercedes. However, they are still involved in other types of manufacturing, such as building engines and ceramics, with factories in France, Belgium and South Africa along with 3 in the United States.

It seems that all Saurer has to do to be the "complete" embroidery machine supplier is to offer machines for right hand as well as their speciality, left hand operation.

With the new electronic readers of their 2040 machines, it no longer makes any difference what type of tape you have for your Schiffli machine. The computers can read any of them in the old form or with discs, thus preserving huge libraries of irreplaceable art in tape form.

Newest of the labor saving devices available at Saurer is the Ketmat, a simple device to assist in laying out goods for the preparation of spans. One end of the goods is attached to an electronic donkey which pulls the goods the length of the spanning table. The spanner then sets the automatic self-contained chain stitch sewing machine to the selvage. The person operating the Ketmat walks before the moving machine to line up and feed the selvages and/or side bands, which are sewn automatically. The end result is neat, clean spans, which lay flat and are properly sewn. This adds to a trouble free spanning process on the Schiffli machine.

Saurers new color change

HUGO SIEBER

Hugo is that rare breed of Master Mechanic who knows the Saurer embroidery machine inside out. His dream in retiring was to build his own machine, and it has materialized in the industry's most requested sample machine. Built only for the Saurer system, his new machine utilizes 68 needles in 4/4, and is 5400 mm in length and 2550 mm in height. He has already built a 2 tier machine, although he prefers the single. His spotless machine shop and sophisticated equipment are testimony to the professionalism he puts into each machine he builds.

The drive mechanism used can be an older Saurer mechanical automat, although Sieber admits the disc drive will also be available. His new machine uses the Saurer Pentamat system.

Hugo Sieber Sampler

Parts are supplied by Saurer and many modifications designed by Sieber are now used by Saurer themselves. The basic design is that of a 2S55.

Although he has many orders for the samplers, Sieber still takes on jobs of modifying existing machines. At present he is working on such a job for Jacob Rohner, which he estimates will take a year. Patience is required in order to wait for one of the sampler gems.

One of the unique advantages of the Sieber machine is that it does not require a foundation and therefore can be set up anywhere.

CHAPTER III

THE EVOLUTION OF SEWING MACHINES

The most popular embroidery work of the 1800's was "tambour" work made by hand with a small device resembling a crochet hook. This embroidery was similar to a chain stitch made on net or material stretched over a frame. This comprised a major hand embroidery industry from the late 18th century. The development of a sewing machine was the next logical event.

There were two avenues of development of the sewing machine. One was the chain stitch machine; the second was the lock stitch machine.

In 1804 an Englishman, John Duncan, took a patent for a tambouring machine similar to an embroidery machine. It was not widely used. 1830 saw Barthelmy Thimonner obtain a patent in Paris for a chain stitch machine. This required a barbed needle and worked with a treadle, using thread wound on a shuttle. A mob, however, destroyed his workshop for fear of mass unemployment within the sewing and embroidery industries.

Most advances took place in the United States. In 1815, W.O. Grover patented a double needle chain stitch machine. A single needle was patented in 1856 to E.A. Gibbs, who used a revolving hook or looper underneath a feed plate to form the chain stitch.

The lock stitch was first made by Walter Hunt of New York City in 1830, using two threads, one above in the needle and one below in a shuttle. This met with little success. However, its continuous development finally awarded Elias

Howe of Massachusetts a patent for the first successful lock stitch machine in 1846. It could sew a straight line up to 15cm in length. By 1851, a better machine using similar principles was invented by Isaac Singer of Pittston, New York. Rotary shuttle and continuous feed were features added by Allen B. Wilson of Michigan. The machine was now practical.

Elias Howe, Jr

Isaac M. Singer

Early Sewing Machine

The chain stitch machine was perfected around 1865 when a French engineer by the name of Bonnaz invented and patented a machine that had a needle which could be rotated by a handle under the machine table. These were manufactured by the Cornely Company. They proved to be the most practical chenille machines and today the company is operated by the Macpherson Co., agent for the Barudan Co.

By 1862, an exhibition in London had no less than 30 different sewing machines on display. The earliest mention of embroidery made on lock stitch machines was in 1878. The possibility existed but still needed much refinement. A beading attachment was developed by Cornely in 1898.

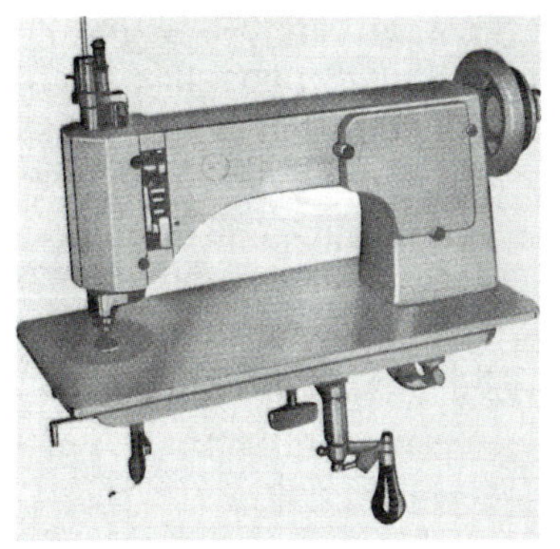

Cornely A3

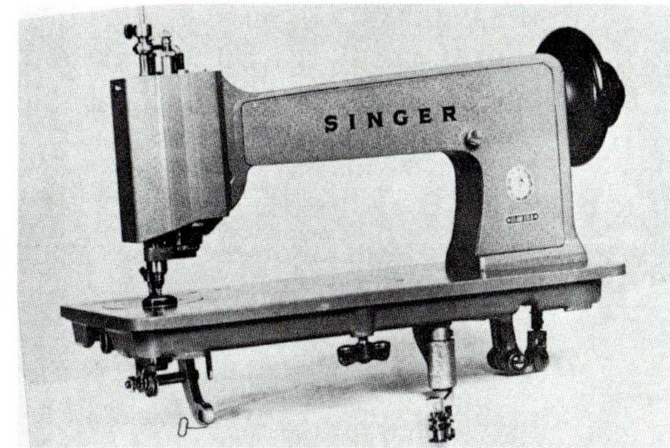

Singer Model 114 B 103

Most any sewing machine with an oscillating hook can be used for purposes of embroidery by an experienced operator. The foot is removed in some cases to allow the fabrics freedom of movement under the needle. The goods to be embroidered are either held in a wooden hoop or held firm by the operator.

Singer Models 3115 or 3139 are familiar to the American embroidery factories. Many sewing machine manufacturers have similar sewing heads.

Singer Model 107 G 307

The Singer Model 107G and comparable models from other companies embroider by setting the motion of the needle to oscillate. This is set by a special cam on the head to maintain a desired stitching width, or by an arm, under the machine, which can be controlled by the operator's knee to vary the size of the oscillation. In such a manner the operator can move the goods, following the design, while using his/her knee to vary the stitch. Needless to say, a great deal of experience is required.

A Schiffli machine maintains its running speed even if a shuttle thread becomes loose or a needle or thread breaks, thereby causing a damage or missed stitches which must be repaired by mending. Machines are stopped to replace broken needles, usually after some embroidery is missing. Broken threads are rethreaded into the needle while the machine keeps stitching, but some stitches will be missing, requiring repair.

The missing part is repaired by mending since it could appear in the middle of a full piece of embroidery measuring 40″ to 120″ by 10 to 20 yards.

These 'misses' can be marked with pins or, if the goods is to be further processed by dying or bleaching, the 'misses' can be marked by a wax pencil. This saves much time for the mender in discovering where the misses have taken place and what has to be mended.

Mending the missing stitches of Schiffli embroidery is usually done with a single head monogram machine. The idea is to replace the misses so that they look exactly like the machine made stitches. Therefore, the operator has to know something about the stitching of the Schiffli machine. The highly experienced menders that were trained in Europe could repair misses in embroidery that would never be seen or noticed by the embroiderers themselves.

Some monogram machines can be operated with a pantograph, so the operator can follow a pattern, thereby producing an acceptable monogram with little experience.

Cornely was the original fancy stitch machine, but today many companies build machines to do fancy work with various attachments. With these machines, it is possible to embroider braids, ribbons, cords, soutache, sequins, etc. Another possibility is the stitching of moss or chenille embroidery. Many chain stitch machines are available and can be adapted to make moss stitches since they use only one thread. The best machine is still the Cornely A3.

These machines are universal feed machines producing a chain stitch or, with adjustments, a chenille stitch. Fabrics do not have be turned. A handle under the sewing table, moved with one hand by the operator, directs the feed while the operator, holding the goods being embroidered on the top of the table, follows a stamped design on the goods with his/her free hand. The needles are similar to crochet hooks and are available in various sizes for different thicknesses of threads.

Award letters used by many schools for athletic teams might be a familiar example of this type of embroidery. These are the chenille, moss, or pile stitches made with a wool or floss yarn. The needle is turned, making small circles of dropped stitches, one next to the other, to fill in areas to form the design.

The Cornely Company was recently purchased by The Barudan Company of Japan and has been incorporated in their Model Belm.

INTRODUCTION OF MULTI HEAD EMBROIDERY

The duplication of hand embroidery by machine was first accomplished with the introduction of the handloom machine in the early 1800's. To further meet the demands for embroidery, a newer more productive machine was invented by Isaak Groebli in the 1870's. Until this time, sewing machines were not utilized to make embroidery.

The development of Multi-head machines was a natural sequence of events involving experimentation and mechanical development of many interested parties. The purpose was to build a machine that would automatically stitch small orders on cut goods or garments economically. The cost of production and the run required by the Schiffli machines, which were built in nearby Plauen, were too expensive.

The Singer Sewing Machine Company first advertised in 1911 the development of a Multi-head embroidery machine consisting of 6 heads with a pantograph attachment. It was discontinued in the late 1930's.

In the mid 1920's, Mr. Wurker of Dresden, Germany, owned a company making zig-zag and buttonhole attachments. He needed a machine that could stitch the single motifs of embroidery his clients requested, in small quantities.

He acquired the services of 2 engineers, Mr. Brettschneider and Mr. Scheibel, to design and build a card reading automat for sewing machines. The result was a Multi-head embroidery machine with a small mechanical automat.

The First Wurker Multi-head

The prototype was run in 1926. A small number of single head units were built, but 3 sewing machines joined together became the standard model. Production started in 1927 with 2 different gear ratios known as Models 5 and 7. The maximum stitch on Model 5 was 4mm (5/32″) and on Model 7, 6.6mm (9/32″) The machine consisted of 3 lock stitch embroidery heads in a row joined by a common drive shaft. The pantograph was guided by a mechanical jacquard device. With the use of prepunched jacquard tapes to guide the frame holding the parts to be embroidered, the design was stitched automatically. In this manner, the embroidery could be stitched, based on the quality of the punching, with no special skills required other than the loading and unloading and making the normal adjustments, that any sewing machine operator understood, to the thread and the bobbin.

The designing and punching of jacquard tapes is similar to that of the existing Schiffli tapes, using special size tapes and punch machines developed for the purpose. The frames holding the cut parts are usually wooden hoops, similar to those used by home embroiderers. Metal arms attached to the wooden hoops were used to hook onto the embroidery pantograph. The universal motion given to the pantograph by the jacquard formed the design. When the machine is in the neutral position, with the needles up, after the release of the automat lock, the pantograph can be moved in any direction. This is required for loading and unloading or to locate the start of a new patterns.

The first machines had only individual hoops or frames, but, after World War II, when the sizes of the machines grew into 6, 8, 10, 12, 15, 18 heads, it became practical to load and unload frames in sections, attaching many hoops to one frame. Frame sections are usually duplicated so one set can be loading while one set is in the machine being stitched. Therefore, the loading time is greatly reduced. The machine does not require constant attention. One operator can load and unload frames and still may have time to attend other machines. Constant improvement was made. The machines were designed to stop should a thread break, reducing damages to a minimum.

The Wurker Company built about 3000 of the 3 head machines by 1940. Distribution was world wide. Some of the machines are still in use today as sample machines in the U.S.A.

The Wurker factory in Dresden, Germany, was about 60% destroyed during World War II, and dismantled during the Russian occupation. Shortly thereafter, the building was confiscated by the State. All production ceased.

When the author first became a distributor for the Zangs machine in 1962, he took over the parts and machines from the previous agent, Robert Reiner, Inc., of Weehawken, N.J. This agency only lasted a short time. The 3 Wurker machines he had were sold to Jerry Diamond of Creative Embroidery in Bloomfield, N.J. and are still used for sampling.

In 1938, Mr. Brettschneider left the Wurker Company and decided to design and build, with his own capital, a mechanical automat for a machine that would compete with the Schiffli machine in producing yard goods on a continuous length basis similar to that of a quilting machine. After a huge personal investment, he sold all his rights to the Barfuss Company of Wilhemshaven, Germany, where such a machine was produced.

Zangs 20 needle, yarn goods machine

Zangs built a 20 needle Multi-head machine which in 1965 was shown by the author at many exhibitions in the U.S.A. The machine stitched well on firm fabrics but had many minor problems. Zangs discontinued their manufacture and the sample machine was returned to Germany.

At the 1990 Bobbin Show in Atlanta, Tajima also demonstrated a similar machine with 2 separate rolls of fabric running at one time.

The market for Multi-head embroidery machines developed in many countries in the post war era. All of the new machine manufacturers used the basic ideas of the Wurker machine, such as a group of sewing machines mounted in tandem on a table with an exact copy of the Wurker automat. Therefore, all the tapes were in the 5 or 7 format and could be read by all automats, and therefore easily transferable. Because the ideas incorporated in the Wurker machine were proven sound and all the engineering was complete, it was easier to improve upon it than develop something new.

The first to build new machines were the Markscheffel Company in Hamburg, Germany and the Zangs Company in Krefeld, Germany. In the

United States, machines were built by Erick Gross Embroidery Automat, Inc., in Bergenfield, N.J. In 1952 a totally new Multi-head embroidery machine was designed in East Germany, with a different jacquard device, based on the design work of Brettschneider. A 15 head unit was constructed but not marketed. The East Germans then went back to the original Wurker card system and produced machines similar to the standards of the 1950 models manufactured by others. In the years since the introduction of electronics and computers the East Germans have maintained mechanical machines. (Textima D.D.R.)

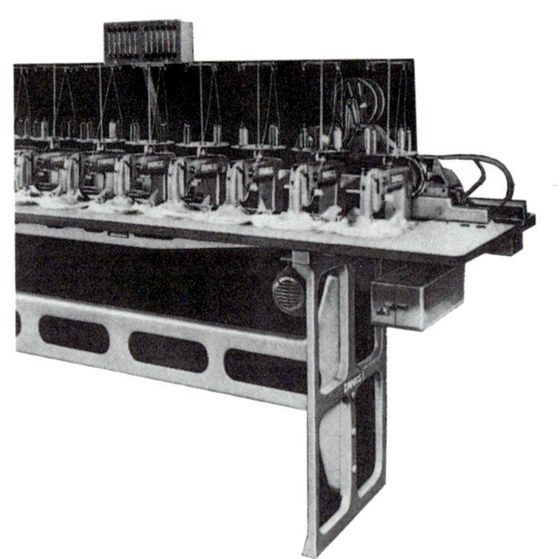

Zangs 12 head

Marco Model 3511 11 head

Textima 15 head

Beginning in 1928, the Adolph Markscheffel Company represented the Wurker machine in Northern Germany. Following the peace in 1945, they sent Ludwig Tragaser to the Wurker plant to learn to repair and maintain the units in existence. He became the only engineer in the West with such a broad knowledge of the Wurker machine. Spare parts and mechanical services were severely lacking, but he was able to put more than 150 machines back into production without the help of the Wurker Company, by having Wurker parts remanufactured in Hamburg, Germany.

During the postwar period, many of the knowledgeable people in the East emigrated to West Germany. Among them was the entire company of Gunold, which had operated a card design and punch center in Plauen. They relocated to Stockstadt, near Frankfurt, where they now maintain one of the largest card centers in the world.

During the reconstruction of Germany, the demand grew for new machinery and card punching machines. Carl Zangs of Krefeld was the first to produce a new Multi-head and card punching machine for Gunold. Mr. Tragaser became quite a popular engineer and was approached by all the companies starting to build machines. He decided to stay with the Markscheffel Company where they began the manufacture of the Marco Multi-head machines.

Both Zangs and Marco were the main suppliers to Japan until the late 1960's when the Japanese began to develop their own machinery.

Erick Gross had purchased a full set of drawings from the son of the founder of the Wurker Company and proceeded in 1951 to construct the first Multi-head embroidery machines in the U.S.A. Zangs was already in production

Gross Embroidery Automat

with the assistance of the original Wurker engineers and displayed their first machine at the Hanover Fair in 1952. Within a short time, Marco also displayed its first machine, at the Stuttgart Fair in 1953.

Both Marco and Gross used the Adler sewing head from Bierfeld, Germany.

The first 6-8-10-12 and 18 head machines were built by the Erick Gross Automat Inc., with the assistance of their engineer, Stanley Semco. Following Gross's lead the other companies also enlarged the number of heads used in their machines. In 1962, Gross developed a jump stitch device, so that the frame would move without the needle penetrating the goods. He gave up the device a few years later.

Barudan purchased a Gross machine in 1957 for their apparel business, but they had purchased the wrong model. Instead of returning the machine, they dissected the machine and developed their own.

For 20 years the Multi-head machinery manufacturers have enjoyed almost full production and, with the addition of so many new machines, expansion of sales to almost every country in the world continues today. In the middle late 1970's, Japan had 13,000 Multi-head machines, mostly mechanical, and was feverishly switching to Japanese computerized equipment. Machines could not be produced fast enough for local and export sales. The introduction of the newer Japanese machines practically eliminated the sale of new German machines in Japan.

The number of heads varied with various models offered, since the use of the machines varied from the stitching of small motifs to that of large motifs such as bed linens. The maximum length of the machine was basically standardized because of the drive system employed. Within this length they built 23 head machines (Eltac) with a small side movement, to the 4 head (Zangs) with a wide side movement.

A bridge machine was introduced, where the sewing heads were hung from a bridge instead of resting on an arm attached to the table. This became an important step in the development of emblem and applique production, as well as in the stitching of large appliques, which no longer needed to be limited by the size of individual hoops. With this new machine, it was possible to stitch the area fully between the heads where the design could form a complete border of embroidery from head one to the other end, an application popular in Europe for tablecloths and bed linens.

The Multi-head machine companies became vertical manufacturers offering all the services of production and pattern making, as well as punch machines and duplicating machines. In the late 1970's, trimming devices were offered, automatic 7 to 9 color change was available, as well as an electronic reading device which made the 7 channel tapes standard. Each manufacturer used their own code for their tape reading device. Therefore, the interchangeable tape of the mechanical machines disappeared.

Electronics quickly developed into computerized reading of tapes. A new era had arrived, and the various tapes could once again be universally read.

THE MACHINE

The machine is built on a flat table of standard working height, higher in the West, lower in the East. This facilitates loading and unloading and attendance to the machine. The sewing heads are on the table, set at specific distances and joined by a common drive shaft. This type of head would serve for embroidering individual motifs, jackets, cut parts, caps, etc.

The heads are usually home style sewing machines to which the Multi-head manufacturer might make major changes according to the demands of his program of construction. Specially designed heads might be mounted on a longitudal beam to allow the frame to have a larger lateral movement as well as allow it to move horizontally the distance from needle to needle without obstruction. This served the linen industry with bordered embroideries and served the emblem industry by allowing the spanning of one piece of goods for production, which could be completely filled with the stitched designs. In many cases, the machine manufacturers set the needle distance at the French inch measurement to conform to the Schiffli machine.

A mechanical jacquard reader placed on the right side would read the pattern which directed the frame. There were many drive systems: direct, belt, or servo motor. Today the reader is electronic, the design usually contained on a 3.5 inch disc or cassette which appreciably increases the speed at which the machine can operate.

The thread is in the form of cones, mounted above the heads and threaded through tensioning springs and a take up lever. Individual machine lighting is available by some manufacturers.

The power system varies, since the machines have become longer and heavier. Current is supplied that meets the requirements of the local power supply.

The whole machine stops automatically each time a thread breaks. A light might indicate the head. The stop sets the needle in the exact position for rethreading. This facilitates a quick repair, with a minimum of stitches missing. Once the thread is fixed, the machine can be restarted and usually no repair is necessary. Machines can now retrace stitches, thus making repairs automatic.

The automat drives a pantograph which holds the frames of fabrics to be embroidered. Each model of machine has a fixed area in which the frame can move.

Various attachments have been developed for cording and boring. Imitation of chenille embroidery was a prime challenge; everyone had an idea. The best solution, of course, is to use the original Cornely machine which now is supplied with the Barudan machine.

Thread trimmers for top and bottom threads assisted production by cutting and holding threads. They have made unloading and color changes easier and quicker.

Automatic color change heads have simplified the manufacture of colorful embroideries, eliminating the tedious rethreading of each head. This has speeded production appreciably. The newest machines are built for automatic changes of up to 9 colors.

The elimination of the mechanical automat, the addition of electronic readers, along with better frame drive systems had immediately doubled the speed of all machines. However, the speed is governed by the size of the stitch, so variations are required. Small stitches can be run at higher speeds than larger stitches.

The loading and unloading of frames set into the pantograph have been assisted by many new framing devices, some of which just snap in and out.

The costs of machines vary with the attachments and extras that the customer requires. Also, in today's complex world, cost is also governed by where the machine is manufactured. Do you pay in dollars, yen or marks?

Service is something that should be considered. We hear all kinds of stories about good and bad service. Check this out with someone who is already operating the machines you intend to purchase.

The following information about the manufacturers and machines they build will give you an idea of the various types of equipment available. They are offered in alphabetical order. We are not comparing machines or advising which are better or more efficient than others; the market has already solved that problem. This information is solely for your own evaluation. Suffice it to say they are all good machines, built to rigid specifications and built to perform the specific embroidery tasks efficiently, using standard, easily available threads, requiring minimal maintenance.

It is important that you choose the correct machine for your purposes, the market you intend to serve.

What volume do you expect?
How many heads do you need?
What is the maximum stitch area you will require?
What type of embroidery will best serve your customers?
Do you need automatic color change?
Do you need thread trimmers?
How many of the expensive extras will you really use?

In addition to the machine, you will need the discs or tapes that contain the designs. Are these readily available? See Chapter VI on computerized punching for information on all the available equipment for tape or disc creation. In some cases the computerized tape equipment can cost more than the machine.

Major changes in machines and tape units have taken place in the last 10-12 years. Be careful, since the cycle is not yet complete. Computerization has opened a Pandora's box for the embroidery industry, and there is much more to come. The basic machine we see today will suffice for the foreseeable future. What will change are the uses the machine is put to, and the added extras that may look nice but may have little real value. These are necessary for the few who actually need them, but otherwise they just keep embroiderers buying new machinery.

A mixture of different manufacturers' machines in one plant is possible. Tapes can be interchanged, with the computerized converting of the Q.D.T. and other built in converters; however, it does not make for an easy operation. The number of parts and services needed is duplicated.

Those Departed Manufacturers

Even though the Multi-head industry is less than 40 years old, considering it really started its main development in the 1950's, most of us know of companies that are no longer part of the industry. This run down should keep you up to date.

The Eltac Company, formed in the 1960's in Japan and developer of the first electronic machine, closed through bankruptcy. The new manufacturer is the Happy Machine Company.

The Erick Gross Embroidery Automat, Inc, was the prime supplier of machines and new developments in the U.S.A. from the 1950's to the early 1970's. It finally folded due to inside problems and not keeping up with the times.

The Marco Embroidery machine, began manufacturing mechanical machines in Germany in the early 1950's. Bankruptcy took them in 1988. In 1989 a new company was formed by the former owner to carry on the tradition with a completely computerized machine. The author is happy he did not delete them.

The Marcus embroidery machine was another German company lost through attrition.

Micro Seiki Co., in Japan was lost through attrition.

The Zangs Multi-head machine, due to problems within the company not involving their embroidery machines, was sold to ZSK.

Hiraoka of Japan was involved in the manufacture of mechanical multi heads in the late 70's. They have since discontinued this line.

This proves that manufacturers must always stay one step ahead of the competition, or try to. New ideas must continuously be developed, and investments made to improve existing machines.

OPTIONS AVAILABLE ON ALL MULTI-HEAD MACHINES

There are numerous options available for embroidery machines. Some are essential, some are helpful, and some look pretty and may never be used.

Most machines are supplied with more than a tape reader for the machine to read and produce the embroidery.

Some of the items that should be included as part of your machine package are:

Automatic color change:

The number of colors is up to the buyer, but the use of colors declines as the number increases. 6 colors seem to take care of 95% of normal patterns; 9 colors may NEVER be required.

Thread Trimmers:

All embroideries require trimming, when there are jump stitches or color changes or when the frame is loaded and unloaded or reset to repeat a design. A trimmer is a great time saving device, most of the time.

Jump Stitch:

This allows separated parts to be embroidered with one long joining thread instead of being confined by the machine's maximum stitch, which is limited.

It is much easier to trim one long stitch than hand trim many small stitches. Some machines have automatic trimmers that cut and lock the threads as the jump stitch is made.

Automatic repeat of designs:

This is important should you be stitching an applique or emblem; it saves the time of resetting the frame and the design upon each completion. If you are monogramming or stitching cut parts or jackets, the function might not be important.

Pattern Rotation:

This function might be of help if you forget to instruct the tape maker as to which direction you wish to stitch the pattern. Also, if you find you can't run a certain design the way you planned, then the change of direction might be necessary.

Mirror Imaging:

This provides the ability to make a mirror image or a right and left design without reprogramming should you require matching designs on a garment.

Back up of pattern for repairs:

This can help you fill in missing embroidery should your machine not stop or stop too late after a thread or needle break or bobbin tension problem.

Scaling:

This changes your design by increasing or decreasing its size. It is important to remember that the thread execution also requires some adjustment. If you substantially reduce the size of a design the threads might become cramped and the pattern will not run well or look good. Likewise, enlarging a design may require more stitches to retain its original composition.

Lettering Functions:

Buy those lettering styles you need. Just as in buying all the candy in the candy shop, there are some you can buy that you will never use. Lettering requires some periferal program features such as arcing, centering, clockwise and counterclockwise, slanting, scaling and the ability to change the length and width. Stocked designs are sometimes added, via the keyboard, to complete a customer's requirement. Such provisions and designs should be available.

Borer Device:

Will you be stitching designs that require bore holes? Bore holes will always be limited to symmetrical cuts and require experienced pattern makers. If you are not going to use it (and most stitchers in America never do) don't buy it. See the section on Hot Knifing or Laser cutting. These might perform the same function for you.

Cording or sequin devices:

The same thought applies. Will you use it? These special devices are usually required in the fashion industry where new ideas are always being developed. If this is your business, then these special features will be there when special situations arise.

Monogramming keyboard:

If lettering is part of the package you will need it.

Monitors:

Each machine can have a monitor and editing program. The operator can follow all the movements as they are stitched, thus actually viewing every stitch and being able to make corrections for improving the quality of the embroidery.

Displays indicating time, speed and stitches:

Costs are going to be based on the speed your machine will stitch. Your machine should stitch according to the design, larger stitches requiring slower speeds, smaller stitches faster. The amount of stitches at a fixed speed equals the total time. Time is the basic method of figuring costs. For proper pricing it is an asset.

CHAPTER IV

MULTI-HEAD MACHINE MANUFACTURERS

Note: All measurements are in millimeters (mm) and centimeters (cm) To convert to inches: 25.4mm = 1 inch; 2.54 cm = 1 inch. rpm = revolutions per minute, spm = stitches per minute.

Addresses, phone and fax numbers listed under "Index of Addresses" in Chapter IX.

Macpherson Monogram, Inc.

Barudan Co., LTD. Macpherson, Inc.

The Barudan Company was founded as an apparel business, and when they built their first embroidery machine in 1959, it was the first Japanese Multi-head machine built. Since then, Barudan has become one of the leaders in the manufacture of Multi-head embroidery machines. In 1972 they introduced the jump stitch device and the automatic color change. By 1977 their first computer controlled machine was displayed. By 1981 they had developed their first monogram machines; 2, 4, and 6 head 5 color automatic color change.

During November 1985 they purchased the Meistergram Company. Barudan assumed the manufacturing role of Meisergram and Neil Macpherson took the marketing group to Greensboro, N.C. This move was the first by a Japanese Company to develop American production in Cleveland, OH. They have expanded their production to include Monogram machines as well as the largest Barudan machines. They are the only company to have production facilities in each of the three major industrial regions in the world; Japan, the United States and Europe. Production has reached 400 machines per month.

Barudan Company is a leading manufacturer of Multi-head machines world wide. They have developed and brought to production many new ideas. The following list of the Barudan stock machine program illustrates the broad range of embroidery equipment available.

Thinking of what no one else
has thought, creating what no
one else has created.

Barudan

MODEL BEMX

HEADS	NEEDLES	SPACE	EMBROIDERY WIDTH FRAMES	AREA CONTINUOUS DESIGN
8		380mm	320 x 380 mm	320 x 3040 mm
10		380	320 x 380	320 x 3800 mm
10		480	320 x 480	320 x 4800 mm
12(WF)	UF..5	300	320 x 300(600)	320 x 3600 mm
12		320	320 x 320	320 x 4840 mm
12	OR	380	320 x 380	320 x 4560 mm
15		320	320 x 320	320 x 4800 mm
17(WF)	UG..7	240	320 x 240(480)	320 x 4080 mm
17		320	320 x 320	320 x 5440 mm
20		240	320 x 240(480)	320 x 4800 mm

MODEL BEMXH

HEADS	NEEDLES	SPACE	EMBROIDERY WIDTH FRAMES	AREA CONTINUOUS DESIGN
10		480	450 x 480	450 x 4800 mm
12(WF)		300	450 x 300(600)	450 x 3600 mm
12	UF..5	400	450 x 400	450 x 4800 mm
15		350	450 x 350	450 x 5250 mm
17(WF)	OR	240	450 x 240(480)	450 x 4080 mm
17		300	450 x 300	450 x 5100 mm
18	UG..7	300	450 x 300	450 x 5400 mm
20(WF)		240	450 x 240(480)	450 x 4800 mm
24(WF)	UF..5	135.4	450 x 135.4(270.8)	450 x 3249.6 mm
26(WF)	UF..5	165	450 x 165(330)	450 x 4290 mm

MODEL BEMS

HEADS	NEEDLES	SPACE	EMBROIDERY WIDTH FRAMES	AREA CONTINUOUS DESIGN
8		380	320 x 380	320 x 3040 mm
10		380	320 x 380	320 x 3800 mm
10	UF..5	480	320 x 480	320 x 4800 mm
12(WF)		300	320 x 300(600)	320 x 3600 mm
12	OR	320	320 x 320	320 x 3840 mm
12		380	320 x 380	320 x 4560 mm
15	UG..7	320	320 x 320	320 x 4800 mm
17(WF)		240	320 x 240(480)	320 x 4080 mm
17		320	320 x 320	320 x 5440 mm
20(WF)		240	320 x 320(480)	320 x 4800 mm

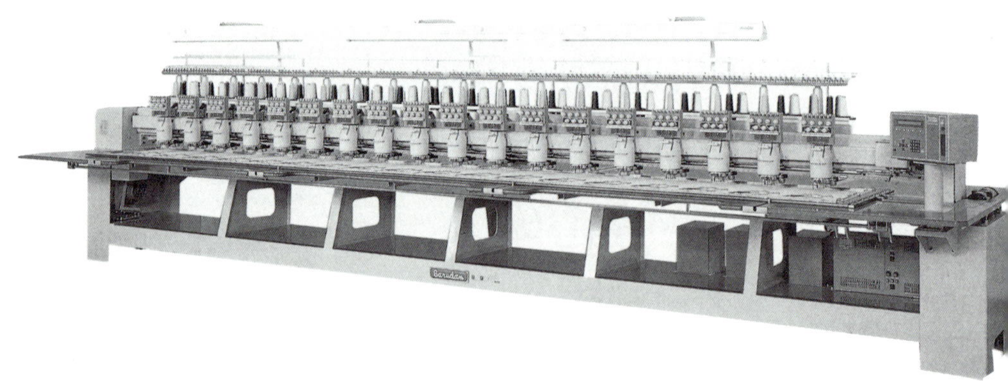

MODEL BEMSH

HEADS	NEEDLES	SPACE	EMBROIDERY WIDTH FRAMES	AREA CONTINUOUS DESIGN
10		480	450 x 480	450 x 4800 mm
12(WF)		300	450 x 300(600)	450 x 3600 mm
12	UK..5	400	450 x 400	450 x 4800 mm
15		350	450 x 350	450 x 5250 mm
17(WF)	OR	240	450 x 240(480)	450 x 4080 mm
17		300	450 x 300	450 x 5100 mm
18	UG..7	300	450 x 300	450 x 5400 mm
20(IF)		240	450 x 240(480)	450 x 4800 mm
24(WF)	UF..5	135.4	450 x 135.4(270.8)	450 x 3249.6 mm
26(WF)	UF..5	165	450 x 165(330)	450 x 4290 mm

MODEL BEMR

8		380	320 x 380	320 x 3040 mm
10		380	320 x 380	320 x 3800 mm
10	UF..5	480	320 x 480	320 x 4800 mm
12(WF)		300	320 x 300(600)	320 x 3600 mm
12	OR	320	320 x 320	320 x 3840 mm
12		320	320 x 380	320 x 4560 mm
15	UG..7	320	320 x 320	320 x 4800 mm
17(WF)		240	320 x 240(480)	320 x 4080 mm
17		320	320 x 320	320 x 5440 mm
20(WF)		240	320 x 240(480)	320 x 4800 mm

MODEL BEMRE

The cylinder arm embroidery machine is adapted for the embroidery of caps, and tubular parts such as sleeves, pockets etc.

MODEL BEMRH

10		480	450 x 480	450 x 4800 mm
12(WF)		300	450 x 300(600)	450 x 3600 mm
12	UF..5	400	450 x 400	450 x 4800 mm
15		350	450 x 350	450 x 5250 mm
17(WF)	OR	240	450 x 240(480)	450 x 4080 mm
17		300	450 x 300	450 x 5100 mm
18	UG..7	300	450 x 300	450 x 5400 mm
20(WF)		240	450 x 240(480)	450 x 4800 mm
24(WF)	UF..5	135.4	450 x 135.4(270.8)	450 x 3249.6 mm
26(WF)		165	450 x 165(330)	450 x 4290 mm

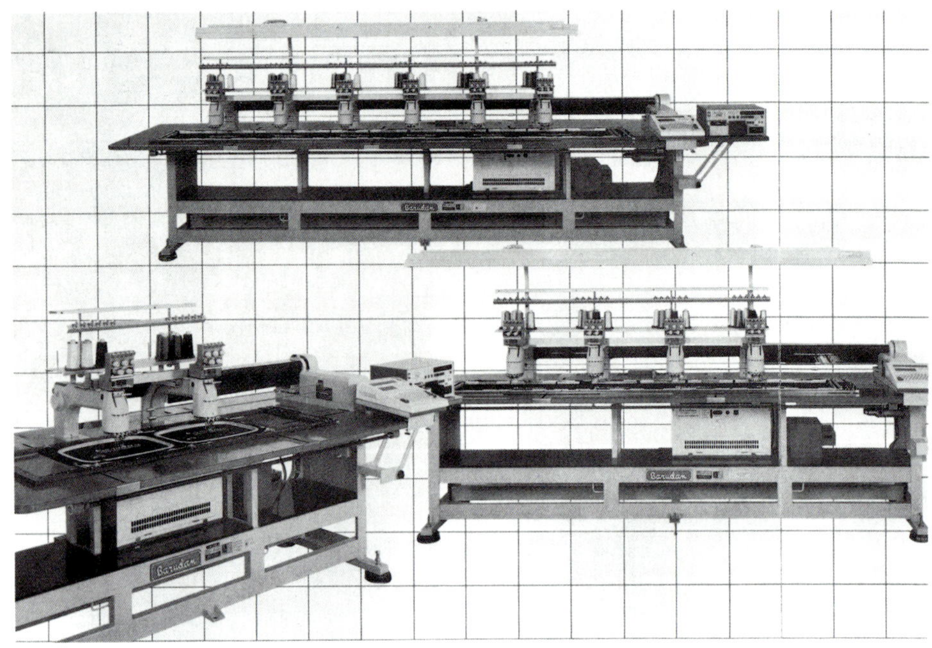

PROFIT 800

Cylinder arm allows for the stitching of flat goods as well as caps and other tubular parts.

2	UF..5	300 x 450 mm
4	UF..5	300 x 450 mm
6	UF..5	300 x 450 mm

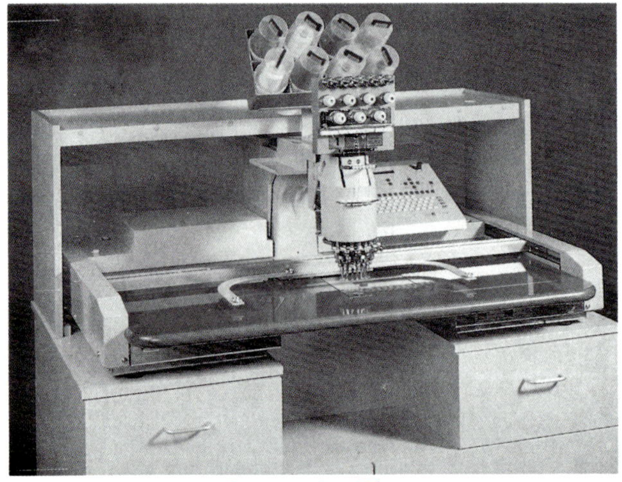

Prosperity Plus

PROSPERITY PLUS INCLUDES:

3 Alphabets, stitching speeds from 300 to 1000spm. Cylinder arm for caps, pockets, sleeves, hard to reach places. Complete pattern programming is part of the package. Single head machine with 7 color automatic change. Area of 300mm x 450mm.

MODEL BELM

Barudan had been buying Cornely machines for the development of various chain stitch machines, and in 1990 purchased the Cornely Company. Cornely has been known from the early 1900's as a superior Moss stitch or chenille embroidery machine. It is very versatile and was one of the most important sewing heads for the fashion industry.

The BELM uses the original Cornely LG 3 head specially designed by Barudan with from 1 to 4 heads. Chain stitch, Moss stitch, Taping, Cording with a multitude of various threads, cords and filaments can be used. This represents the type of embroidery made by the most highly skilled craftsmen which had almost completely disappeared. Now one can recreate those special designs of the early 1900's without skilled craftsmen to bring them to life. Automatically, the Barudan recreates the fashionable embroidery of a by-gone era. Speeds from 200 to 500 spm.

BELM 1 Head, area 800 x 500 mm
BELM 2 Head, area 800 x 500 mm
BELM 3 Head, area 800 x 500 mm
BELM 4 Head, area 800 x 500 mm

MODEL BELM A3

A special machine designed to use heavier threads on a broader range of fabrics. Chain and Moss stitch with the ability to change from one style to the next. Single needle now can reproduce new fashion designs, bringing new life to embroidery.

Speeds vary from 200 to 500 spm.

BELM 6A3 6 Heads, Embroidery area 600 x 500 mm
BELM 8A3 8 Heads, Embroidery area 600 x 500 mm
BELM 10A3 10 Heads, Embroidery area 600 x 400 mm
BELM 12A3 12 Heads, Embroidery area 600 x 320 mm

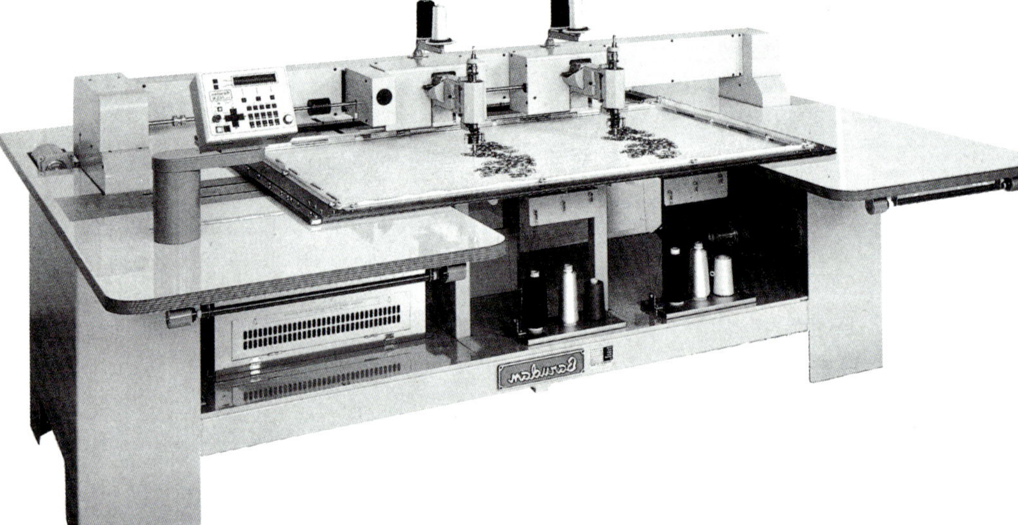

MODEL BEATH RS 802 UF

Rhinestone and Monogram embroidery machine using a heating element to fix rhinestones or other attachments to a frame of fabric in the form of designs guided by standard tape input. The machine can fix rhinestones alone or stitch embroidery alone. It is a very versatile machine.

Heat sealed rhinestones can be applied to cotton, silk, nylon, polyester, vinyl, leather. For the apparel trade the ideas are unlimited. The embroidery area is 600 x 600 mm, speeds from 200 to 600spm with 5 color automatic color change, with or without the special attachment.

BEATH RS 702 2 Heads, embroidery area 600 x 600 mm
BEATH RS 704 4 Heads, embroidery area 600 x 600 mm
BEATH RS 706 6 Heads, embroidery area 600 x 600 mm

MODEL BEATH SS 802 UF

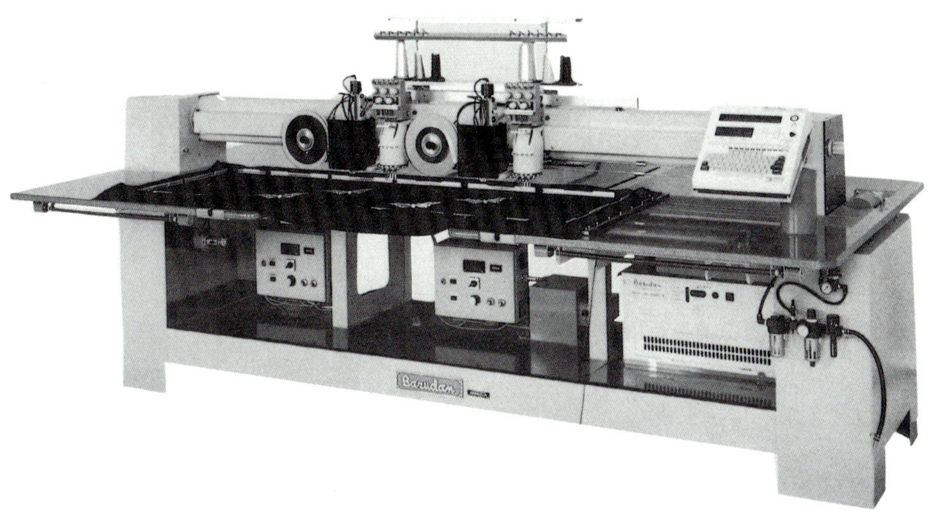

Another machine for the fashion industry, developed for sequins, stars or other shapes. Strips of glitter are stamped by special dies and automatically heat sealed according to the punched design. The final product can be a combination of embroidery and heat seal shapes and designs. The machine can always stitch regular embroidery in 5 color automatic color change without the special attachment.

BEATH SS 702 2 Heads, embroidery area 600 X 600 mm
BEATH SS 704 4 Heads, embroidery area 600 X 600 mm
BEATH SS 706 6 Heads, embroidery area 600 x 600 mm

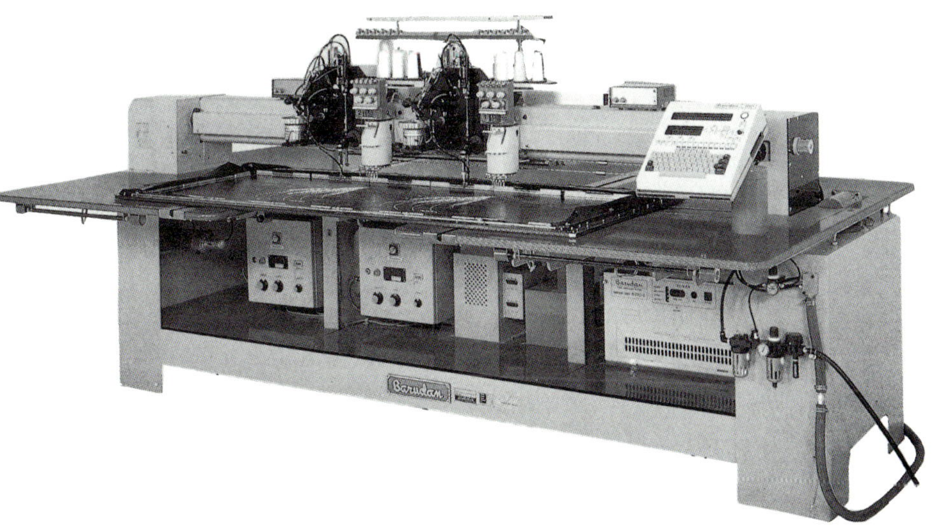

Hirsch International

The Model BAS-410 is a single head, computerized, 9 needle automatic color change machine with all the goodies. The computer assist includes editing, and the ability to run units independently or in a series up to 5 machines. This allows the embroidering of single designs on individual machines or one design running on all machines. The machine includes a cylindrical bed for use in embroidering pockets, sleeves, socks, and caps.

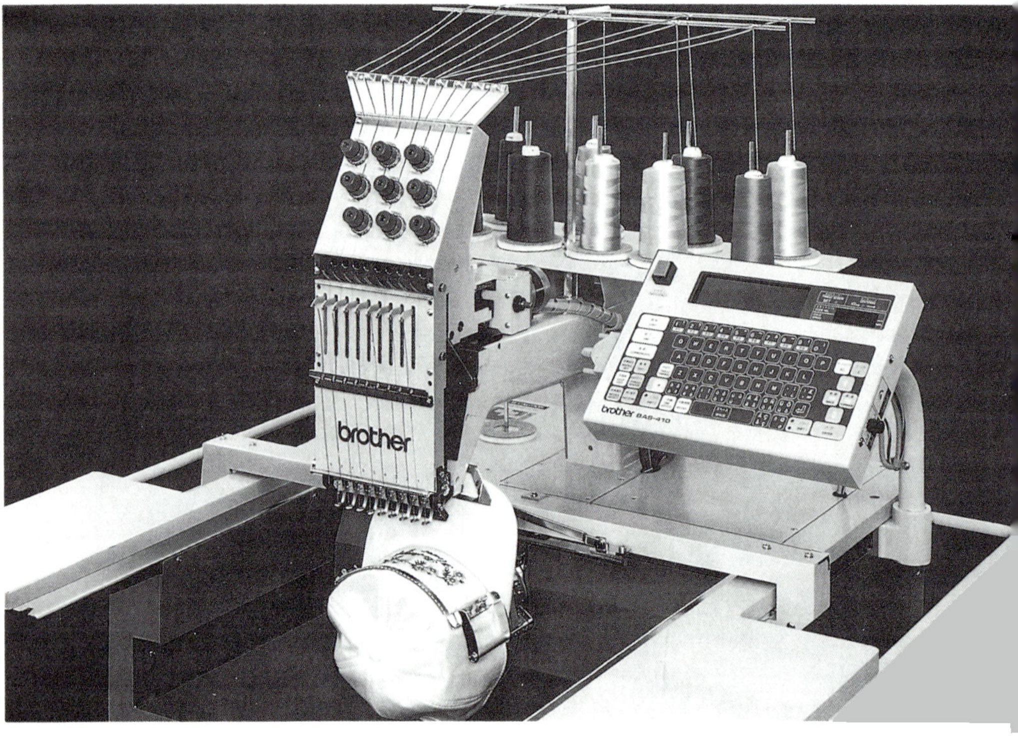

Included are a thread trimmer and a removable table that allows the addition of a cap frame. Embroidery programs created for all Multi-head machines on floppy disc or even 8 channel tape can be read into the machine. Recommended speed 1000spm.

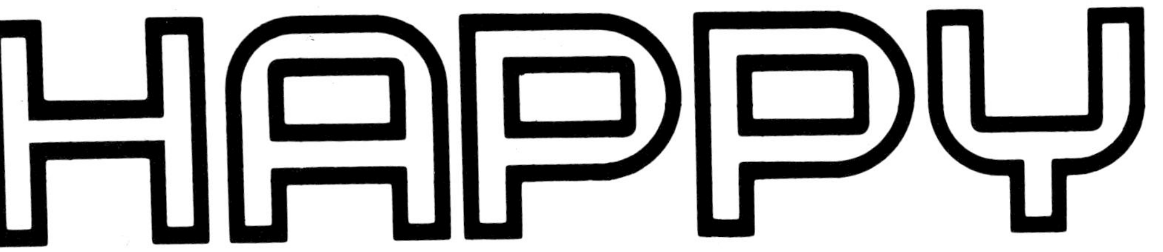

The Happy Multi-head embroidery machine is the outcome of the demise of the Eltac Embroidery Machine Company. The machine offered has all the computerized state of the art programming and a well designed machine with up to 24 heads, boring device, thread trimming, computer, pattern editing and memory to 131,000 stitches.

For emblems, an automatic repeat sewing program allows for continuous running to fill up the frame of goods without resetting the pattern. Automatic frame return saves hand resetting of the frame after each run.

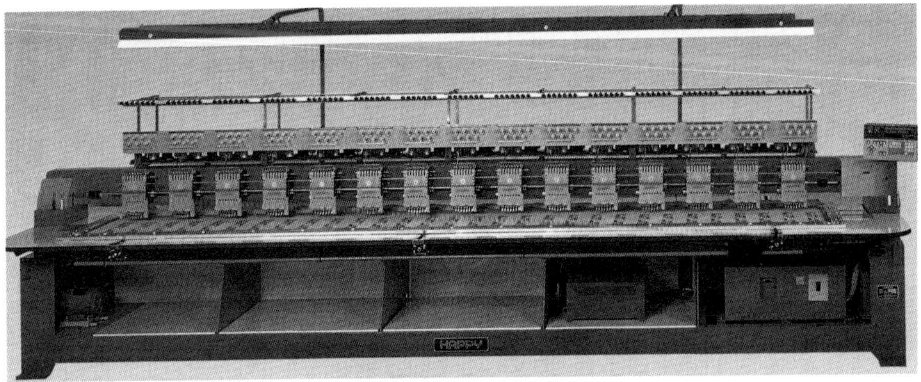

Control box

The control box is easy to use.
Even people new to electronic embroidery machines will be able to easily master the functions.

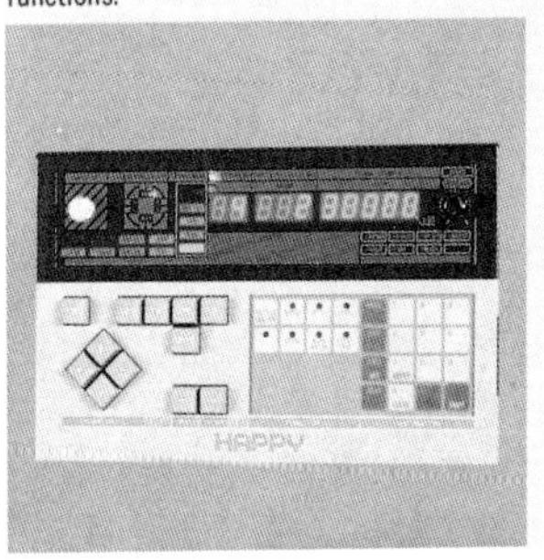

Tape reader

When operating the machine by direct "tape drive". it is still possible to use the "frame back" & "pattern convert" function.

Rotary type thread break detecting device (option)

Improved rotary type detecting device has been adopted.

Model: EM3 Series

MODEL	HEADS	EMBROIDERY AREA	ALTERNATE
		cm	cm
L424A	24	480 x 200	400
L720A	20	480 x 240	480
L816	16	480 x 310	
L812	12	480 x 400	
L810	10	480 x 480	
K718A	18	480 x 240	480
K815	15	480 x 300	
S715	15	480 x 275	
S812	12	480 x 335	
S810	10	480 x 400	
S808	8	480 x 485	
HAMS 702C	2	450 x 330	sample machine

Speeds: 300 to 700 spm.
7 color change

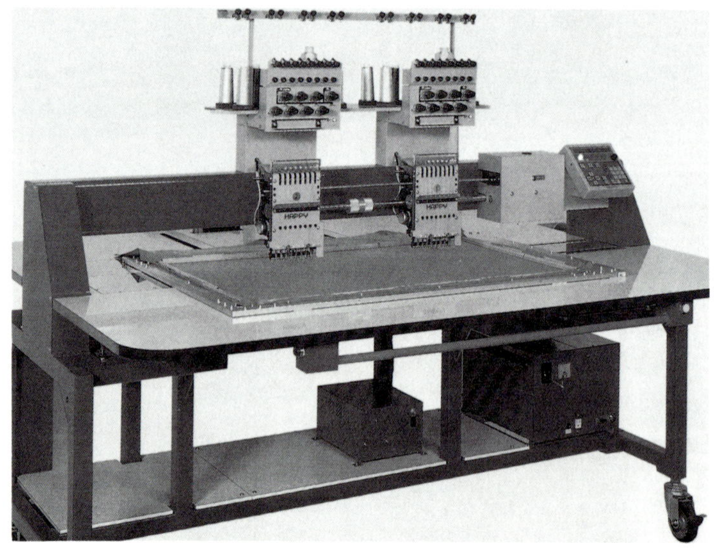

Model: HM4 Series

MODEL	HEADS	EMBROIDERY AREA	ALTERNATE
		cm	**cm**
L720A	20	480 x 240	480 x 4800
L816	16	480 x 310	480 x 4960
L812	12	480 x 400	480 x 4800
L810	10	480 x 480	480 x 4800
K718A	18	480 x 240	480 x 4320
		580 x 240	580 x 4320
K815	15	480 x 300	480 x 4500
		580 x 300	580 x 4500
S715	15	480 x 275	480 x 4125
		580 x 275	580 x 4125
		780 x 275	780 x 4125
S812	12	480 x 335	480 x 4020
		580 x 335	580 x 4020
		780 x 335	780 x 4020
S810	10	480 x 400	480 x 4000
		580 x 400	580 x 4000
		780 x 400	780 x 4000
S808	8	480 x 485	480 x 3880
		580 x 485	580 x 3880
		780 x 485	780 x 3880
HMS 802 58T 2 head		580 x 480	

Capable of stitching with thick yarn, 7 color change
Speed: 300 to 700 spm

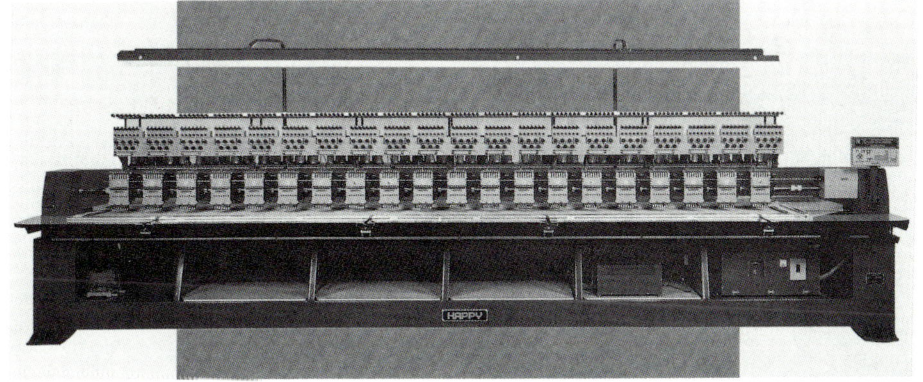

JUKI

The Juki AMS Series cycle machines have programmable pattern capability with computer controlled cycle machines. Straight, arc, zigzag embroidery can be made with an IBM personal computer, as well as pattern storage, and enlargements and reductions from 1% to 400% horizontally and vertically. Self diagnostic controls cover all major functions.

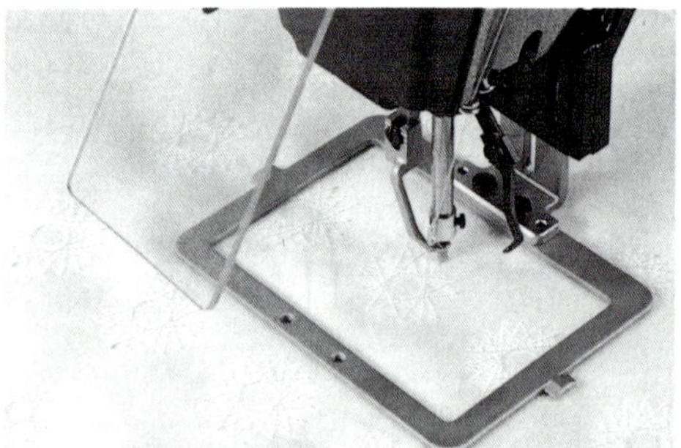

AMS	Stitching Area
220B	145mm x 200mm
210B	60mm x 100mm
212B	60mm x 125mm
205B	40mm x 50mm
206B	40mm x 50mm
229B	195mm x 600mm
224B	145mm x 400mm
222B	190mm x 200mm

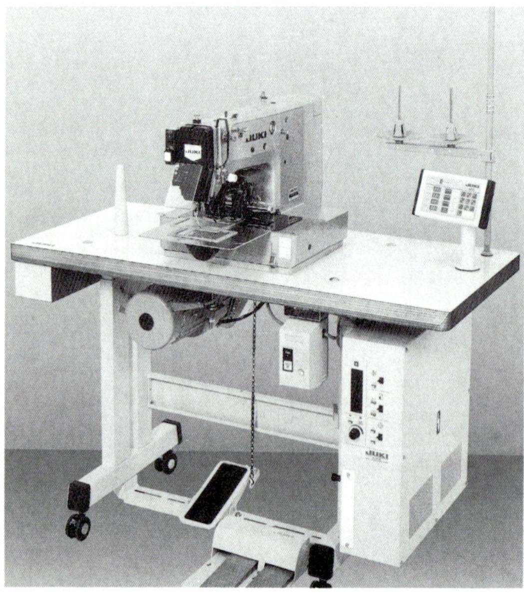

AMS-210BT is a standard machine for attaching labels.

AMS-210BJ is designed for heavy weight materials.

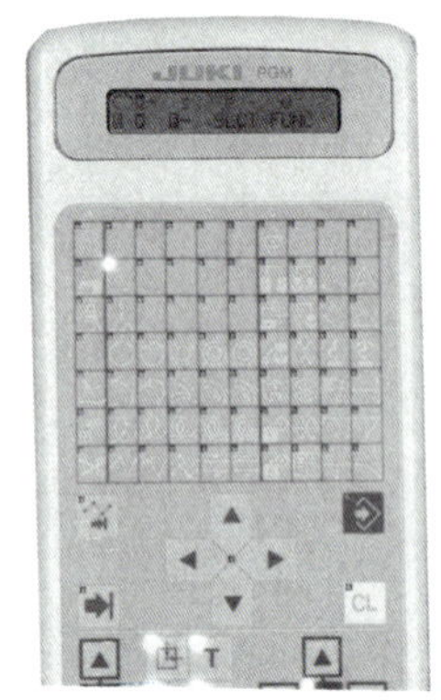

Juki Portable Programmer

MARCO

We know from the history of Multi-head machines that the Markscheffel Co. was the representative of the Wurker Company in Northern Germany from 1928. Ludwig Tragaser was the chief engineer and active in supplying parts for Wurker machines. Wurker was destroyed during the Second World War and no intention was made to resurrect the earlier company. They began to build a completely new machine known as the Marco Stickautomaten. Thousands of Marco machines were sold to more than 60 countries. As U.S. agent for Marco, the author sold about 100 machines in the U.S. in the late 1960's.

Many times during this period, the author had difficulty scheduling delivery since Marco's prime customers were the Japanese. With the introduction of their domestic machines, and the coming revolution in computerization, their business gradually shrank.

The factory management reverted to George Tragaser after the passing of his father and machinery sales continued to decline. The business was terminated in 1989. However, Horst Markscheffel took on a new partner, Dr. Rainer Bischoff, and they again are reviving the Marco name and quality.

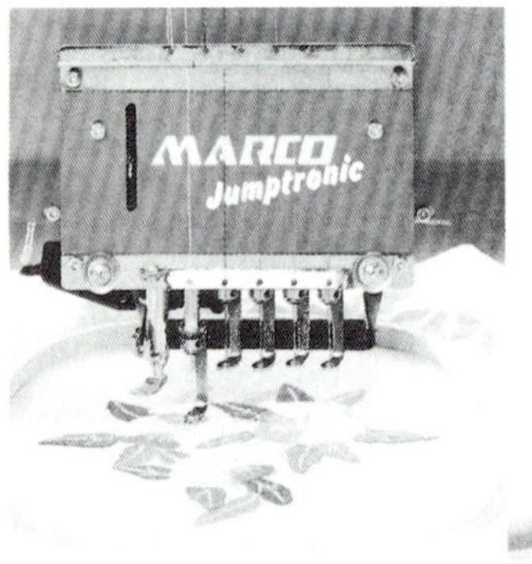

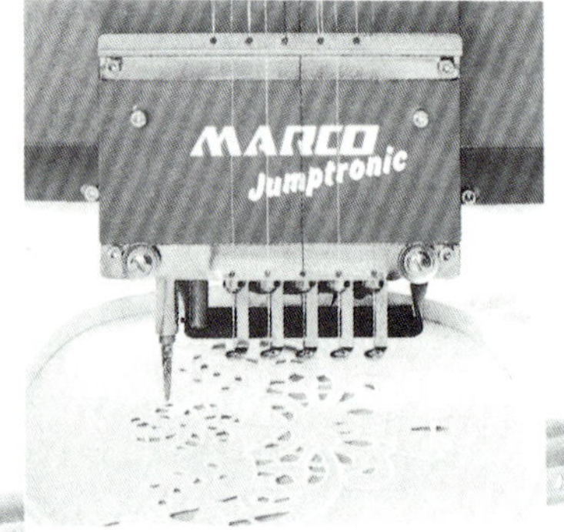

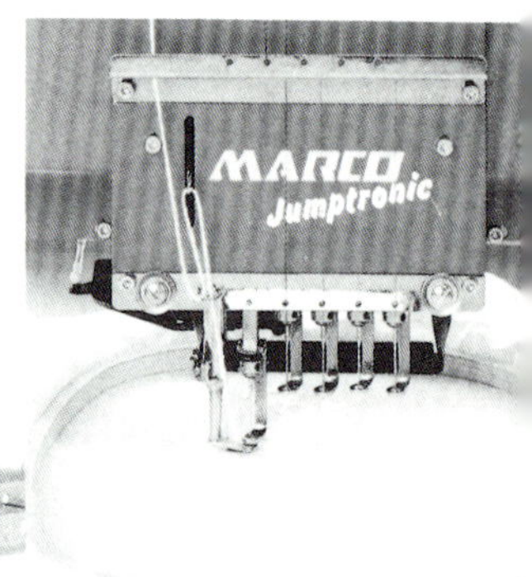

Series: Berlin

MODEL	HEADS	COLORS	STITCH AREAS FRAMES	STITCH AREAS BORDER
5008	8	5	400 x 500mm	400 x 3200mm
5010	10	5	310 x 500mm	310 x 3100mm
5012	12	5	255 x 500mm	255 x 3060mm

Recommended speed for all machines is 700 spm. Additional equipment includes upper and lower thread trimmers, disc drive, rotation, up to 250% size variance, mirror images, position return, alphabet keyboard, display in various languages, single head disconnect control, up to 500 stitch return repair, speed control, design repeat and power failure return. Options available: reading device for monogram discs, boring device, cord device, second disc drive and tape reader.

Model: Hamburg, now in the testing stage, will be offered at the Cologne Show in 1991.

Cooperation now exists between Marco and Textima, the former East German manufacturer of Multi-head machines known as Maschinenfabrik Weissensee.

Macpherson/Meistergram®

Meistergram machines were first introduced in March 1933 by the Meister Bros. in New York and Cleveland. They were the first monogram machines produced in the world.

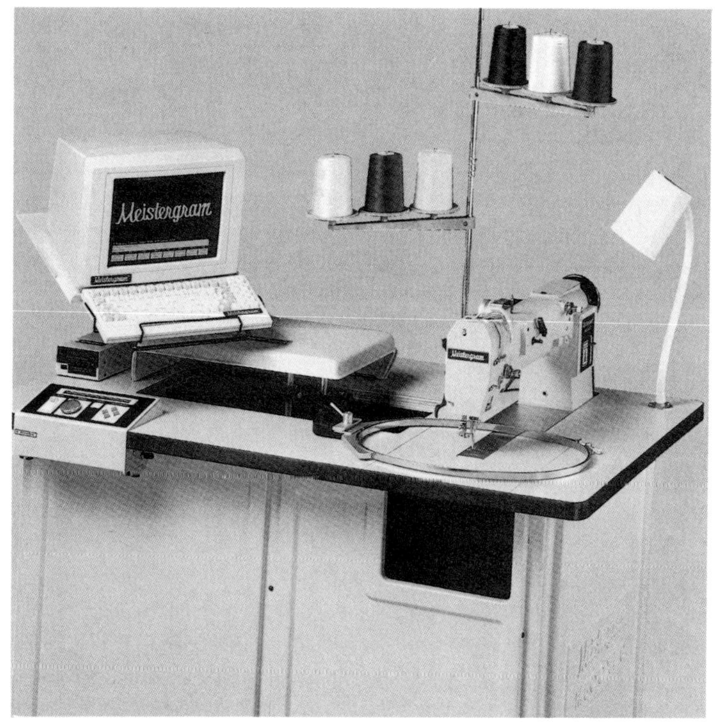

The 800XLC single head monogram machine operates at 1800 stitches per minute with a cylinder arm for caps, sleeves and pockets and a 2 1/2″ x 6″ sewing area. It quickly converts to a tabletop machine with a field of 18″ x 9″. Completely computerized with floppy disc technology. "Help" key offers instruction on garment preparation, sewing techniques, preventive maintenance, etc.

Computer design storage and lettering allow for the creation of original designs.

Saurer Textile Systems

Melco began in the early 1970's, creating computer software for various companies. Both partners had moved to Arvada, Co in the late 1960's for the skiing, thinking, why not work in an area you love? Their first jobs were for the Auto-Trol Company which built Digitizing tables. They were hired by Bill Barnes to help with a system ordered by the author, to be the first computerized embroidery punch system. Bill Childs was hired for his experience in programming computers, Chip for his previous work in electronics in the aircraft industry. The original company, Auto-Trol, was sold and the project was dropped. Then Bill and Chip formed their own company, known as Melco, and phoned the author to ask if they could complete the outstanding contract for the first computerized punch system for embroidery machines. They hired Marty DeSantis to assist in the programming.

They had asked the author if there were other businesses they could supply and were directed to the Ultramatic Company in New Haven, Conn., which was developing and producing electronic and computerized Multi-head embroidery machines. They built many electronic components for Ultramatic. They finally finished an acceptable punch system in 1976. Programming was in a condensed form since Plauen, Saurer and Marco Multi-head machines were in use. Melco built an enviable business with good management and suppliers and became a well known name in the Multi-head embroidery industry.

In 1989 Melco sold to the Saurer Company of Arbon, Switzerland, one of the foremost manufacturers of Shiffli embroidery machines in the world. Under Saurer's direction, Melco is moving forward with deliberate speed to becoming a major competitor in the Multi-head embroidery machine field. Some of the problems being addressed include the replacement of Tajima heads with new Melco heads. Replacement of existing representatives in the U.S. is progressing at this time with newer Saurer selected agents being considered. Saurer's two established embroidery locations in New Jersey and South Carolina are now actively serving the east coast. A survey of the industry is under way, to discover what the Melco embroiderer is really looking for and to improve his equipment, costing and production.

We believe that with the new Melco, Saurer, with its vast expertise will bring the embroidery industry to new heights of production, quality and fashion accomplishment.

C H 1

A single head chenille embroidery machine with the Epicor computer. 26 variable needle heights allow different stitching effects. Features chenille lettering capabilities and allows for creation of original custom designs. Design sizes can be enlarged or reduced to 20%.

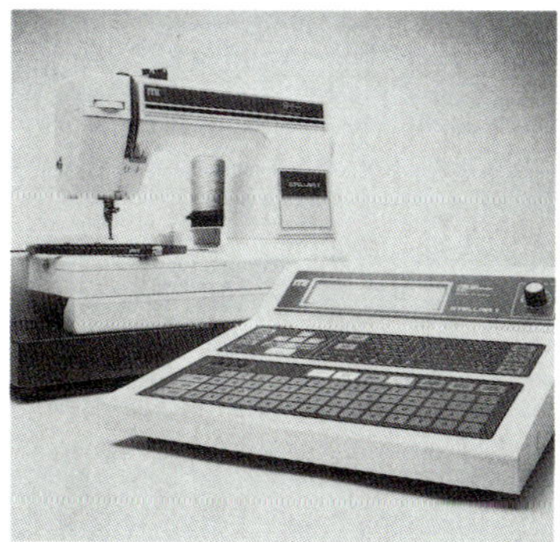

STELLA 1

Ideal for retail monogrammers, a small portable unit for lettering and designs. Included are 5 alphabet styles, hoops, thread and bobbins.

E M 1

A single needle, single head embroidery machine for flat goods.

E M C 6

A 6 color automatic change, single head embroidery machine, with a cylinder arm for embroidering caps, sleeves, pockets, etc.

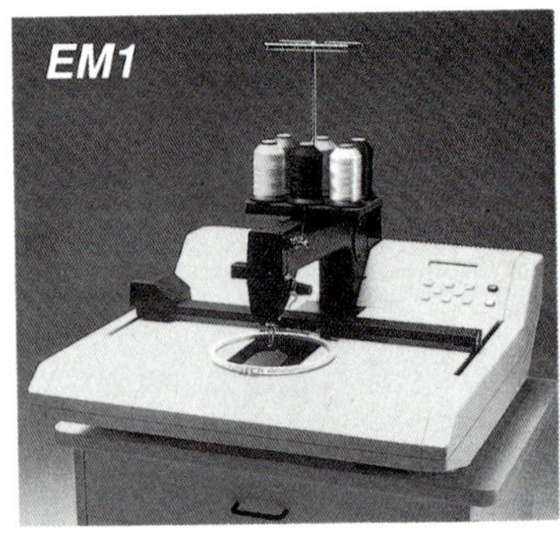

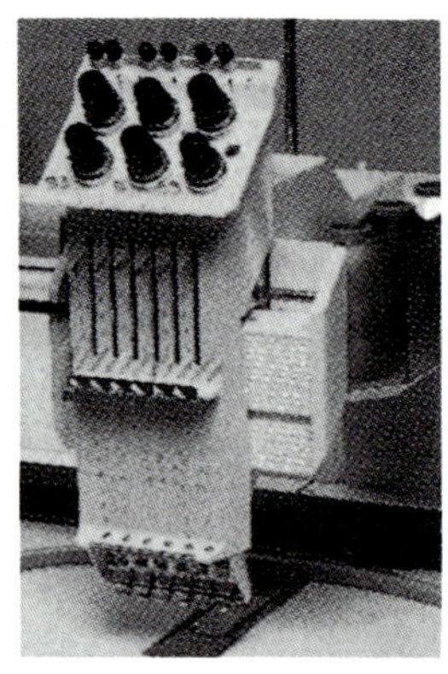

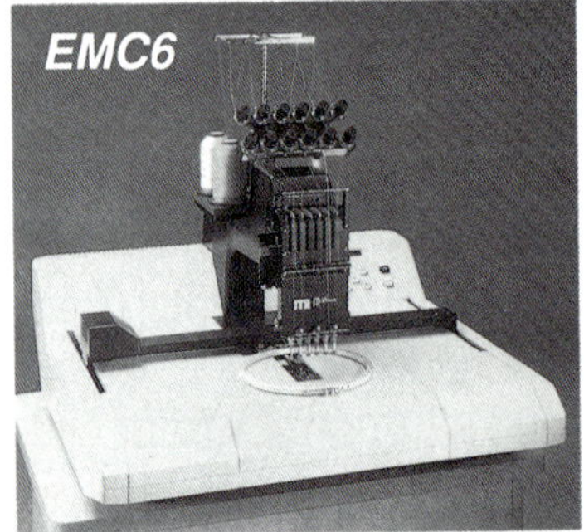

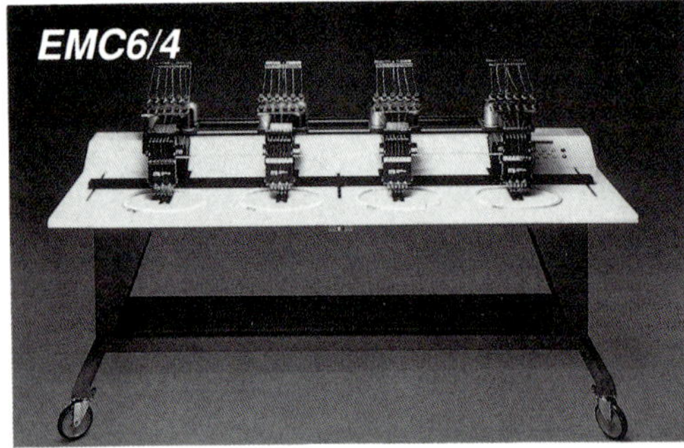

E M C 6/4

The Melco EMC 6/4 with 6 heads, the largest machine now made by Melco. 6 needle automatic color change with cylinder arm for caps.

E P 1

The EP1 is a single head, single needle, portable sewing machine weighing 67 lbs. and stitching at speeds to 600 spm.

Features include automatic thread break detector and low bobbin sensor. A bobbin winder is included.

It measures 20 1/2″ x 18″ and can embroider designs within a sewing field of 9 1/2″ x 5 1/2″.

The EPI embroiders expanded design, letter and monogram files. Additionally, lettering and design from Stella 1 formatted discs can be used and enlarged up to 4 times.

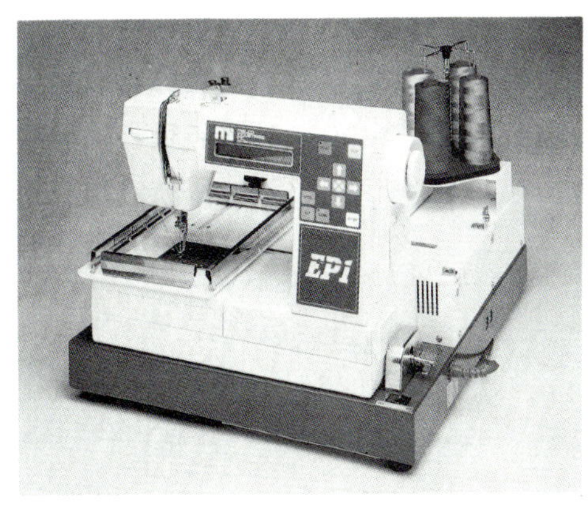

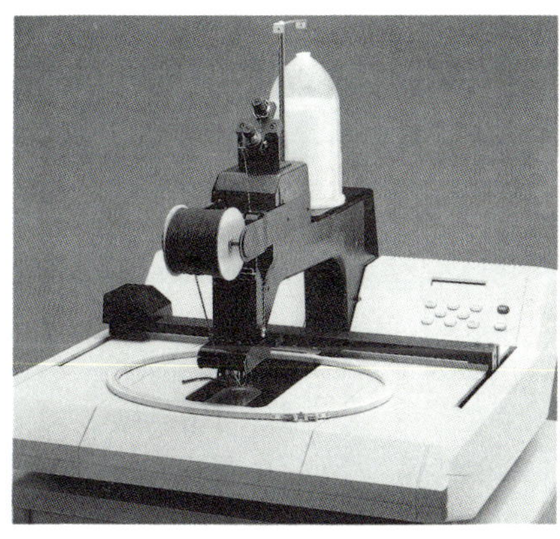

O S 1

Stitching a 3 dimensional design with an Epicor computer, the OS1 is used specifically to embroider a cord or other heavy textured yarn to form a different look in embroidery. Embroiders designs from 16″ in width to 11″ in height at 750 spm.

Pantograms®

Manufacturing Company, Inc.

A combination of a Toyota embroidery machine, IBM technology and Wilcom digitizing. Additions to form a modular embroidery system are possible. Complete stitching capabilities with state-of-the-art stitching machine, color monitor, computer with punching capabilities and 6 needle automatic color change. Frames for stitching with hoops on a flat surface or with a cylinder arm for caps or tubular goods, such as sleeves, pockets, etc.

PFAFF®

Innovative Kompetenz

SCHAFTEX, INC.

Pfaff is the largest sewing machine manufacturer in the world. The company was formed in 1862, and their main factory is located in Kaiserslauten, Germany.

Pfaff had embarked on a program of building Multi-head machines in the late 1970's and has gradually, on a planned expansion, built their delivery to 100 machines per month.

The Pfaff model KSM is a basic bridge type machine with unobstructed workspace and 5 to 28 heads. It is one of the quietest machines in the industry, with many advanced features. Spacing of heads can be adjusted at the factory for larger or smaller repeats. Normal distance between heads is 108mm to 162.42mm all in Schiffli repeat with a 450mm to 750mm field depth.

5 to 8 colors are normal with a unique threading system. Thread monitors report both needle and bobbin breakage. In case of thread breakage, the machine will stop after 3 to 8 stitches and the embroidery frame can be repositioned to any place to restitch the missing design. Top and bottom thread trimmers do not affect the thread monitors. Hook lubrication is standard.

The presser foot (retainer) height from the needle plate can be infinitely varied according to the thickness of the fabric being embroidered. Such features can be adjusted to puff embroidery similar to the Schiffli machine look. These units are standard on all machines.

The new bobbins contain 60% more thread than conventional embroidery machine bobbins.

The control unit has a full conversion program for punched tapes and memory for 250,000 stitches.

Functions of the Pfaff machine are included when tapes of other manufacturers are converted. Pattern rotation, reversing, and scaling from 50% to 200%, power failure protection, and menu guide in your own language with important functions controlled by individual keys.

Other options include an 8 channel tape reader, 3.5 inch Disk-drive and coding and lettering input device system and 3.5 double disk station.

Two extensions for memory capacity to 375,000 stitches and 500,000 stitches.

Border frames as well as frames for single motifs are available. The pantograph frame has a quick release mechanism to assure that a frame can be easily removed while a second frame is inserted.

Pfaff has a unique thread feed which saves much time and safely transfers thread from the cone to the head.

The quietest machine in the industry also offers a large bobbin for longer runs.

Pfaff Thread guidance system

PFAFF MODELS

MODEL	COLORS	FIELD DEPTH	HEADS	SPM
F800/M7	7	460 x 460mm	1-2	1200
F800/370	1	370 x 200mm	1	1100
F800/500	1	500 x 430mm	1	900
F800/320	1	320 x 200mm	2	1100

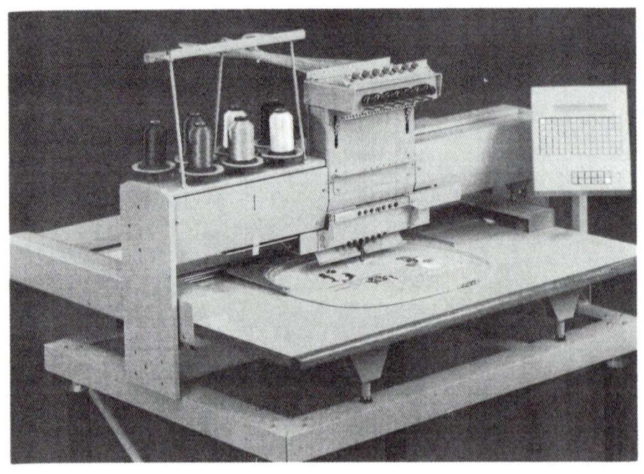

MODEL	COLORS	FIELD DEPTH	HEADS	SPM
F810/370	1	370 x 200mm	1	1100
F810/500	1	500 x 430mm	1	900
F812/320	1	320 x 200mm	2	1100
F900	1	290 x 200mm	1	1000
				Needle Dist.
KSM 200	6	450 x 520mm	5-28	108.28-
KSM 201	6	750 x 520mm	5-28	
KSM 210	5	450 x 520mm	5-28	108.28-
KSM 211	5	750 x 520mm	5-28	
KSM 220	8	450 x 487.26	6-18	162.42-
KSM 221	8	750 x 487.26	6-18	
KSM 230	7	450 x 487.26	6-18	162.42
KSM 231	7	750 x 487.26	6-18	

KSM 210, 211, 230 and 231 include boring. One year warranty. Recommended speed is 700 spm.

Boring device

HIRSCH INTERNATIONAL

Tajima was founded in 1944 as the Tokai Industrial Sewing Machine Co. for sales and service of industrial sewing machines. In 1964 they began manufacturing Tajima Multi-head embroidery machines. Through continuous growth, Tajima established a technical center in New Jersey, an assembly plant in Nottingham, England and service centers in Hong Kong, Shanghai and Guangdong, China.

Tajima is a leading manufacturer of Multi-head machines world wide with offices and distributors in most every industrialized country. Many innovations and technical advances are due to the advanced engineering capabilities of the Tajima Company.

Tajima machine features begin with the simplest computers. All features are increased (none eliminated) as the models grow from EH to G.

TMEH	TMEHC	TMMHC	TMEFH	TMEFHC	TMEG	FEATURES:
X	X	X	X	X	X	Automatic thread trimming
			X	X	X	Jumbo bobbin
X	X	X	X	X	X	Ind. take up lever/thread control
X	X	X	X	X	X	Reads binary/ternary tape/disc formats
X	X	X	X	X	X	800 spm operating speeds
					X	850 spm operating speeds
X	X	X	X	X	X	3, 4, 6, or 9 needles per head
X	X	X	X	X	X	Automatic needle sequencing
X	X	X	X	X	X	Multiplex memory up to 99 designs
X	X	X	X	X	X	Frame back stitch for repairs
X	X	X	X	X	X	Frame forward
X	X	X	X	X	X	Automatic repeating of stored designs
X	X	X	X	X	X	Scaling of design size, up or down
X	X	X	X	X	X	Design rotation
	X	X		X		Cylinder type for caps or tubular goods
X	X	X	X	X	X	Utilize Tajimas 1″ tape reader
X	X	X	X	X	X	TFD II, Tajima floppy disc drive
X			X		X	UTC, bobbin control
					X	Individual head control
X	X	X	X	X	X	Boring
X	X	X	X	X	X	Cording

TME-H series is a standard cylinder arm machine with automatic thread trimmers. (all measurements are in mm)

	Needles	Heads	Head Interval	Embroidery Space Frames	Embroidery Space Border
H606-906	6/9	6	500	300 x 500	300 x 3000
H608-908	6/9	8	400	300 x 400	300 x 3200
HH610-910	6/9	10	345	300 x 345	300 x 3450
H610-910	6/9	10	400	300 x 400	300 x 4000
H612-912	6/9	12	275	300 x 275	300 x 3300
H612-912	6/9	12	345	300 x 345	300 x 4140

6 or 9 color automatic color change.

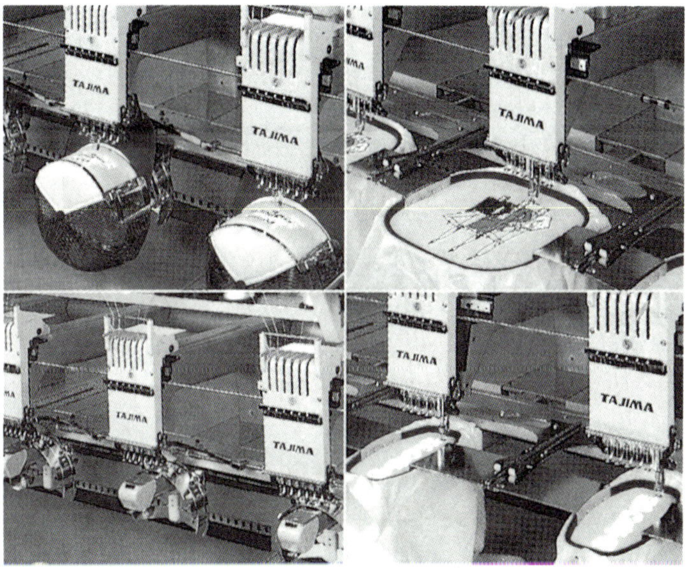

TME-HC series combines a standard Tajima embroidery machine with a detachable frame table plus a range of specialized frames. This machine is the basic Cap machine. The frame is easily detached for flat stitching of separate cut parts or for the use of the border frame. Automatic thread trimmers are included.

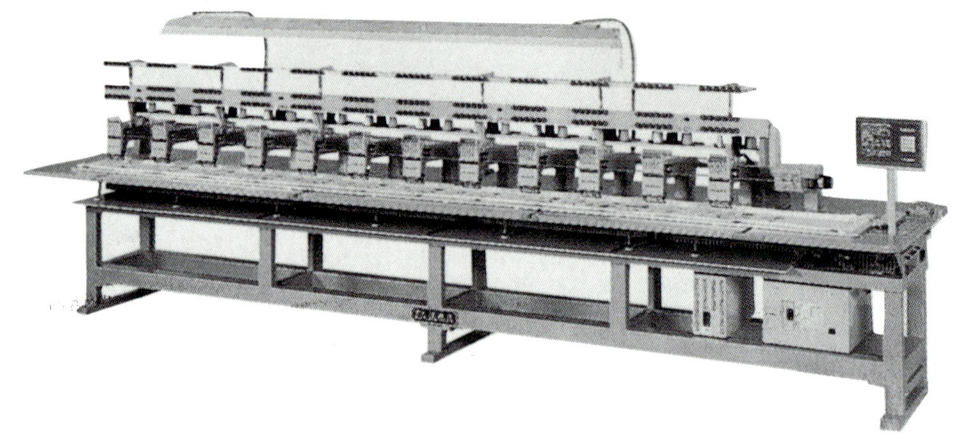

TME-HC

	Needles	Heads	Cap Frame	Tubular Frame	Table Frame	Border
EHC-606,906	6/9	6	70 x 140	300 x 300	300 x 500	300 x 3000
EHC-612,912	6/9	12	70 x 140	300 x 300	300 x 360	300 x 4320
EHC-918	9	18	70 x 140	240 x 240	300 x 275	300 x 4950

TMM-HC series, features a lettering keyboard control panel.
Cylinder arm models.

MHC-606	6	6	70 x 140	300 x 300	300 x 500	300 x 3000
MHC-612	6	12	70 x 140	300 x 300	300 x 360	300 x 4320

TMEF-H series bridge machines can be loaded from the front or back, and all are equipped with automatic thread trimmers.

			Head	Embroidery Space	
Models	Needles	Heads	Interval	Frames	Border
FH-608 908	6/9	8	400	450 x 400	450 x 4220
FH-610 910	6/9	10	345	450 x 325	450 x 4195
FH-610 910	6/9	10	400	450 x 400	450 x 5020
FH-612 912	6/9	12	275	450 x 275	450 x 4470
FH-612 912	6/9	12	345	450 x 345	450 x 5110
FH-615 915	6/9	15	275	450 x 275	450 x 5020
FH-616	6	16	240	450 x 240	450 x 4960
FH-618	6	18	230	450 x 230	450 x 5010
FH-620	6	20	200/400	450 x 200/400	450 x 5020

TMEF-HC A bridge machine also includes a cylinder arm.
Equipped with automatic thread trimmers.

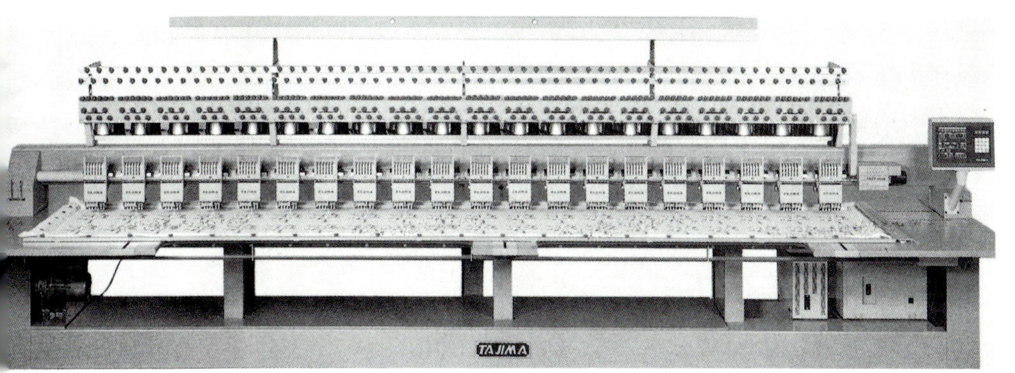

TMEF-H620

Models	Needles	Heads	Head Interval	Border	Cap	Tubular
FHC-606,906	6/9	6	500	450 x 500	70 x 140	400 x 430
FMC-608,908	6/9	8	500	450 x 500	70 x 140	400 x 430
FMC-612,912	6/9	12	360	450 x 360	70 x 140	400 x 290

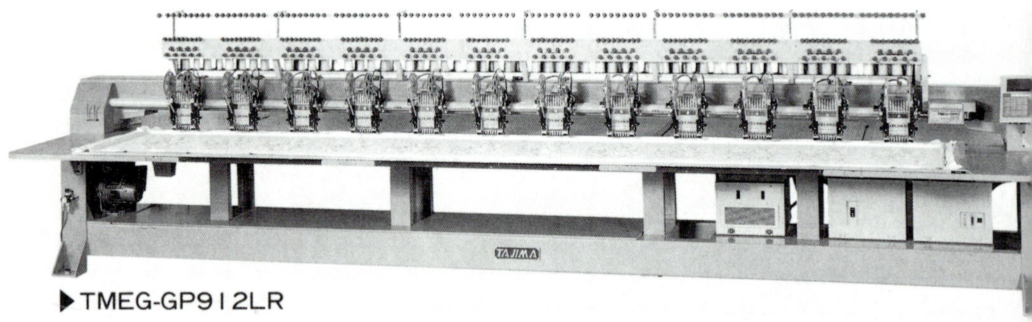
▶TMEG-GP912LR

TMEF-HCA 18 Head Cap Machine

TMEG SERIES

	Needles	Heads	Head Interval	Embroidery Space Frames	Border
908-610	6/9	8	480	450 x 480	450 x 3840
910-610	6/9	10	345(W)	450 x 345(690)	450 x 3450
910-610	6/9	10	400	450 x 400	450 x 4000
G910-G610	6/9	10	480	450 x 480	450 x 4800
912-612	6/9	12	275(W)	450 x 275(550)	450 x 3300
912-610	6/9	12	345	450 x 345	450 x 4140
G912-G612	6/9	12	400	450 x 400	450 x 4800
G912-G612	6/9	14	345	450 x 345	450 x 4830
915-615	6/9	15	275	450 x 275	450 x 4125
G915-G615	6/9	15	330	450 x 330	450 x 4950
616	6	16	240(W)	450 x 240(480)	450 x 3840
G918-G618	6/9	18	275	450 x 275	450 x 4950
620	6	20	200(W)	450 x 200(400)	450 x 4000
G620	6	20	240(W)	450 x 240(480)	450 x 4800
G624	6	24	200(W)	450 x 200(400)	450 x 4800
424	4	24	162.5(W)	450 x 162.5(325)	450 x 3900
324	3	24	135.4(W)	450 x 135.4(270.8)	450 x 3249.6
G430	4	30	162.5(W)	450 x 162.5(487.5)	450 x 4875

A whole new era opens with the introduction of the Tajima Roller Traverse model for fabric roll feed. Yard goods as we know it can be performed on certain fabrics in endless length. Quilting as well as embroidery including novelty devices used on other Tajima machines can create a whole new use of embroidery manufacture with Multi-head machines. The only limitation will be the fabrics selected to run. Competition with Schiffli machines is a reality.

The machines feature 3 color automatic change with 99 selections available. Automatic repeat can be preset. Stitchback eliminates the need for mending as the machine will stop at a thread break, and, by stitching back up to 5 stitches, repairs can be made automatically. For single head operation the repair can retrace as many as 1000 stitches. Upper and lower thread trimming is available.

Designs can be scaled up or down from 50% to 200% in 1% increments.

Designs can be rotated, stitches can be expanded from .1 to 1.0 mm. Head use can be selected which basically allows different repeats through the stitching process. This also allows several heads to make one larger design.

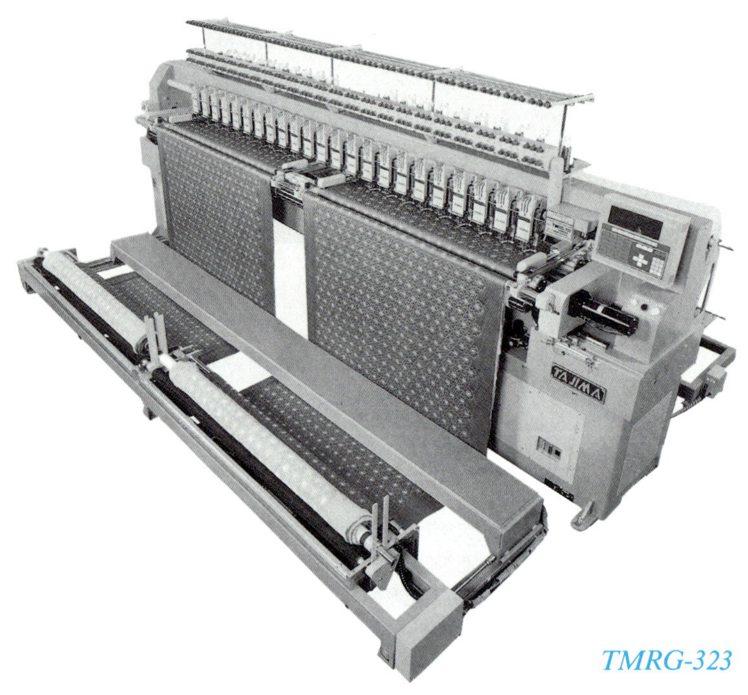

TMRG-323

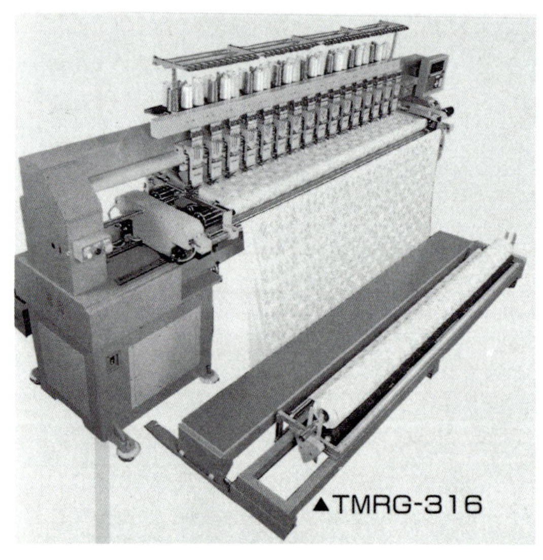

▲TMRG-316

TMLE-114/70WF

MODEL	HEADS	HEAD INTERVAL	EMBROIDERY AREA	WIDTH
TMRG-323	23	135.4	180 x (135.4 + 44.6)	3158.8 x 1
TMRG-316	16	135.4	270.8	2301.8 x 1

TMEG/AFC Frame changer
TMEG-100WF 24 135.4 Max. fabric width 1524mm (60″) 2 rolls
TMEG-160SF 18 135.4 Max. fabric width 2325mm (92″) 1 roll
TMLE-111 Automatic frame changer
TMLE-110SF 11 135.4 Max. fabric width 1850 1 roll
TMLE-70WF 14 135.4 Max. fabric width 1200 2 rolls

TMCE-S100 SERIES is the Tajima version of a chenille embroidery machine. It can use Moss and/or Chain stitches as well as cording. The needle height is adjustable in 10 steps for higher pile fabrics. Upon completion of stitching there is an automatic tie-off to avoid loosening of the threads. Special frame software for curved stitching keeps the design precise.

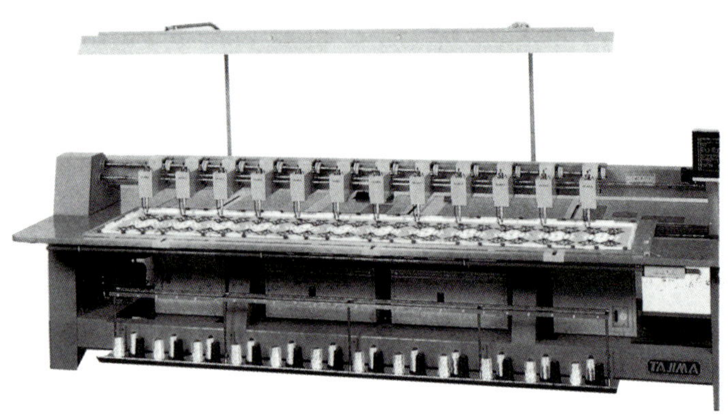

Model	Heads	Head Interval	Embroidery Space Frames	Border
TMCE-S106	6	460	450 x 460	450 x 2760
TMCE-S108	8	360	450 x 360	450 x 2880
TMCE-S110	10	295	450 x 295	450 x 2950
TMCE-S112	12	275(550)	450 x 275(550)	450 x 3300

TMEG-P Series is the Tajima's sequin machine, which can stitch with normal threads as well as sequins, becoming a multi-purpose high fashion unit. The machine can be set with 2 colors of sequins and 7 colors of rayon or polyester threads.

6
5
TAJIMA

8

	Heads	Head Interval	Embroidery Space Frames	Border
P908-P608	8	480	450 x 480	450 x 3840
P910-P610	10	345(W)	450 x 345(690)	450 x 3450
P910-P610	10	400	450 x 400	450 x 4000
GP910-GP610	10	480	450 x 480	450 x 4800
P912-P612	12	275(W)	450 x 275(550)	450 x 3300
P912-P612	12	345	450 x 345	450 x 4150
GP912-GP612	12	400	450 x 400	450 x 4800
GP914-GP614	14	345	450 x 345	450 x 4830
P915-P615	15	275	450 x 275	450 x 4125
GP915-GP615	15	330	450 x 330	450 x 4950
P616	16	240(W)	450 x 240(480)	450 x 3840
GP618-GP618	18	275	450 x 275	450 x 4950
P620	20	200(W)	450 x 200(400)	450 x 4000
GP620	20	240(W)	450 x 240(480)	450 x 4800
GP624	24	200(W)	450 x 200(400)	450 x 4800
P424	24	162.5(W)	450 x L62.5(324)	450 x 3900
P324	24	135.4(W)	450 x 135.4(270.8)	450 x 3249.6
GP430	30	162.5(W)	450 x 162.5(487.5)	450 x 4875

With the TMLE-100 stitching thread, core thread and coiling thread can be used in combination; this should be a designer's delight. There are so many more thread combinations possible than those shown, to leave the imagination unrestrained. The novelty yarns are tacked by a series of zig-zag stitches, 6 variations are easily selected from the stitch processor.

MODEL	HEADS	EMBROIDERY SPACE
TMLE-106	6	680 x 540
TMLE-108	8	680 x 460
TMLE-110	10	680 x 400
TMLE-112	12	680 x 275 (550)

Options include sequin attachment.

TMLE-112 D5	12	680 x 540 (135)
TMLE-112 D5	12	680 x 600 (135)
TMLE-116 D5	16	680 x 470 (135)

Tajima has a large staff working on new ideas, continually finding better uses for embroidery as well as better ways to build machines, automating the industry and continuing their advances of the last 15 years.

Models can be seen under construction in their plant, not yet on the market, of 32, 34, and 36 head Multi-head machines.

TOYOTA
apparel equipment

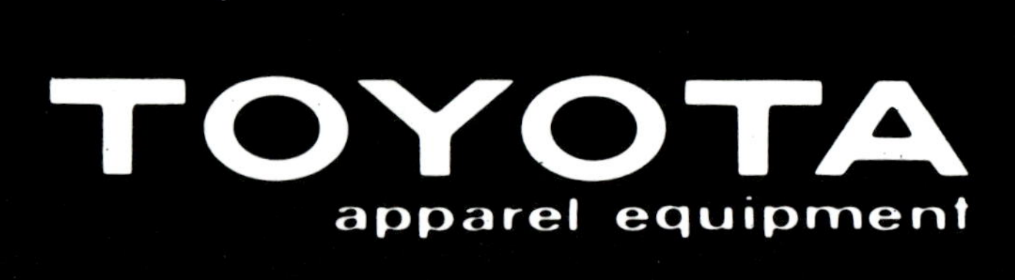

Nomura (America) Corp.		Aisin Seiki Co., Ltd.
Model AD 100-510	1	6¾ ″ x 15½ ″ Portable
Model AD 510	1	6¾ ″ x 15½ ″
Model AD 800	6	240mm x 400mm
Model AD 820	6	267mm x 432mm

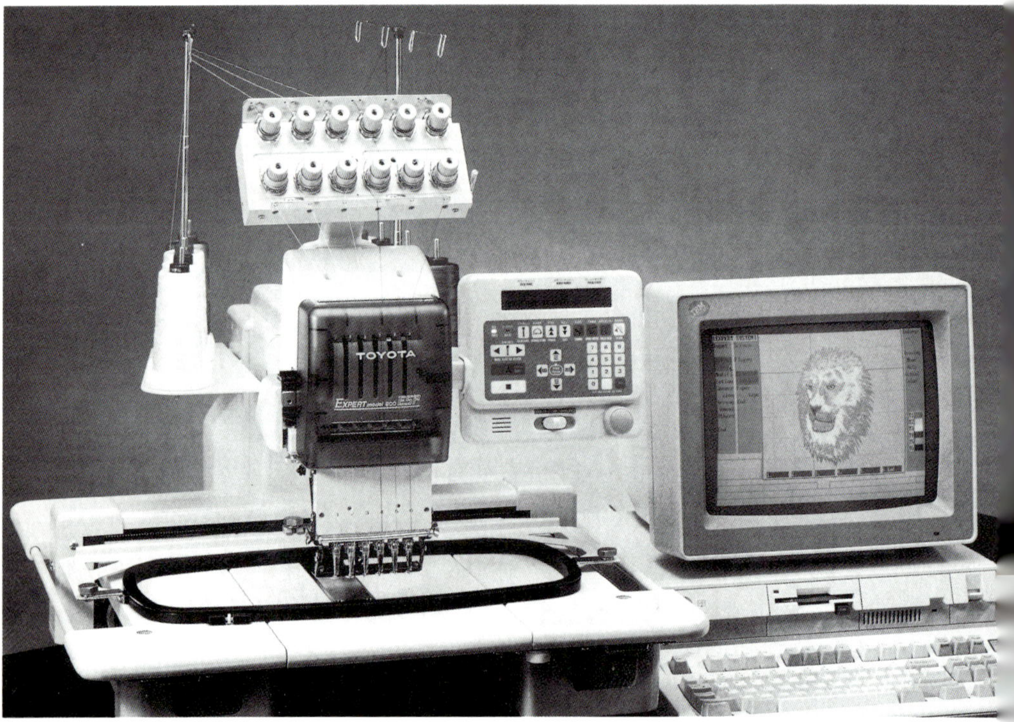

All Toyota embroidery machines are built with state-of-the-art electronics. Two models (800/820) have automatic 6 color change with thread trimmers and provide adequate space for all types of articles, including a cylinder arm that allows for the stitching of caps, socks, sleeves, etc.

Model 380 'Expert' Computer directed module. This is the original modular embroidery machine system patented in the USA, a system which will operate more than one machine at one time with different patterns or the same design.

The computer has the ability to enlarge or reduce designs and change density as required. Original designs with lettering and existing art can be created, edited and changed with the use of the mouse against the menu displayed on the screen.

These machines are the basis of the Pantogram units shown.

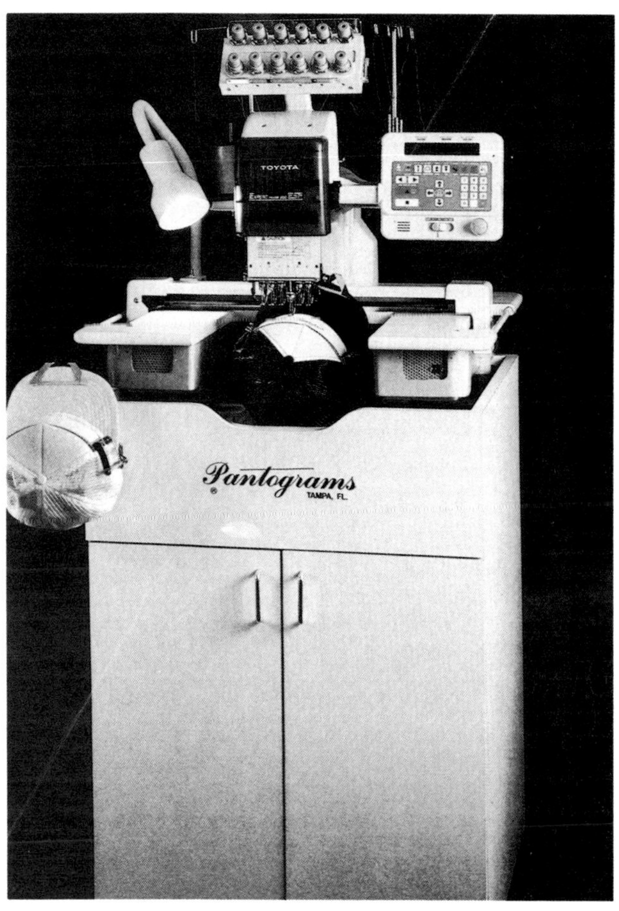

ULTRAMATIC

The ultimate monogram/embroidery machine

The Golia family has been involved in the embroidery business since the founding of their original company, New Haven Embroidery, in the 1920's. Thus, they have acquired quite extensive knowledge of the industry and its machinery through their years as a machine embroiderer, distributor and manufacturer of embroidery machines and through the operation of their design and tape center.

In the 1970s, Dominick Golia and his son Kenneth formed a company known as Marco-American after purchasing the Marco machine agency from the author. This firm distributed Multi-head mechanical embroidery machines manufactured by Marco of West Germany. Marco-American also had a punch center which programmed jacquard paper tapes of embroidery patterns for use with mechanical Marco and other brands of Multi-head machines.

Also in the early 1970's , the Golias conceived of an idea for an electronic embroidery machine, and by 1974 had developed their first machine. Ultramatic began as a division of Marco-American.

The Ultramatic was the first Multi-head embroidery machine developed in the U.S. and remains so to this day.

The first Ultramatic machine was the only one at the time to utilize stepping motor drives to move the embroidery frame along the X and Y coordinates. Accuracy of this drive precluded other Multi-head machines then in existence. The machine used one inch, 8-channel computer paper tape.

Ultramatic introduced a six head model of their electronic embroidery machine at the 1975 Bobbin Show and ran it at twice the speed of the mechanical embroidery machines. These unique electronic machines were sold by Ultramatic from 1975 until 1977. Marketing this new technology was a difficult task, and the machine was initially met with skepticism and fear of electronics. However, after a short period of time, the Ultramatic electronic embroidery machines became stable products in the industry.

Soon after the success of the electronic embroidery machine, Ultramatic began expanding their equipment lines's capability. Development of an Ultramatic punch system began in 1976. This system enabled users to design and punch their own custom embroidery tapes and to use it to verify the design while it was being programmed. Thus, when the programmer was finished, they had a sewn sample of the design.

With the basic components of the electronic embroidery system complete, Ken Golia developed a system where the embroidery machine could automatically stitch letters stored on computer chips. Alphabets were selected which would best serve the monogramer and embroiderer.

Ultramatic engineers created artwork, the particular stitch configurations and techniques for translation of stitching from letter to letter and then digitized the selected alphabets. Each character was stored in memory and defined as having a variable width and height, this data was then programmed onto electronic boards.

A keyboard input system was then devised to interface with the existing embroidery machine. They then began to build and market the Ultramatic Keyboard Machine by combining the electronic keyboard assembly with a mechanical embroidery machine component. Letters and characters would be able to be stitched from memory.

The first Ultramatic keyboard machine had a great impact on the embroidery industry. It simplified the creation of embroidered lettering by allowing the operator to type in the letter, and select the desired size with automatic spacing electronically controlled.

An early 3 color manual color change led to further development of 6 color automatic change device.

Standard machines are supplied with a top thread breaker and lighting.

The machine features the computerized keyboard with 24 character display, speed control, automatic return to origin, individualized thread take up device, lettering on an upper and lower arc, automatic centering, variable slant, italicized and vertical letter arching, stitch width variability, speed readout and many more features. Thread trimmers are available on all models.

The basic machines are individual sewing heads that are ideal for embroidering cut parts and full garments. The variety of equipment available fills a definite niche in the American market.

There are 6 machines from the single head to the 12 head machine, a single head 'portable' machine and the new 2 head cap machine.

The only machine that claims to use right or left twist threads, including Schiffli rayon yarns 100/2, 150/2 rayon, DMC 50 through 20/2 and rayon.

Electronic 6 needle color change, automatic color change embroidery and monogram machines. Cap frames for single and 2 head machines.

ULTRAMATIC

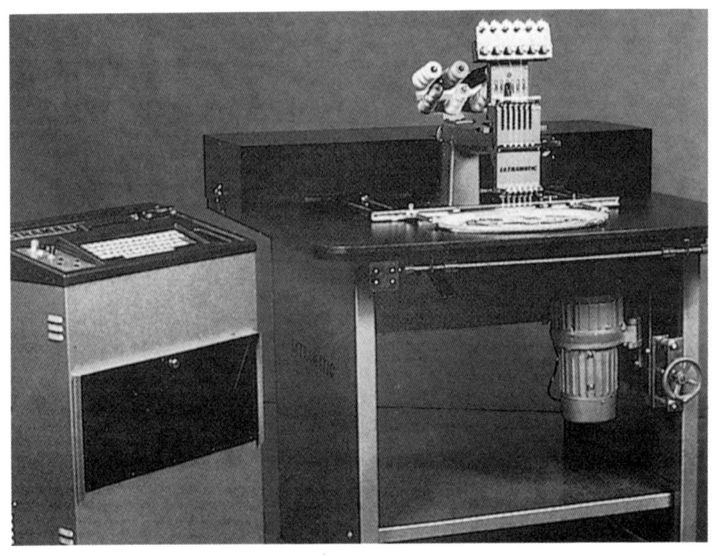

Ultramatic	Heads	Stitch Area
100c/c	1	11″ x 16″
200c/c	2	11″ x 16″
400c/c	4	11″ x 16″
600c/c	6	11″ x 16″
800c/c	8	11″ x 16″
1200c/c	12	11″ x 8″

Single needle electronic and monogram machines.

Ultramatic	Heads	Stitch Area
100	1	8″ x 16″
200	2	8″ x 16″
400	4	8″ x 16″
600	6	8″ x 16″
800	8	8″ x 16″
1200	12	8″ x 8″

Ultramatic Jr. is a single head portable computerized sewing machine in a suitcase with wheels. Sewing area is 9″ x 6½″. Take it directly to your customer or craft fair if desired.

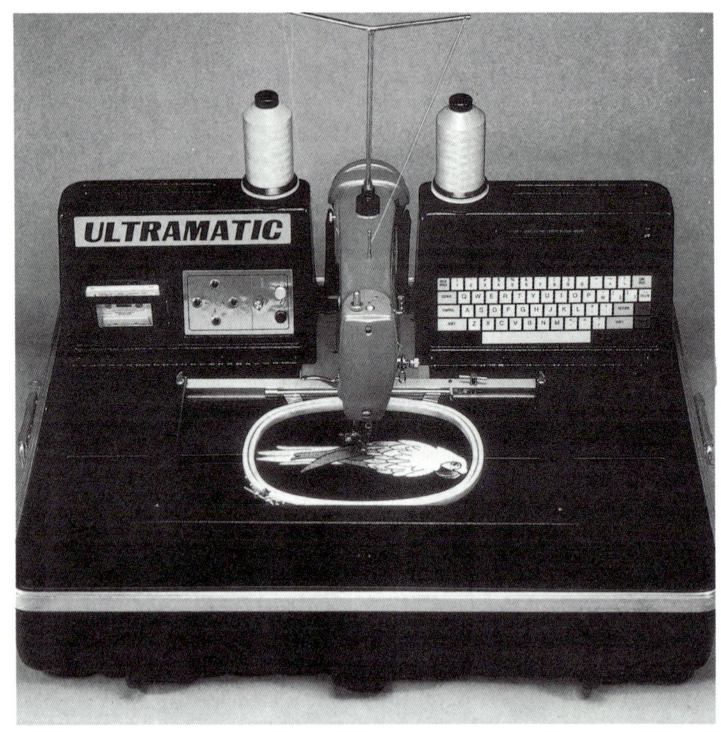

Portable Ultramatic Jr

Speeds 500 to 1000 spm.

The keyboard has all available programming including back up system to correct missing stitches, and variable stitch density from 10 to 99 stitches. The computer with 128K memory allows you to combine custom designs with any alphabet style, and allows the complete job to be stored on a cassette. Hundreds of stock designs are available with many alphabet styles, all stored in memory for instant use.

The Ultramatic single and double head machine has an extra long cylinder arm machine for flat goods, and a drop table that also allows embroidering on sweatshirts, pants-legs, bags, caps etc. It has 6 needle color change, a keyboard with all of Ultramatic's programming and available library with hundreds of stock designs and lettering styles. The embroidery stitch area is 11″ x 16″. A new machine has been developed with a field area of 11 ½″ x 24″.

Ultramatic 2 head cap machine

Ultramatic can also supply prestitched chenille and a pre-programmed keyboard alphabet that is set up to accommodate many sizes and styles of tackle twill lettering.

Ultramatic offers dozens of alphabet and hundreds of design panels for your Ultramatic monogram machine. You can use these designs with the alphabet panels to create your own designs.

A Chenille program has also been developed using premade chenille type cloth which is stitched by the yard in 14 colors. Various size athletic letters can be die cut and purchased for your mascot panels for use with your monogram machine. With the use of the chenille alphabet panel, an outline of the letter is stitched, the chenille letter is placed on a garment, and the outline of the letter plus any mascot is stitched onto it.

MULTI-STICKTRONIC

Z S K is the outcome of the bankruptcy of the Zangs machine company, a famous manufacturer of Schiffli and Multi-head machines. Z S K took over the sales and manufacturing of the Multi-head division. Their heavy duty machines are state-of-the-art designs and fully computerized, selling world wide but very strong in Europe.

Model 172 with boring device

Up to 9 needle color change available on the models

MODEL	HEADS	NEEDLES PER HEAD	FIELD BORDER	FIELD HOOP
170	6	1	not available	200 x 300mm
170	12	1	not available	200 x 120mm
172	12	9/4	700 x 2880	700 x 240mm
			500 x 2880	500 x 240mm
172	8	9/4	700 x 2880/3200	700 x 360/400mm
			500 x 2880/3200	500 x 360/400mm
172	6	9/4	700 x 3960	700 x 480mm
			500 x 3960	500 x 480mm
172	4	9/4	700 x 2400	700 x 600mm
173	1	1	not available	900 x 900mm
174	12	9/4	700 x 3960	700 x 330
			500 x 3960	500 x 330
174	10	9/4	700 x 4000	700 x 400
			500 x 4000	500 x 400
174	8	9/4	700 x 3960	700 x 495
			500 x 3960	500 x 495
174	4	9/4	900 x 3600	900 x 900
			500 x 3960	500 x 495
175	1	1	900 x 3600	900 x 900
			500 x 3960	500 x 495
201	1	9/4	900 x 3600	500 x 500

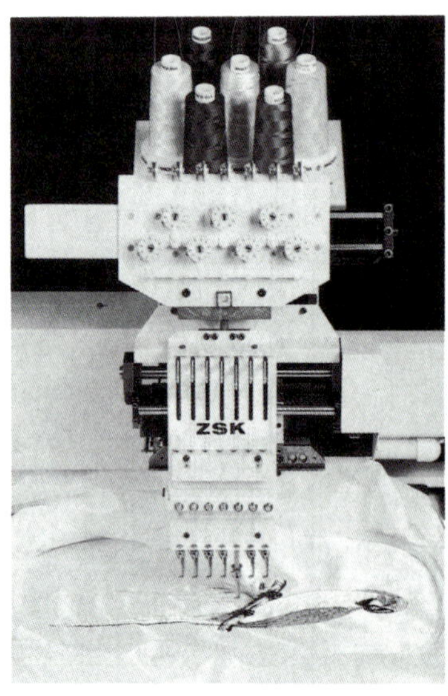

Model 201

Model 202 Monogram machine has a 4 letter style. The letter size is variable from 5mm to 100mm, and it has a lettering line spacing variable from 5mm to 100mm. The stitch density is fully controllable. With the letter separation variable, letters can be varied from straight to 15 degree slant forward or backward. Letter width is variable from 50% to 150%, and both automatic fill or satin stitch can be used.

Additional features include: horizontal and vertical line with start position control, descending and ascending line with height interval control, top arc with radius adjustment, and reverse arc with radius adjustment.

Model 174

MODEL	HEADS	NEEDLES PER HEAD	FIELD BORDER	FIELD HOOP
202	2	9	450 x 450mm	
210	10	9		
215	15	9		
218	18	9		
220	20	9/4	700 x 4800	700 x 240
			500 x 4800	500 x 240
224	24	9/4	700 x 3960	700 x 165
			500 x 3960	500 x 165

Model 224

The customer can select either 4 or 9 automatic color change heads upon order. Recommended maximum speed is 750 spm. Thread trimmer and borer are available on request.

Cord loop device available for all machines on request. Sequin device available for models 172, 174 and 220.

CHAPTER V

DESIGNING AND PATTERN MAKING

The DESIGNER is the artist who creates the idea. He or she should know the capabilities of embroidery and what it can do to enhance fashion. However, without an understanding of the basic machine language involved, they will not create beautiful embroidery. It would be like handing an engraver a palette and brush.

The ENLARGER is the person who interprets the artist's wishes and draws the enlarged technical drawing (cartoon) with all of the machine language from which the tapes can be cut.

The embroidery designer and enlarger are many times the same person. The enlarger should be both an artist and a drafts person. In many cases he or she creates the original design in sketch form, applying their knowledge of the capabilities of the machine which will produce the end product.

Unfortunately, many people have no idea of the limits of the embroidery machine. It is certainly not a printing machine or a weaving machine. There are limits to the size of the stitches in length and width, and color possibilities. Of course, price is also a consideration.

Embroidery design consists of a library which represents the accumulation of thousands of years of hand work through hundreds of cultures. Therefore, we have a huge amount of material and experience to draw upon for guidance.

Embroidery is always the addition of art to a finished fabric, but it is not simply the addition of stitching or color. It can create a whole new feeling, a romance of style with texture, color, and dimension using many types of stitches. Embroidery can be used to create tapestry, laces, pictures, motifs, stories in yarn, trims and allovers.

The use of embroidery on virtually any fabric will help to make it more beautiful and more saleable.

All types of embroidery machines are wonderful to work with. They have been designed specifically for the task. Not only will they be able to stitch most any yarn, but will do so on most any base cloth, from the lightest sheers and knits to light weight vinyl and leather.

The limitations that might arise are the limits of the machine on which the embroidery is to be stitched.

Is the frame area sufficient? Is it sufficient for the design? Is the design cost effective?

New ideas can be presented in many ways. A sketch in color can be drawn as an inexpensive beginning, with specific yarns and fabrics attached. Then a hand sample might be made, provided you have an experienced sample maker, or an actual punch sample, using the customer's fabrics and colors. In the apparel trade the next step might be "salesman's samples" which require an investment in actually producing yardage so that samples for salesmen to show their prospective customers might be provided. Should the item be interesting to the buyers, then orders will follow.

Sketches must be accurate. We can not sketch one design and deliver something else because what we drew first was not practical. If the design is repeat work, then enough repeats of the design should be shown so the customer can envision the finished product. If designs are symmetrical, they should be drawn mechanically with a compass, dividers and a steel rule.

Threads can vary as much as the base cloths on which we embroider. There are many textures, colors and sizes which can add to the story of the design. Other ornaments are available such as sequins, stones, metal, wood and leather, which can further enhance the design.

Dimension can be added by building up certain parts of a design with underlay stitches, flowers can be made to appear three dimensional. Appliques, partially stitched into a fabric, part hanging loose, can seem to flutter on the fabric.

With all of the above, one factor must always be taken into account, and that is the eventual cost. Beautiful embroidery does not necessarily have to be expensive, but consider when making your drawings that stitches can be converted into time, which is the main cost factor for embroidery. Never skimp or spread stitches so far apart that they destroy the design. It is better to redesign the product than ruin it with cheapening or reducing the stitches. All customers would like to pay the least amount for embroidery trim, so consideration of your client and a meeting of the minds should tell you how much you have to work with.

Yard goods can be made less expensive by reducing the repeat of a design. It may look great as a 16/4 but if your customer can't afford it, you might be able to keep the same theme and quality by reducing the design to 12/4.

We understand that all designs are not original, many might be direct copies of ancient or not so ancient art, or adaptions of previously made or competitors' embroideries. However, copies are becoming a thing of the past. Today, without the requirement of a copyright notice, you must assume all designs are protected.

When President Reagan signed the Berne Convention Implementation Act of 1988, it made effective the date of March 1, 1989 after which time, if a design is registered with the Library of Congress, then full copyright protection is granted even if the design is not marked. This gives an International protection to members of the Berne Convention which includes the U.S. and dozens of other countries.

The enlarger must present the puncher or programmer with an accurate drawing. To do so, he requires certain tools of the trade. Certain well tested materials are suggested. Jute tag paper (.21mm .008″) is smooth and thin enough to draw proper enlarged designs. An opaque projector can be used for enlarging drawings: the sketch can be inserted and the machine adjusted for projection to a wall or a table to make the 6 time enlargement. Make a point of checking the image size each time you use the projector if you wish an accurate six time enlargement. When the author first began in business he had a blouse design enlarged and punched, then ran the complete order. Something looked strange - the design was only enlarged 5 times! All punch machines are set mechanically to record stitches 1/6 the measurement of the enlargement.

For Schiffli enlarging, a French rule is necessary. This measurement is the basis of the needle spacing on all Schiffli machines today. Six French inches, or one Zoll, is the enlarged distance of the smallest repeat, needle to needle, equaling 4/4, pronounced four quarter. (In the early 1900s, machines were built for 3/4 and 6/4.)

Schiffli Yields and Measurements

All embroidery on Schiffli machines is produced with two lengths of fabric; a 10 yard machine will yield 20 yards; a 15 yard machine will yield 30 yards; a 21 yard machine will yield 42 yards.

The calculations used for the repeats are: 1 french inch = 1.0648 inches = 2.7045 cm.

ACTUAL SIZE				6X ENLARGED SIZE			10 YARD		15 YARD		21 YARD	
QUARTER	FRENCH	METRIC	INCH	FRENCH	METRIC	INCH	NEEDLES	DOZENS	NEEDLES	DOZENS	NEEDLES	DOZENS
4/4	1	2.7cm	1-1/16	6	16.2cm	6-3/8	684	57	1024	85-1/3	1416	118
8/4	2	5.4cm	2-1/8	12	32.5cm	12-3/4	342	28-1/2	512	42-2/3	708	59
12/4	3	8.1cm	3-3/16	18	48.7cm	19-1/8	228	19	342	28-1/2	472	39-1/3
16/4	4	10.8cm	4-1/4	24	64.9cm	25-1/2	172	14-1/3	256	21-2/3	354	20-1/2
20/4	5	13.5cm	5-5/16	30	81.1cm	31-7/8	138	11-1/2	206	17-1/6	282	23-1/2
24/4	6	16.2cm	6-3/8	36	97.3cm	38-3/8	114	9-1/2	172	14-1/3	236	18
28/4	7	18.9cm	7-7/16	42	113.6cm	44-3/4	98	8-1/6	148	12-1/3	202	16-5/6
32/4	8	21.6cm	8-1/2	48	129.8cm	51-1/8	86	7-1/6	128	10-2/3	176	14-1/6
36/4	9	24.3cm	9-9/16	54	146.6cm	57-1/2	76	6-1/3	112	9-1/3	156	13
40/4	10	27.0cm	10-5/8	60	162.3cm	63-3/4	70	5-5/6	104	8-2/3	140	11-2/3

Schiffli Lace

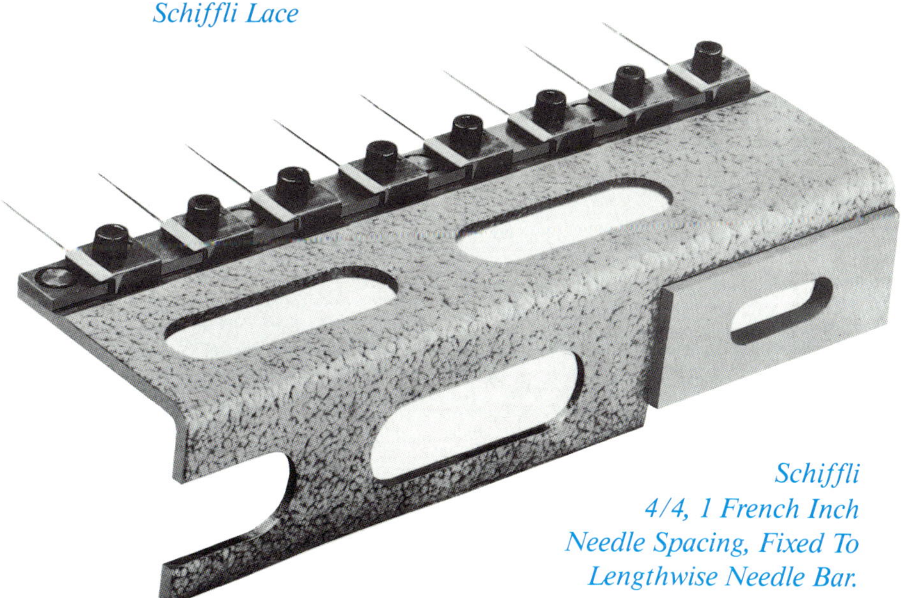

Schiffli
4/4, 1 French Inch
Needle Spacing, Fixed To
Lengthwise Needle Bar.

Use metal rulers for enlarging distances over 10″ since wood may warp. A 90/45 degree triangle for drawing perpendicular lines and geometric divisions is a must. #2 drawing pencils are excellent for enlarging; keep them sharpened. A kneaded eraser will help keep the drawing clean.

A complete drafting set is required for the enlarger. A compass and set of dividers will be in constant use and virtually become an extension of the enlarger's hand. These tools are necessary to draw circles, subdivide them into equal parts and draw symmetrical curves as part of the design. Free hand does have its place; however, there are enlargers who will enlarge only with tools, drawing every curve of the design with a compass. Keep a sanding board at hand to keep the compass lead sharp.

Extenders for the compasses are necessary and should be included with your set.

The compass can be used easily to subdivide circles into 6's or 12's. Compasses with screw adjustments are not efficient. You should be able to use your compass as you would a set of chop sticks. The finger motion is similar.

Small screw type compasses can be used for sketching.

If you are working from a sample which has to be duplicated, then you must constantly measure the widths of steils and blatt stitches and leave nothing to your eye or to judgment. In short, be accurate.

The first accurate measurement is to make the enlargement 6 times larger than the sample so it is the same proportional size as the sample you want to copy. Has the sample shrunk because of bleaching or dying? If it is an aetz, then it has definitely shrunk with the removal of the base cloth. Has the bleaching or dying process twisted the design? All of this must be assessed if you want the design off your machine to be the same as the one you are cloning. Constantly look and check the sample, keeping it before your eye. When you have the enlargement completed, set it on the floor, and standing before it with the original in your hand, use this view to check the proportions.

When every required stitch had to be drawn, a designer's wheel was effective, which could automatically mark the paper by being rolled over the jute, in accurate stitch measurements. The wheels are available in sizes 4, 4 1/2, 5 etc., to 18, measuring the number of stitches per French inch. The enlarger had to use his judgment when the length of the stitches varied. Today you will set the density by computer, as lengths change, remember the density should change also.

Example of required stitches per French inch:

60/2 cotton	blatt stitch 8 wheel,	steil	5½ wheel
40/2 cotton	blatt stitch 7 wheel,	steil	5 wheel
20/2 cotton	blatt stitch 6 wheel,	steal	4 wheel
150/2 rayon	blatt stitch 7 wheel,	steil	5 wheel
100/2 rayon	blatt stitch 9 wheel,	steil	6½ wheel
00/2 rayon	blatt stitch 11 wheel,	steil	7 wheel
00/3 rayon	blatt stitch 10 wheel,	steil	6½ wheel

The 00/2 rayon (Multi-head thread) is equivalent to 150/2 rayon (Schiffli thread) in weight but with a slightly tighter reverse twist.

A blatt stitch is a wide zig-zag or satin stitch requiring more stitches per inch. As the stitch becomes narrower, to the size of a steil, the smallest zig-zag stitch, the amount of stitches per inch should change proportionally. There are no hard and fast rules. The designer has to use his or her own common sense. If stitches slant, the stitch becomes longer and the coverage will require more stitches.

Embroidered emblems require more stitches simply because they are always viewed at close range, and therefore demand a better quality.

Previously, after the enlargements were penciled accurately and inked with straight pen and inking compasses, they became part of the records and could always be used over and over as changes occurred. Since many designs were symmetrical, the particular green ink used was transferred by wetting-off part of the jute, folding the paper and rubbing off the design where required. The ink could be erased with normal household bleach if mistakes were made.

When inking is needed today, most people use 'Flair' pens. They are handy, comfortable to hold and have a large supply of ink.

Opaque tracing paper is used to transfer parts, for example: duplicating identical flowers to various parts of a design, and for masking repeats. A rubbing bone is helpful to 'rub off' or transfer parts of the design when copying by wetting paper, or to transfer from the opaque tracing paper.

These are the basics, but in the 1970s these routines began to change. So much could be done with use of photocopy machines to change sizes, copy identical parts and reverses. Parts can be drawn on tissue and copied, eliminating inking. In the 90s, we accomplish so much with the use of the computer as far as the drawing of the enlargement is concerned.

However, keep in mind that what has been proven and tested for the last 100 years has great value for the enlarger. 6 times is still the best size and covers many mistakes in digitizing. One to one is unsuitable. It can be done in rare cases but most of the time your work in one to one will not be professional.

But today, we do have a choice of size, thanks to the computer. Copying, reverses, using the same or similar size figures, moving them, twisting and turning, and editing them, is all feasible.

The average designer and enlarger is not a puncher. If you want to do all three, i.e., design, enlarge and punch, then you have to study and be proficient with all three. You have to be an artist, make a mechanical drawing, and know your machines inside out to take what you have created, drawn and punched and see it come to life as you want it.

We suggest you have the proper instruction and experience for each of the stations, in depth, to become truly professional.

Fortunately, when it came to drawing the art, the author had natural talent; the ability to draw the enlargements came from high school mechanical drawing class; and the punching was self taught through punching for 4 separate and different systems. For 20 years he and his staff were the leading pattern makers for Groebli, Saurer, Plauen Schiffli and for Multi-head mechanical machines. Therefore, it is all possible.

CONSTRUCTION OF EMBROIDERED EFFECTS

Sometimes it is difficult to see the difference in some embroidered effects by eye. The following designs are enlarged drawings of all the effects that can be made by stitching on a flat plane. All stitches are filled in an area, but the drawings only have to contain the required stitches if drawn for computer interpretation.

Embroidered designs become more interesting when different effects are used in the same design. The effects can be larger, smaller or together with other effects or redrawn in any form.

The enlargement of any stitch is only showing one movement. The second movement, to complete the stitch, is assumed. Otherwise, the drawings would be too confusing. All the stitches in a running stitch are drawn together in full, as if you were stitching a single straight line.

STEIL STITCH

This is any back and forth (zig zag) stitch which is very narrow. On your sketch it might appear as a thin line. It can be straight or curved as long as it is back and forth in a tight stitch. Steils are sometimes used for straight edges for cutting, because they are strong, tight and offer an edge to cut against. Scallops are sometimes steils, or sometimes a steil might be stitched with a Blattstitch scallop to act as reinforcement. They are also used on the edge of an odd shaped emblem as a reinforcement to protect the blatt stitch. They are a safety factor should the cutter's scissor slice into the edge, protecting the wider blatt stitch. The dotted line represents the return stitch, which is not normally drawn.

Slanted Steils require less stitches and add form to flower stems and other designs.

BLATT STITCH

This is simply a wider steil, usually over 1/8″ in width. It is also known as a satin stitch. This would appear on a sketch as a solid filled in area, in the form of a wide steil, a leaf, a dot or part of a design, but only one stitch in width. Stitching tension is usually loosened for these larger stitches. This stitching will show color and sheen, for dress goods and decorative fabrics.

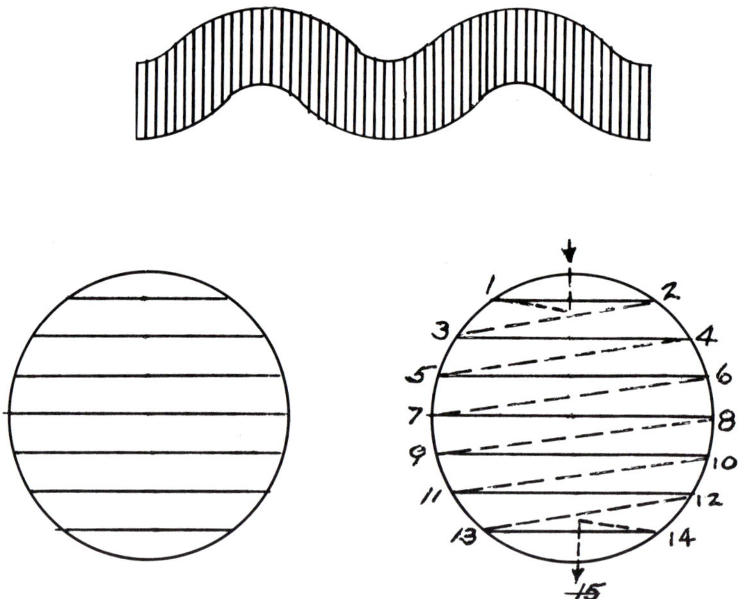

RUNNING STITCH

The running stitch is any stitching, regardless of its direction, which forms the design with only the thickness of thread, with no back and forth steil or blatt stitch effect. A seam in a suit or shirt would represent a running stitch. Additional design treatments utilizing running stitch patterns create interest. No design should be drawn with only one type of stitching, unless it happens to be the effect you are looking for. Running stitches can be used for shading, backgrounds and other effects. Since all running stitch lines are individually drawn on the cartoon, the stitch length, if not set by computer, is 'tipped off' with a small mark showing the length of the stitch. Excellent for light weight fabrics and with coarser yarns for heavy weight fabrics, it can create a light airy pattern.

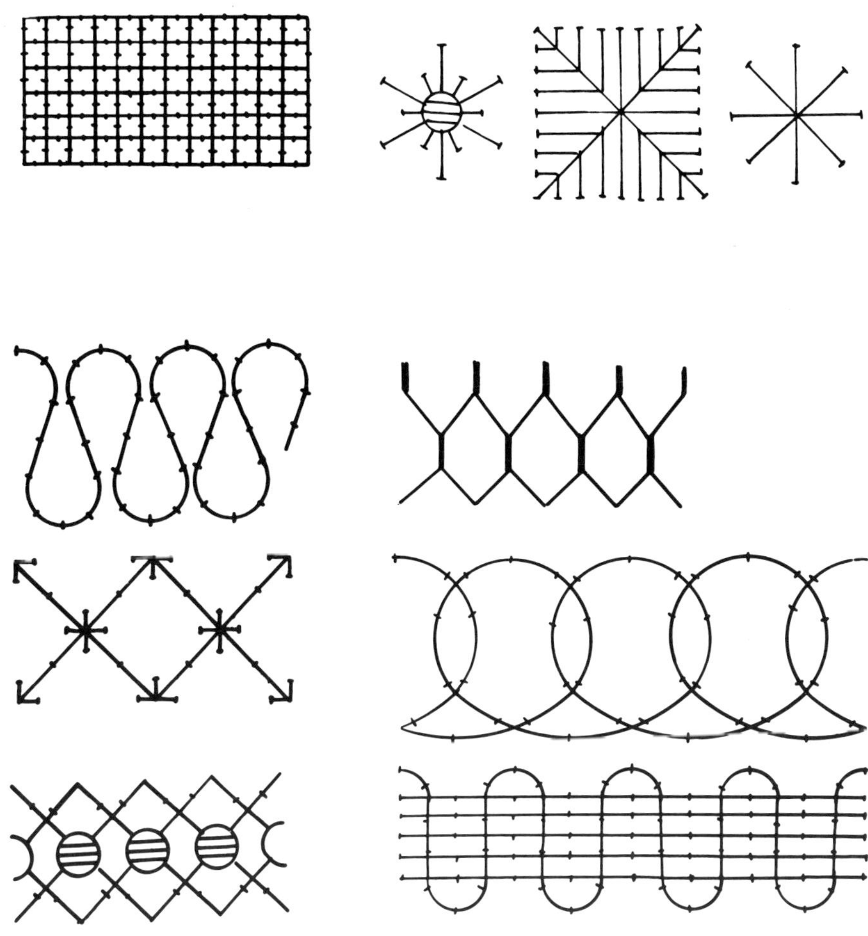

UNDERLAYS

Underlay stitches are travel stitches that can not be seen in finished embroidery. Some underlays are running stitches used to travel to the end of a leaf or to connect parts of a design as one progresses through the punching process. However, underlays also have the important function of creating three dimensional effects.

There are sometimes more underlays than cover stitches when one is punching a lace. The whole design depends on the web construction of underlays over which the blatt stitches are made.

A steil is just a flat zig zag without an underlay. It is possible to see through the tightest steil stitches unless an underlay is made first. It serves to create a binding, thin solid band. For example, a white steil on black goods requires one or two running stitch underlays.

Underlays can also be blatt stitches. One layer over another will appreciably change the look of the embroidery and form a beautiful rounded three dimensional effect when overstitched with Blattstitches.

Underlays are a necessity in the construction of emblems. They serve to reinforce borders, build figures, and 'engrave' a design on the base fabric. Underlays also hold embroidered shapes on fabrics where tension and fabric construction might tend to distort the embroidered design. They are stitched just inside the shape, then the overlaying cover stitches stitch over the underlay.

The number of underlays desired by the designer is not necessarily shown in drawn lines but in numbers. Alongside steils the numbers would denote how many times the puncher should travel, i.e., 3 X would indicate 3 tours or rows of underlay. A blatt stitch flower requiring underlay to build dimension might be marked 12 alongside or inside the design. This would indicate the total movements desired by the designer for the proper execution of the design.

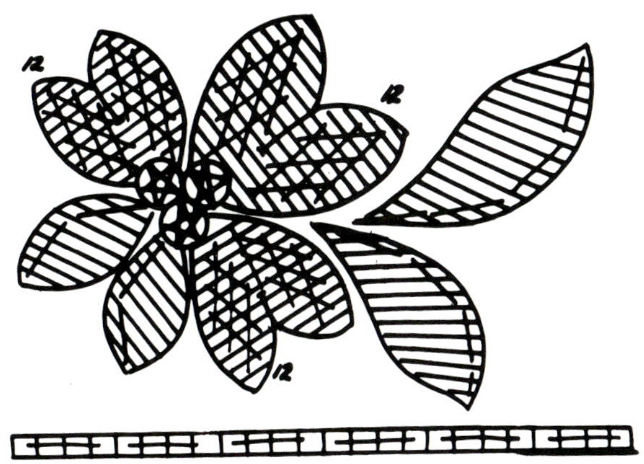

WITH AN UNDERLAY

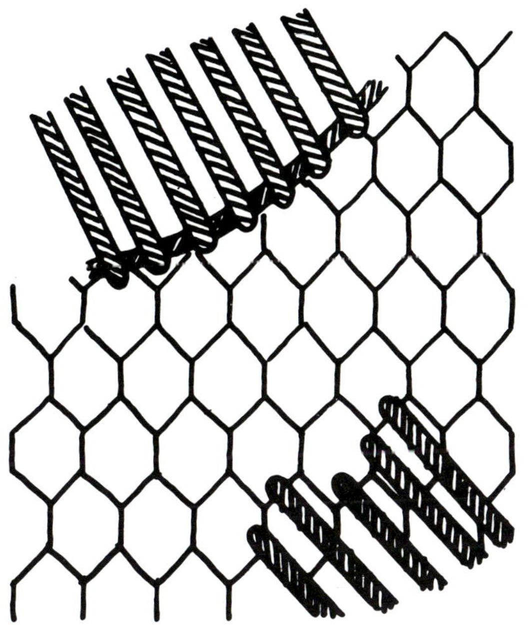

WITHOUT AN UNDERLAY

FRENCH DOT

The French Dot can be made with as few as 5 running stitch lines, which crisscross to give a third dimension to the embroidery, placing 5 threads one over the other. The look is a small raised dot. By increasing the number of stitches, the dot becomes progressively higher. Small French Dots with slightly enlarged dots superimposed are commonly used for lace effects which require loft. These dots are always drawn with an odd number of stitches so the following of the stitches start and stop at the same point. They are good to use on medium weight fabrics and laces.

BEAN STITCH

The bean stitch is made with one stitch out in any chosen direction and the return stitch back directly over itself to the same starting point.

This effect builds as the number of stitches increase to give raised three dimensional effects. Joined together they can form all types of designs and are used in many embroidered effects.

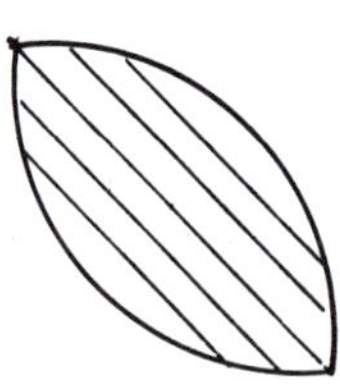

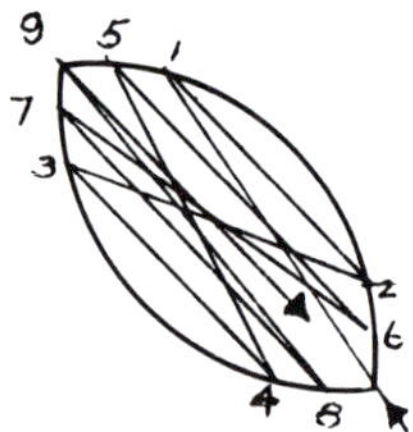

CROSS STITCH

Cross stitches are regular bean stitch movements forming 'Xs' in rows, or within a box shape to form geometric designs. This effect is very popular in the blouse trade, used for imitating peasant style embroideries.

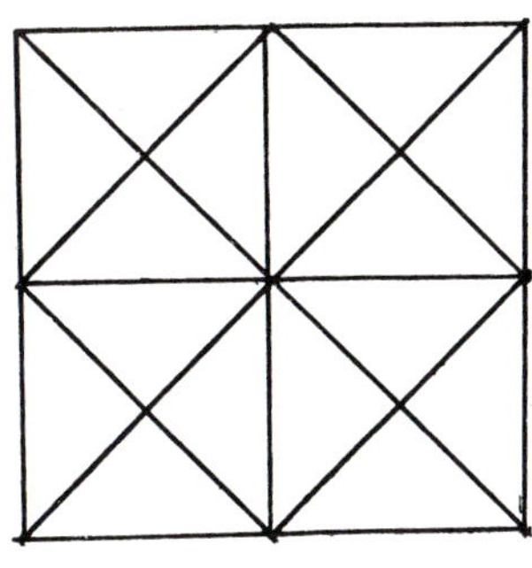

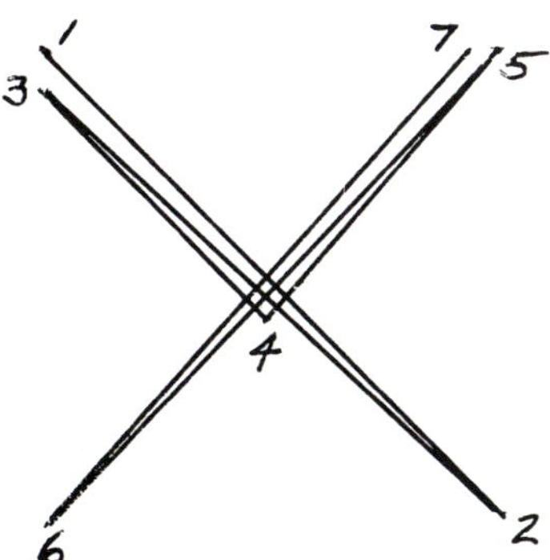

FRENCH KNOT

Start off with drawing, in the center, a small dot about half the size of the knot. A bean stitch around the perimeter will give a raised effect, like a button. Be sure to start and stop at the same point, otherwise, it will not form a balanced design. This is best used on medium weight fabrics.

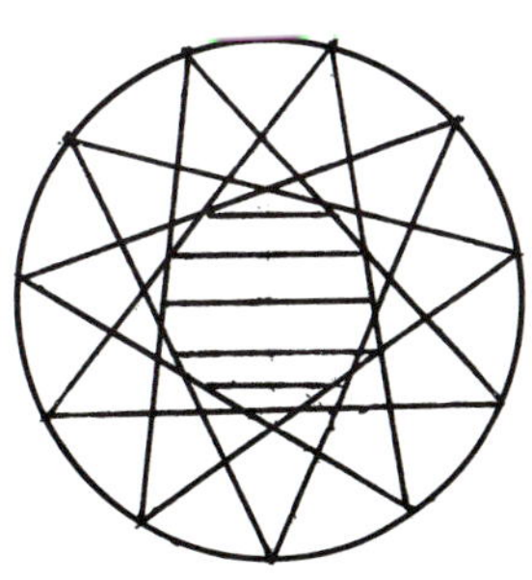

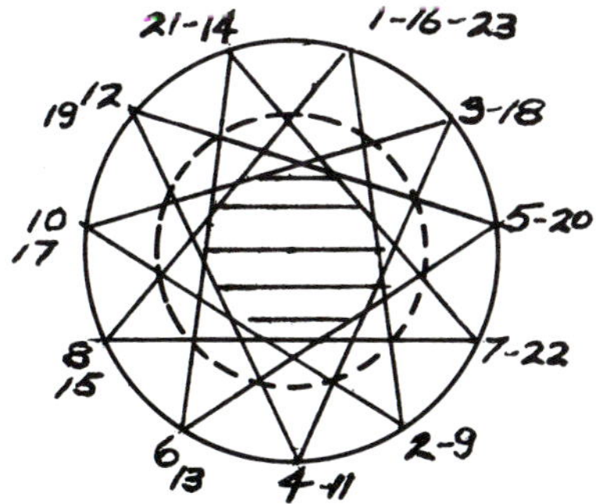

WIGGLE (WICKEL) STITCH

This is a series of running stitches, overrun with a narrow zig zag stitch, which forms a cheap steil as a guide for cutting. It is used most frequently to connect and hold together lace designs. The Wickle also is used in forming the net background as base for Lace stitching. The effect has a light look and does not impose on the basic lace design.

FESTOON STITCH

The festoon stitch is used as a reinforcement for cutting — it forms a strong edge for the cutter's knife to slide upon. It saves one movement for the blatt and steil combination over the separate steil stitch. Make sure an underlay is used when stitching festoons.

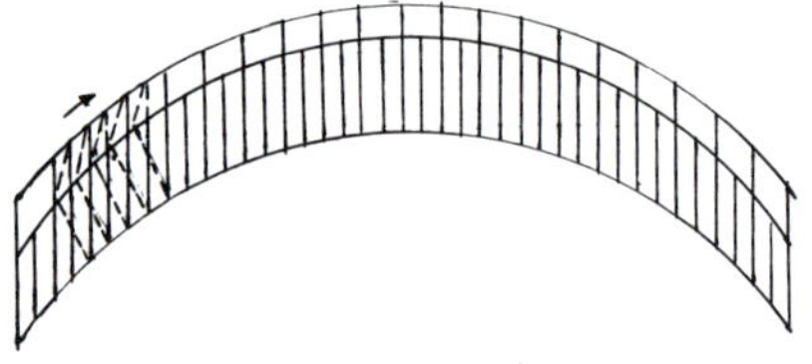

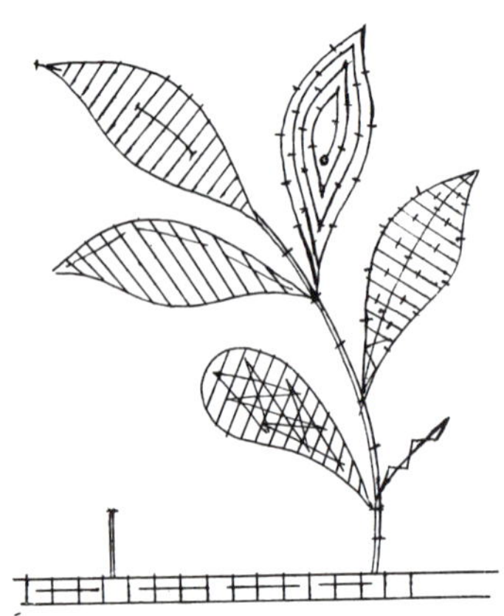

BLATT STITCH
SPLIT STITCH
RUNNING STITCH
GEFLECT STITCH
PICO, WIGGLE
STEIL
UNDERLAY

ROSELI

This stitch is a combination of blatt stitches for effect, giving an excellent three dimensional look. The center dot is designed first, then each 1/5 of the design is punched separately as a blatt stitch. Used in bands and flounces with other effects, it is best for medium and heavy weight fabrics.

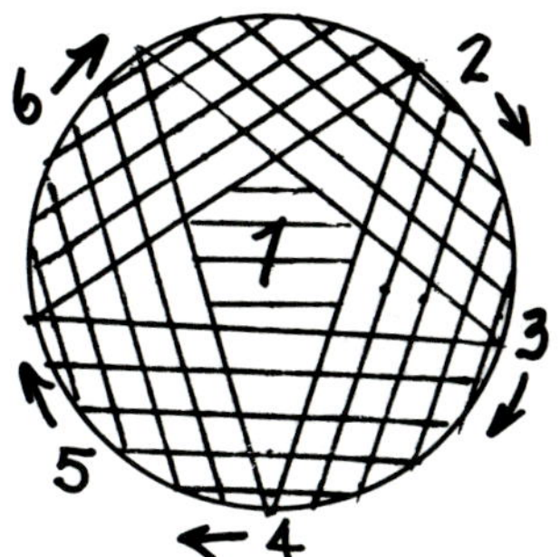

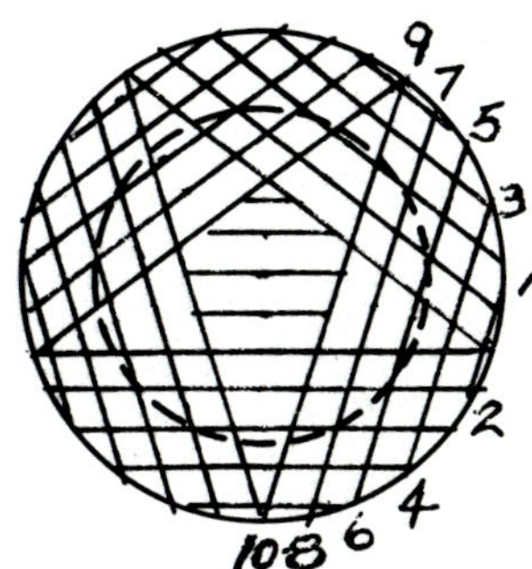

PICO

This running stitch has one stitch, stitched into the fabric at intervals away from the cut edge. It is used as a reinforcement to hold a running stitch along a cut edge. For multi head machines it is used to stitch and hold the cut edge of appliques so they do not pull away while the balance of the stitching is made.

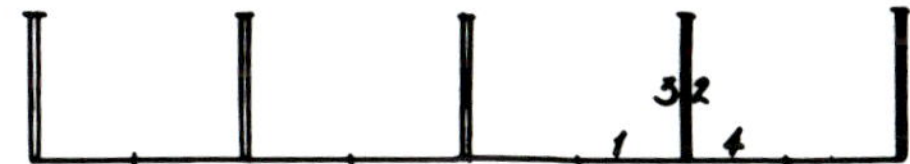

SNORKEL

This stitch is created by using any type of basic stitch to form a spiral, such as a single running stitch or steil without an underlay, into the center and then returning between these lines to the outer edge of the spiral.

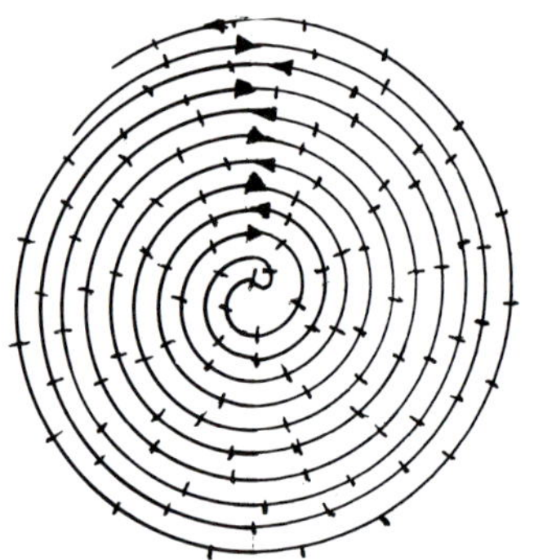

PETIT POINT

Petit point stitching consists of a series of bean stitches all in the same direction, tightly placed so the travel stitch connecting the beans is lost in the design. Many different floral designs lend themselves to this geometric form of stitching. The tight stitching makes the embroidery very durable. The bean can be made with 3, 5 or 7 movements. It is popularly used for shoes and handbags.

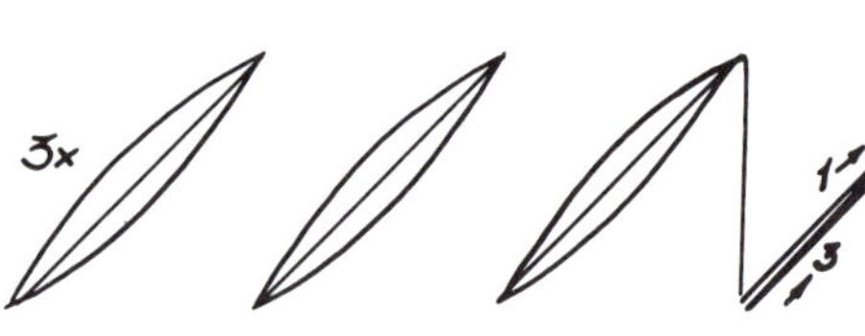

ZUCHOLE

The zuchole is a running stitch in a geometric form which can be used in many effects. Added design character is achieved by adding bean stitches. With every fourth stitch, the needle should penetrate a previously stitched point, thus forming a small hole with the tensions pulling the thread in opposite directions. When the design is back to back, as in the first and second sketch, then the needle will penetrate the same point 4 times with 4 opposing tensions. If the tension is properly set a fine hole will be formed. This light weight stitching enhances lingerie.

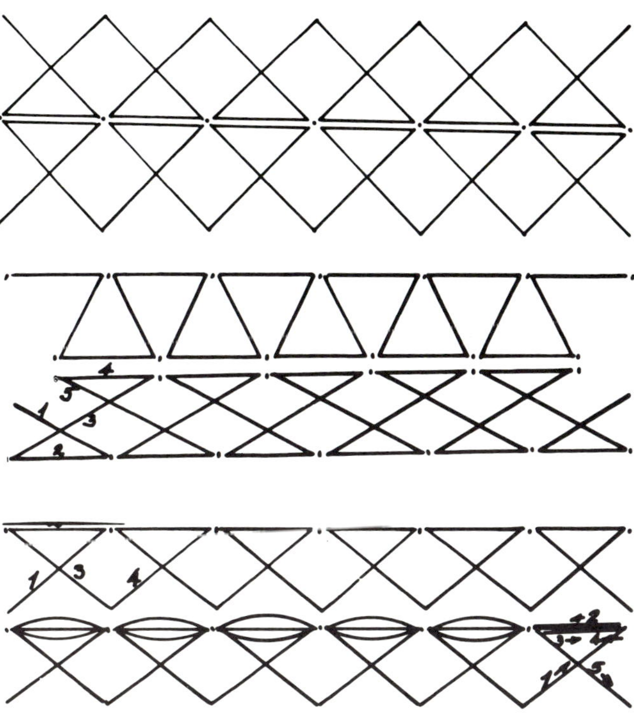

GEFLECT STITCHING

Geflect stitching is used to lightly cover an area. A running stitch outline of the design is made, then the over stitched fill stitch holds onto the outline. Goods should show through the running Geflect. Very popular for use on light weight fabrics, lingerie, bras, and quilting.

CHAIN STITCHING

The chain stitch is another form of the running stitch, duplicating the stitch made with a Cornely sewing machine. With heavier yarns it makes beautiful embroidery for drapes and furniture fabrics.

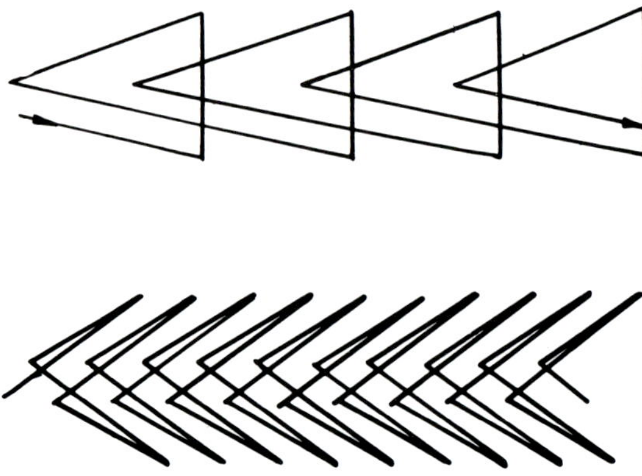

FEATHER STITCHING

Feathers are light weight designs with running stitches, in many forms or shapes for tricots, nylons, and taffetas.

TOLEDO STITCHING

A famous stitch used for handkerchiefs, napkins and table linens, the Toledo is formed with beans stitches at right angles to one another. Tensions on the thread cause the needle to pull tiny holes as it penetrates thc same points as the design is formed.

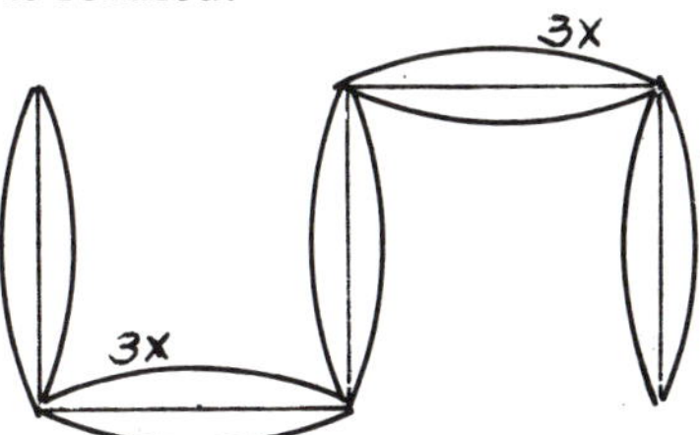

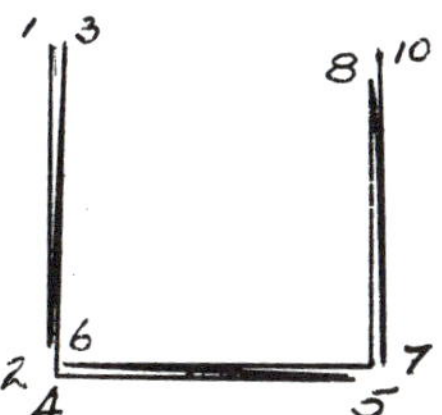

TASSELS

A tassel is usually a group of long threads, hanging free. To achieve this a large blatt stitch should be made to simulate the actual tassel. This should be longer than the maximum stitch the machine can make; it could be called a group of jump stitches. Therefore, to exaggerate the length of the tassel a blatt is made to a straight line. First a steil is stitched on top, to which the stitches will hang. A tassel's desired length must be determined, and a single stitch drawn to that length. Stitch as many movements as necessary to form the length and make as many of these long jumps as necessary to achieve the thickness of the tassel. Then tie in the top end of all the stitches with a French Dot, usually a small dot of 7 movements covered by a larger dot of 13 movements. A steil with 2 underlays, should secure the top of the tassel and cover the joining of the blatt stitch to the tassel. With a sharp knife, the bottom edge of the tassel should be cut forming the loose ends. Tassels serve as decoration for drapery and ladies' fashions.

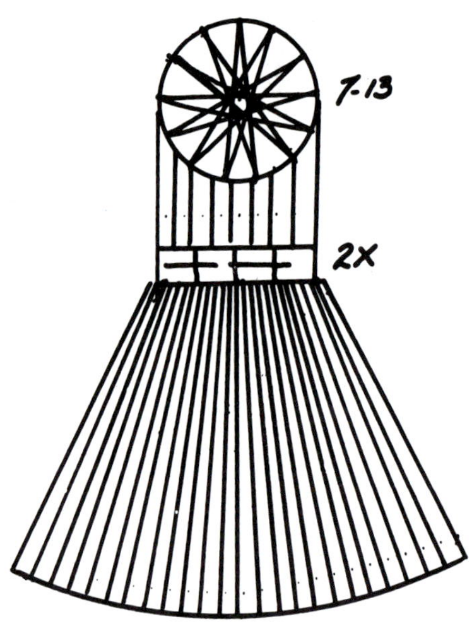

FRINGE

A fringe is formed with like stitches to that of the tassel, first a steil, then long lengths of jump stitches from repeat to repeat for the size you choose the fringe to be, each fringe stitch over stitches the top of the steil. Another steil is stitched on top of the fringe to tie the threads together. At this point a design can be added to the head of the fringe. Then the long fringe threads are slit across the bottom to form the fringe. Fringes might be used for period dress trims or drapery.

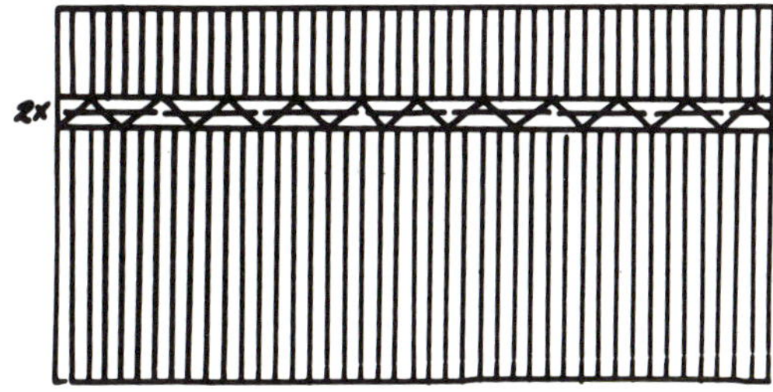

SCHRAGE STITCH

When stitches are slanted, they give more thickness to the steil or blatt stitch. Larger stitches lay looser than small stitches. The coverage for either requires less stitching and looks softer. It is easier to interrupt art, form, shape and graceful curves by stitching with the flow of the design. Steils sometimes employ Schrage stitches for cutting edges, however, the direction of the cut has to be with the stitch, not against it.

STITCHING IN DIFFERENT DIRECTIONS

Blatt stitches when stitched with a high sheen yarn, like rayon, in different directions reflect light in ways to change color tones. It would appear the drawing for this square is stitched with 8 separate shades of yarn.

INTERLOCKING STITCHES

When some areas require stitches larger than the machine can move, or when very large stitches might cause a problem (stitches that are too long, may easily catch on something and break, causing a damage) the same blatt stitch or satin stitch can be retained by stitching it one into the other. (See background fills "C" on page 162). This technique is often used for background fill stitches by Schiffli emblem manufacturers.

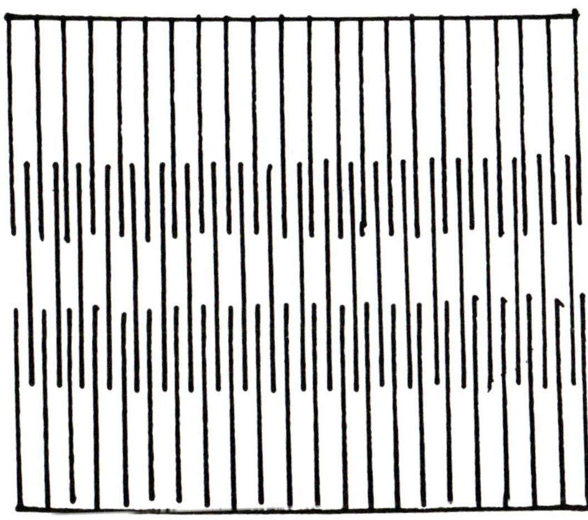

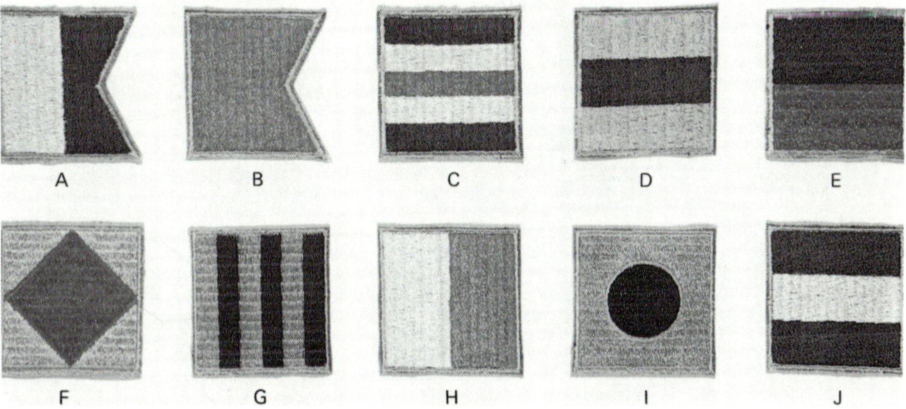

BACKGROUND FILLS

(A) Background fills are used to add texture and color to designs. They can replace appliques, add a third dimension, and add strength to fabric. At times a solid fill is used for emblems when the requested color of a background fabric can not be found. The density of the stitching is relative to the use required. When drawn at a 30 degree angle the fill stitching appears to have better coverage. The top drawing would be the enlarged drawing while the bottom is the actual stitching sequence.

(B) A lighter background known as a 'chicken scratch' is sometimes used to add an additional shade of color to a fabric. This is often used for emblems.

(C) Blatt or satin stitch backgrounds for the U.S. Military require total close coverage with no fabric exposed. Columns of vertical blatt stitch, interlocked into each other, form a solid background. The coverage is stitched from A to C as a blatt stitch in column form, then punched A to D, again for the whole column. The same progression is followed; B to E, C to F, D to G etc., filling in the entire area in double stitching. The background coverage is solid, over which various designs are stitched.

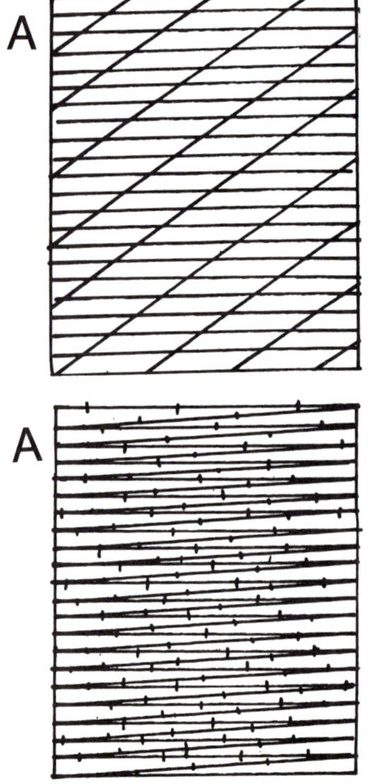

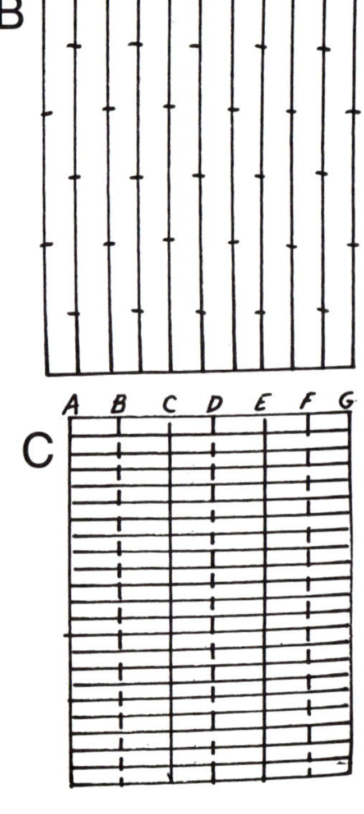

VERMICELLI STITCHING

The vermicelli stitch is used to fill in areas with light running stitches. Evenly dispersed stitches in a multitude of designs add texture to plain fabrics. This stitching is popular for lingerie, bras, and quilting.

SINGLE RUNNING STITCH ALLOVER

One of the most difficult brain teasers the author ever had was to figure out the problem of filling a piece of goods with squares where all the lines were single lines, never doubling any stitched line, yet cover the fabric completely. Repeat this design over and over to solve the puzzle.

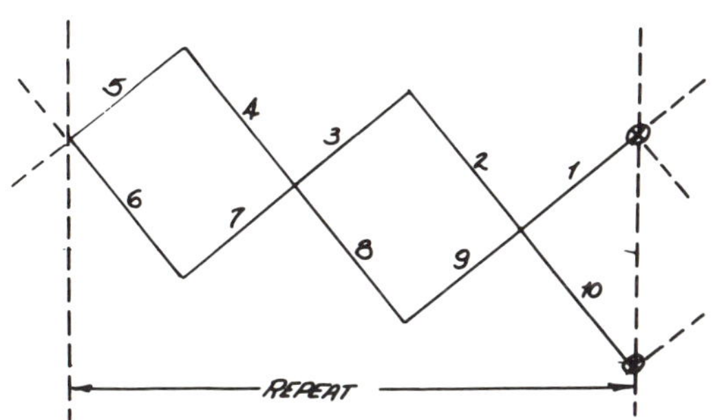

SHADING OF COLORS

One of the most difficult stitching formats to understand is that of color shading, i.e., reproducing an embroidered design from a 4 color process photo or from a painting of many colors. It is really simple if you mentally disect the colors and plan the drawing accordingly. It is best to program this stitch for stitch.

Develop a short area stitch pattern and repeat it to fill the area.

For example: as the following drawing demonstrates, assume we want to shade a black to a white. We draw the stitches at various lengths so that, stitching from the solid black, we add in some long white stitches in various lengths. The appearance will be black, gray to solid white. Yes, you can do this with three colors or as many as you choose. Make sure you do not bunch up the threads, which would change the texture of the embroidery and might cause stitching problems. Remember, you are shading the design with 2 or more colors of thread.

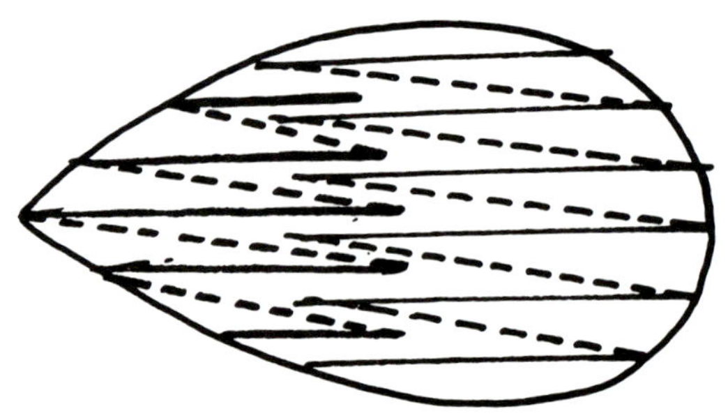

SPLIT STITCHES

When cleavage or short tight stitches are required to cover an area of a blatt stitch, as in laces, it is necessary to 'break' or split the stitch into 2 parts. This is another design effect for any type of stitching.

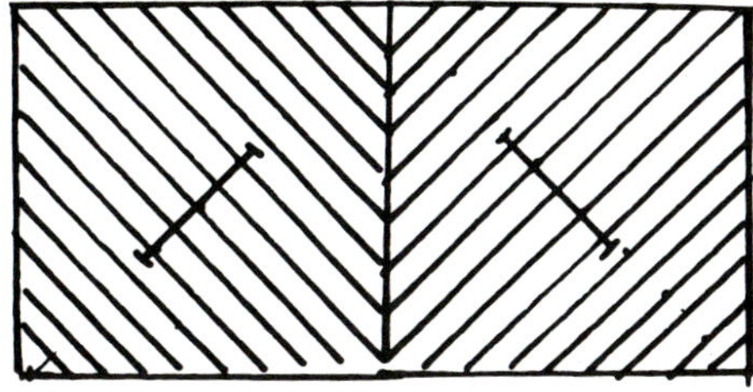

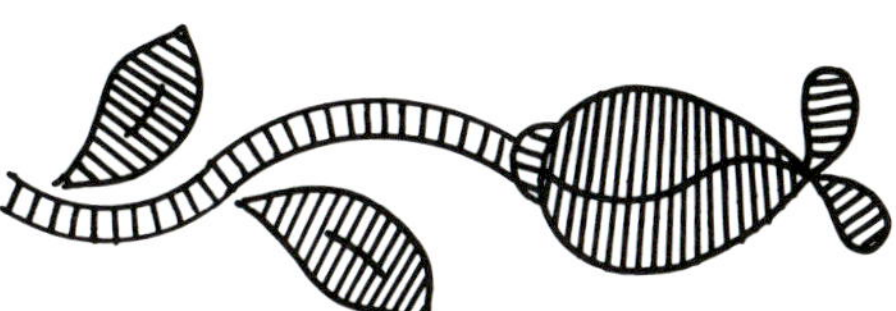

SPIDER

Spiders give geometric form to running stitches, and are usually found in designs for lingerie inserts and allovers.

PULL HOLE

A small eyelet effect can be made with needle and thread by stitching the needle in the same place as the design advances around a circle.

BORING

Boring effects are made by a special device standard on the Schiffli machine, now available for Multi-head machines as well, which is used to puncture the spanned goods as required to form holes in the fabric. Stitching is necessary to clean the hole, pull the loose goods together to open the hole and give it shape. A steil is stitched around the hole to hold its size and shape. Depth can vary from a pinpoint to 1/2″. The eyelets are limited to symmetrical shapes, diamonds, squares, ovals, triangles, circles and also works with tear drop designs. There are many ways to form designs with eyelets and groups of eyelets.

Uses include airy summer cotton designs for lingerie, and blouses, and effects for bedspreads and pillow cases.

Programming the bore hole is done by activating the borer into the goods. If the hole is small underlay support may not be necessary, but if the hole is large an underlay should be used. The firmness of the fabric should also be a determining factor.

First, position the borer to punch in the proper part of the design. The borer and needle are in different positions on the machine, therefore we can not assume normal punching, and a superfix must be made. All manner of machines have specific adjustments to carry out the exact repositioning. Bore the hole with a minimum of punctures. Only experience will determine how many movements to use for a particular goods and what area to punch. Reposition the needle and stitch from the center of the hole to the outer edge, to clear the hole with a steil to reinforce the edge to avoid unravelling of the fabric.

There are many tricks to achieving a clean eyelet, heavier goods may require you to stitch every other stitch, twice around to stitch all the stitches, this will clean the hole better. You are really cleaning the loose threads twice.

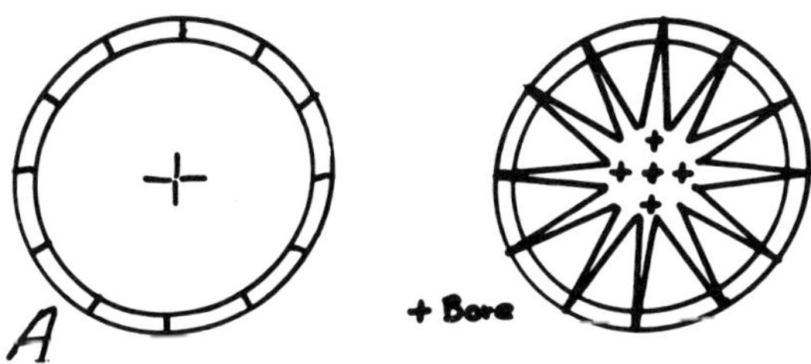

Boring in itself adds design to any creation. All types of eyelets can imitate flowers, by stitching around a design. Leaving the goods to form the design for allovers and with various types of stitching will add interest to designs on all types of fabrics. Boring is used for dress goods, blouses, and tablecloths.

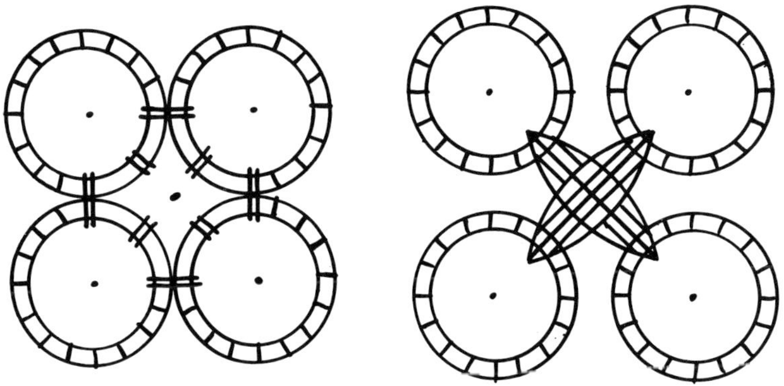

MOCCA

This is the addition of running stitches over a completed boring hole to add additional interest to eyelets. The row shown demonstrates the drawing, 1) the punch motions for clearing the hole, 2) the motions to form the mocca.

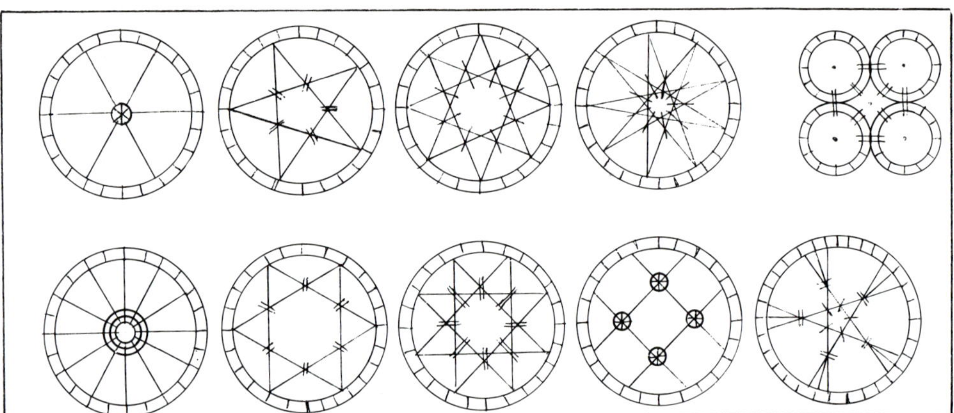

Other geometric mocca designs formed with running stitches are shown. Moccas are not limited to round borings.

Moccas are not easy to create in embroidery and require a great degree of exactness and proper tensions. They are popular in cotton goods for blouses.

STEFFELS

A steffel is any group of boring, side by side. They can be designed in a line, curves or circles, but always in a chain effect. Figure A shows the 7 steps required in forming the steffel. 1) The drawing, 2 and 3) the underlays to hold the shape of the design, 4) the boring points, 5) the base stitches to open the hole, 6) the final stitching, 7) recouping all the motions.

Do not bore too many holes at one time, or you can cut the goods into pieces and lose all tension of the span on the machine. The following designs show various effects including combining rows. Just remember to clear all holes in all directions and you will be proud of the results. Steffels are mainly used in lingerie, blouses and dresses.

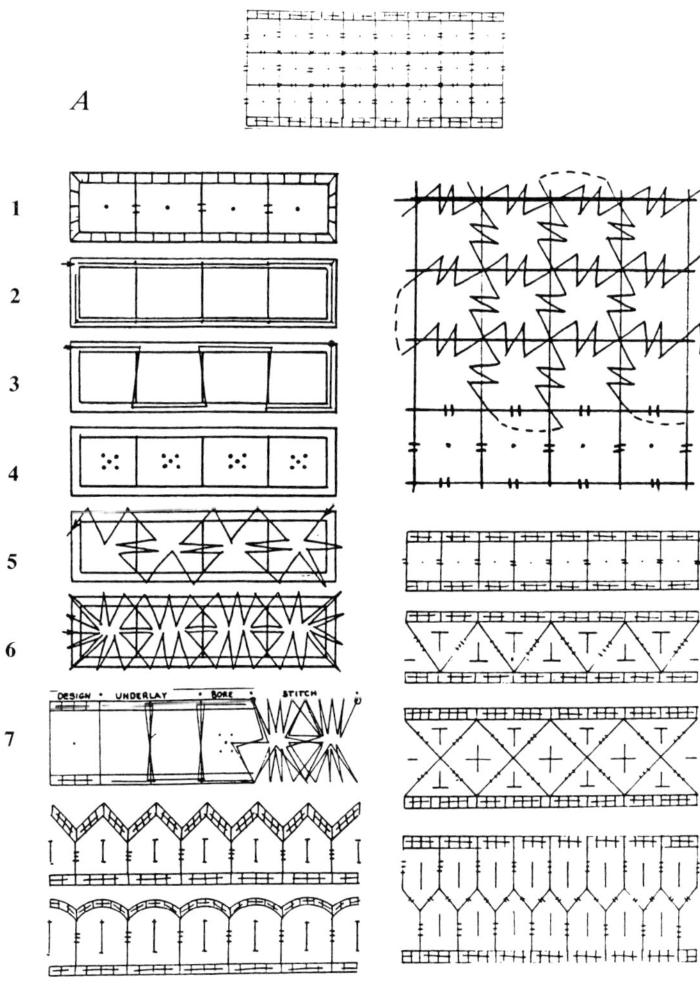

CHECKERBOARD BORING

An interesting background texture is created with this boring design. The stitching is very inexpensive and requires no underlays within the embroidery. Figure A denotes the enlarged design, figure B the method of punching.

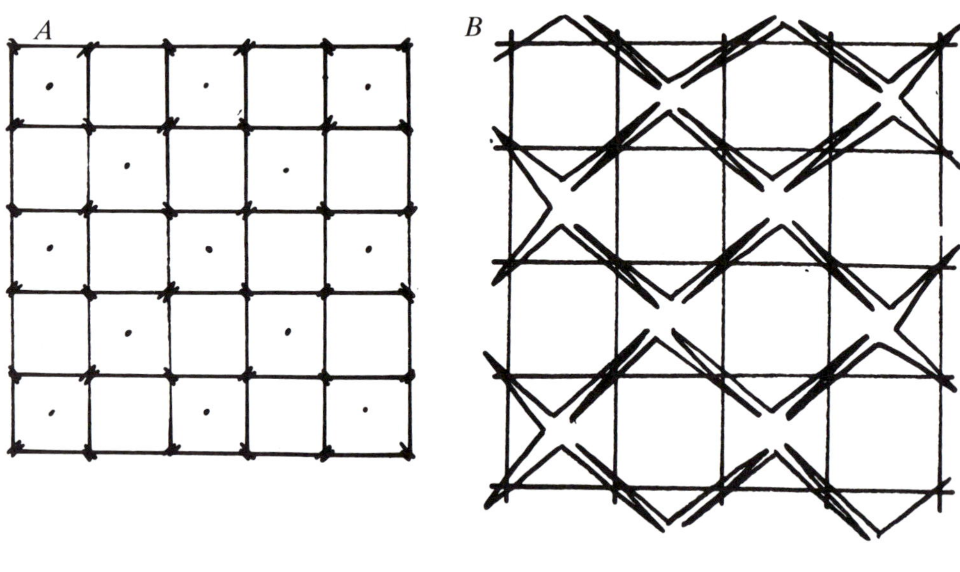

IN BORING

In boring, the stitching of picos within an empty space of an eyelet, is a tricky procedure. It is costly to stitch and requires great skill in punching and stitching. It is best stitched on firm fabrics for blouses and linens.

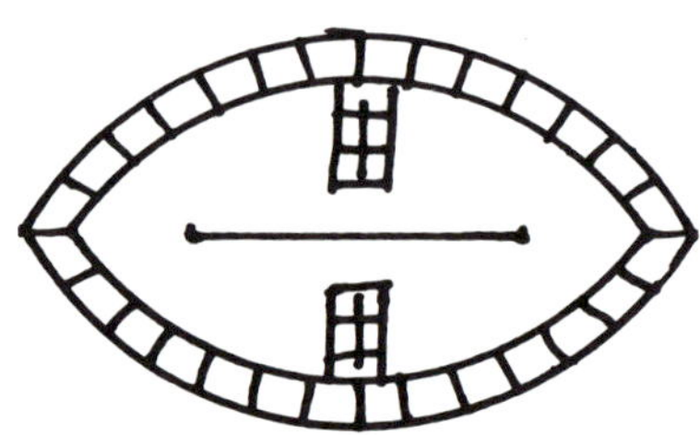

TASSELS OVER EYELETS

Try this one for fun, and at the same time achieve a beautiful effect. Cut a line of steffel holes and over them stitch a tassel. Imaginative design can add character to all embroideries. Don't cut the tassel stitches.

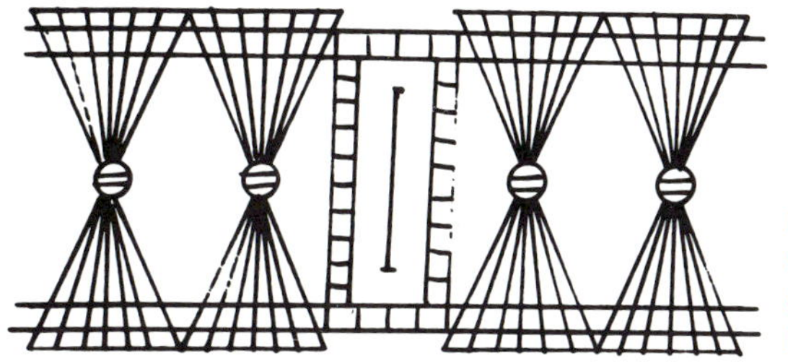

BORED
STEIFEL
(STEIL HIDDEN
BY TASSEL)

BEADING HOLE

A set of beading holes are inserted into designs for the purpose of adding an extra trim and color. Beading holes are necessary to add a ribbon insert into a design. The holes are always in pairs so a ribbon can be threaded into one hole and out of the other for the length of the fabric. This is very popular for cotton lingerie.

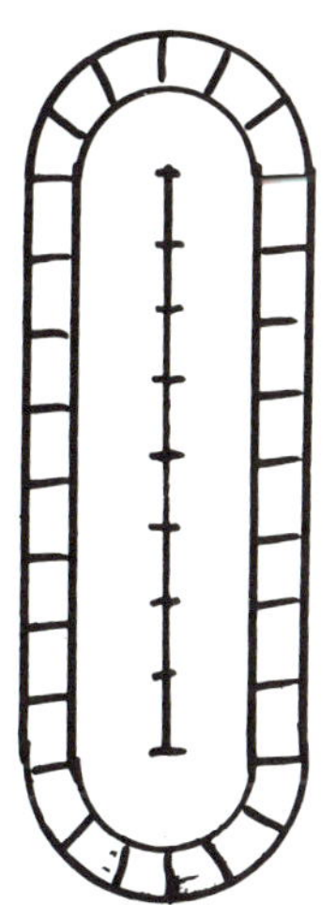

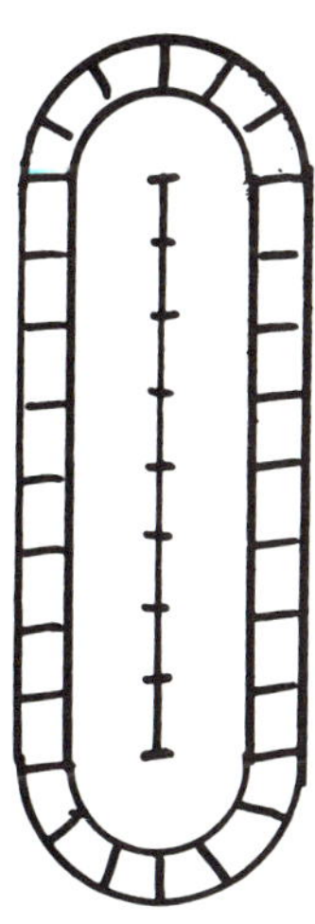

IMITATION FABRIC EFFECTS

Combinations of stitching that include running stitch, bean stitches, blatt stitches and various design constructions can imitate linens, cottons, woven effects, satins and other basic fabrics. The range is greater than any weaving machine can make. Imitation of appliques, adding textures, using some of the fancy stitches discussed, all add to the beauty and versatility of embroidery machine.

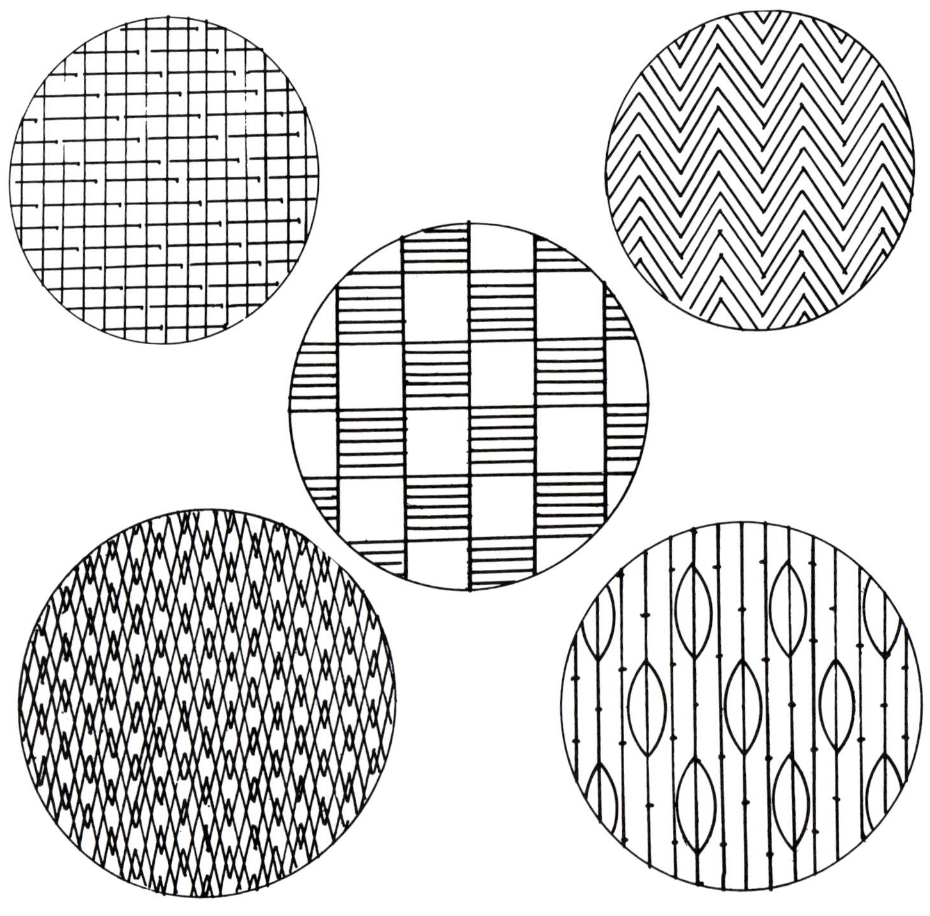

ALTERNATING

Two or more colors offer a design, production and cost increase on a Schiffli machine. Until the advent of automatic color change, each color had to be changed by hand. One way to overcome this problem was to alternate colors on the machine, i.e., if you were stitching a 3 color design, you could combine the 3 colors in each figure without the tedious work of changing colors. The yarns are threaded in a predetermined order in repeat. Following the sequence of the drawing you will note that each needle stitches simultaneously, therefore, the first needle might stitch red the second pink the third white. Thus, in a flower, the leaf and stem will have 3 different colors in the 3 repeats. By moving the frame one repeat, we have the adjoining color now in the next repeat. Here we stitch part of the bud, we again move the frame one repeat and stitch the third color, and now we have all 3 colors in the flower example.

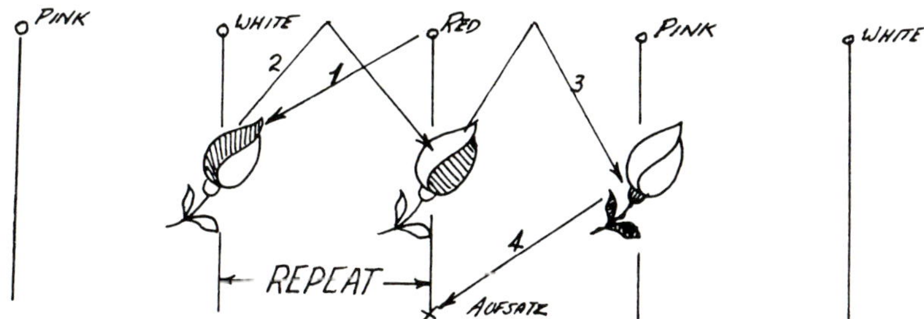

LACES, BURN OUTS, VENICE AND GUIPURES, known in the trade as aetz, this process includes stitching on a firm degradable fabric. A special fabric is spanned, embroidered and then the base cloth is eliminated by desolving in water or with heat. The remaining embroidery is a duplicate of a lace, with threads only, no fabric. Environmental controls in most countries do prohibit the use of caustic sodas or other chemicals that were used to degrade the various base cloths in the past.

Imitating Fabrics with Embroidery

COTTON GOODS

LINEN

BACKGROUND LACE EFFECTS

Embroidered lace effects also duplicate the construction of fabrics. They are necessary as a base for design. Lace design was locally-oriented with different designs developed in different countries.

The names or areas where these designs developed are used for the names of the lace styles, such as Chinese, Duchess, Irish, Vale, and Venetian, among others.

Embroidered laces require accurate designing as well as punching. Lace is constructed only of thread, and in the embroidered effect we stitch on a base cloth that will later be removed by heat, water or chemicals. Therefore, each thread must tie in with others so the whole design will hold together without the support of the base cloth. It is extremely important to tie deep into repeats for the same reason. Therefore, more designing is required than the motif itself, since we have to accurately show those repeats to which the design will connect, in detail and in depth.

Designing requires all stitches to be straight within their shape, whether a steil, blattstitch, or flower. Never use a slanted stitch that might loosen once the base cloth is removed. Stitching must be tight and well underlaid.

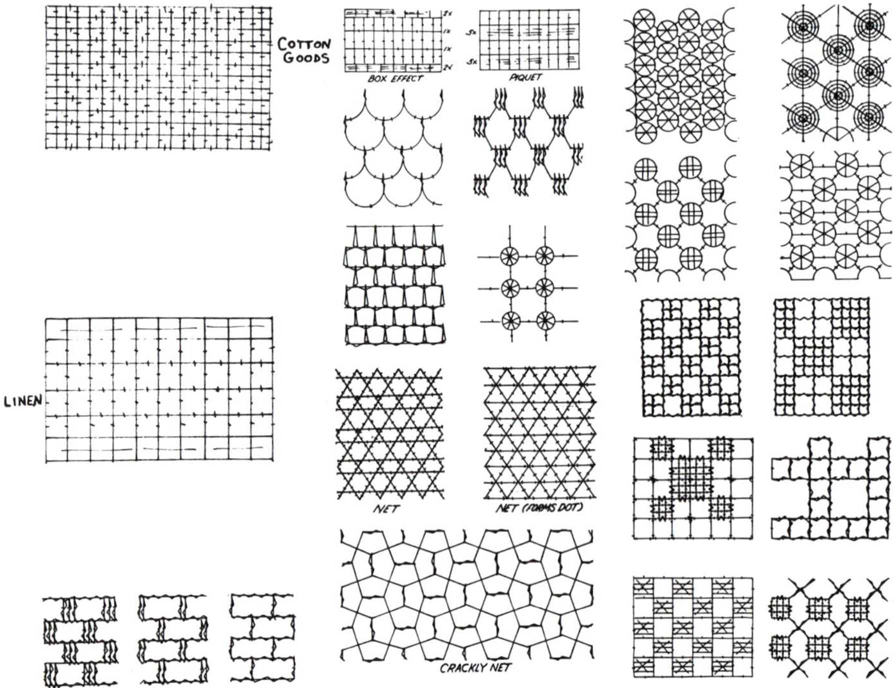

Almost any style of lace can be reproduced on the Schiffli machine if the basic yarns are used. Background areas are used in most laces, to add net effects on which the designs will be stitched. Costs in many cases may be prohibitive. The most economical laces, because they wear so well, tend to be Venetian laces, which can be reproduced for the type of apparel that is currently in fashion. Blouses and dresses become more feminine decorated with Schiffli Venetian laces.

Lace motifs are used as appliques, lace bands, collars, allovers and edges.

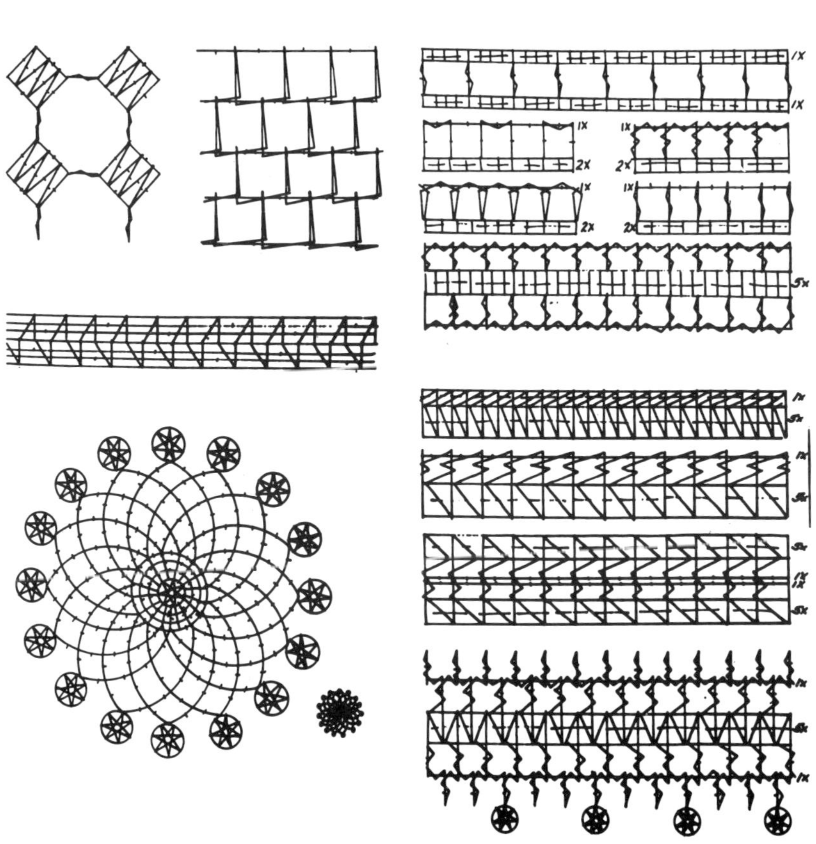

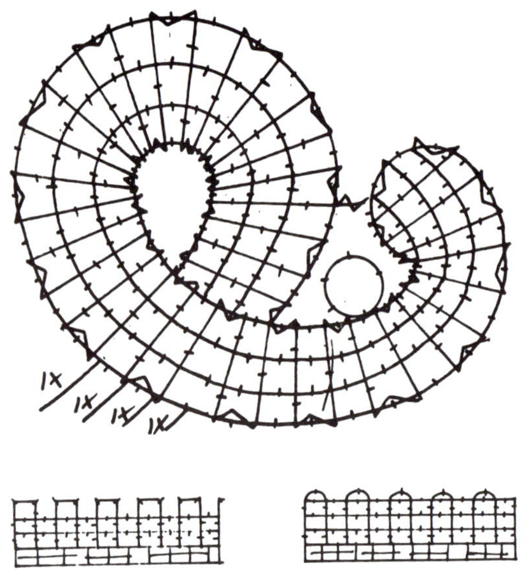

Various laces lend themselves to the Schiffli machine, the existing designs can be formed in repeats. If those repeats are reduced in size, the costs are reduced accordingly. Some laces use yarns as thin as hair, some use heavy wools and cords. Names of some particular laces may originate from the yarn used. Most laces can be reproduced on the Schiffli machine for a price.

Dutchess Lace

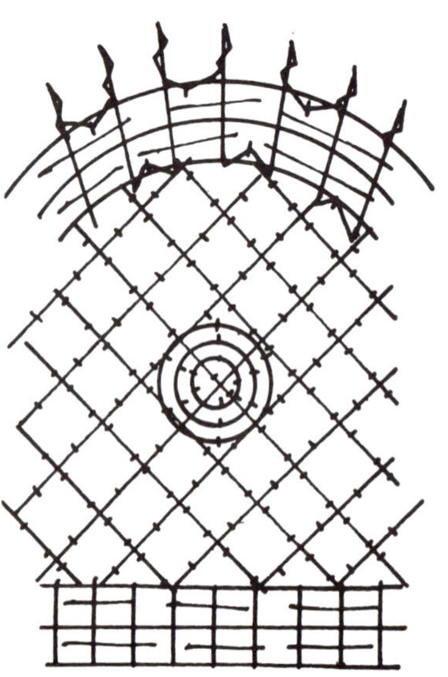

Irish Lace

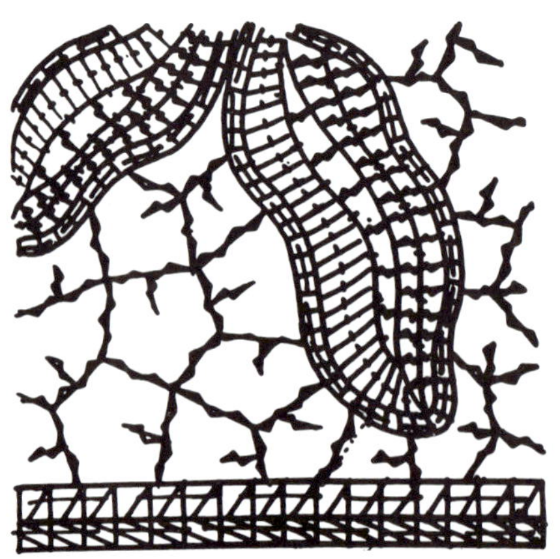

IMITATION LACES

Various lace designs can be made inexpensively as an imitation by stitching on a net. The net looks like the background used in lace but does not require the same kind of special stitching to hold the design together, thus saving time, stitching and money. The net takes the place of the ground stitching construction that an aetz would require. No aetzing, no special stitching. Thicker yarns can be used to give the effect of some laces. These "tulle" effects are always in fashion.

LACE ENLARGING

Laces require more drawing for the puncher. Since he has to tie in stitching in other repeats, in the case of Schiffli, it is necessary to accurately draw the corresponding outlines of all repeats wherever the embroidery must connect. It is not necessary to show the stitching because the puncher is only interested in the design and outlines. This 'mask' is just as necessary if the design is part of an allover, and in such cases it is necessary to draw the repeats on all 4 sides.

JAKOB SCHLAEPFER

This is the leading creative design and embroidery company in the world! Embroideries are created for the most discriminating Haute Couture houses in more than 80 countries. The house of Schlaepfer was founded in 1904 in St. Gallen, Switzerland. Branches exist in Paris, London, Los Angles and New York. A pioneering center has been created in Tognano in southern Switzerland specializing in creative design.

With unlimited possibilities, ideas are created and followed to ultimate completion by hundreds of dedicated employees in handcraft, weaving, embroidery and textile finishing. They continue to develop innovative production engineering techniques and methods, machines, and patents which are employed in their factory in St. Gallen and Marina del Rey in California. Global communication with their CAD-CAM system keep all segments in constant communication from idea to design to prototype to production.

Their success is based on creativity and skill. They continually endeavor to improve upon their own creations which include four new collections yearly. They are open to all challenges put forth by the textile market.

The present Director, Robert Schlaepfer, is involved in the everyday activities and loves his work. He was kind enough to provide 2 original books of their 1990-1991 collection and allowed the author the honor of selecting some designs for this book.

He believes that the few designs shown here, representing a small fraction of their million dollar investment in new ideas this year have brought embroidered novelties to their peak. Never before have so many novelties been used by the fashion industry. "It has been the best year ever," says Schlaepfer. Lace allovers in large repeats and designs with as many as 17 colors have added to the glitz and glamour of their fascinating line.

Their motto: To win each day anew — as creative, skillful people — confidence, consent and success.

The following photos are those selected by the author representing some of the most difficult, charming and the best in novelty embroidery design. It would be difficult to estimate the time of developing such a line; in no case has expense been limited in creation or stitching, thus delivering the finest man and the machine can produce.

Their creations for Haute Couture houses are personally designed for the fashion houses shown, but many more in many countries were part of their collection.

Chanel, Paris

Pierre Balmain, Paris

Pierre Cardin, Paris

Pierre Cardin, Paris

Ted Lapidus, Paris

Lecoanet Hemant, Paris

Hanal Mori, Paris

Emanuel Ungaro, Paris

Pierre Balmain, Paris

Paco Robanne, Paris

Emanuel Ungaro, Paris

Emanuel Ungaro, Paris

Emanuel Ungaro, Paris

Pierre Venet, Paris

Pierre Cardin, Paris

Hatteras
Yachts

Save The Earth
Save Our Wildlife

Statesville
Balloon Rally
Bass
Tournament

SPECIAL ADAPTIONS AND EFFECTS WITH THE SCHIFFLI MACHINE

Special effects with embroidery can be obtained with yarn combinations, color changes, special attachments and settings of tension to accomplish different stitching effects. In most cases a stitcher will specialize in some form of embroidery. Some attachments are part of the machine, and others have been developed individually for special purposes and effects.

Originating a special effect is costly, and usually borne by the stitchers themselves. It not only requires farsightedness and financing, but the ability to merchandise the product developed.

All stitchers are capable of running one color yarn in repeats from 4/4 to 40/4 or to the limits of any particular machine. We could call this the standard set up. Stitchers may specialize in 4/4 cotton stitching, 8/4 white rayon stitching or any of dozens of other combinations that they feel are practical and can keep their machines busy.

A change in repeat requires changes in yarn, tensions, needles, and shuttles, but all of this is feasible with the standard machine and part of the normal order processes all stitchers live with.

Machines are "set up" when ready to run on any particular type of work. This is known to the jobber or merchandisers who will place work of a particular type with special stitchers. In this way one could set up 4/4 natural or 16/4 cord and find they can keep this set up for years, supplying many jobbers.

ALLOVERS: Any continuous pattern which covers the whole width and length of the goods being embroidered, from selvage to selvage, with a similar design. The design could be in any repeat and the figures could be connected or disconnected but the effect is an "allover". Best uses include dresses, lingerie, wall coverings, upholstery, and bed linens. However, it competes with any fabric.

EDGE: A narrow trimming with scallops on one side, raw edge on the other, cut into strips. Used as trims in lingerie, blouses, dresses, to finish off allover edges.

BAND: Same as the edge but with a straight edge on one side, usually finished with a straight steil.

FLOUNCE: (also known as a ruffle) Any wide edge utilizing the whole width of the goods where one edge is stitched as a design.
Uses: slips, skirts, curtains, bed ruffles.

FLOUNCE

GALLOON: An edge of any size with scallops on both sides. Instead of sewing into the garment, it is usually stitched onto a garment.

Uses: blouses, lingerie.

INSERT: A trimming where both sides have straight edges and are sewn into the garment

Uses: lingerie, blouses, dresses.

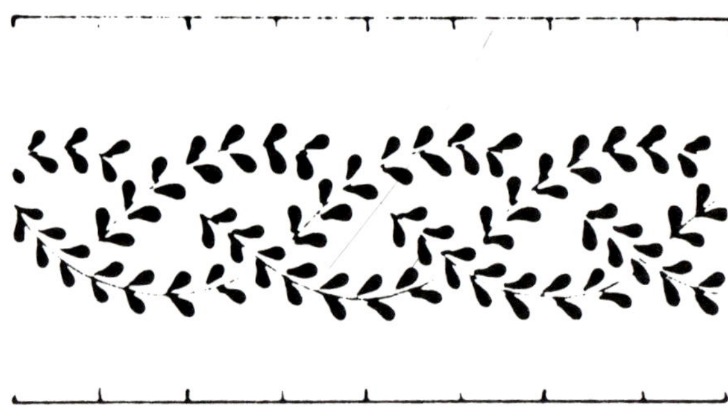

BORDERS: Can be made along the full length of the fabric, cut out or stitched up side down at a specific distance, to be used as curtains, drapes, bedspreads or table linen. End pieces can be joined to finish a 4 sided tablecloth, pillowcase or drapery.

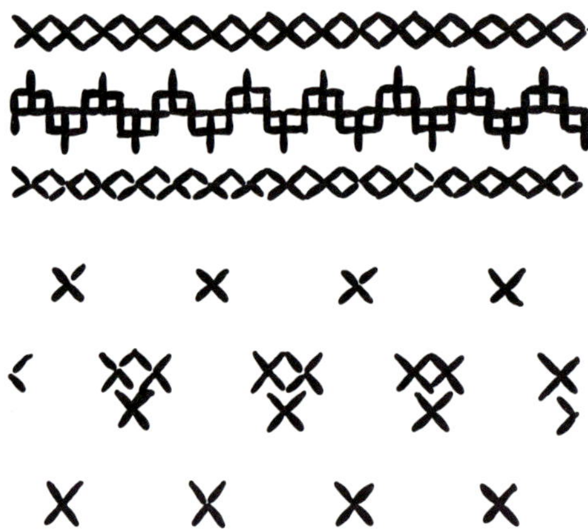

Stitching a border completely around a specific item requires the length to be determined (to fit your machine equally). If you had a 10 yard machine you might fit 4 3 yard pieces or 5 2 yard pieces in the length.

Space is allowed between the pieces by eliminating needles. Determine how far the border should be from the edge. After this part is complete, eliminate all the needles so those that will form the upright part of the border are left. Consider how you will treat the corners. 4 special punchings are usually required, or you can work out the design to form a corner without special work.

Stitch the upright part to the width of the embroidery desired, then reverse the process by making another corner, add the needles for the lengthwise part of the border, and you have a completely stitched rectangle.

This is used for handkerchiefs, scarves, bed linens etc.

NEEDLE SET-UPS: Patterns can be varied by setting the needles in a pattern of repeat set-ups, i.e., 2 in 4/4 with an 8/4 spacing or whatever might suit your design ideas. This is good for draperies, dresses, blouses, etc. The purpose of needle set ups is to envision more embroidery in a larger repeat but in a 2 needle set up the stitches that determine the cost are only half. Borers can be used in conjunction with needle set-ups.

DRAWN OR PULL WORK: This type of stitching can imitate color change work. One color yarn is in the shuttle and another is used as the front yarn. By setting the tensions of the front yarn tight and the shuttle looser, it is possible to set the sperrzeug to stitch at a normal tension and then activate it to tighten the tension at a particular part of the design, which will pull the bobbin yarn to the front, making it appear as the dominate color. For example, if you were stitching a small flower with red, you could then pull a green bobbin to the front, thus the new embroidery stitching what would appear as change work. Reactivate the tension and you have the front yarn dominate again.

There is a limitation to the size stitch that works best, usually 1/8″, but the whole idea is based on accurate bobbin and front yarn tensions.

SHADOW OR PUFF WORK: Another trick with tensions and the superior controls of the Schiffli machine is reverse of the drawn work above. The front tension is looser for shadow stitching while the bobbin is tighter, but the front is controllable with the sperrzeug. On a sheer fabric, the front yarn is in the loosened mode while the bobbin (always) remain slightly tightened. If a small loop is made, the bobbin will pull the front yarn to the back, giving a shadow effect to the front stitching, simply because you can see through the fabric. This design usually consists of all running stitches. Care is required when making curves in your design since the bobbin will always be pulling the front to the back. If you take great care you can set the front and back once and leave it.

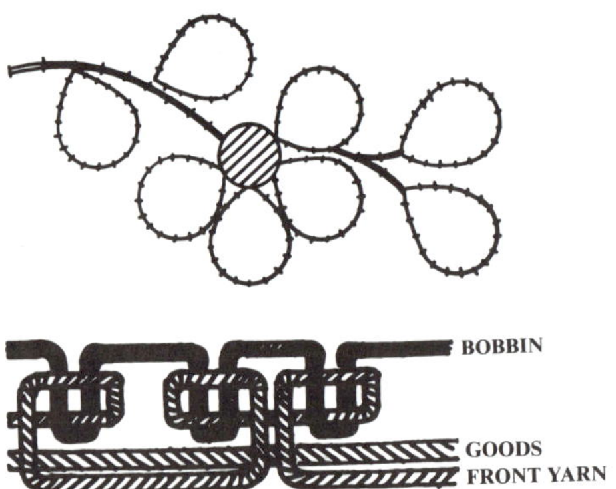

PUFF WORK is created by setting a greater tension on the front and back yarns so that small loops actually make the goods puff out. In this case it is not necessary to make the fabric too tight in the frame. Knits or any loosely woven goods that has some stretch works well.

Both Shadow and puff designs must use small closed loops to achieve the effect.

RUBBER BOBBINS: The goods should be a knit or any fabric which is not tightly woven. It is stretched firmly on the frame. The bobbins are special wound rubber bobbins. The design will consist mostly of running stitches in geometric form. The strength of the rubber bobbins will crinkle an allover pattern when the tension of the fabric is removed. Additional crinkle can be achieved by steaming the finished stitching to cause the bobbins to shrink further. This is a popular effect for swim suits and outerwear.

MATLESSIE: This gives another type of designed crinkle to base fabrics. By spanning a stretch fabric tightly in the frame, with a stable fabric like a light woven goods laid over the front or back of the spanned goods, not spanned, but pinned to lay loosely, then stitching in an allover pattern, the result will be, after the tensions are released, a crinkled design into that of the pattern used.

QUILTING: Quilting can be stitched on a Schiffli machine by spanning the face fabric with a second fabric, a filler, pinned to the back, not spanned. The filler can be cotton wadding or foam type goods. A third piece is usually pinned on the back of the filler, similar to a netting or gauze. The needles stitch through the 3 pieces and the tension of the stitching pulls the goods together, causing it to puff or quilt the design. This type of work is labor intensive and prices are based more on labor than on stitches. Limitations on the amount of goods that can be spanned at one time also add to much down time for spanning.

RIBBON INSERTS: As the stitching process takes place, a ribbon can be stitched into the design as follows:

A design is made and punched with a stop at predetermined point allowing a small loop into which the ribbon is placed, as many yards as the machine is long. The stitching process starts slowly, by tacking the ribbon on its top edge, stopping and checking that all is OK, then stitching a design over the edge.

Jump across the width of the ribbon and again make tacking stitches in slow motion. It is possible that the first few stitches on the top or the bottom will pull the ribbon out when the needle comes out. Walk the machine and check that the ribbon is off the needle so the stitch can be completed, then complete the design.

Stitch the desired design over the bottom edge.

REVERSE STITCHING: This is a method of stitching that solves the problem of adding heat seal to an embroidery as it is being stitched. In this method, the yarn that would normally show as the embroidery is wound as a bobbin while the front yarn is a monofilament low melt fiber that acts as a heat seal.

The normal thread in a bobbin is much thinner than the front yarn, therefore, a thinner yarn is required in the shuttle, meaning more stitches for proper coverage.

The front monofilament does not have to be spooled but could remain in cone form for long running times. Should the embroideries be motifs or appliques, the work can automatically be heat sealed.

BORE OUT: An allover where the main motifs are prominent because the surrounding fabric has been completely bored and stitched in a net effect, it can have the appearance of a lace. Uses include blouses, outerwear, and bed linens.

BEADING: A set of elongated eyelets which serve to thread ribbons into the design, the double eyelet holding the ribbon in place. Used frequently in edges, bands and flounces, on blouses, lingerie or other intimate wear.

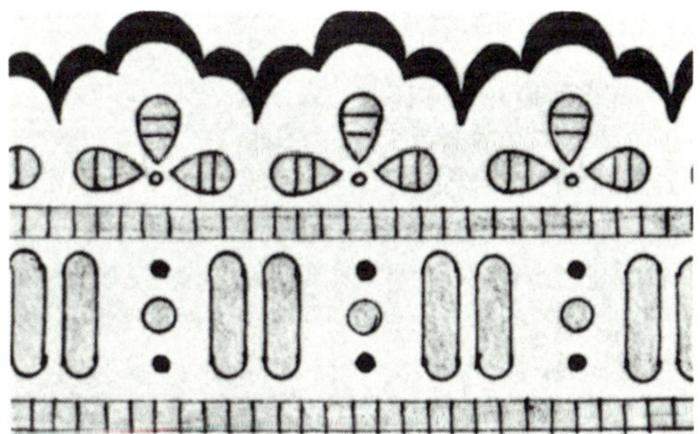

COLOR CHANGE: Using 2 or more colors to enhance a design like a flower and a leaf. There is no limit to colors that can be used if the costs can be absorbed.

Few Schiffli machines have automatic color changes, therefore, each color must be changed by hand.

There is a spindle for each needle setting. The smallest setting is 4/4, in which one spindle per needle or one color per needle would be used.

Color changes are used for repeats of 8/4 or larger, allowing for 2 spools of thread or 2 colors. 4/4 would not be practical because of the time required to change it as well as space for the yarns. 12/4 allows 3 different colors to be preset, 16/4 4 colors, etc.

Colors are twisted individually on the thread rollers. When one color work is stitched, the thread is normally wound 3 or 4 times around the roller. When more than one color is stitched, the thread is usually twisted one time around the stopped roller so the color in use will slide, pulling the yarn off the spool, while another color is stitching. In other words all thread colors to be used are threaded at one time. Therefore, changing colors only requires that the next color needles be threaded, one at a time.

For many color stitching, the first color is stitched for the full frame. For example, if you are stitching a 3″ patch down the frame on a 24″ machine, you will stitch color #1 7 full times or until the frame reaches a safe limit, then cut off and rethread with color #2, stitching up the goods 7 full times, and checking after each emblem is stitched that the colors are fitting properly. Color #3 would stitch down the frame again, following the correct sequence until the design is fully stitched. This is not as time consuming as it might sound since a color change might take approximately 15 minutes when everyone in the plant joins in to expedite the change. 3 colors might cost 45 minutes in time but the machine with a 3″ patch x 7 would produce 2394 patches on a 15 yard machine. In our emblem factory we have already stitched 14 color change work in a like manner.

The fabric has to be firm for many colored change work. If the work is very delicate it is possible that instead of 7 rows at a time, only 2 may be stitched, for proper registration and accuracy.

Many tricks have been tried (unsuccessfully) to make change work easier.

1. Figure out how much of each color is required for a particular design with some extra length, dye the yarn accordingly so you can start with color #1. At the time for change, pull the excess thread through the needle so the machine will start with color #2.

2. In the 1960's a stitcher set up a dye process on the machine, so that the thread could be dyed and dried as it was stitching. Run 'X' amount of one color, move the dye holder to another color, pull through the excess color not needed and start with another color.

Now we know the basis for automatic color change and why it is so valuable.

TRAPUNTO: This embroidery is three dimensional, the area to be raised is usually a front applique stitched to the design which will be filled with cotton or a wadding. The applique acts as a sack to be packed.

At one time we recommended a Trapunto gun, which would shoot thread into such an area. Unfortunately, we haven't seen them in the last few years or know where they can be purchased, but a filler is the answer to Trapunto. It is also possible to stitch a trapunto design with excessive underlay or make a yarn change and substitute a heavier yarn to both build and fill the area, but there is the possibility of broken needles.

STUMPWORK: Popular in 17th century fashion and art, Stumpwork is elaborately colored embroidery with intricate designs and high relief. It can not be accomplished entirely with thread but uses fillers of cotton, wood or other materials. The overall embroidery could include laces, other embroideries, beads, furs, jewels, feathers, etc.

Puffed embroidery up to ½ inch thick stitched with silk, containing many semi precious stones

For the U.S. Army and Navy, this type was effective in duplicating the hand made Bullion embroidered insignia made in India. It was very difficult to stitch and caused many broken needles, experimental stitching included patterns, adjustments and special needle settings.

Should you attempt this on an embroidery machine, apply many, many underlays or a filler as you would in an applique. Adjust the pressers, so movement can take place without the presser getting caught or the needle being bent on the filler.

There are beautiful effects to be made with Stumpwork.

APPLIQUES: For Schiffli, appliques are applied after the direct or basic stitching is completed. They are usually in the form of cut pieces large enough to cover the applique area completely. Die cut pieces of the exact size are impossible for Schiffli. The pieces are pinned onto the spanned goods. In some cases the applique for a 4″ figure might be 6″ wide, the length of the machine. After the goods is off-spanned it is hand cut as close as possible, but unless laser cut it will never be entirely clean, and if woven goods are used the possibility of fraying always exists.

For Multi-head machines the pieces can be die cut. The pattern should contain a stitched outline over which the applique will be fitted. A stickum of some type, heat seal or pressure sensitive will hold it in place. The pattern is programmed to stitch an outline around the shape to hold it in place while the edge is stitched. Unlike the Schiffli above, the embroidered steil will be stitched over the edge, making it perfectly clean without any fabric showing along it.

Multi-Head Applique

CONTINUOUS LENGTH EMBROIDERY: The length of a machine was always a problem for the garment trade. If goods were stitched on a 10 yard machine and the garments required 3 yards per panel, then 1 yard would be wasted. On a 15 yard machine 2 yard parts require 14 yards, and again a yard is lost. The best solution is continuous stitched goods.

One company in France stitches this normally, with a 15 yard machine. Once the 15 yards is completely stitched the goods is shifted length wise adding goods from one side, rolling it up on the other. Of course, the design has to fit to itself and the time needed for moving and fitting would be an issue.

Another method we mention is discussed in the "Future Ideas" section. In doing research for this book we found photos supplied by Herb Petermann, which shows the idea isn't so new after all.

LARGE REPEATS: the length of a Schiffli machine and the side movement of its frame are limitations to the length of any embroidered motif a machine can stitch. Machines vary from 40/4 up, but if you really want to make long repeats with sideways stitching beyond the machine's capability, it is possible. Many times we have designed patterns for machines that pull 32/4 to stitch 60/4. The trick is to set up the machine for a specific workable repeat, stitch with the space that is available, stop, move the frame and reset the needles once again to another workable side movement.

One of our orders our first year in business was to stitch a pattern 120″ long, along the selvage. That is a tough problem when the machine's side motion was only 15″. This was punched on a small board machine with a stitching distance of 40 inches (actual embroidery size 6.5 inches). The Schiffli frame only had a 15″ side movement. The 15″ maximum movement was enlarged 6 times, making the drawing 90 inches long. This required folding the jute enlargement, sliding it under the fixed cross bars of the punch machine (mechanical of course), punch and move, punch and move etc.

To make the task more complicated it was a 5 color change work, by hand. We were overjoyed when our first stitching joined our last stitching after 40,000 motions.

Today, thanks to computers, the whole problem does not exist, because we are not limited to the 6X enlargement, and the digitizing board has eliminated the cross bars.

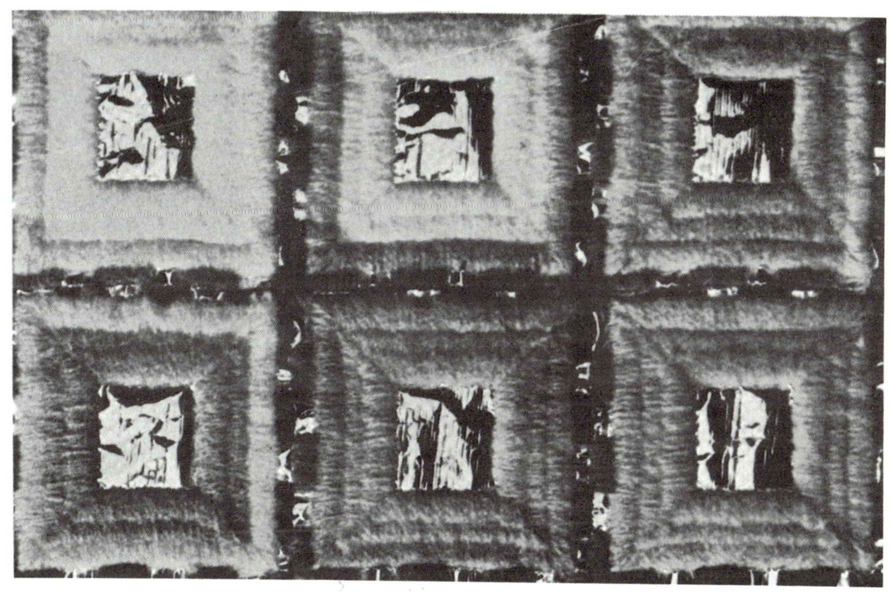

Schiffli Applique

STITCHING ODD SHAPES: Sometimes it is necessary to stitch oddly shaped pieces, such as animal skins which are irregular.

They are pinned or attached to a base cloth, already spanned. Stitching over the full area with an allover design is the most practical method. Then the goods are unspanned and cut apart.

PAINTING: Appliques and allovers have been made where color is added by dye or paint spraying. The design is stitched with special areas outlined. A mask or stencil is placed over the designated areas while the goods is still spanned, then a color is added. The same can be accomplished after the goods is unspanned and spread on a work table.

TWO SIDED EMBROIDERY: Used specifically for stars of American flags. The purpose is to make the stars look alike on each side of the flag rather than in normal stitching where we always use more front yarn than bobbin yarn. Yarns of the front and back are similar in size and color.

The answer to this problem lies in the exceptional advantages of the tension controls offered by the Schiffli machine. By using large shuttles and setting the tension to be equal on both sides, the joining point of the shuttle and front thread should meet at the fabric line.

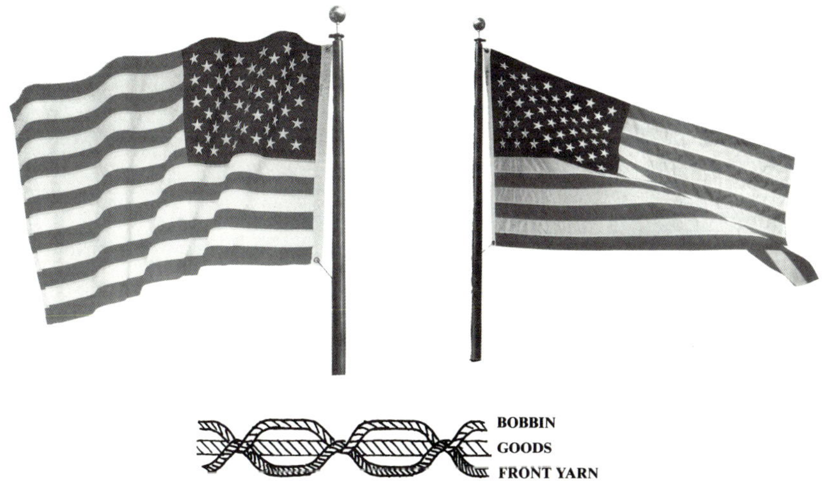

SINGLE APPLIQUES, MOTIFS AND MEDALLIONS: These are any embroidered design items that are self contained designs which will later be hand cut, die cut, aetzed or hot knifed.

PERSIAN LAMB: A special attachment is used to stitch imitation Persian Lamb which looks as good as the lamb did when it originally grew its fur. A ring holds and guides a specially developed curled yarn inside the circle.

By turning the ring, guided by the punching, in a backward and forward motion causing the ring to revolve, the spun type yarn is moved to the right and left over which a stitch is made by the needle attached to the needle bar. The needle is centered on the bottom inside of the ring, which ties the Persian Lamb yarn in place.

The sewing needle is usually threaded with a clear monofilament yarn. The design is usually a full allover, thus the finished curled product actually looks and feels like the fur of a Persian Lamb. The design possibilities are numerous for borders, allovers or anywhere a fur trim might enhance wearing apparel.

With the same device, it is possible to feed other yarns, ribbons, beading etc., into allover designs.

PERSIAN LAMB

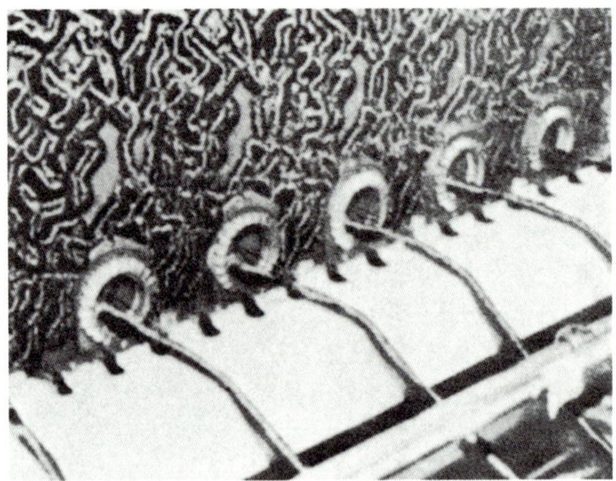

CHENILLE EMBROIDERY: This is created with a specifically designed attachment, without shuttles or bobbins, a hook mounted on the shuttle rail which actually catches the loop of the chenille yarn and holds it to form a loop in the back while the needle is retracted. This imitation of the Cornely moss stitch machine is very effective, but instead of producing one at a time, as with a single head machine, the machine will produce 172 automatically.

CUT PILE: Created with another special attachment used without bobbins, having a small scissor mounted on the shuttle rail which moves into the loop and actually closes and cuts the yarn in the formation of the stitch. The yarn has to be heavier than normal and the stitch as large as possible to gain the desired effect. After the embroidery is unspanned it requires a special starching treatment so that the threads do not come out of the base cloth. This is used mainly for bedspreads.

TUBULAR EMBROIDERY: How do you embroider ready made gloves, stockings or hosiery? A special attachment was originally designed by an unknown North Carolina embroiderer. It has been used successfully by Joe Gilodone, a Schiffli stitcher in Virginville, PA. The author has never seen the machine but the drawing shown was based upon telephone conversations. A 10 yard Schiffli machine is the basic stitching unit. The shuttle rail "A" supporting the shuttle boxes was lowered about 6". Below this, a driving platform "B" was constructed to drive the shuttles through a bar "C" with pins attached. A hole is drilled in the shuttle rail allowing the bar to drive the shuttles up and down. The shuttle box "D" is supported on the pillar "E". The shuttle box is in exactly the same position as when we started. By lowering the rail and compensating for the drive, an isolated shuttle box over which we can place a cylinder frame can be used to span the tubular item.

The frames are supported by pipe "F", in the same manner as the previous section of frame embroideries connected directly to the lower support of the Schiffli frame "G". A strip of metal is attached to this pipe as the base into which the frame is locked for stitching. The single frame "H" is a curved metal attached to a bar to form a group of frames for easy handling. The curve is open in the front and the rear, over which the tubular item is spanned.

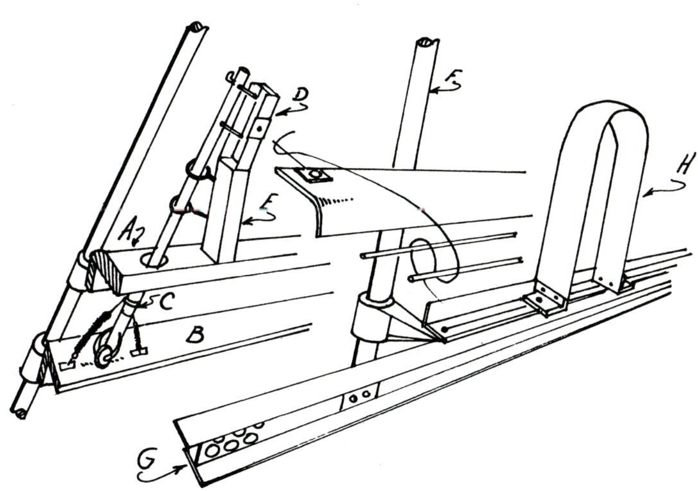

SEQUIN EMBROIDERY: The addition of sequins to any embroidery is another form of designing novelties, familiar to hand embroiderers. The first embroidered design on a Schiffli machine utilizing sequins was made in New Jersey in the late 1950's.

Attachments now exist in many countries as the patents expired. Most machine manufacturers will provide sequin attachments as options.

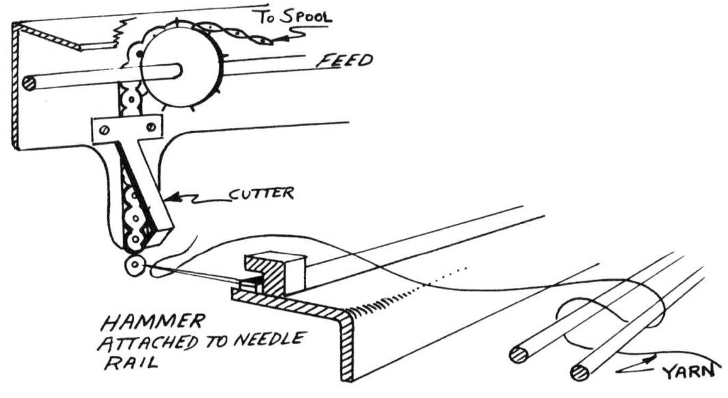

Subsequently a US Patent was awarded to Arnold Oschner for a device that presets sequins where needed for the machine to lock in with a stitch through the center of the sequin to the outer edges. Design possibilities are limitless. US Patents 505358 and 3922399 and Swiss Patent 432213 covered the details of this invention. (Now expired)

The sequins are prepared in one string on a roll and set on the machine. The first sequin is set in position. As the needle makes the first penetration in the center of the sequin a mounted hammer on the needle bar acts as a cutter to separate the sequin from the roll. The design is controlled by the punching in the normal stitching process. Special functions of the card can cause the sequins to feed or stop feeding. Thus, normal stitching can be combined with the sequined effects.

Other types of sequin attachments have been developed in the last few years.

AETZING: This is the method of finishing embroidery as laces. It was developed by Herman Dietrich in 1887 while at the factory of the Vogtlandische Machine Company in Plauen, Germany. The basic idea is to be able to disintegrate the base fabric on which the embroidery is stitched, leaving the embroidery in the form of a lace. This has been successful with the use of silk goods embroidered with cotton. A bleach bath of caustic soda is used to dissolve the silk. This has no effect upon the cotton stitching. Other methods have been used, such as chemically treating the base cotton goods, to be gassed or disintegrated by heat with the same result. The term "burn out" is derived from this process. Transfer embroidery uses this method.

Whether aetzing is done with a dry or wet process, the resultant lace must be constructed so that the stitching remains in one piece. The design must be punched so that the design will hold together allowing the finished product to be handled as embroidery in one piece.

The embroidered goods are rolled onto drums at the aetzing plant, placed into the bath for a specific time, then washed and dried. Bleaching or dying is done separately. Shrinkage is to be expected with this process and must be anticipated in the design of laces. The same applies to finished laces by the yard where the shrinkage will account for a loss in length of the embroidery. The less the amount of stitches used in designing and punching, the greater the overall shrinkage.

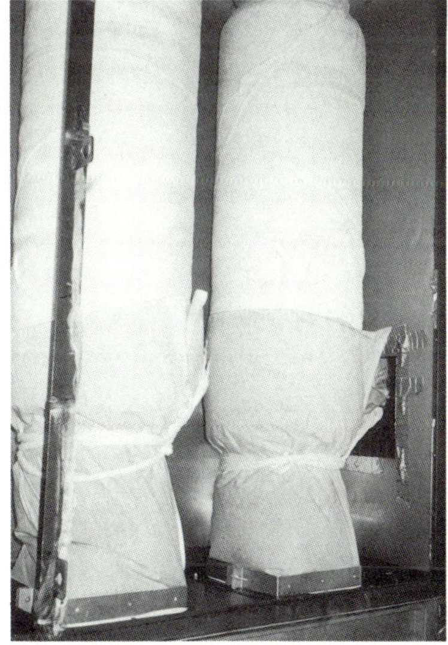

EMBROIDERY PRODUCTION

There are few instances where embroidery will not make a garment more distinctive, more colorful, more stylish or more feminine with the addition of embroidered trims, allovers or appliques. Not only are they more pleasing to the eye but they are more saleable and more profitable.

Distinctive examples include the Izod alligator, the Champion C, the Munsingwear penguin as appliques.

Colorful and stylish wearing apparel are visible when we examine the most famous designs of the early 90's in the previous chapter. The limits are not just womens wear, but extend into all wearables and home decorations.

The creators of this art today are not just the Swiss, who excel, but all designers in all countries are actively creating new styles daily, putting ideas into needle and thread.

For all practical purposes, we have to stitch the embroideries by machine. Mass production makes it available to everyone at reasonable prices. Hand embroidery might still be employed by some special companies but it is generally not affordable to the average person.

The embroideries we study here, made by machine, are more accurate and distinctive and have the same, if not more beauty than hand made stitching.

The merchandiser and manufacturers have huge libraries to draw from for art and uses of embroideries. Ideas are their stock in trade. By referring to the libraries, ideas are kindled, not necessarily copied.

We have so much to work with, the fabric designers base cloth of a hundred textures, colors, weights and hues. To this, the embroidery designer can add additional color, texture, dimension and create a whole new fabric.

Use of embroidery requires both imagination and interpretation. The delicacy of fine Swiss flowers can contrast with the boldness of peasant embroidery. It is an art like no other. All of this beauty can be produced by the yard with the Schiffli machine.

Embroidered designs can fit any mood or historic period of time. As romantic trends in design develop, it is necessary to seek designs that might be applicable.

It is not necessary for the designer to create the trend since that would be a great undertaking and a huge cost. For example, if Egyptian art is "in", then it is necessary to research appropriate Egyptian art.

Logos, animals or popular sayings can also be creative art and are another example of stitching for specific markets. The embroidered patch or emblem is a tested method of identification that is washable, dry cleanable and long lasting. In many cases the embroidered emblem will outlast the life of the garment on which it is attached.

Machine stitching can duplicate the finest hand made embroideries and styles created by other forms of stitching. Laces made by hand are impossible to buy, they are all in the museums. The time taken to make a lace by hand is unbelievable, the skills just about have disappeared, resulting in poor and inconsistent quality. Most of it is programmed into Schiffli tapes. As styles change, new ideas are punched, making laces available to everyone economically.

2S55 Saurer 15 Yard Schiffli Machines

Saurer 1040 21 Yard Schiffli Machines

Other mechanical means do exist to imitate laces.

Raschels are made inexpensively on the Mayer machine which is also used to knit tricot fabrics. They can not imitate the Schiffli laces.

Embroidered yard goods can also be stitched in small amounts of yardage, an asset not available to other types of machines. The set ups and designing and pattern making are relatively inexpensive.

Schiffli manufacturers usually specialize in one or two types of embroidery, therefore, designers and embroidery jobbers have to know the industry to find the right stitcher for his work. One stitcher will stitch laces, another emblems, or novelties, one may specialize in 4/4 natural while another in 4/4 white. The reasoning is that specialization will cause many jobbers to know that he is set up for a particular type of stitching and direct that production directly to him.

Production of embroidery is not difficult if the customer works with a stitcher who knows his machines, production capabilities, and performance. Reasonable time for deliveries should be allowed, the garment industry is always expecting deliveries "yesterday". There is much planning required for all parties and the end result is usually less time than other types of stitching might require.

New designs are always necessary because of the various uses of embroidery in many trades and competition with rival trims and designer fabrics. Imagination and creative ideas are what keep the best items in use. Embroidery, often known as the highest form of art in many periods of history, still requires constant attention to design and production to remain first in decorative use of trims and allovers.

In the U.S. price plays an important part of garment decoration, that is because we use the best pricing for many more trades and do not limit ourselves to fine embroideries in the expensive Haute Couture trade. This can be accomplished only by designing and stitching embroideries to fit a certain cost structure. If it is too expensive it will be eliminated as a trim. Credit to the American stitchers is deserved since they have created marvelous designs that every level of the population can afford. This is difficult embroidery to create and bring out to the correct price. Much creative design and punching are required.

Design is important to create the fine Swiss embroideries we all love. Punching is basically following the lines drawn by the designer, however, making something inexpensive requires more careful design and extremely sharp punching techniques. Transplanted Swiss have a difficult time programming inexpensive American embroideries.

PRODUCTION FLOW

The process of embroidery manufacture in the USA begins with the merchandiser or jobber who is familiar with the industry and which stitchers (contractors) are qualified to produce certain types of embroidery. They would know which machines are stitching certain repeats, yarns or processes. The flow of the order is important to follow step by step from the origin of the design to the final delivery of the finished product.

From the first submission of the idea in sketch form to the enlargement, punching and sample and the final approval from the customer, the proper stitcher is located to schedule production.

The embroidery manufacturer must be selected, he is one who is familiar and experienced with the particular type of stitching required. With an approved punching, yarns selected and base cloths supplied, the embroiderer is basically ready to begin production. 10 yard machines are ideal for novelties and small runs, 15 yard machines require longer runs because of set up times and the 21 yard machine is ideal for staple goods.

Fabric requirements must allow for spanning and "hanging in", a 10 yard machine requires a minimum of 21 yards of full width goods, a 15 yard requires 31 ½ yards, while a 21 yard needs 43 ½ yards.

Stitching takes place at the embroidery factory but many finishing processes require the goods to be moved from point to point. Laces require aetzing, bleaching, and or dying, thread trimming, joining, processes which are always subcontracted. These scheduled processes also take time and have to be considered in the total delivery picture.

A look at the flow chart will show those necessary steps for laces and embroideries. Usually these services are performed by specialized companies who cater to the Schiffli industry.

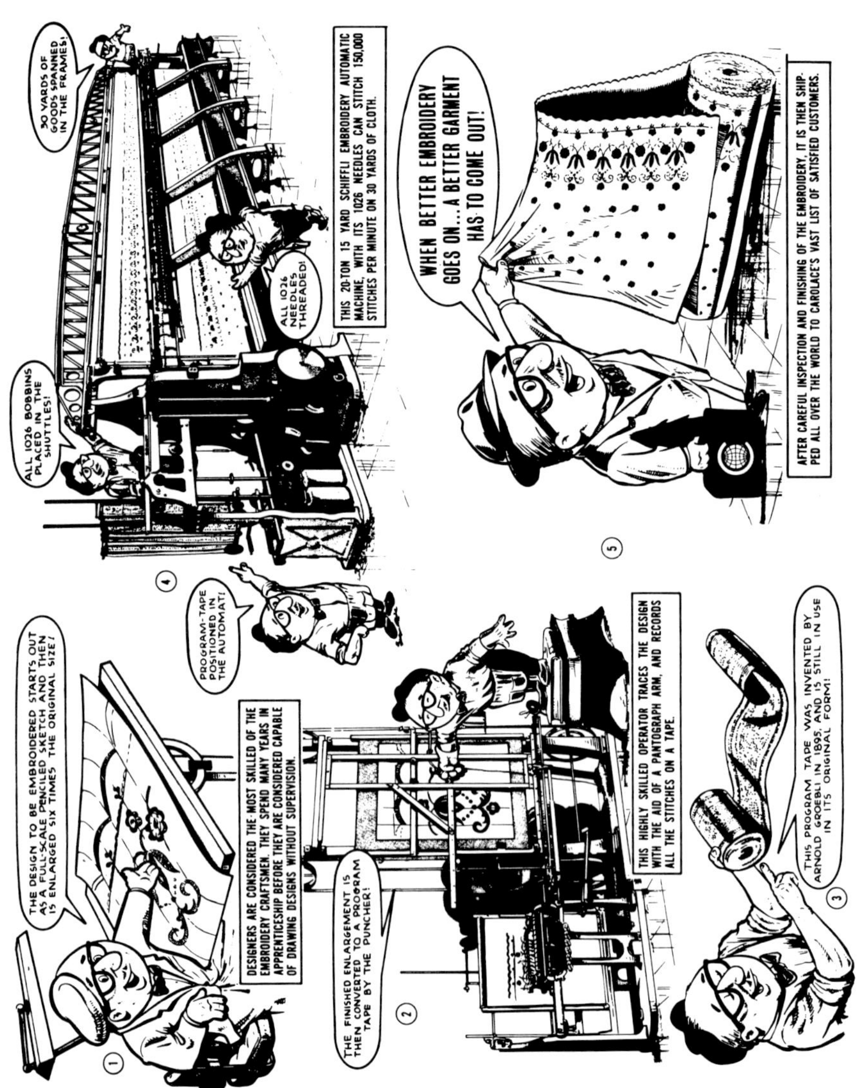

Courtesy of Carolace.

FLOW CHART FOR YARD GOODS

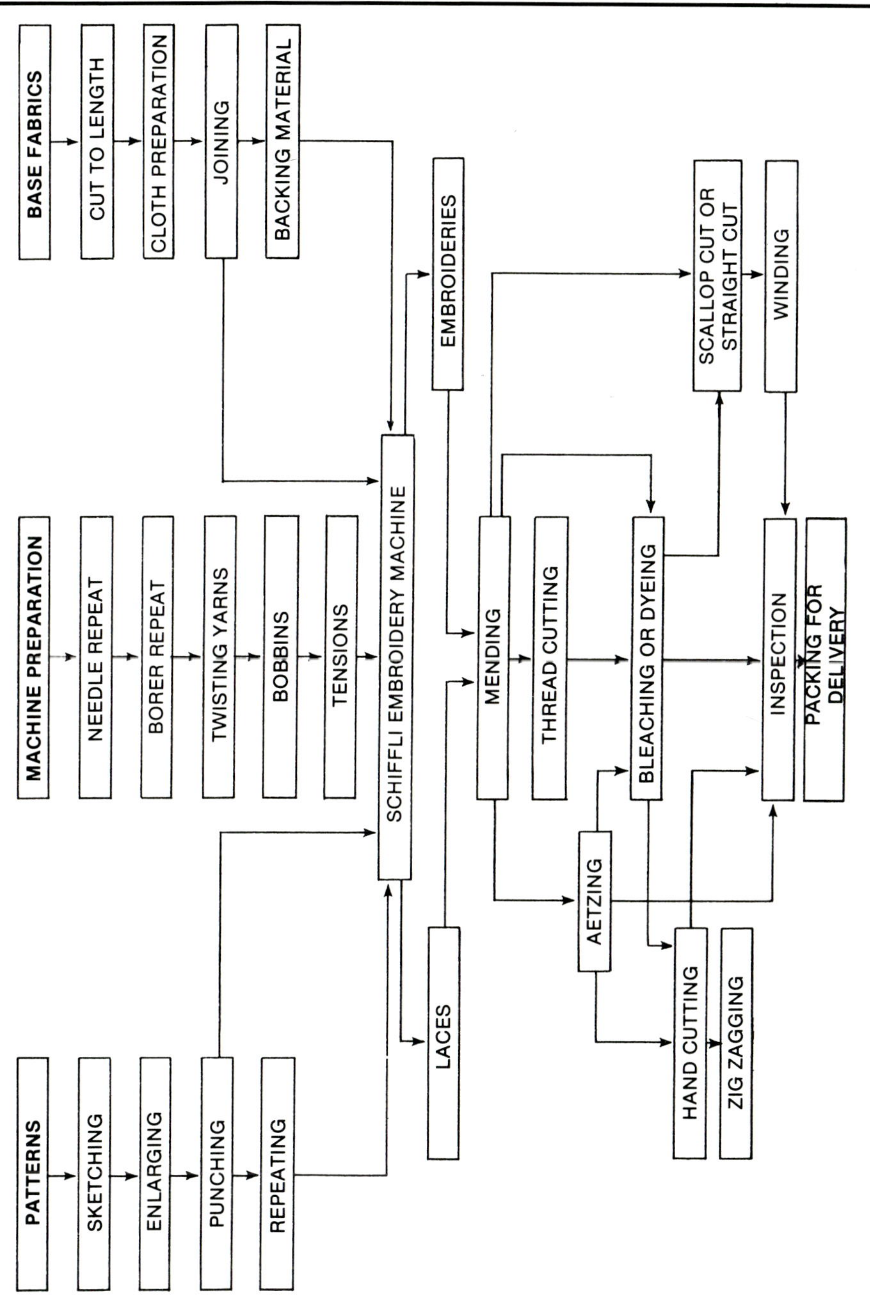

CHAPTER VI

BASIC PUNCHING FOR THE EMBROIDERY MACHINE

Punching is a general term denoting the punched card, the tape or the disc, or the process of preparing the design through digitizing, indicating to the production machine all of the functions to be activated and the frame movements required by the design.

The programmer of the design is known as the puncher, the term carries over from the mechanical machine when each stitch was recorded by a punched hole in the paper tape.

The recording of the stitch, whether mechanical or electronic, is recorded for the embroidery machine to read and perform. It may be recorded with a stylus, attached to vertical and horizontal bars as with the mechanical machines, or with a mouse, the more modern way, to record those points needed to form the design.

The basics of punching have not changed. We still need a drawing to work from, drawn to 6 times its normal size. The inaccuracies disappear when the computer and or mechanical machines both reproduce the embroidery 6 times smaller in normal size.

Place the drawing on the digitizing board in the same direction you would want the pattern to stitch on the production machine. Line it up so it is straight and tape it to keep it from moving while you are working on it.

The most important part of punching is to study the enlargement, plan your starting and stopping points, the route to be followed in the design, plan your sequence of color changes and your jump stitches.

Take the time to do it right now, to save redoing or spoiling your work. Plan the stitch densities the design will require. Always keep in mind the total concept of the design.

Since this book deals with Schiffli and Multi-head machines it is necessary to understand that the punching used for a design would be essentially the same for both of these machines, but that the techniques required to produce it are vastly different.

For Schiffli, a puncher must have expert knowledge of the machine for which the design is to be used. In many cases it is necessary to interpret what this particular machine will perform differently from the drawn design. Some machines will make large stitches larger and small stitches smaller, thereby distorting the design.

Even machines from the same manufacturer will stitch differently since over the span of machine development many changes were made affecting the way the embroidery is reproduced. Some machines in use still date from 1895; they remain the same because the improvements in many cases were not transferable. Many of the older factories have various machines from different manufacturers, and this causes differences in embroidery from the same tape on different machines. The condition of the machine, and when it had its last overhaul will affect production. Different fabrics, such as knits, twills, shirting, fleeces, will cause different results. Another difference could be the multitude of yarns which a Schiffli can run, heavy cottons, wools, cording, fine yarns, cottons, silks, and polyesters all reproducing differently.

For Multi-head, the differences also exist, only not to the same degree as with the Schiffli. The main problem is that the Multi-head puncher does not have enough basic experience with various yarns and fabrics that are required as well as the huge expanse of framed goods and its inherent problem that exist in Schiffli: otherwise the basics are the same.

The enlargement should be an exact reproduction of the sketch or embroidery from which it is drawn. The puncher is responsible for interpreting the drawing for a particular machine. No skill is more important in the whole industry than that of the puncher, in bringing out the designer's idea, and ensuring the quality and appearance of the embroidery. A properly made enlargement with the proper number of stitches and a properly spanned machine with the correct tensions are the basic requirements.

At this point the puncher is in a position analogous to that of a diamond cutter. For, depending on the programmer's skill, the resulting design can either be lost or all its beauty and detail brought to life.

Every design brings with it new problems which have to be thought out in advance. The puncher is continually presented with new ideas which must be interpreted based on his experience. As he proceeds with the stitching various programs are utilized for stitching or functions of the machine such as color change, tightening and loosening of the tensions, boring, stupfel, slow, fast speed or any other function he might require. It is necessary to interpret the design, feel the flow of stitches, add or take away stitches, compensate if required. This interpretation can only be gained by experience.

No punching can be just a mechanical drawing which is programmed 1-2-3-4 without feeling. If this is the method you use, you are still a learner and will not produce art in embroidery.

If drawings are made accurately, then punching for Multi-head is simple since the accuracy of the machine along with the smaller area of spanned goods allows the puncher to correctly follow the design without the thought of compensating for size of stitches. Only as the machine grows old from use and parts become worn, does it become necessary to compensate as required.

No two punchers will follow designs in exactly the same way. Each will lay out the design according to his experience. However, there are certain rules to follow.

The fabric to be embroidered is a knitted or woven group of threads. When framed on any embroidery machine it is under tension and will react differently to various types of stitching. Since the fabrics are held only on their perimeters, the balance of the goods is left to shift or move according to the stitching.

This will be minimal in a hoop, but it will increase with a larger frame and becomes very important on a Schiffli machine where the perimeter will measure more than 700 inches by 70 inches.

We discover mighty fast the differences in fabrics the first time we punch on a knit goods. This is where experience is important to the ultimate design. The possible problems are not shown on the enlargement.

Stitches will react differently according to the direction of the knit, a stitch right and left will look different from a stitch up and down of the same size.

Compensation has to be used to conform to the original design. Such fabrics can also cause thread problems whereby not only direction but execution becomes a factor both in the design and the harmonious running of the stitching. Broken threads, looped stitching or needle breakage are some of these.

In addition to following the pattern, the puncher has to know how to tie in laces, place jump stitches so they are not in the way of other stitches and can be cleanly cut, make tie-ins for bands, scallops, and lock jump stitches in and out. The puncher has to make sure the design does not run out of its assigned area, that all colors fit, that the machine is properly threaded and ready for the punching.

Unfortunately, one of the most important sources for progressive information was the sample machine. Spanned with the proper fabric, threaded with the correct yarn and colors, this was a source of constant information for the puncher as he progressed with the design. Most mechanical machines had one yard samplers attached. Even some Multi-head machines (Gross and Zangs) had single needle samplers.

With the advent of the computer, these units were an impractical accessory. Therefore, there is no longer a practical way to produce a sample while one is punching a design. The puncher can check through the use of a monitor or plotter.

The substitute is the single head Multi-head sample machine. However, it is impossible to produce an accurate sample, the same yarns and tensions do not exist for Schiffli and a single needle is not going to produce repeat stitching.

2½ yards and larger sample machines do exist for proofing the tape and making the sample for presentation to the customer. However, they are very expensive and most use their production machines to provide accurate samples.

Patterns then, are progressively viewed on a CRT or a printer or not at all.

The fabric to be embroidered is a mesh of threads, some woven, some knitted. When spanned on an embroidery frame in their full width from 10 to 21 yards in length, the various fabrics will react differently to tension in spanning. We know the fabric is held along its perimeter under tension. With this much pressure there is always some minute internal movement of the fabric due to the size, density and direction of stitches. We assume each thread tension is equal at the needle, and the same should be true with bobbin tensions. Therefore, the proper framing and tensions are of utmost importance to prepare the machine for stitching.

Considering that as many as 1400 needles will penetrate the fabric at one time, 150 times per minute, with the thread tension drawing back and forth as tensions are made, there has to be some give to the overall embroidered fabric and therefore the design.

These are some of the problems the puncher must take into consideration:

How much does the fabric pull in because of the spanning? What distortion can you expect?

How small can a stitch be made, how will the thread react?

These questions are not answered on the enlargement.

How will the particular machine to be used react to this stitching? Does the programmer make the larger stitches slightly smaller?

In which direction should the design be stitched, horizontal or vertical?

Should smaller stitches be made slightly longer to compensate for little or no frame movement which might cause broken ends or needles?

Does the fabric being used require a backing? In the front or in the back? Should the backing be framed with the fabric or set on top? How tight should the fabric be spanned?

After the tape is made and assigned to a machine, it is up to the puncher to critically evaluate his work. If it is not correct then it must be fixed or redone to meet his criteria. Experience is the best teacher.

There is no study of punching which can answer these questions or solve all the possible deviations in design. When one has to punch for a Schiffli machine they should first operate the various jobs that are part of the machines operation, watcher, shuttler and spanner and learn these thoroughly. At the beginning of his punching career, it is possible he will have to redo his work until he learns the machine's normal reactions under all conditions. Originally, punchers gained extensive punch experience by stitching on a pantograph. Today, with so few pantographs, he or she must learn their trade from actually running the machine by trial and error.

Experience is the key. Newer factories train punchers at a young age. The author has seen a dozen young women in Taiwan, about 19-20 years old, punching by themselves. Some were punching very difficult and intricate laces, proof that age alone is not a factor in becoming a good puncher. This factory had only one model of machine, all the same age, so the problems were reduced.

When the punched design is completed, it is the job of the puncher to check the tape and sample to see that no parts were left out and that all functions are recorded in the proper sequence, and properly mark his pattern and see the finished product in production.

SCHIFFLI CARD SYSTEMS

GROEBLI

The first Schiffli card system was the Groebli, designed and built by the son of Isaak Groebli in New York City. The system moved two separate sheavers, like the parts of a scissor, whereby, moving the frame straight up or down required the movement of each sheaver equally. Moving sideways required one to move up while the other moved down. The punch machine was operated by holding two leather strips to move the cursor, which rested on 2 sheavers and a third to move and record the combination by punching the card. The punch system was good, the board on which the 6 time design was attached was narrow, catering to the smaller designs used for trims. However, it was possible to 'superfix' the design to move the drawing and continue side or up and down movements. Boring was also available by shifting the board the fixed movement required for the borer to be in its proper position.

Functions (other than frame movements) to start the needle motion, alter the speed or activate the borers were punched alongside the edge of the tape.

Even a sampler was supplied, approximately 10″ wide and 20″ high with the original double pointed shuttle running right to left. It was a fun machine to work with and once you developed a rhythm you could swing along at a rapid speed.

ZAHN

The second system required a different size tape. It was simpler to read since the movements were not a combination of motions as in the Groebli, but only right and left, up and down. The system was easier to punch but achieved the same results. The center of the tape recorded the frame movements, a punched hole along the edge of the frame controlled the direction: up or down, right or left. Functions for starting stopping, boring, tension controls and stupfel were on the right and left sides of the tape.

SAURER

The Saurer system was a combination of motions in punch form with all the function punching in the middle of the tape. Again, it was a different size tape, not transferable. It seems it was developed to be different, possibly because of patents of the time.

These were the main systems, and each required a separate mechanical punch machine. With the introduction of electronic drives, combined with the machine manufacturers' desire to sell all factories regardless of the machines style they were using, it was practical, electronically and with computerization, to read anyone's tape into the machine to operate it. Therefore, today all these machines read all tapes.

Older machines even now are being transformed to computer assisted, electronic servo drives. They have become more efficient and faster. Age offers no hindrance to conversion.

It is not necessary to remove the mechanical automat from any machine. A simple "Electra Card" reader is the easiest and least expensive first step in converting the older machine. This unit can be tied in with your automat and direct the platines by use of solenoids to deliver pattern information to the machine without the use of a paper tape. The automat acts in its normal fashion, performing all its special functions and moving the frame. Your older punchings can be converted into 3.5 inch discs which you will use instead.

Storage of tapes is simplified, repeating ends, and other problems associated with paper tapes disappear. Conversion of tapes from others machines can be read into the 3.5 inch disc.

MULTI-HEAD CARD SYSTEMS

Originally, we had only to contend with one system, the one developed by the inventor of the Multi-head machine, Mr. Wurker. His system's tape, modeled on that of the Schiffli machine, was 2 11/16″ in width, mechanically punched.

Before the computerization of punching, we had this mechanical card system for all the machine manufacturers. Naturally, all automats read the same tape, in two formats; 5 or 7 for the two gear ratios. 5 had a maximum stitch length of 5/32″ while 7 had a maximum of 9/32″. These tapes were not interchangeable, they were two distinct models manufactured by all the machine builders.

With the advent of electronic machines this all changed. Originally all Multi-head machine manufacturers developed their own 8 channel tape code, which was not transferable from one machine to a competitor's machine. Even Ultramatic thought they could own a system outright (to capture all the tape business for that type machine) by having the machine read only cassette tapes. With the introduction of electronic and computerized punching it was simple to change the code of the 8 channel 1″ tape for each machine manufacturer.

Today, most machines will allow the reading of competitors' tapes, but not all of them. One of the answers to this problem is the QDT by Moritz Embroidery. This quick Disc Design Transfer unit reads any tape directly into your machine's format and it's economical too! Therefore, any tape can operate your machine. Other such converters are available.

Differences in Schiffli and Multi-head counts of stitches for the same design vary as follows:

Schiffli in the U.S.A. count every movement as a half stitch, thus we say rpm for revolutions per minute. Every stitch count in the U.S.A. requires 2 movements to count as one stitch.

Schiffli in the rest of the world count every movement as a stitch, the same as Multi-head, therefore, we say spm for stitches per minute.

Other differences for Multi-head comparisons with Schiffli will show up in the number of stitches for the same pattern since a Schiffli stitch can be longer in one motion while Multi-head is limited and might require 2 or more movements to gain the same length.

Another difference is the amount of stitches of the same length used to cover a certain area. Schiffli has a yarn twist which lays soft while a Multi-head yarn is a tighter twist, requiring more stitches to cover the same area.

DEVELOPMENT OF COMPUTERIZED PUNCHING

The idea for computerized punching was conceived by the author in 1967. The first unit was operable in 1976 and has become the standard method of punching embroidery tapes throughout the world.

From 1951, the author had made his living by establishing the company C. Schneider International which supplied embroidered designs and punching to the Schiffli and Multi-head industry in New Jersey and many parts of the world, and as a designer and a puncher for many years for all types of Schiffli machines and mechanical Multi-head machines. Punching was very time consuming, but mechanical punch machines were all that existed, and that was the method everyone in the industry used. Sometimes patterns would be on the machine for a week because the best we could punch was 8,000 Schiffli stitches per day (16,000 movements). Multi-head was somewhat faster, with approximately 20,000 stitches per day.

This is the reason the author was looking for a faster method of making punchings for all machines.

If the embroidery tape consisted of punched holes indicating a numerical value in X and Y directions, plus and minus, that meant that all stitches consisted of straight lines. The basic idea was to develop a method of electronically digitizing an enlargement that was able to drive a mechanical copy machine to transfer these values to the existing blank Schiffli tape.

Since the author was very familiar with the economic situation of the average Schiffli manufacturer, he immediately decided to work on the computerization of the punching and leave the mechanical embroidery automat alone. The manufacturer might invest in a punch system but the automat would be too expensive at this time. First prove the punching, and then the computerized automat would follow. Electronics were too new to the stitcher, he knew how to fix his mechanical machine and many good mechanics were available.

The mechanical copy machine, we estimated, was too slow to punch the information the computer could provide. So we started to build a complete new copy machine, using electronically driven solenoids that would activate the punches as directed. After investing a lot of money we gave up on a new machine and settled for an electronic adapter which fit the existing copy machines.

The first programming information included all the machines we punched for at the time: Groebli, Saurer, Plauen and mechanical Multi-head, plus all types of stitching programs used for embroidery.

We searched for a contractor who would be willing to develop this embroidery system. Many had no concept of what we were trying to accomplish.

However, on Oct. 12, 1967 we were lucky in meeting Tasmin Barnes of Armada, Colorado whose company, Auto Trol, a manufacturer of digitizing equipment, was willing to try and understood completely what we were attempting to accomplish. They selected a 16 bit 8K memory Varian computer to start off the system. We proceeded to build a large digitizing table at Auto Trol, using a T bar similar to the existing mechanical punch systems, with an electronic reader which was the counter for the X and Y movements.

Meetings took place with the author and many ideas were discussed, as Mr. Barnes struggled with the formation of the original concept. One idea was to lay graph paper over the enlargement and type out the coordinates of each stitch. We felt this would stifle creative punching, and it was dropped. We also considered punching directly to the embroidery automat, but eventually decided to use an 8 channel tape as the primary product of the computer.

We had the advantage of working with a company that devoted much time to the project, and was in the forefront of advances taking place in the electronics industry at the time. The U.S. was also where computer technology was most advanced and information was flowing at a fantastic pace.

Our goal was to build a machine that would not scare the existing puncher, one he could easily make the transition to from the mechanical without trepidation.

The function, stitch, even the M and W of the Zahn automats had to be retained. It was, in fact, designed by a puncher for punchers.

The first sample was stitched in October 1970 in our studio in West New York, NJ, witnessed by Mr. Cataletto who operated a card punch center in Italy. He immediately placed an order for a similar system, but another downturn in the embroidery industry caused a delay in further development.

Mr. Cataletto went on to try to develop his own system.

We supplied him with an electronically controlled mechanical Multi-head copier. Others who assisted were Dominick Golia of Ultramatic and some card centers in Greece, Spain and Switzerland.

Others were also active in developing their own systems, Gunold of Germany, August Heinzle of Austria and Goda of Japan. Not all were successful.

The Pfaff agent in Japan, along with Tajima and Eltac in Japan and Saurer of Switzerland also developed electronic punch machines. Faul Coradi of Switzerland also developed an electronic punch machine for Penn Emblem in Philadelphia.

These machines increased the speed of punching by at least 20% but contained none of the programming the author envisioned by computerization.

Auto-Trol sold out in 1970 and the new buyers did not do well.

Meanwhile, the author discontinued his design and punch business because of a severe downturn in the Schiffli industry. He formed the All American Company as a manufacturer of embroidered emblems. Within 6 months a partnership was formed with a Schiffli stitcher.

Some of the employees of Auto-Trol formed their own company and finally contacted the author in 1972 to restart the uncompleted project. One knew the electronics, the other programming, but neither knew anything about embroidery.

We again started to develop the computer punching system with 2 former Auto Trol employees who had done some of the work on the original units. The author acquainted them with all the intricacies of design and punching, supplying all the existing data on punch tapes for Saurer, Plauen and Multi-head machines.

The advantage of computerization over an electronic punch system was the programming of stitching, curves, reverses, rotating, curved lettering, editing, executions, enlarging and reductions and memory of sub routines. Then the importance of electronics came into play to transfer this programming to the finished tape.

The author called for computerized punching to be the standard of the entire embroidery industry 12 years ago and it has become that standard, but computerized punching has developed far beyond what he envisioned in 1967.

The first computerized punch system was completed in 1975 and the final bugs were removed by the end of the year. The first machine installed at The All American Company was more sophisticated then those offered to the competition a short time later. Ours punched a condensed tape because our company used contractors with various card systems. After a month without serious problems the builders phoned and asked if we would represent them. We asked how many machines they would like to sell and their reply was that 3 or 4 a year would be great.

Beginning in 1976, the author offered the machine to all Schiffli manufacturers and we sold 13 units the first year. The builders felt they were giving too much away and agreed to build and sell machines programmed for any one of the specific machines. Thus the author sold Multi-head, Saurer and Plauen separately many different stitching programs were available.

Initially, we digitized the design, then converted it into the machine punching for the required machine code. This was accomplished by converting the existing copy (duplicating) machines to electronic punchers, reading the computer tapes into the copy machine which produced a machine punching (mechanical tape) for the production machines.

At this time, the author was President of The All American Emblem Company and used the services of Saurer, Plauen and Multi-head machine contractors. We required the tapes to be punched in condensed form, then expanding them to the machine of our choice.

The hardware was easily available from many sources and the whole key to the computerized punching system was the software programming. The genius in this division was Bill Childs of Melco Industries, and Marty De Santis who really put the whole thing together.

Any stitch can be programmed, but some are very seldom used, therefore the author was to work out the most commonly used embroidery stitch combinations, estimating about 90% of what a puncher would require on a daily

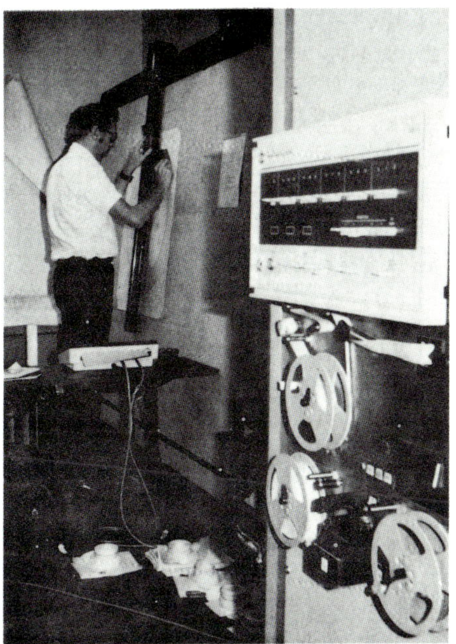

The first computerized punching system.

basis. He figured this would be most useful and most economical. We digitized the remaining stitch forms for the time being, stitch by stitch. Later, the programmers could add all the seldom used data.

We found we could punch up to 1000 times faster with the computer, and we helped local stitchers, making punchings which would have cost thousands of dollars to enlarge and punch and require as much as 8-10 days to complete in as little as 4 hours. Embroidery fills became the easiest and most profitable programming. All other programs added to the realization of a successful development. We hit a total of 140,000 stitches in an 8 hour day. However, our business at this time was not as a card center. All we did for others was to prove various possibilities for the machine.

SAMPLES

An expensive way to provide samples was to transfer the design to a fabric and have a sample mender, i.e., have an experienced sewing machine operator, follow the design by eye. For Schiffli, it is difficult to find the older experienced menders and only the best could make the embroidery look like machine made samples. Usually, the samples of today are poor substitutes for machine made goods since the training of expert samplers no longer exists in the U.S.A.

Samples were provided by a sample machine on most mechanical Schiffli punch systems. You could frame the proper fabrics, stitch with Schiffli yarns in actual repeats with a maximum of 14 needles in 4/4. Larger machines did exist. This sample could be submitted to the customer for approval. Schiffli computerized punch systems do not provide samples. Some with a monitor provide computer images, some use color printers, but for the Schiffli operator it is necessary to break down a machine to provide the proper sample, or to purchase the ready made sample machines that exist in 2 to 4 yard lengths.

Gross and Zang Multi-head mechanical punch machines did have a single head sampler attached, that stitched as one punched.

Today it seems you either depend on a CRT or run the sample off after the pattern is punched. At least that sample gives an idea of what the actual work will look like, even if it has the wrong yarn and repeats are not stitched.

Of course, with Multi-head machines the one head sample machine will run the tape to satisfaction with proper threads and goods.

Saurer Schiffli Sampler.

THE IMPACT OF COMPUTERIZED PUNCHING

There were two main advances during the 1970's. The first was the introduction of electronics to the Multi-head embroidery machines, followed by the introduction of computerized punching. This was a bonanza to the embroidery industry. The machines became easier to repair, faster in speed, easier to program. The machine manufacturers jumped into a vast open market as identification became popular, embroidery art became popular and it seemed everyone could become a computer artist.

That is exactly what happened. Today, in the U.S.A. we have about 10,000 Multi-head machines in a whole new industry. It is now up to that industry to keep innovating, inventing, and designing, to keep forging ahead.

Multi-head is not as sophisticated to program as the Schiffli. Their frames are smaller, they are not old machines with outmoded frame systems or frames that are so heavy they continually over and under stitch. Once a firm goods is framed on Multi-head it will remain stable, but some considerations are still required, of a lesser nature than on the larger machines.

Thread tensions are more controlled and losses from mistakes are minimal, when compared to the larger Schiffli machines with 21 yds of goods to replace.

Multi-head programmers need different experience to punch for Schiffli, likewise, the Schiffli puncher may be a poor Multi-head puncher.

Most Schiffli embroidery manufacturers world wide now use computerized punch systems. Starting the older punchers with computers was like teaching them to fly, since they had walked all their life.

The only area slow to adapt to computerized punching is where it all began, in the heart of the Schiffli area in New Jersey. After 15 years there are only 3 or 4 systems operating among 222 factories. Perhaps this is indicative of the state of the industry in New Jersey.

SCANNERS

The next logical step in the computerized punching revolution would be to create the drawing you wish to punch with the computer. The scanner will eventually provide that service, but as of today it works only with camera ready art, clip art or line drawings. As soon as you use an actual free hand drawing in color and scan it into your computer, you will find you need much assistance to bring forth a clear drawing from which to actually digitize an accurate tape. We have not as yet replaced the artist's drawing with scanning. In the future many advancements will make the scanning process more accurate. However, keep in mind that computer generated art, just like punchings, will never replace the talents of the artist or the puncher who can add creative "feeling" to either of these methods.

COMPUTER PUNCHING EQUIPMENT

There are many computerized punch systems available, all continuously try to improve and keep up with the latest technology. Therefore, what is shown here as standard equipment may change in the foreseeable future.

The hardware in all cases is 'off the shelf', used in many industries for various purposes. The warranties of the individual hardware manufacturers cover all the punch systems: the computer and accessory hardware such as printers, tape punches, plotters, scanners, etc.

What do you want from your punch systems? Easy to read and efficient software, the basic programs that will complete your tapes without causing you to take a special computer course.

There are many software programs available including total design capability, conversions to other systems, enlarging, reducing, editing, in tapes, discs or cassettes. It is up to the buyer to decide where the limit is. There is much more available than anyone really needs. If the system you are considering is for internal use only, just for your equipment, you can leave out a lot of extras, but if you want to supply the embroidery industry you will need much more. Remember, you can always add to your equipment and software. All the companies will keep you informed of new developments.

When the author first figured the programming necessary in 1967, it was to save time by programming area fills, steils, satin stitches, in any configuration on a plain surface. At that time, he estimated he would complete 90% of all the programming necessary at a fixed price, whereas, if they added those which were used "once a year" programs to try to complete all the available designs routines, we would spend ten times the cost.

You have to consider the same values when you estimate the system you choose. Buy what you need, not what you want. Of course, one of the most important things to consider is the service and technical backup a particular company can offer.

Computers and software are growing as fast, if not faster, then they did in the 1980s. Newer, faster and easier methods are being developed almost daily. In the next 10 years, you will look back at this era and many will call it primitive.

For example, in business computers, we are now installing our 5th successive software package in 10 years to keep up with growth and provide all the information we feel we need.

SCHIFFLI PUNCHING

Mechanical Schiffli punch machines might still be used in small factories that still have experienced punchers available, but even these will soon be replaced by the computer. Schiffli is still not easy to punch, it is entirely different from Multi-head because it is necessary to have the Schiffli experience behind you before you start. Almost every machine is different depending upon its age, model and condition. It is certainly not possible to punch a pattern as drawn and have it reproduced exactly without knowing the machine on which it is to be used.

SCHIFFLI PUNCH SYSTEMS

Casati Carlo AG is a name well known for 70 years in the Schiffli embroidery industry for the manufacture of Plauen & Saurer copy machines and other finishing supplies such as scallop cutters and accessories.

The author was surprised to come across some 21 yard Comerio Ercole Schiffli machines (along with 44 Plauen machines) in Kalish, Poland that were operating with a Casati Carlo computerized punch system. Casati Carlo is looking forward to delivering complete modular systems to convert automated Schiffli machines to electronic control, from consulting and planning to service. This is planned to include all manufacturing functions including designing, punching, machine production and administration, all in one computerized system.

The punch system at the Polish plant included a large digitizing board, colored printer, and state-of-the-art softwear. The management seemed satisfied and planned the conversion of many years of punched tapes into a disc format.

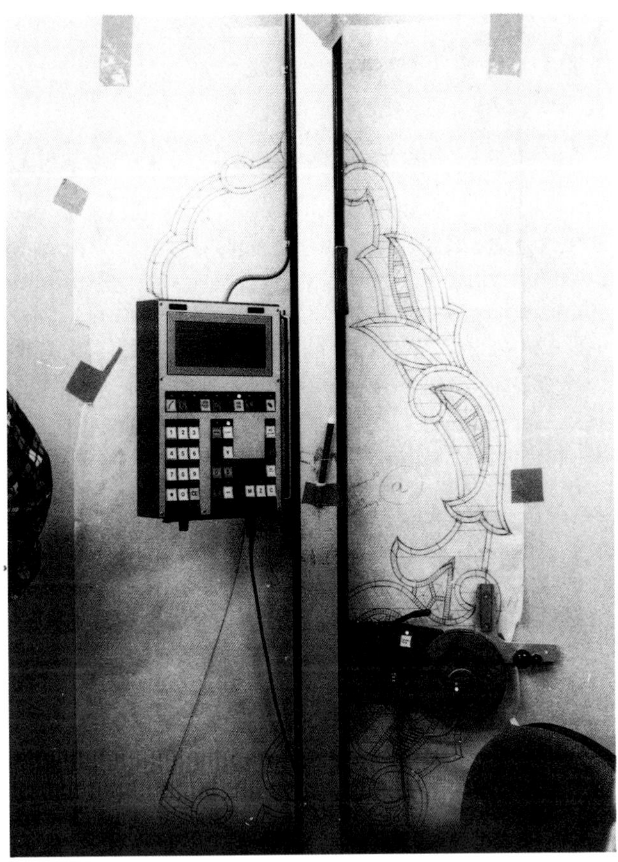

In keeping up to the minute, Carlo Casati has developed a Plauen and Saùrer copy machine to convert paper punchings to 3½″ discs. The units are rented to manufacturers, conversion is charged by the meter.

Casati Carlo issues a newsletter 4 times a year known as INFO, keeping the whole Schiffli industry informed at no cost.

GUNOLD + STICKMA

Punching tapes for more than 60 years, the Gunold Company also has been active in Schiffli punching. Experimenting with one German company where they provide a Gunold Schiffli system, they will soon expand into the Schiffli market worldwide. They will start as equals with the existing Schiffli computer systems now available.

Saurer Textile Systems

The first company to build the computerized Schiffli and Multi-head punch systems developed per the instructions of the author. Now part of the Saurer Company which also has the more advanced Semco punch system, whose advanced software is attuned closely to the needs of all Schiffli machines.

Melco systems are used in more than 100 card centers and manufacturers. The software contains all the basic programs needed for all embroidery formats, Saurer and Plauen Schiffli, and most every Multi-head machine.

Programming is in condensed or expanded form.

EMBROIDERY COMPUTER AIDED PUNCHING SYSTEM INC.

E C A P System, Inc.

Heim Sasson

Heim Sasson is a leading embroidery manufacturer, creative designer and shrewd business man with Schiffli machines and an active bleachery. His brother-in-law, Morris Assarf, who is an exceptional programmer for NASA, has written many original programs that have been developed for the Schiffli industry.

His computer system has been delivered to 6 major manufacturers and card centers, his software to many more.

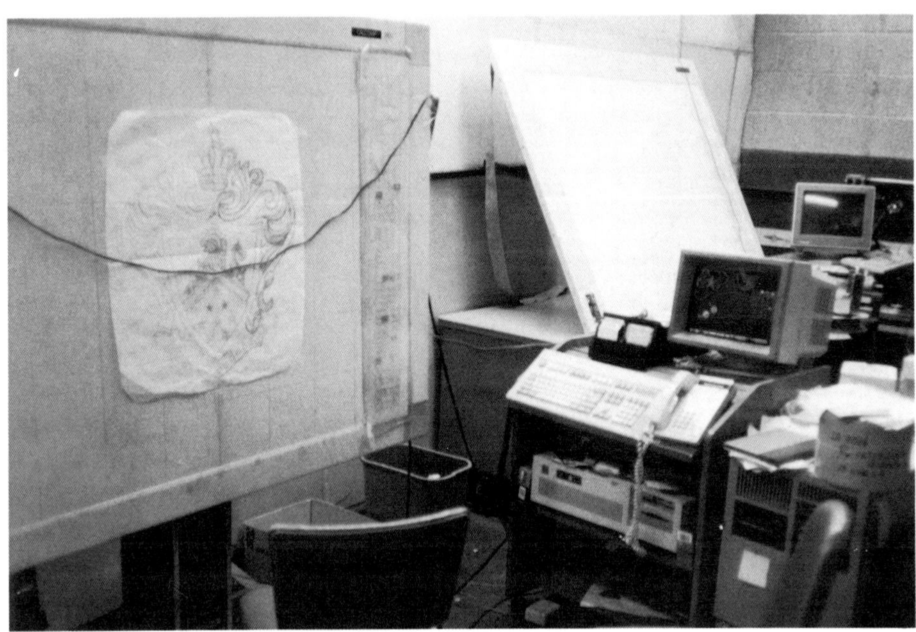

Development of other electronic equipment, including the first to convert Schiffli punchings to 3.5 discs. A demonstration is an experience. The reader operates at 1200 stitches per minute, read into the computer where it can be converted into any required format. If transfered Plauen to Saurer or vice versa, the tape is automatically being checked by the computer for the exact motions and functions called for in the original tape.

The units are for sale, he does not have time for rentals.

Reading a Plauen tape into the computer

Punching a Plauen tape from a computer conversion of a Saurer tape.

Also under development and soon to be released is a new electro card reader for the Plauen automat, which will surely be followed by the Saurer unit. This unit fits above the platines and becomes a permanent part of the machine. Should the stitcher decide to or be required to use a paper tape or a 3½″ disc a simple switch will allow either to be read.

These conversion units as well as the punching system are being supplied to other companies who are offering the systems under their own names.

SEMCO COMPUTERIZED PUNCH SYSTEM

SAURER

Saurer Textile Systems

Erick Schoenenberger developed a sophisticated punch system for Schiffli machines early in 1980. 100 have already been delivered to such countries as China, Taiwan, Japan, Korea, and Russia, in addition to western countries.

The development of a punch system for Schiffli machines requires the expert intelligence of an experienced Schiffli puncher. There is just no way to create a software system for yard goods and trims stitched on a Schiffli machine without those skills.

For emblems, it is possible to use this system for Multi-head punching, which is the simplest type of punching.

Yet, there is much to consider when 3 dimensional work is required and the design will end up being used on a Schiffli machine. Keep in mind that Multi-head punching is like building a Tinker Toy and Schiffli punching is like building the first manned space shuttle.

Schiffli punchers don't all agree on the method of stitching certain designs. Therefore, the job of programming for Schiffli becomes even more difficult.

However, Erick Schoenenberger, an experienced puncher who was also employed for some years in the U.S.A. has the expertise it takes to actually program computers for Schiffli work. We say that partly because the center of embroidery for Schiffli (quality) is Switzerland, and if you can make it there, you can make it anywhere. At the same time, punching in the U.S.A. is an entirely different type of punching. Here the bottom line is pricing, so you must produce not only an acceptable quality, but use only as many stitches as the customer can afford.

Semco has developed a multi use system for all Multi-head machines, known as System IV. It will be shown for the first time, fully tested, at the forthcoming ITMA exhibition in Hanover, Germany in September, 1991.

The system's graphic softwear can now produce designs via a plotter not only for computer punching but also for the many mechanical punch systems still in existence in Schiffli factories. These graphics show every stitch in the design on a six time or smaller enlarged drawing.

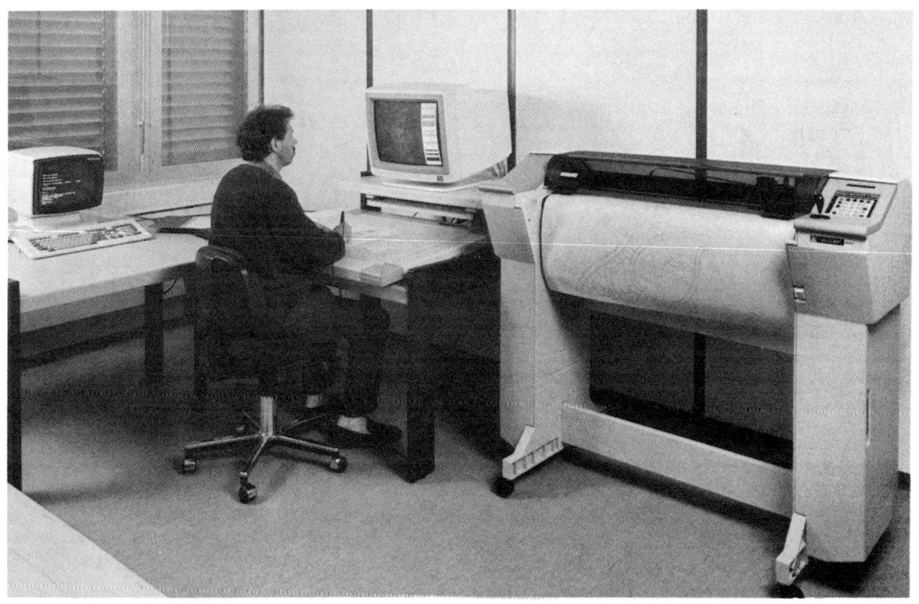

The basic equipment consists of a Data General workstation, 32 bit, 4MB memory, 70 MB disc, 737 KB floppy station, a Color screen 1024 x 800 x 8 bit, D 214 Alphanumeric terminal, cassette tape drive 22MB, a CalComp 91240 digitizer, and 1041 GT plotter, 8 colors and 10 formatted tape cassettes with 6 months manufacturer's service on all hardware. Upgrades in hardware are available.

The software package includes a dialogue system in many languages, plotter programs for the Semco system, and drawing and working programs for anything an embroidery machine can produce. Programs tailored to fit your special requirements are available.

Training in Arbon, Switzerland and installation in your factory are included.

The Wilcom Company is largest supplier of computer generating pattern equipment for Schiffli, Multi-head and monogram embroidery machines. One of the first to realize the potential of computer generated tapes for the embroidery machines, they actively pursued programming for all types of machines and peripheral equipment. They are attuned to your requirements and have built a substantial software package based on the input of various embroiderers.

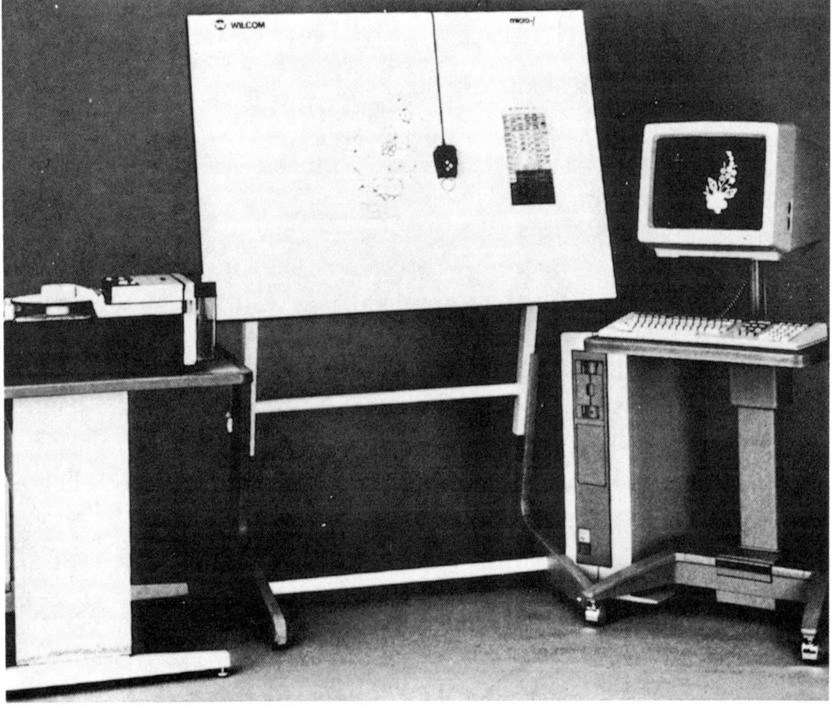

Components include IBM PC (AT or 386) or compact (20MB), communications software and Level 1 stitch processing software. Other options include mouse, Schiffli tapes for Saurer and Plauen machines, 8 channel tapes, 3.5″ and 5 ¼″ floppy discs, cassettes and 68mm jacquard, readers, plotters, printers, and modem.

Installation, 4 day training on site and 1 year software and hardware warranty are included. Staff available for consultation.

Wilcom's programming for Multi-head and Schiffli is about the most complete you will find anywhere.

Programs of training for various equipment are available for beginners to the most advanced.

ELECTRO CARD SYSTEM

The Electro Card System is the next step to computerization by the Schiffli Industry. This unit attaches directly to the Schiffli automat, eliminating the paper tape and within a short time your tape reading system is computerized. If necessary the unit can also be removed in the same time frame.

All the old tapes can be converted into 3.5 inch discs which will save hundreds of square feet or meters of storage space.

The advantages with the addition of the CED punching station allow the full use of computer technology to alter patterns, edit designs, enlarge, reduce, change density of stitches. automatic rewind to next row, set the number of rows to be stitched, and do it all quickly. The tapes can be stored on the hard disc of the computer and called to use at any time.

Conversions from Saurer to Plauen and all Multi-head formats and vice versa is another advantage.

Savings include: rewinding patterns for large repeats or rewinding for repeats within one span, setting up and removing the punching, finding designs from the shelf, insurance for paper tapes and safety in overrunning the frame width.

Safety of loss of designs can be achieved by computer back-ups which can easily be stored in a fire proof cabinet or out of the building.

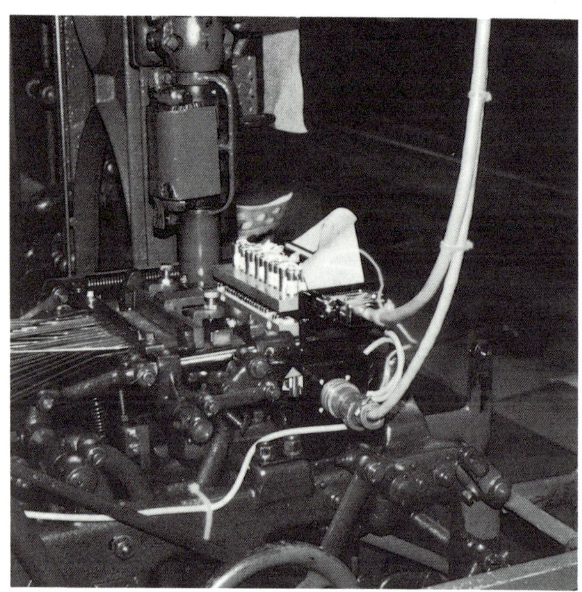

Wilcom Electro Card System

This should be the first step by the Schiffli manufacturer to computerization of his Schiffli machine. The next step, of course, is to replace the whole mechanical automat with electronically driven components.

MULTI-HEAD PUNCHING

Multi-head punching for mechanical machines was simple once you got the knack of using the 2 handles; one moving the stylus right and left, the other moving the stylus up and down. A foot switch recorded the stitch and neutralized the drum, making it ready for the next stitch.

The introduction of the computerized punch system with all its programming simplified the punching even more. Now you can use the programming from the starting point to the end. It does not change the special attention that the machine required. The best way to train a potential puncher is to have them work first as machine operators, so that they become familiar with the start, stitching, framing of goods, fixing of needles and threads, and study punchings made by professionals. Only then can they start, make the mistakes and learn from experience what is required of the puncher. The number of Multi-head punchers has grown, from perhaps 10 in the U.S.A. in 1978, to near 1000 today.

MULTI-HEAD PUNCH SYSTEMS

BROTHER

BAS-IS 5091 386SX/16MHZ computer 40MB hard drive and 14″ color monitor. Condensed or expanded disc or tape formats for all popular machine types. Direct interface up to 8 machines.

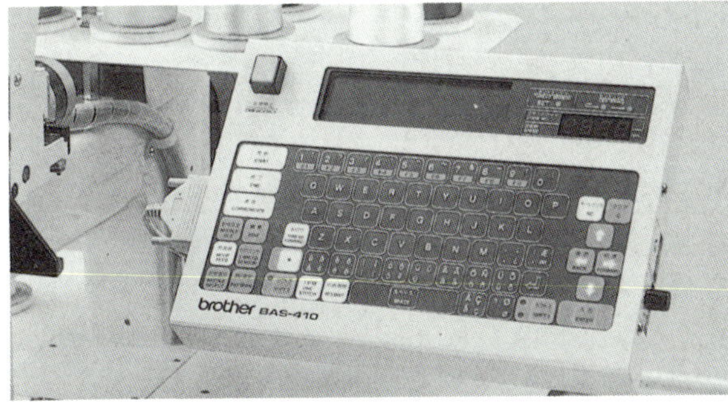

CORBETT SYSTEMS

EMBROIDERY DESIGNER

This is a state-of-the-art computer punching system, offered in various formats for most Multi-head systems. It uses IBM PC/XT, PC/AT and compatible 286, 386, 486 computer. Video training is available.

Corbett Systems offers freehand design, zoom levels to complete verification and many fill patterns to choose from for regular and irregular shapes. The system can read ready made tapes and edit them. Alphabets can be created, lettering rotated, moved to any position with use of rulers, crosshairs, coordinates or grids.

Barudan

Macpherson Monogram, Inc.

EMBROIDERY EXPERT

MACPHERSON ASSOCIATES, INC.

The hardware consists of an Apple Macintosh IIcx computer system, 40 MB HD 2-4 MB RAM, color monitor, 8 bit video card, extended keyboard and ADB mouse, Summagraphics Digitizing tablet or Sharp JX-450 color scanner, Facit N4000 tape reader/punch, and direct interface for Barudan (MUR).

A range of programs is available from novice to advanced punch center.

Features include condensed or expanded format punching, scaling, many stitch formats, editing, with mirroring, deletions, enlarging and reducing and building a library of designs. Step and repeat saves much punching time should parts of a design be repeated within a pattern.

The author has found the Apple MacIntosh is by far the best computer with easy and multi varied programs for drawing. Add this advantage to your computer punch system. Through hundreds of interviews we find most people with draw and art and computer ability are familiar with MacIntosh computers.

EMBROIDERY PLUS

The Apple Macintosh computer can be part of your production machine. Full programming for making tapes, seeing results, storage, density, and editing. Keyboard lettering and various drawing designs are compatible.

GEMINI

This is a state of the art Italian computer punch system with IBM hardware and full programming features for edit and all stitch programs. A scanner is included with an upgraded system.

MEISTERGRAM EMBROIDERY DESIGN

The M E D computerized digitizing system allows you to create custom cassettes and 3.5″ discs, for use with Meistergram 600/700/800 machines.

The MED has a Wilcom support package. The programs in this case would include all the basics for good design.

Included is an IBM PC with color monitor, 20″ x 24″ digitizing board and hard disc storage. It can also edit designs, and has zoom capabilities up to 80 times original size.

gunold+stickma 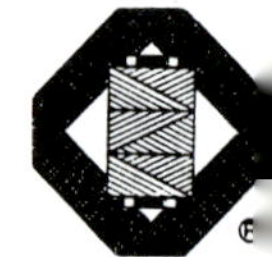

GUNOLD+STICKMA

Gunold+Stickma, the oldest company in the embroidery industry to provide custom tapes to owners of Wurker Multi-head machines, did so for many years before the onslaught of other machine manufacturers starting in the 1950's. They saw the potential in developing an easier method of making tapes. While the author was utilizing his new computer system successfully, he visited Gunold in Germany where experiments were under way to develop their own computer punch system. He met with the owners but never got further than the reception room. In time they surely did develop a computerized punch system and today offer it to the industry as the Manager I and II and Pro Stitch. Also available are Advanced Punchmaster and Advanced Punchmaster Plus for experts and punch centers. There are many units in use throughout the world.

State-of-the-art programming is included, with well laid out programs and many windows to assist in adding, deleting and editing.

Utilizing an NEC 286 Plus computer with 5 1/4″ and 3 1/2″ disc drives, 42MB hard disk and colored monitor.

They are only too happy to visit your factory to give demonstrations.

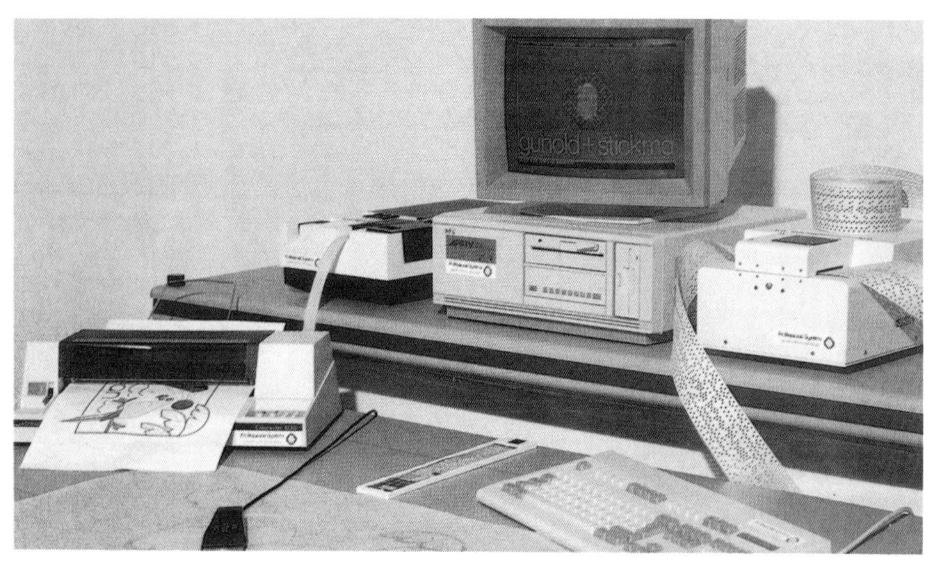

JUST RIGHT MODEL NO. JR-10

Chinese, English and Japanese Language display, the #1 Asian computer punch system for Multi-head machines. State-of-the-art software, features automatic running stitch, single or triple with selected lengths. Satin stitches made with half and full stitches, automatic fill in 4 directions and slanting. All machine functions can be added. Editing, copying by angles in all directions. E stitch and chain stitch functions available. Rotation, scaling, density adjustments for all or part of designs. 2HD floppy disks store a maximum of 400,000 stitches.

The computer employed is NEC/EPSON 32 bit PC, includes 21″ color monitor, 4 different size digitizers. Available: plotter, punch and plotter buffer and automatic voltage regulator to 1000 W.

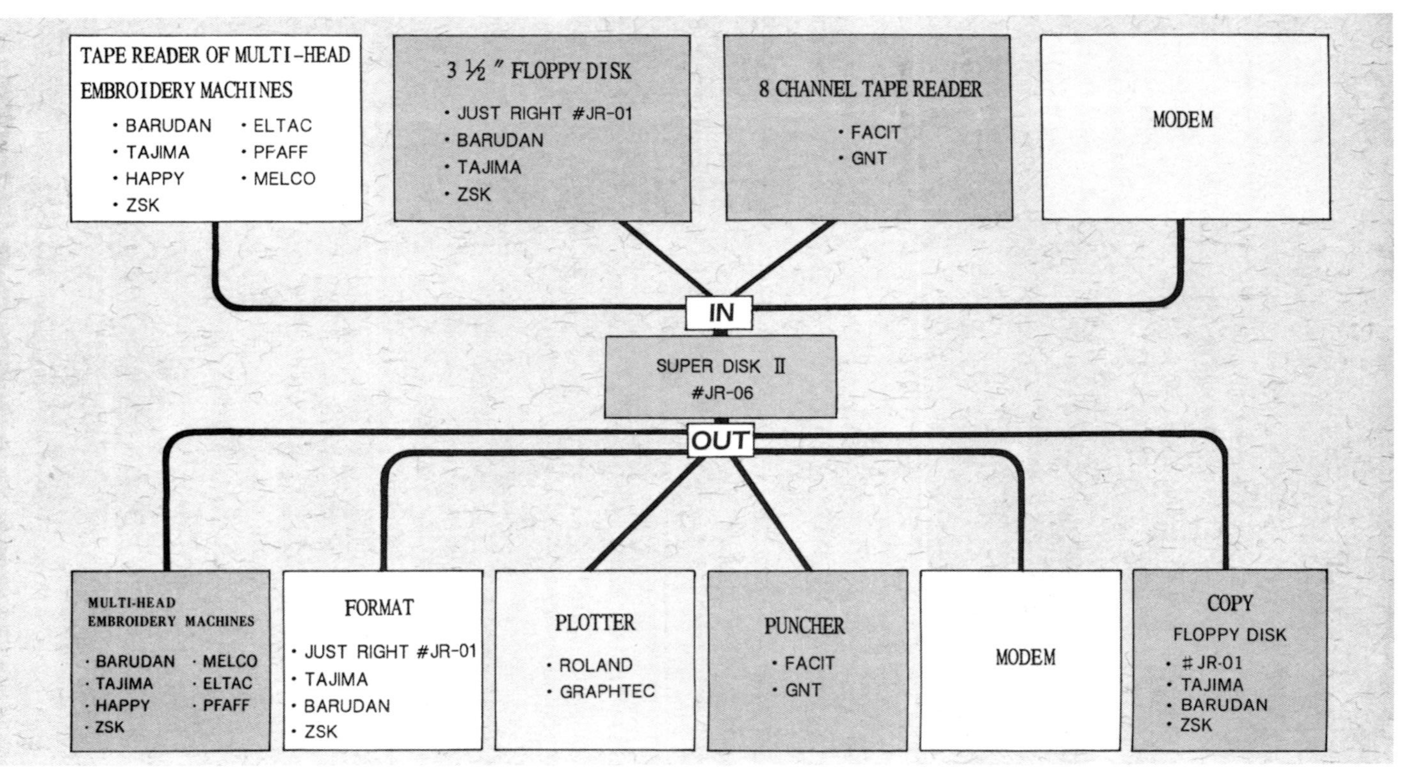
TAPE READER OF MULTI-HEAD EMBROIDERY MACHINES
· BARUDAN · ELTAC
· TAJIMA · PFAFF
· HAPPY · MELCO
· ZSK
3 1/2″ FLOPPY DISK
· JUST RIGHT #JR-01
· BARUDAN
· TAJIMA
· ZSK
8 CHANNEL TAPE READER
· FACIT
· GNT
MODEM
IN
SUPER DISK II
#JR-06
OUT
MULTI-HEAD EMBROIDERY MACHINES
· BARUDAN · MELCO
· TAJIMA · ELTAC
· HAPPY · PFAFF
· ZSK
FORMAT
· JUST RIGHT #JR-01
· TAJIMA
· BARUDAN
· ZSK
PLOTTER
· ROLAND
· GRAPHTEC
PUNCHER
· FACIT
· GNT
MODEM
COPY
FLOPPY DISK
· #JR-01
· TAJIMA
· BARUDAN
· ZSK

Just Right offers free updated software.

KASHMIR PUNCHING SYSTEM

This is a computer punch system for Meistergram machine diskette or cassette programming models M600 - 800 XCL, and includes IBM compatible PC. Software package is complete with all major programming. Includes free upgrades for 3 years.

Saurer Textile Systems

D G Digitizer

Melco provides tablets and digitizing boards for its EDS and Epicor systems from table top to free standing boards. When used with these computers the stitching programs are easily controlled through the use of the cursor and the menu attached to the board itself.

PREMIER

The simple Premier computer, a light weight portable keyboard controller, can operate and control up to 4 peripherals at one time. It is compatible with Melco's EM1, EMC6, EM6/4, EDS and the Epicor. This can be used to control any of Melco's units.

E D S

This digitizing computer for design creation and storage can be used with all Melco and Tajima equipment. 29 separate digitizing functions are listed on a movable design menu set on the digitizing board.

With the use of a 13″ color screen with 64 colors, you can punch and view your work as you digitize any design, enlarge the pattern to 32 times its original size for editing, or proceed to store your design.

Since you digitize in a condensed format, it is easier to edit and add and subtract parts and move them around. You can add lettering to stored designs, and make all the changes necessary before setting the designs to the desired density. You can look at it on the screen, make any changes and save them, and correct older designs as you choose.

EPICOR

This is an advanced computer which can control as many as 16 single head machines each running different designs, or all stitching one design. It is also the main unit to use to digitize designs for all makes of machinery.

M C I

The MCI Multi-head controller serves as a link between EDS/EPICOR computers and Multi-head embroidery machines, translating design information into the correct Multi-head formats. MCI units enable the stitcher to centralize all production decisions and design information at the EPICOR computer. As many as 16 Multi-heads can be controlled individually from a single EDS/EPICOR using the MCI. It can store to 120,000 stitches and as many as 16 designs.

E S S Embroidery Scanner System

With this system, artwork can be scanned and projected onto the computer screen. Special features allow you to smooth rough edges automatically. The design is transferred into a computer format, prepared to receive stitching instructions. You can select the stitch pattern, type, length and direction, and check the pattern on the display.

In some cases it is possible to scan, digitize and complete a pattern in record time. However, scanners are not the final answer, since the art must be camera ready or relatively good and accurate, and if it is in color, the colors should not be shaded. If the art is not good, it may take you longer with a scanner than without.

S R 1

This strip reader can read your tape into the EDS or Epicor computer, enabling you to transfer tape designs to disc.

Q.D.T.

Moritz Embroidery Works, Inc.

The QDT (Quick Disk Design Transfer) system developed by Moritz is an inexpensive unit which will convert any tape code to any other tape code.

You can transfer your designs via QDT's 3.5″ disc to most Multi-head embroidery machines. Connect your Multi-head embroidery machine tape data cable to the QDT output port, and the other end to your Multi-head embroidery machine input port, and the system is now ready to transfer to your machine or to the hard disc for storage.

The system consists of an XT Turbo computer with 20 meg. Hard Drive to store your designs, one 3.5″ floppy disc drive, a monochrome monitor and a 101 key keyboard. It also includes DOS, QDT and screen save already loaded and ready for transferring, and a one year warranty.

QDT comes from the world's most advanced embroidery factory, having 7 Plauen Schiffli machines and many Multi-head machines, where all production and design transfer originates in one controlled central location. There are no paper tapes in existence in the whole factory.

All machines are tied into a master computer. The mechanical Schiffli automats are controlled by electronic readers, and a QDT is on each Multi-head. A CRT monitors each machine so that the machine operators can see every stitch being made.

SEMCO COMPUTERIZED PUNCH SYSTEM

Saurer Textile Systems

This is a newly developed punch system for Multi-head machines developed by Erick Schoenenberger, the experienced Swiss puncher now associated with the Saurer Company, developer of the newest Schiffli machines and Melco Multi-head machines.

Considering the vast experience of SEMCO, the newer Multi-head system will prove a great success.

STITCHITIZER

Data Stitch, Inc.

A system developed by one of the leading card library companies, it has state-of-the-art software.

Atari ST Computer with 16 Mhz processor, 2MB RAM, 3 1/2″ disc drive with mouse and keyboard.

A complete lettering and design system. Editing of designs by stitch, block or condensed format.

The system is compatible with all popular machine formats.

Hirsch International

The Tajima data control system is state-of-the-art, with all the equipment and programs necessary to save you time and expense in cutting tapes, making print outs, editing, adding and subtracting from design, enlarging, or reducing. A NEC Powermate 286 Plus with 2 3½″ disc drives and 4MB memory. A color monitor makes it easier to see display, colors, grid and zoom functions.

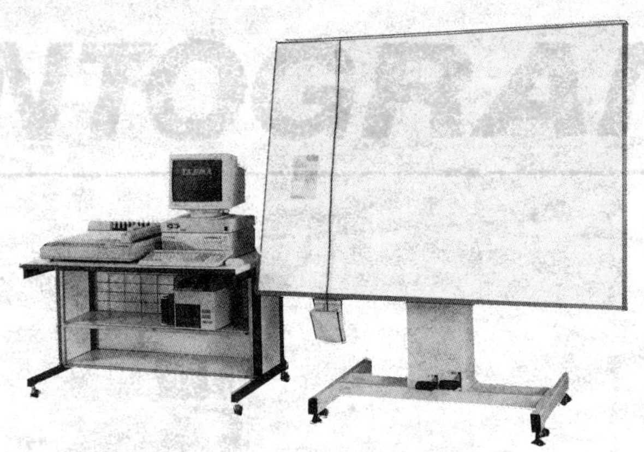

Tajima Punch System

PANTOGRAMS

IBM compatible with 1MG RAM, limited programming with design scaling, editing and merge designs with keyboard lettering.

ULTRAMATIC

The ultimate monogram/embroidery machine

As a punch center, Ultramatic began the switch to computer generated tapes in 1976, and when Melco cut off their supply of electronics (to compete in the embroidery machine field) they were ready to develop their own systems. Ultramatic has been at the forefront in developing computer generated tapes as well as components for their Multi-head machines.

Their present machine consists of a 20″ x 24″ digitizer with mini computer. You can have your choice of a cassette and/or paper tape punch, and verifier. Verifiers for this system are the CRT, a single needle embroidery machine or a 6 color automatic change single head machine. 8 various formats can be read or digitized.

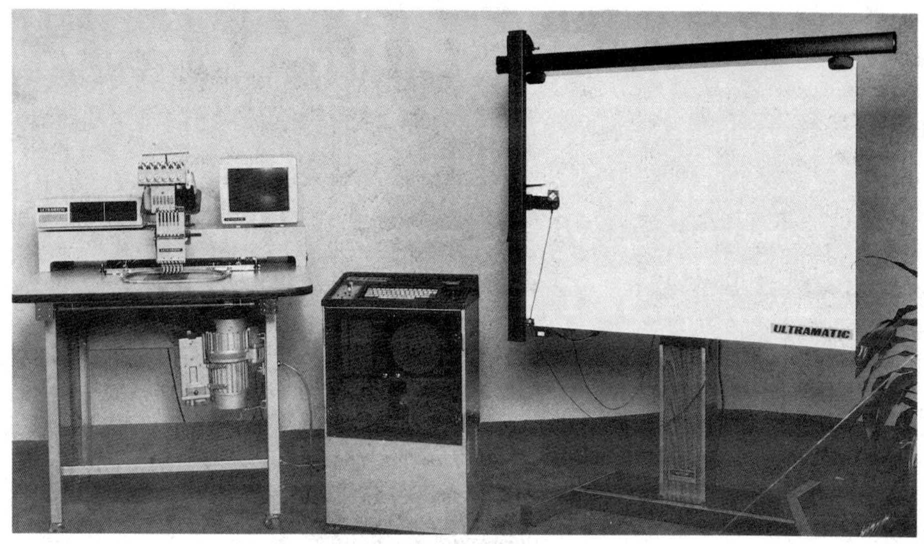

Programs for digitizing include all the basics to eliminate hand stitching, with editing, scaling and reading everything into memory. Options available include condensed or expanded formats, and many more.

The newest programming unit includes the 20″ x 24″ digitizer, cassette reader, 256K memory, CRT, 14 color monitor, 2 alphabets, and a single head 6 needle automatic color change embroidery machine. Now you can punch and verify at the same time and also produce a sample with the proper colors on the customer's goods, in other words, produce embroidery while cutting the tape.

The embroidery machine can stitch on a flat surface of 11 1/2″ x 24 1/2″. The removable table top allows use of an extra long cylinder arm for bags or sleeves. A cap frame is provided. The machine is also a production machine at the same time.

Wilcom has been active since 1980 in the development of the most sophisticated punch systems for all Multi-head machines. They are state-of-the-art and offered internationally.

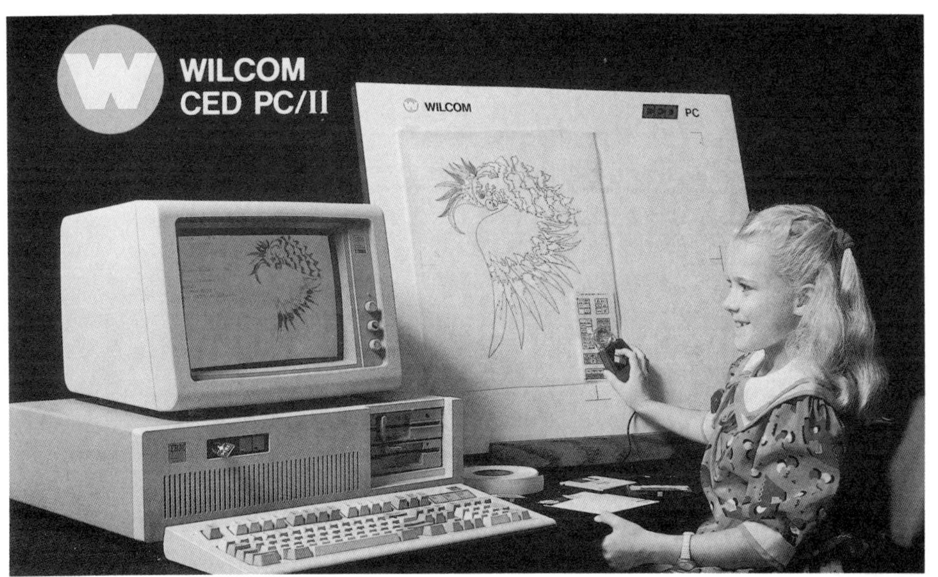

IBM compatible 386 PC with mouse and keyboard. All major machine formats are included with condensed or expanded capability. Units available for the beginner to the expert in Schiffli or Multi-head.

MED system for Meistergram programming.

MULTI-STICKTRONIC

These are state-of-the-art programs with Hewlett Packard hard disks up to 85Mg and 12 inch graphic screen, offered in two models with user-friendly menu guided softwear for beginners to experts.

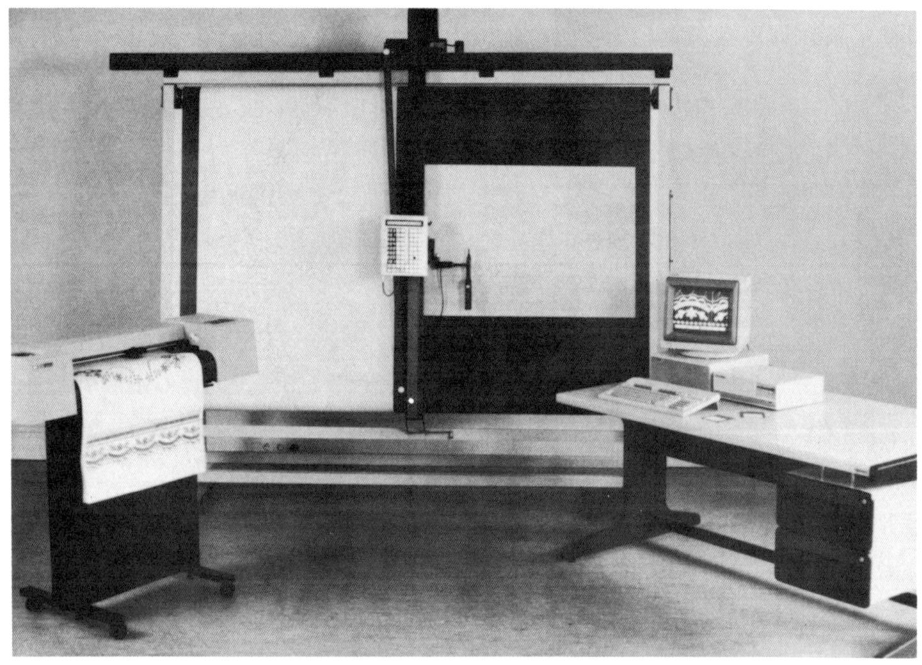

Similar to all Multi-head systems the Z S K offers a printer, monitor, and fully programmed embroidery routines for all major stitch forms, editing, lettering origination, curving & reverse, mirroring, and movement of punched parts to various places within the design. All machine functions are programmable. 8 channel or 3½″ disc adaptable to all punch formats.

CHAPTER VII

EMBROIDERED EMBLEMS

Emblems are insignia, badges, or patches made of any base material such as cloth, metal, or plastic. They are a means of identification or association. We in the U.S. are in an era of identification, when everyone wants to show their feeling or identity in some form.

Organizations have long used emblems to indicate achievement, position or membership. How else could you identify a sergeant, a general or a pilot?

The purpose of this chapter is to acquaint you with cloth emblems, specifically those known as Swiss embroidered emblems, which account for 90% of all cloth emblems in use today. The term "Swiss embroidered" is applied here because embroidery attained its highest standard of quality in Switzerland, where the original machine embroideries were produced. The Swiss, who built the embroidery industry, are still most active embroiderers.

Embroidered emblems are popular for uniforms and wearing apparel, mainly because of their durability. Usually stitched on strong cotton and poly twills, the construction of the stitching, colors and finishing tend to make them strong enough to outlast the uniform to which they are attached.

Swiss emblems are made on Schiffli and Multi-head embroidery machines, which exist today in every technically developed country. However, the technology for the manufacture of emblems made on these machines is strictly American. To attest to that fact, many foreign governments have the insignia of their armed forces manufactured in the United States.

The quality of embroidery reaches its peak with the emblems that are manufactured on Schiffli machines in the United States. Unfortunately, they are quickly being replaced by Multi-head machines, which can compete economically with them. However, it goes far beyond that. The Multi head-machine is basically a group of sewing machines, greatly improved over those that existed when the Schiffli machine first started embroidering. The tensions are tighter, the frame is lighter and therefore more accurate, and it can make a much smaller stitch, thus stitching smaller letters. The yarns are a tighter twist, the tapes are all computerized and more accurate. The investment required is much smaller. Smaller orders are easier to manufacture, and because of thread controls there are fewer damages, and loom runs become a thing of the past.

Look at any serviceman and you will find embroidered emblems made on Schiffli machines that still can not be duplicated in any other country. In the U.S. it might be made on a Swiss, German, Italian or Japanese machine, but the method of designing and punching and the resulting product is strictly an American achievement.

The Multi-head machine embroidery is still not accepted by the Government purchasing organizations. The manufacturers here are still small, but one day soon they too will be the major suppliers to the American Armed Forces.

There are about 35 Schiffli manufacturers in the U.S., dozens of small Multi-head manufacturers and scores of importers of Multi-head emblems. Their distribution touches everyone's life. The average purchaser of embroidered emblems knows little about how they are made. The secrets are usually closely held by those involved in their manufacture. We hope to give you some insight into the designing, punching, stitching and finishing of embroidered emblems.

Insignia are a modern form of Heraldry. They are distinguishing marks of authority, rank, office or service. The variety and uses of insignia in the armed forces, the U.S. Army, Navy, Marines, Air Force and Coast Guard, number in the hundreds. The serviceman's insignia denotes his specific service and indicates rank and skill.

Insignia, a form of shorthand, are similar to fancy jerseys of football players and pins of Fraternal lodges and colleges. Anyone wearing an insignia displays his associations and his place within them. Sleeves, shoulders, lapels, collars, backs of shirts and jackets, hats and breast pockets can be so adorned.

Insignia can be made of metal, cloth (both woven and embroidered) and even multi colored three dimensional plastic. Each branch of the armed services uses a different mode of identification in their insignia. The army has its own system, the Navy a different one and the other services use variations of the two. Commercial emblems might show designs, logos, and lettering that designate products or services. They are used for promotional purposes, identification of employees, awards, etc.

Why is there so much attention paid to the wearing of insignia and their proper display? Why does each have its individual identity? It is because they are an aid to recognition, a means of establishing and maintaining discipline, and a display of pride. Obviously, recognition of individuals in connection with their organizations and positions of authority is simplified by insignia worn on their uniforms. Surely there could be an easier and less colorful way, such as the 'PW' worn on the backs of Prisoners of War, but this would not convey beauty, color, and romance the way insignia can.

Insignia express a warmth and fraternity which men and women know from experience. Emblems are very often a source of pride which enhances discipline, the essence of self respect, service and patriotism.

During America's war of independence in the late 1770's, an order given by George Washington reads as follows:

> As the Continental Army has unfortunately no uniforms, and consequently many inconveniences must arise for not being able to distinguish the commissioned officers from the privates, it is desired that some distinction may be immediately provided; for instance, that the field officers may have red or pink colored cockades in their hats, the captains yellow or buff; and the subalterns green. They are to furnish themselves accordingly. The sergeants may be distinguished by an epaulet or stripe of red cloth sewn on their right shoulder, the corporals by one of green.

A few days earlier Washington directed for the purposes of preventing mistakes that:

> The general officers and aides-de-camp will be distinguished in the following manner:
>
> The commander in chief by a light blue ribbon worn across the heart between his coat and waistcoat; the major and brigadier general by a pink ribband worn in a like manner; aides-de-camp by a green ribband.

After the orders were issued, Washington directed that Major Generals' sleeves be distinguished from those of Brigadier Generals by broad purple ribbon.

The original order was the beginning of a series of orders and regulations, all calculated to mark the uniforms of the members of the armed services with designs in symbolic form as insignia of identification. The development of military insignia has continued along with that of the armed services themselves. They illustrate battles upon the sea and land and reflect the achievements of the science of war. Examples include all the space flights, from Mercury to the latest Atlantis. The same holds true for commercial insignia.

Originally, emblems were made with pieces of felt appliqued on a background material. Most used today are embroidered. These resemble the enameled badges that were worn during the Civil and Spanish American Wars.

The first embroidered shoulder insignia is that accredited to members of the 81st Division, in 1918. They developed the design of a wildcat and were given permission to wear it on Oct. 19, 1918. Soon all units were directed to adapt similar original insignia. During the invasion of North Africa in World War II all the American armed forces wore U.S. flag arm bands or flags on their helmets to distinguish them as part of the American army in Africa.

Authorities consider insignia not only as aids to recognition and spur to pride, but as a means of establishing and maintaining discipline. Remember the knight of the Middle Ages, with his individual crest upon his shield? He was the forerunner of the modern serviceman and his insignia.

As a white carnation may distinguish a certain person waiting to be identified at an airport, so also do insignia identify a person or group.

One of the most popular emblems since the early 1970's has been the U.S. flag emblem. Colorful and distinctive, it is worn by many regardless of politics, signifying pride in the United States.

As of this writing we have seen Desert Shield, Desert Storm and Desert Calm, all designating phases of a war where all Americans, whether in Saudi Arabia or home in the U.S. identified with the American flag. Yellow ribbons and other patroitic novelties abounded as a show of support, all demonstrating the use of embroidery as a form of identity, mostly on wearing apparel.

Police and Fire companies have used the flag extensively, identifying themselves as law abiding citizens. It has also been popular world wide. It is colorful and represents freedom and the type life style many aspire to.

TYPES OF EMBLEMS

Early emblems were made with pieces of cloth, appliqued in layers one on top of the other and cut to show color and design. Because embroidery is the art of ornamental needlework, it is natural that these emblems, made with cloth, would include sewn designs and lettering. Unlike other methods of decoration with textiles, such as weaving or knitting, embroidery is something added to an already finished fabric. Today, some emblems are still made by hand, some are made with the operator on a single head sewing machine and large quantities are made by Schiffli and Multi-head embroidery machines.

WOVEN EMBLEMS

Woven emblems can be compared to labels on shirts or in suit jackets. In large quantities, label machines can make emblems that look and feel like labels. They lack the three dimensional effect of embroidery. Colors are expensive to use, and wearing ability is not as good as embroidery. Their main advantage is that the lettering can be made very small, smaller than with any other method. Woven can be inexpensive if made in large quantities. In small runs the set up and pattern costs are very high. Usually, they are soft to the touch and require a stabilizing backing for merrowed borders.

Woven emblems are manufactured by a weaving process, therefore, the design is woven at the same time as the fabric is woven. Colored yarns of the warp and weft, controlled by the jacquard, form the design.

PRINTED, FLOCKED AND SCREENED EMBLEMS

These methods of adding design, color and lettering by screen printing to cloth through the use of dye and paints can also be used to create emblems. However, the durability and wearability leave much to be desired. Their advantage is that they can be made in small orders since the screen costs are small.

BULLION

BULLION (or Zari) emblems are hand made, either in Pakistan or India. The delicate stitching utilizes gold and silver wire type thread, stitched by hand directly in a base cloth on which the design has been transferred. Some common examples of this embroidery include the scrambled eggs found on the visor of Naval officers' caps, from Commander to 5 star Admiral, or the insignia on the jackets of some golf and country club members. These emblems are extremely tedius to make, and although there are many solicitors for this work, it is hard to find quality workmanship.

HAND EMBROIDERED (other than Bullion) emblems with normal sewing threads are stitched for individual appreciation. Few people today have time

to make 'that old time embroidery'. There are emblems made one at a time, free-hand, by sewing machine with threads similar to those of the Schiffli machines. They require the skills of an artist.

The art is transferred to the fabric either by perforating the sketch and powdering the design onto the goods or rubbing from a sketch made with soft pencil. The sewing machine artist then moves the hoop holding the goods by hand and operating the sewing machine in time with the needle. You need a steady hand and a good eye, but even more importantly, long experience to achieve good workmanship. Small orders and samples were sewn this way until computers developed inexpensive tapes and became available in the middle 1970's. It has become a lost art because computer tapes give a perfect reproduction in much less time with Multi-head embroidery machines.

PHOTO EMBLEMS

PHOTO emblems require a 4 color negative which is separated and printed on a polyester cloth by sublimation. The emblem is stiffened with heat seal film and merrowed. In this process a color photo is directly imprinted on a fabric and finished as an emblem.

CHENILLE

CHENILLE emblems are made from wool or thick yarns forming a chain stitch of loops with a special bobbinless sewing machine. The Cornely single head machine, which requires a highly experienced operator, is the most popular machine for this type of work.

There is only one specially developed Schiffli machine that can stitch a good copy of chenille. However, many Multi-head machine manufacturers have devised machines to do a similar type of stitching, imitating the Cornely. Barudan Multi-head chenille machine which actually utilizes the Cornely head in tandem, recreates the true chenille embroidery.

Chenille patches are used on outerwear and usually combine Multi-head Swiss embroidery stitching with the heavier yarns. Most popular are the award letters worn by athletes on high school and college jackets.

MANUFACTURING EMBROIDERED EMBLEMS

Multi-head embroidery machines can automatically manufacture from 1 to 30 emblems at one time at speeds to 800 spm. They consist of a tandem group of sewing machines stitching in unison. Now fully computerized, they are perfect for small orders and successfully challenge the long standing Schiffli machines which dominate the present Swiss embroidered market.

10 and 15 yard machines producing from 342 to 512 2″ emblems at one time at speeds to 160 rpm have only in the late 1970's been challenged. This machine, which is the leading supplier of mass produced embroidered trims and allovers for the garment and sewing trades, has been adapted to emblem manufacture. Beginning in 1918, many manufacturers discovered the lucrative emblem market and today we have about 35 emblem specialists with 50% of American Schiffli machines engaged in their manufacture.

The author has found in many cases, that embroidered emblems can be less expensive than woven, flocked or screen printed. The costs of Multi-head embroidery have been reduced dramatically with the newer, larger Multi-head machines. Automatic 9 color changes, speeds to 800 rpm and electronic and computer controls have helped the Multi-head to successfully compete with any 10 yard Schiffli machine. Efficient operation will cause these Multi-heads to compete favorably even with the 15 yard machines. Their advantage is not only speed, but the elimination of color change costs and the quality available.

STEPS IN THE MANUFACTURE OF EMBROIDERED EMBLEMS

STEP 1. The first item needed is the design or sketch, which should be a drawing, photograph or actual emblem previously made that is to be reproduced by machine. For embroidery reproduction it is not necessary to have camera ready artwork or artwork in the exact size the finished emblem is to be. We just need to know the idea or rough sketch, colors and size desired. From there, unlike in other modes of emblem manufacture, the design has to be redrawn for the machine to reproduce it. We say 'redrawn' since anything that might be drawn can not necessarily be embroidered. There are restrictions, therefore someone with the knowledge of embroidery and a machine's capability is required to reproduce the art.

A sketch is made, swatches of fabrics and colored threads to be used are provided for the customer's approval.

STEP 2. After the design and colors are approved, the design is drawn into technical form 6 times larger, from which the pattern can be punched to direct the embroidery machine. The skills of the enlarger are those of artist and draftsman. The stitches are indicated for the type of yarn to be used, and colors are noted, along with any other pertinent information the puncher might require.

STEP 3. The puncher now cuts the tape by a special machine or computer. There are many methods of directing the specific machine, from tapes to discs, and the puncher will be familiar with the specific machine within his factory. But all tapes today, no matter what format they originated in, can easily be converted to any other format.

The human element is most important at this stage, and only highly skilled and experienced punchers are employed as emblem programmers. Tapes can be proofed in various ways, for example on a Schiffli mechanical machine with a sample machine that stitches a sample in time with the puncher so that he can constantly see what is being stitched. In contrast, with computers, samples are usually made only after the tape is cut by actually running it off on a sample machine. So the puncher doesn't get lost, it is possible to have an active monitor engaged for checking progress.

In some cases, customers require samples for approval, but the machine operator also needs a sample to see what his work is to be.

STEP 4. The proper goods are spanned in the embroidery frame, the proper colors are selected, the tape or disc set into the reading device, the frame placed in its proper starting position and the machine started. The pattern should be programed to automatically stop for mechanical machines to change colors or automatically shift needles for computerized color change units. The process continues until the design is completed.

STEP 5. The goods is now removed from the machine and spread on a table to be trimmed. Floats, jumps, or spring stitches, used to advance the separated parts of the design without the needle penetrating the goods, as well as for color changes, are now to be cut and removed. This is known as 'hand splitting' on a Schiffli machine, but they are usually removed entirely on Multi-head machines, either during the stitching process or by scissor at this point.

Emblems from the Schiffli machine, unspanned and laid out on the table, usually have the floats sliced off by hand from the emblems themselves, while the other end, attached to goods around the emblem is left attached. The emblems in the full piece of goods are then sheared to remove the floats completely removed by a thread cutting machine. This is very time consuming.

Multi-head machines have optional automatic thread trimmers which are activated by the pattern to cut the threads as the embroidery process continues. Therefore, no hand splitting is necessary, and this is a real time saver.

STEP 6. The goods is now sized or plastic-coated, and heat seal film or pellon are added as backing. Up to this point the goods have remained in one piece.

STEP 7. The emblems are cut. If the emblem shape is irregular then they are hand cut. If the emblem is symmetrical with a stitched border they can be either hand cut or die cut. Die cutting requires a hydraulic press or hand stamping. A die is made in either case from the emblems after they are backed.

Considering the elasticity of the fabric being stitched, the tension caused by tightening the fabric in the frame and the continuous penetration of the needle and the tensions of the yarn, all emblems need to be cut individually. Many manufacturers have tried the quick method of group die cutting or laser cutting but so far nothing has proved helpful. Therefore, all emblems are die cut one at a time. You will find that after a time, you may have a dozen 3″ dies, just because of little idiosyncrasies in shape. Damaged emblems are put aside at this time.

There is no way to hand cut an emblem close enough to avoid the edge from becoming frayed. A heat seal backing helps somewhat, but even then by scratching your fingernail along the edge you can pull some threads loose. Laser cutting is the next best method for cutting odd shapes.

To cut the emblem properly, it should be die cut. The emblem requires a backing of nonwoven material such as Pellon or a plastic, a heat seal or similar application. Years ago, a wet starch application was applied while the goods was still on the machine, and left overnight to dry before being unspanned.

Hot Knife, Laser Cutting

Developed in Japan in the mid 1970's, the art of hot knife cutting has changed the look of embroidery. No longer do we have to hand cut shapes that do not lend themselves to overlocked edges. The fraying of twill edges can be avoided with the use of polyester fabrics and rayon yarns. Polyester yarns do not work for this type of cutting. Unfortunately, if you laser cut a polyester fabric you will also be cutting polyester yarn. Rayon requires more heat and is therefore safe from immediate burning. This simple cutting requires a polyester, nylon or man made fabric base for cutting with a rayon or cotton stitching yarn. The heat of the knife will melt the poly fabrics and if moved at a specific rate will not burn the rayon yarn, which will only scorch at a higher temperature. This cutting takes place after the embroidery is completed. The completed embroidered fabric is placed over a sheet of heat seal film. The 2 pieces cut well on a smooth hard surface like glass.

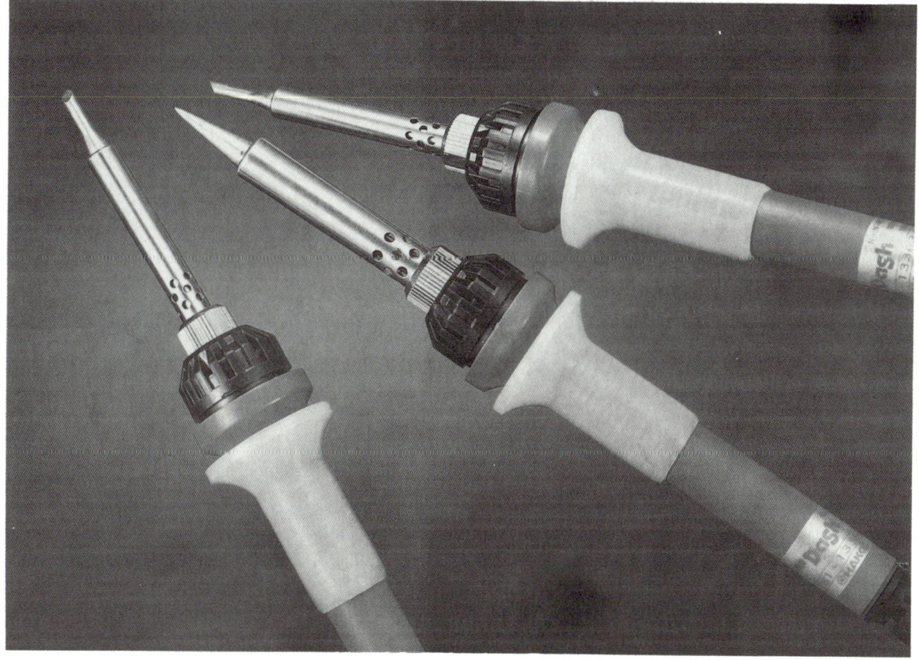

The knife is similar to a soldering iron with a long needle-like point. The cutter traces the outline of the design at a pace which does not affect the embroidery. Hesitation, or moving too slowly will burn and discolor the embroidery thread. While the heat is melting the fabric, it is also melting the heat seal film, binding the film to the applique.

If your choice is 100% embroidery, appliques, or lettering, a taffeta or nylon can be chosen as the base fabric. This gives the effect of direct embroidery when heat sealed to a cap or garment.

With a hot knife, the cutting is clean, and the edges bound with no residue or thread showing as might be the case with hand cutting.

STEP 8. Die cut emblems require a merrowed border as a finish. Overlocking or merrowing is performed on a merrow machine individually. Only symmetrical emblems lend themselves to this method of finishing. The merrow operator places each emblem against a guide and triggers a switch to start the merrowing process. The overlock stitch really stitches around the edge of the emblem, therefore, there can be no fraying. The operator runs the merrow about ¼ inch over the starting point and cuts the end, leaving a tail.

The amount of stitches per inch can be set and some bid contracts and the U.S. Government require a minimum amount of stitches per inch. Damaged emblems are put aside.

It is extremely difficult to merrow plain goods; it must be firmed up with some kind of applied backing.

The Merrow machine is the standard of the industry.

It operates at 5500 spm with special parts such as a short presser foot, a short feed dog and an edge guide. The operator takes one emblem at a time holds it against the guide, starting at a preselected point on the emblem. The pressure starts the machine and the operator follows the shape of the emblem with pressure against its edge. Emblems with square corners require the operator to stop the machine, turn the emblem at each corner, adding to the cost.

A 3 inch tail is run off so the end can be secure to avoid unraveling. The start of the next emblem will also have a small tail. The operator cuts the emblems apart as they finish each one.

Merrowing

STEP 9. The stump left by the merrow yarn must be secured in some way. The end is trimmed to about 1/4". One method is to paste the ends to the back of the emblem. Another is to pull the remaining end through the merrow where friction will hold it in place, this is known as 'pull through'.

If the end is trimmed clean, there is the chance the merrow can be pulled loose. Damaged emblems are put aside.

STEP 10. The emblems are inspected for quality, counted and packaged. The investment in each emblem is increased as each process is added. Damages can be caused at any point of the operation from the original stitching process onward. Damages are normally discarded, not repaired.

ON WHAT ARE COSTS BASED?

SCHIFFLI

All emblems are worn on clothing, and are subject to sunlight, washing and dry cleaning. It is therefore necessary to use the best sanforized fabrics to prevent shrinkage, and fast dyed (colorfast) yarns to prevent the colors running in washing.

The basic costs are the tape and machine set up, both one-time costs. Add to that your overhead and profit, based on time. The cost of the fabric, backing, cutting and merrowing are all based on quantity. These are easy to figure.

The major cost will be based on yarn and stitches, since that is easily transcribed into time. Therefore, the major unknown cost is the time needed to stitch the emblems.

The amount of embroidery will determine the price. A few letters on a patch are inexpensive, as the coverage increases, so does the amount of stitches, so does the stitching time. Stitches vary considerably, thereby affecting the cost.

Schiffli and Multi-head costs vary considerably. Schiffli machine production is based on running all needles in the machine. A 10 yard machine uses 20 yards of fabric, a 15 yard machine 30 yards.

The number of needles varies with the size of the emblem. Using the narrowest width, we figure the repeat. For instance, on a 10 yard machine a 2″ x 3″ emblem can fit in an 8/4 repeat which is 2 1/8″ between needles, for a total of 342 active needles at one time. A 3″ x 3″ fits in 12/4 or 3 3/16″ between needles, for a total of 228 needles active at one time. One row of emblems is known as a loom run. In the case of a 15 yard machine, the amounts are 50% greater.

On a Schiffli machine you will always span 2 pcs. of 10 yard or 15 yard goods, no matter how small the order is. Small orders, in this case, waste a lot of fabric. If the goods is 48″ in width you will only need a minimum of 13″ of goods times 20 yards for a 10 yard machine. The goods is normally striped to 13″. The cost of hanging in the goods top and bottom and both ends counts for at least 5″ on top and 5″ on bottom besides ¼ yard on the 4 ends (right, left, on the both 10 yard cuts). The loss of goods for hanging in is the same to stitch 14 rows; on a 10 yard machine, a 2″ emblem, 342 needles, 14 loom runs across the width or 4788 emblems, with the same loss as 1 loom run.

The cost of the finishing: thread cutting, heat seal or other backing, is basically the same for all orders. Cutting and merrowing are fixed costs per item. Colors are fixed costs added to the emblem. 95% of all Schiffli machines do not have automatic color change, therefore the laborious job of changing colors requires hand twisting and rethreading each time a color is changed. However, since these machines can stitch a full width of spanned cloth from 22″ to 40″ at a time, the color changes only have to be made at that time. Color change costs are nominal. Automatic color changes can only count in pricing for the set up of the machine.

For example, if we are stitching a 3″ emblem in 4 colors, we will stitch it 5x for the first color, one row below the other within the 22″ span. That raises the frame to its highest point. At that time, the machine will stop and we will change the yarn color and stitch color #2 up the 5 rows. These yarns are usually twisted on the rollers and laying in preparation. Each row will have stitched guides as part of the pattern to see that the colors register and fit properly, and are in the right position for each successive row.

At the highest point, again the machine will stop for the #3 color, which will stitch down the 5 rows. Now we have another problem. The most colors that can be twisted on a machine is equal to the needle spacing. For a 3″ emblem only 3 colors can be set and ready. If there is a 4th color, as in this case, it is necessary for the operator to remove one set of color while the machine is running color #3 and replace it with the 4th color. The twisting of the 4th color can not be done until the machine stops, so this change takes longer.

Stitching the 1st color down the span.

4/4 needle set up, which is only spaced at 1 1/16″, is never used for emblems because of the time required to set such a machine. The time is quadruple the time and cost of setting up 2″ spacing and only one color work can be done. It is only done when an order reaches monstrous proportions, but is very common for other types of Schiffli stitching in one color.

Those machines that have automatic color change usually stitch one row at a time with all the colors. If they had a 3″ emblem with 4 colors they would run the machine in 16/4 with 4 1/4″ spacing, (instead of 12/4) which would allow 4 spindles for spools of thread, and wasting the fabric costs less than the time lost in color changing. Therefore, all the colors would be in place. The risk involved in stitching 4 colors completely, one row at a time, is minimal for fitting compared to stitching 14 rows at a time.

The other costs are based on quantities and stitches. The design and tape costs are based on the stitches. The cost of fabric is based on the quantity, the cost of stitching on the total number of stitches which translates into time (based on the speed of the machine), on which the cost is figured. Yarns can be based on stitches also, since the average factory can easily judge the consumption of yarn by looking at the design and knowing the cost of yarn per 1000 stitches. If the design has many large areas filling in or wide blatt stitches it will be known as a 'yarn eater'. But to be sure, check Chapter VIII, Costing Schiffli Embroidery.

The quality of Schiffli emblem embroidery is acceptable if the machine is in good condition. Tension controls are excellent and the yarns are much softer than sewing threads and the tensions much softer. It is possible to make a true three dimensional emblem on a Schiffli machine, which would be difficult with a sewing machine.

The Schiffli machine is the product of the early and middle 1900's for emblems. These have been upgraded by Saurer's last two models. All Schiffli machine manufacturers are improving these machines to include color changes, and doing away with the mechanical automats, switching to computerized reading devices and electronic controls.

Costing an emblem for a customer is always an estimate until the tape is cut. As stated, most costs are fixed except for stitching time which is only an estimate counted by eye, stitch for stitch, or by experienced judgment.

Some suggestions for economy include using symmetrical designs and designs that are not too intricate. Odd shapes cost more to stitch and cut and always have the problem of frayed edges after repeated washing. The overlock edge eliminates this entirely.

Use as few colors as possible. Remember the base cloth and merrow can also be extra colors at not extra cost. On irregular cut emblems, borders, where practical, should be the same color as the twill.

Keep lettering to a minimum in slogans, mottos., etc.

Too much lettering obscures the emblem and makes it uninteresting. Letters should never be less than 3/8″ (Schiffli). The design may look good as a sketch but the machine, even the best, is incapable of making finer letters consistently.

FLOW CHART FOR EMBLEMS

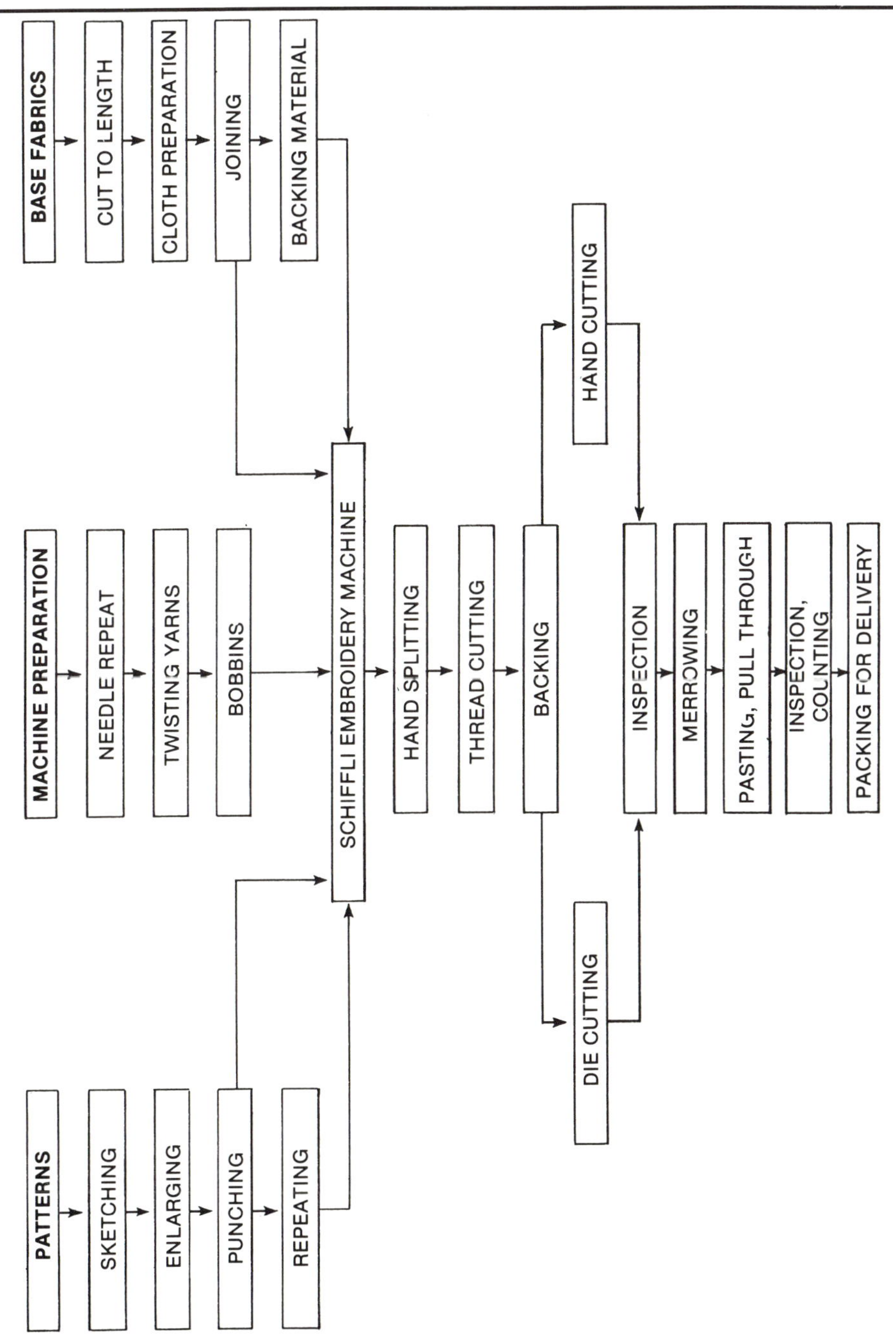

MULTI-HEAD

Multi-head machine embroidery uses the newest technology. The basic requirements for fabric, yarns and tapes are the same, they are fixed costs. The tape cost is based on the number of stitches. Costs for stitching the emblem are based on the total time required. The machines are sewing heads, different from a rack of needles. The heads are placed at varying distances by different manufacturers.

Production is limited to the amount of heads on the machine, from one to 30, but allowing enough room between heads to stitch emblems to 6 or more inches in width. The length is determined by the size frame used.

The fabric is spanned as one piece, the loss not more than 4″ on each side. The speed of the machine can reach 800 spm but practical speeds seldom approach this. All the stitches would have to be very tiny to produce a beautiful emblem at that speed.

Color changes are automatic, threaded at the beginning of production and thereafter controlled completely by the pattern. Automatic colors range from 3 to 9 according to the machine manufacturer and according to the overall size of the machine.

The yarn size is thinner and the stitching tighter than Schiffli, therefore Multi-head machines will require more stitches to stitch the same design. However, the quality of stitching is superior. With a lighter weight frame, the stitching is more accurate and lettering and details can be smaller. 1/8″ lettering is possible as a running stitch, but only with a highly experienced puncher. Normal steil stitching of letters can be as small as 3/16″.

The costs of producing a specific order on Schiffli against Multi-head are similar. The big question is always the amount produced in a specific time. The Multi-heads are competitive with any 10 yard machine, and on small orders they are way ahead. On larger orders they come close and usually surpass Schiffli. However, Schiffli is still ahead on the larger orders stitched on 15 yard machines. But because of overhead costs and the larger factories, the integrated Multi-head operation is not far behind and generally is very competitive.

The Multi-heads beat Schiffli because of the small runs and no overages to cover for damages.

Multi-heads do not have anywhere the number of damages as Schiffli does since if the machine breaks a thread, the whole machine stops and the thread is repaired. Should the thread break and the machine not stop, losing some stitches and part of the design, the machine can backtrack and restitch the missing parts.

Therefore, the amount the customer requires is what is shipped without a 10% or more allowance for damages (which are never repaired). The stitching is sharper and more detailed, and the colors do not add to the cost as they do in Schiffli. Smaller orders are available because fewer emblems are being produced at one time. The investments in yarn are much lower since you purchase enough yarn for the machine, for 30 heads you need 30 cones. On a Schiffli you would order for a 10 yard 3″ emblem a minimum of 228 spools just to run one loom of emblems (1 row). The future of this business is in the hands of the Multi-head embroidery machines.

EMBLEMS FOR THE U.S. GOVERNMENT

The largest single customer in the world for embroidered emblems is the U.S. Government. The orders are always for Schiffli type emblems. They have tried Multi-head emblems, perhaps with inexperienced emblem manufacturers, but for one reason or another have selected Schiffli emblems. It has been some time since they used Multi-head emblems, but the changes in this part of our industry have been so great that it is time for them to try Multi-head once again.

Embroidered emblems for the U.S. Government are designed by:

The Institute of Heraldry, for the U.S. Army.

The Navy Supply Systems Command and U.S. Navy Flags Organization, for the U.S. Navy.

The Air Force Services Office, for the U.S. Air Force.

Some of the finest emblems stitched on Schiffli machines today are worn by the Armed Forces of the United States. With them the Schiffli emblem manufacturer reaches the peak of his machine's capability. The quality is part of the requirement of the Government purchasing office.

All bids demand a fixed number of stitches, usually based on an approved Schiffli tape. Remember Schiffli stitches are based on 2 movements per stitch. When you punch your tape you may find that the stitches you made are less than the number required. This frequently happens with government bids, and therefore you have to add stitches to arrive at the number they require. This may entail just adding underlays in the border or making some round tours under the edging, but sometimes it gets so ridiculous that you make stitches as small as 1/16″ just to raise the number to their request.

The reason Schiffli stitchers wanted a fixed approved number of stitches was to protect themselves from others who might punch the pattern with an approved look that was many stitches less and therefore, offer a better price. Another reason was to have enough work in slow times. They figured the government was paying for the stitching anyway and could afford to pay for it once the pattern was approved. The orders thus became larger. If an actual bid were 100,000 stitches, wouldn't it be better and afford more work for the embroiderer if the same bid quantity could be for 125,000 stitches?

Another strange thing was the inspection the government required. There was always a damage allowance. Why allow for damages, weren't the emblems supposed to be perfect? You will not find this with Multi-head embroidery. We have been counting damages for the past year and find the total delivered is less than .01% after inspection. Savings for the military would be tremendous. Just add up the allowance indicated on every order for the last 50 years!

The Government bids development work which requires a certain number of patterns to be produced annually along with a required number of samples. Beyond the development, if orders are required, they are given for bid only to registered Schiffli embroidery manufacturers who meet certain specific requirements. Bids go to the lowest bidder.

The one receiving the bid is provided with the enlargement from which he must make the punching within a specified number of stitches. A sample must then be submitted for approval. Government inspectors will check the tape for the required number of stitches.

Periodic inspections take place. All items used, such as fabrics, colorfast yarns, require 'end item' tests. The results are part of the requirements for acceptance of finished work. Some contracts require first article acceptance before production can begin. Each contract stipulates a "quality systems requirements manual" report which indicates specific visual, dimensional and packaging inspections prior to acceptance. The contracts are very specific and must be adhered to.

Bids are open to all manufacturers provided the bidder is capable of performing the task required. Prior to acceptance as a bidder, his plant is inspected and his financial position is assessed. Investigations are made to insure that the manufacturer does not discriminate in hiring and that all safety laws are upheld. Bids are solicited by:

Defense Logistic Agency
Headquarters Defense Personnel Support Center
2800 South 20th Street
Philadelphia, PA 19101

STATE AND MUNICIPAL BIDS FOR EMBROIDERED EMBLEMS

Most government agencies including Federal, State, County and Municipal organizations requiring embroidered emblems, issue bids to embroiderers, the purpose being to receive the best price, delivery and quality available. Unfortunately, most purchase agents don't know much about embroidery, so that assistance is usually required in writing the specifications. The embroiderer chosen is usually the one who received the last order, therefore, they write the bids to their specifications, which may vary dramatically from those of other embroidery manufacturers.

Bids to manufacture emblems are not new and preceded today's buying practices. Bids at this time might be given to embroidery manufacturers, uniform companies, sales organizations like the speciality advertising industry, or anyone who requested permission to bid.

The former bid procedure usually was sent only to embroiderers; they were the prime bidders and had little or no competition. When the embroiderer entered his quotation he knew he was only bidding against other embroiderers and according to his production schedule, whether he needed work or not, he fixed his price. At no time did he have to consider anyone adding to his price (like a sales person). In such cases there was no room for commissions or others to earn on securing the bid.

Today we find that most embroiderers still bid in the same fashion. If they have the tape and history of previous orders they already know the costs and the profit margin, and the price might suffice to cover his planned profit.

The Schiffli machine was the only machine used for embroidered emblems until the early 1980's. Many bids still require that the emblems be stitched on Schiffli machines. However, in the last year we have actually received bids that require the emblems be stitched on Multi-head machines. It's about time!

The advantage of the Schiffli machine was the loft offered, because of a softer tension, making the emblem more of a 3 dimensional product. The heavier yarn used (usually 150/2) required fewer stitches but left much to be desired in small details.

The cost effectiveness of Schiffli used to be a factor but that is no longer an issue.

The advent of the computerized 20-24-30 head Multi-head machines stitching at speeds of up to 800 spm makes them competitive with all Schiffli machines.

It is still difficult to surpass a Saurer 2S55 15 yard machine or the 1040/2040 models. However, they require larger runs to be profitable.

The quality of the Multi-head machines is far superior to Schiffli. Instead of pushing a heavy frame around at 170 rpm, the Multi-head has a light frame driven more accurately by timing motors. The yarn is of a thinner denier (120/2), and the tensions are more easily controlled and uniform.

The Schiffli also requires a span of 10 or 15 yards with a width of from 24 inches to 44 inches. This requires more tension on the goods which is not always uniform. Distortions are common. Just picture what is happening to the goods on a Schiffli machine when it is punctured 170 times a minute over 17,200 square inches, as compared with a 2,250 square inches on a Multi-head frame.

Multi-heads with 120/2 denier require more stitches than the Schiffli with 150/2 denier, because the yarn is thinner and the thread tension tighter, requiring more stitches to cover the same area. Fill areas on Schiffli have a thicker appearance, and can use a larger basic stitch than the Multi-head, on which the largest stitch is 5/8 inch, which might require two movements to equal that of the Schiffli. 120/2 denier thread guarantees better quality.

Damages are a factor with Schiffli production. Broken needles and thread break damages are not repaired but discarded, making overages and shortages common. Meanwhile, the more advanced Multi-head has an automatic stop if a thread or needle breaks, limiting the damage, and some machines can retrace a number of stitches, so the missing stitches can be redone. The Multi-head can therefore deliver an exact count, without loss of emblems, to fill the original order.

The Schiffli machine also has to work with a fixed number of needles according to the size of the emblem, with needles fixed at one french inch (approx. 1″) on a 10 yard span (2 spans to one machine of goods). Therefore, a 2″ emblem will produce 342 pcs at a time in one row on this machine known as a loom run. How then can a Schiffli machine deliver 100 emblems or 400 emblems? The same is true with all multiples of 2″, it applies to all repeats; 228 for 3″, 172 for 4″ etc., there is no in-between. Then all quantities are minus damages. Therefore, to reach a fixed requirement it is necessary to run over, thus you end up with overages, which are passed on to the customer.

Other requirements of bids for samples make sense. Let's see what type of embroidery you make, let's see the quality, check the quality of the punching. But when the bid reads 'provide the actual sample with the bid return' you know it is fixed. Who in their right mind is going to make a tape on every bid that arrives on speculation?

Yarn requirements are okay, but what happens if you don't buy your yarn from the designated yarn supplier, or if you use another manufacturer for the base cloth? What about using a buckram that differs from the requirements but still serves the same purpose? How about requiring you to have the goods tested by a special testing company you don't use? You can see how some of the bids can differ. Of course, you can fill these requirements but in many cases it is just not practical. Legitimate requirements indicating a fixed number of stitches per inch or special requirements for merrowed borders assure the quality of stitching coverage the bidder is looking for.

The future of embroidered emblems in the U.S. or anywhere is in the Multi-head machine. The only reason so many Schiffli machines are still used is because of their long established ties to the emblem industry.

Schiffli will not disappear. There are many features mentioned above that make it still a viable means of production for emblems. It has just not kept up with the times.

The Federal government requires only Schiffli emblems for bids on military uniforms. They tried Multi-head and were disappointed, usually faulted by the manufacturer they chose.

We manufacture many emblems used in the same manner for the Air Force, Army and Navy where bids are not required, all by Multi-head. So the newer machines are providing Multi-head emblems for the military.

Our company continually receives requests to bid Government contracts from third parties.

A letter we send to sales organizations attempting to bid for government contracts is as follows:

Government contract bids for embroidered emblems.

We do not bid directly to any government agencies (U.S. State, County or City) however, we do stitch many orders for those who receive these bids.

Give us the opportunity to bid your contracts.

You may not receive any of the orders we quote for the following reasons:

1. The embroidery industry has quoted directly to all the government agencies for many years before there were sales organizations looking for these orders. Machinery has improved ten fold since the introduction of machine-made embroidered emblems. Many Schiffli machines are antiquated, the newer computerized Multi-head produce a 100% better quality emblem for the same cost.
2. In most cases the bid of the average embroiderer (not us) to the agency, and their bid to you will be the same dollar amount, therefore, leaving no margin of profit for the sales group.
3. We request, for your protection, that any bids made by you contain a request for a copy of the bids made and the quotes received so you know who your competition is and what they are doing.

4. This has been the normal practice of embroiderers, who look for large orders to keep their workers employed while making their profits on smaller orders where there is little competition.

We offer you quality, on time delivery and a fair price. Sometimes this isn't enough.

Yours truly

So you can see there is only a slight chance of receiving bids based on the salesperson making a profit if the bid is also forwarded directly to an old time Schiffli embroiderer.

DIRECT EMBROIDERY

On Schiffli machines

Direct embroidery is that embroidery stitched directly into a towel, garment, or other part of wearing apparel. It is not something like an emblem which is added on, either heat sealed or sewn, onto the finished product.

From the beginning of machine made embroideries there have always been products that required direct embroidery such as handkerchiefs, blouses and undergarments.

On the Schiffli machines this was done by adding a frame to hold the cut parts or garments while they were stitched.

Since the frame machines were 10 yards long, consisting of 2 racks of needles, the frames were large, heavy and cumbersome.

Beginning with the first machines, the handloom, frames existed. It was only a short time after the Schiffli machine was introduced that frames were devised to supply stitched cut panels.

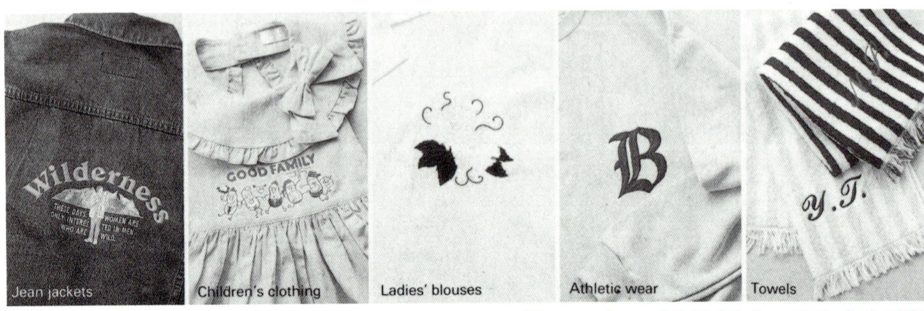

Examples of Multi-head & Schiffli

Frames were built to serve particular industries. The holding rods took space away from small repeats.

The presser foot for standard machines had a single 4/4 presser foot for each needle. These had to be replaced and entirely redesigned with only one presser for each needle. The needle had to be longer to reach the shuttle since the thick frame had to fit between the needle bar and the shuttle rail and to claim this space the shuttle rail was moved.

If a stitcher's main business was handkerchiefs he would use a 12/4 frame which allowed about 2″ for embroidery right to left. The up and down movement reached to 14″.

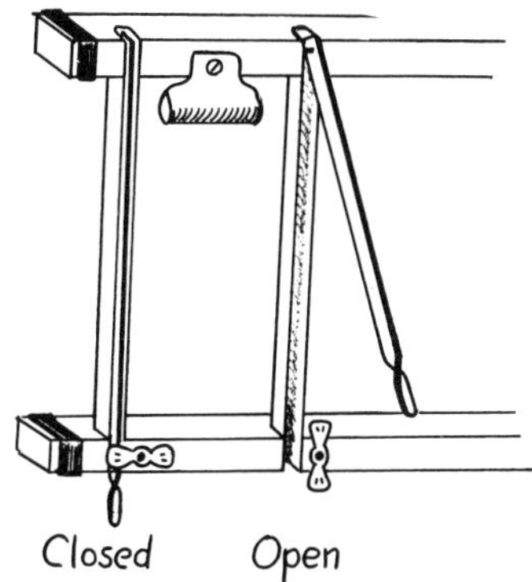

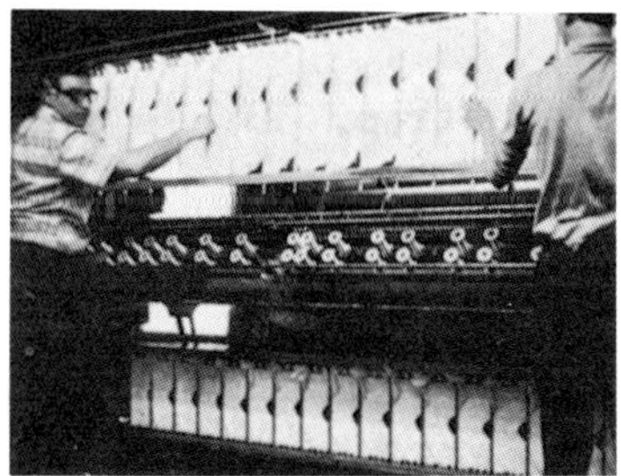

Framing was difficult. A spring loaded clipper was screwed into the top of the frame to hold the top of the cut part. This would hold about ½ the width of the goods. One side of the goods would go into a channel containing a 1/4″ rubber tube, held in place with a clever type of arm which closed into the channel and was held by a swivel latch. The other side had the same type of channel.

The spanner pulled the cut piece tight, pulled the arm down and locked it. This was OK as long as the goods was small but if the cut part were a blouse panel there would be more goods to keep out of the way of the embroidery. In this case, it would be twisted closely to the arm and pinned. The bottom of the cut piece hung free. Some of the problems came from these twisted pieces being 'stitched in' because they were not twisted tight enough or the goods was larger than the frame could safely handle.

There was one channel between each repeat which means each channel had to hold the goods tight for 2 cut pieces, and this required experienced spanners. One side would be set and held by one hand, while the cut piece for the next needle was also placed in the same channel and held till locked, then the overage twisted and pinned.

The twisting had to remain in the front or on top of the frame, because the back of these frames slid against the shuttle boxes.

There were all kinds of pinning and tacking.

Some frames were made larger for wider embroidered motifs. Heavy items, such as pillowcases, would arrive in one piece with the last seam unsewn. Since this goods was so large, special frames were made with a single channel for the right and left, separate for each repeat or each pillowcase. This doubled the weight of the frames.

Change work was still done with each color separately twisted and threaded.

Two sets of frames were used for each machine. When a design was completed the frame was raised to its highest point and the machine watcher and one helper were required to change the frames. Usually, 8 frames were necessary for a 10 yard machine.

Lingerie used 16/4 and 20/4 frames.

Changing frame sizes required replacement of all needles and pressers. If 20/4 was used that meant two sets of 8 frames each for the machines to stitch 128 pieces at a time. Many different repeats were stocked.

On Multi-head machines

Small orders of direct embroidery were made by hand or on single sewing machines. The introduction of the Wurker Multi-head machines were the awakening of a new industry. The machines were used before 1940 as monogram machines in department stores in the U.S. In Europe they were already stitching domestic linens. It was only after the 1950's that machines were used in many garment factories for children's wear, shirts, sweaters, shoes, slippers, and towels. The Gross machine was at the forefront of production in the U.S., while in Europe it was the Zangs and Marco machines.

In the beginning of the 1970's many new machines were introduced. With the advent of electronics and computerization, speed increases and automatic color changes, the machines jumped into the forefront of embroidery production. Now everyone could buy and operate, rather easily, a Multi-head machine. The owners innovated many new uses for embroidery.

The increased speeds made the machine competitive with the smaller of Schiffli machines. Now emblems and appliques could be produced with exceptional quality.

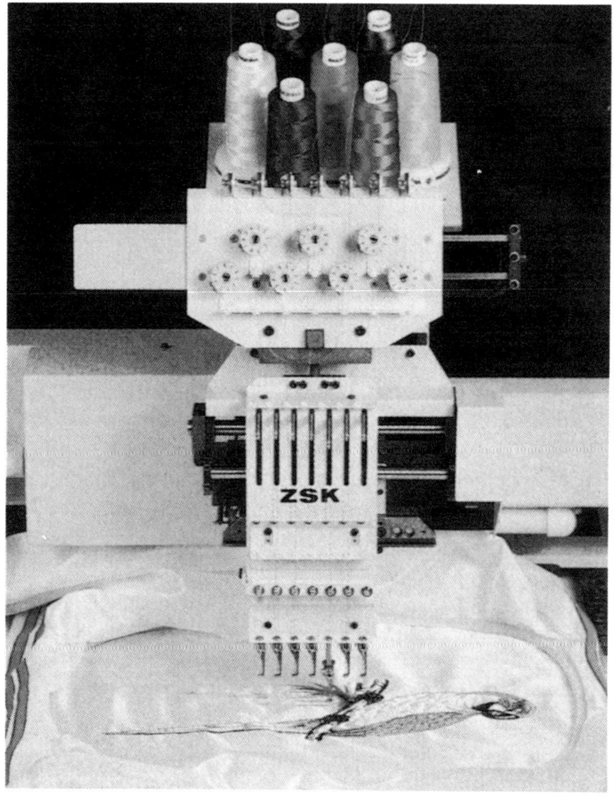

The introduction of the cap machine practically changed everyone's idea of embroidery on caps. No longer restricted to the "patch" look, real embroidery art could be used to decorate and advertise on caps.

The manufacturers were the happiest of all. Production was 50% greater, quality improved and color changing was not the tedious job of the past.

Production changed, not only due to speed alone. but because machines were now not limited to 12 heads. Today many in the U.S. run 30 head machines.

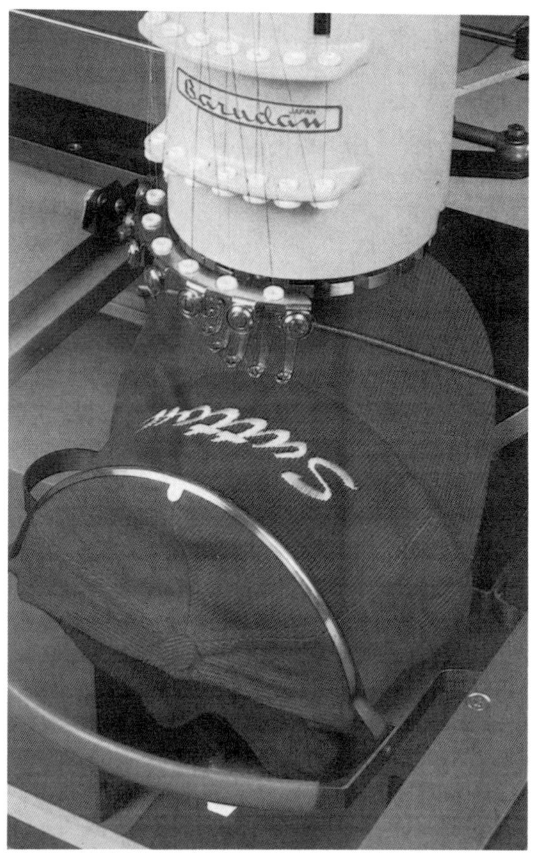

Stitching areas were enlarged enabling one to fully embroider the back of a jacket, the whole jacket being framed in the machine.

There is another interesting point here. Emblems were always cheap. We used to stitch CAT DIESEL, a very popular emblem, and market it for a mere .10 cents a piece. We all realize you can't stitch direct embroidery for .10 cents a piece, but we find that the emblems of this type are not used any longer. Direct embroidery is in full vogue, even with prices more than 10 times higher. Therefore, the lesson is that we don't always have to be the low bidder and can sell embroidery at a higher price if we make a better design, with better quality. The customer has not balked at the higher prices, but instead has demanded more of the better quality direct embroidery.

Newer machines have enlarged the area where embroidery can be used. Styling with sequins, cordings and chenille has opened new avenues for the designer.

CHAPTER VIII

COSTING SCHIFFLI EMBROIDERY

The proper costing of embroidery should be based on the cost of operation of the embroidery factory. We realize the costs will vary with each operation but it is important that the actual cost be known to accurately fix selling prices. The total cost will reflect fixed costs, such as the building, heat, air conditioning, and light; the cost of manufacture, including yarns, labor and machinery; the additional costs of shipping and benefits; and that magic word, profits. Without profits you do not have a business!

It is necessary to take every cost into consideration since the industry is no longer just a cottage industry. Income is not easily divided into costs and profits. Every order for a different design will have a different cost. Keeping records is important as a basis for reference. Without paper work you will not have control of your costs and information for future pricing.

First establish a production order with all information required for the particular item.

Example:

SCHIFFLI

Order #__________ Date __________

Customer ____

Machine # ______________ Yards ______________ Repeat ______________

Stitches per machine ______________________ Yarn ______________________

Production: Hours per day ____________ x Stitches per hour ____________

equals stitches per day ______________________________________

Yarns: Front yarn ____________________ Cost per lb. ____________________

Bobbin yarn ________________________ Cost per lb. ________________________

Fabric Type ______________________ Fabric Width ______________________

Costs and income are easily figured on a stitch basis since stitches easily convert into time. If we took our total production per day and divided it by the stitches produced we would have a cost per stitch.

This is called a stitch rate. If more labor than stitching is required, we could also compute on a yard rate.

YARN, LABOR, FACTORY OVERHEAD, SELLING AND SHIPPING EXPENSES AND ADMINISTRATION COSTS APPLY TO BOTH SCHIFFLI AND MULTI-HEAD BUSINESSES.

YARN: These costs are a combination of front and back yarns. If the cloth on which we stitch is weighed before and after stitching the increase will reflect what was added, which should only be the yarns. By applying a ratio of front and back yarn we can determine the actual yarn cost.

Example:

60/2 or 80/2 cotton front	1 ½ or 2	to back 1 5% waste
40/2 or 50/2 cotton front	2 or 3	to back 1 4% waste
100/2 or 150/2 rayon front	2 or 3	to back 1 4% waste
120/2* rayon or poly front	2 or 3	to back 1 4% waste
30/2 or 20/2 orlon front	4 or 5	to back 1 3% waste
10/2 to 10/3 cord front	5 or 6	to back 1 2% waste

**Multi-head yarns*

If we have the total weight of the yarn, we use the ratio and the cost of the yarns and thereby attain a fairly accurate cost.

Fabric weight _______ before stitching

Fabric weight _______ after stitching

_______ yarn expended

Front yarn weight _______ cost per lb. ____________ cost ____________

Ratio to bobbin _______ cost per lb. ____________ cost ____________

Total cost ____________

% waste ____________

Actual cost ____________

Take the actual yarn cost and divide it by the total number of stitches and we have the cost of yarn per stitch. If special yarns are ordered and the chance of using them again is dim, then the total cost of the yarn is amortized on that one order.

Thread that remains after an order is completed is of negligible value in the normal course of business.

LABOR: Labor costs are not necessarily the actual payment to the employees. To these we have to add all the extras that we pay.

Federal Unemployment	Union Promotion
Social Security	Union Pension
Paid Holidays	Union Welfare
Disability and Compensation Insurance	
Paid Vacations	Bonuses

These costs can inflate hourly rates more than 30% above the amount actually paid. These costs have to be added as part of the overhead and then applied to the cost of production.

regular time		+ overtime	+ night	× rate	= cost
Watcher or	________	+ ________	+ ________	× ________	=
Operator *Shuttler*	________	+ ________	+ ________	× ________	= ________
Piece sewer	________			× ________	= ________
Mender and examiner	________			× ________	= ________
				Total cost	________
				% benefits	________
				Actual cost	________

The total cost of each day's operation can be divided by the number of stitches produced to give us a total labor cost per 1000 stitches.

OVERHEAD: This would include all other costs of doing business. Mainly the factory and selling and administrative costs, the depreciation of machinery and owners' salary.

FACTORY OVERHEAD:	***Per year***
Stitch master or foreman	________
Punching and enlarging	________
Building rent, mortgage, depreciation	________
Shuttles, needles, etc.	________
Personal property taxes	________
Heating fuel, power and light	________
Machinery parts and repair	________
Factory maintenance and repair	________
Janitorial services and supplies	________
Insurance	________
Depreciation on machinery(*)	________
Proprietors salary(**)	________
SELLING AND SHIPPING EXPENSES:	
Samples purchased	________
Advertising	________
Traveling and entertainment	________
Auto maintenance	________
Shipping supplies	________
Delivery expenses, freight, etc.	________

ADMINISTRATIVE EXPENSES:

Salaries	________
Postage, stationery and office supplies	________
Telephone	________
Legal and auditing	________
Credit and collection	________
Association dues	________
Interest and bank charges	________
Bad debts	________
Contributions	________

Total of factory, selling and administrative costs:

(Divided by the number of machines for cost per machine.)

Days per year	365
Sundays	52
Holidays	9
Vacations	12
Saturdays ½ day	26
Down time and slow	10
days from 365	109
Average working days	254

The total overhead divided by the working days will give you the cost per day's operation. This divided by the number of stitches made per day will give you the total cost per 1000 stitches.

(*) Depreciation and obsolescence of machinery:

Depreciation as part of overhead is ignored by the average embroidery producer because it is not a fixed cost which must be paid periodically. The construction of the machinery has extended its life beyond an average age to be replaced. The Schiffli embroiderer has seen machinery of little value more than double its value in a strong season, or new machinery lost because notes could not be paid in a bad season. Nevertheless, for all practical purposes the machine does lose value with time simply because of wear and tear. A cost of obsolescence should be figured into the overhead especially at a time when new machinery will actually make the older machines obsolete. That time has arrived. The value of 10 yard Schiffli machines is depressed, the value of Tajimas and Barudans have held their value, and may never again be as high as it is today. Who is to say that the same will not apply to the other machines with the introduction of newer, more sophisticated machines? How are you going to compete with the slower machines when the newer Schiffli's run at 200 spm and the Multi's all have thread trimmers, etc.

Such considerations must be taken into account, now more than ever.

In the 1990's, the Schiffli Industry is where the Multi-head was in the late 70's, that is, innovation is here for Schiffli machines and investment will be required to keep up with competition. The embroiderer should visit some of the newer factories and see the computer programmed 10-15 and 21 yard machines running only on electronics and servo motors. Instead of mechanical automats, you have machines that run 215 stitches per minute, with automatic color change. How will you compete with this in the future? Such updating costs must be considered in your pricing.

The basic premise that larger machines are not suited to various types of orders is self-defeating. The cost of machine depreciation and obsolescence must be charged to the customer as overhead and the replacement of machines must be considered an inevitable expense. Could your firm absorb a cost of $500,000 to replace equipment today? This might be possible if machine replacement, updating and overhauls were planned in advance and included as part of the overhead costs.

(**) Proprietors salary: This cost is for organizational, supervisory and selling expenses rendered by management. It does not include the return on investment. This is properly part of the overhead. Good management and a prosperous industry are the sources based on which this salary can be increased.

Recapitulation of all costs:

The total costs applied to the stitches will give a fixed rate of overhead per 1000 stitches.

Yarn cost per 1000 stitches . . . . ________

Labor cost per 1000 stitches . . . . ________

Overhead cost per 1000 stitches . . . . ________

Total cost . . . . ________

This is relatively simple since we have figured all costs per 1000 stitches.

Stitches produced daily . . . . ________

price per 1000 stitches . . . . ________

Income . . . . ________

Less any discounts* . . . . ________

Actual income . . . . ________

*Discounts are those that might be customary to certain trades. Schiffli usually allowed a 2% discount on all invoices. Retail chains might have all kinds of penalties, like not following instruction for billing, late delivery, improper marking on the carton etc.

Now take into account the considerable investment in machinery, equipment and time. Nowhere have we considered this, since the salary should not be considered a return on investment. The average Schiffli stitcher who takes the time to cost his embroidery services and applies the basic principals of good business management will show a loss for his operation in normal times. You will not find this in other businesses.

Schiffli pricing is predominately based on supply and demand which varies as styles change. Each manufacturer has determined the bottom price for which he is able to work. Undercutting these established prices serves neither the embroiderer nor the industry.

Cutting prices does not increase the amount of embroidery being used, neither does it guarantee that you will receive stitching orders over someone else who takes a little more time, a little more care and charges a few cents more.

When the owners themselves put their labor on the machines or take over any of the labor costs by doing the work themselves, then they are entitled to both the wages of the employee and the proprietor. When this occurs, we have a cottage industry because the owner usually never takes both wages.

Domestic competition is keen. From the foregoing costs it can be seen that Schiffli embroiderers often do work below cost or do not consider their true costs. Some base their prices wholly on the demand for their services.

Until now it has been rather easy to go into business, but in the 90's rents are not as low, and yarns and other supplies and services might be on a COD basis. Machinery is not as easy to secure, the banks are not ready to lend the large sums required without good collateral. The cost of machines is high because they are based on the currency value of the countries supplying them. With the value of the dollar down, machines are expensive.

COSTING OF MULTI-HEAD EMBROIDERY

Multi-head machines can operate at a speed of 700spm at times, but as stitch lengths increase it is necessary to reduce the speed

The amount of stitches produced per hour is directly related to the costs of operation, a simple comparison of stitches to time.

How long does it take to complete the pattern? Divide that by the time and you have a stitching time. This will vary with different patterns. According to the number of heads you are running you will produce x amount of pieces per hour running time.

Or, compute this on a daily basis. If you are running one pattern steadily, again, a simple calculation will give you the stitches per hour. This should be used as a basis for your costing.

It is not just stitches alone. The cost of setting-up for an order, the changing of frames and spanning the goods, the changing of patterns and how well the design runs are also determining factors. But you will find the simplest method that using the stitches of production to find the cost, which basically includes all of the above.

A substantial reduction in costs can be attributed to thread trimmers, automatic color change and framing devices. Still, the conscientious and efficient operator is of prime importance.

Looking at a typical cost factor, consider the following:

We will use an average stitching speed of 600 spm with electronic upper and lower thread trimmers, 5 color change and pattern containing 2000 stitches.

Number of Heads	Stitching Time	Color Change	Loading	Loss Factor	Total	Time Per Piece
6	3.3	.5	1.0	1.0	5.5	.9
8	3.3	.5	1.1	1.0	5.8	.7
12	3.3	.5	1.3	1.0	6.1	.5
24	3.3	.5	1.4	1.0	6.2	.26

The time per piece should be the total cost factor used in determining the cost of production. Yarn, labor, factory overhead, selling and shipping and administration as described above are the balance of the equation. Don't forget amortization of your equipment as well as depreciation.

CHAPTER IX

SOURCING SUPPLIES AND ACCESSORIES

The most important part of operating an embroidery machine is the sourcing of supplies necessary to perform the services you offer. Alphabetically, you will find those services listed followed with suppliers names, addresses, phone and Fax numbers in an Address Index. No supplier is recommended for any product or service, this is only a list.

All embroidery machine manufacturers supply machine parts and most services and supplies

Computer punch systems are listed in Chapter VI

No sources for embroidery stitchers, contractors, or punch services are listed.

ACCESSORY SEWING AND FINISHING MACHINERY SCHIFFLI

The embroidery machine is not the only piece of equipment necessary to complete embroidered products. Sewing machines, straight and scallop cutting machines, winding machines, overlocking machines, etc., whatever might be necessary to complete your particular product, are part of the manufacturing process.

Cutters Exchange, Inc.: Factory Supplies

Elder Service, Inc.:
Dash type hot knife (laser cutting tool) 15W and 20W models. Mach II 60W model with adjustable temperature control

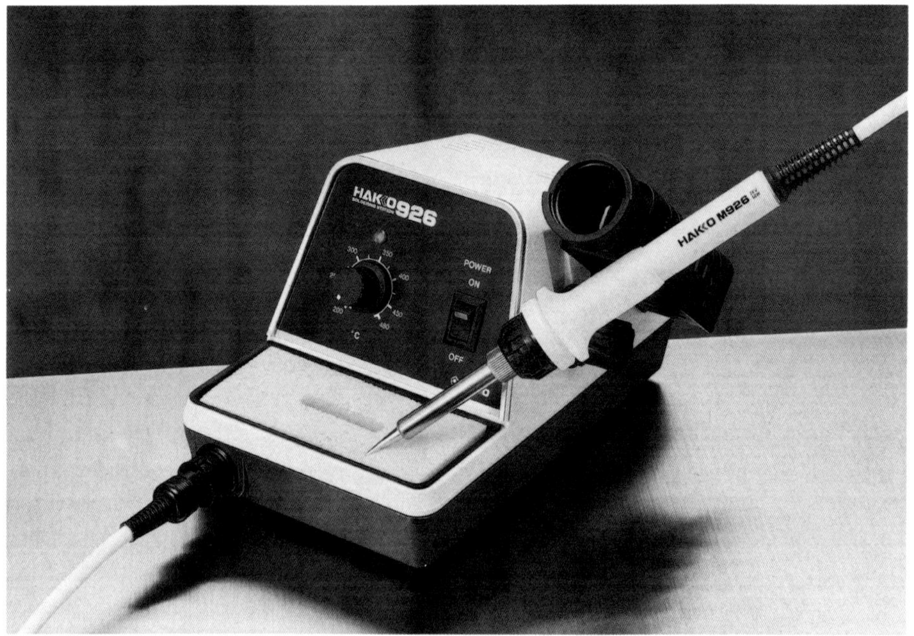

Alfred Heitzman Machine Works, Inc.:

Manufacturers of high speed lace and scallop cutting machines for the Schiffli trade. Hand operated circular knife lace scallop cutting machine.

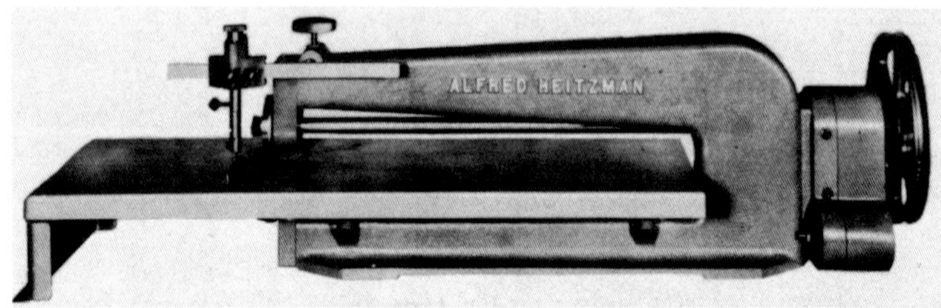

Hirsch International:

TSM-30 Scallop stitch sewing machine operates with cams to make perfect scallops to finish off the edges of border embroideries, or scallop anywhere on the goods. The length of scallops is adjustable from 3mm to 12mm. Stitching speed is 1800spm.

Cam NO.	
1 — 1 2 — 2	
1 — 1 2 — 3	
1 — 1 2 — 4	
1 — 1 2 — 5	
1 — 1 2 — 7	
1 — 3 2 — 7	
1 — 4 2 — 1	
1 — 4 2 — 4	
1 — 4 2 — 5	
1 — 4 2 — 6	
1 — 7 2 — 1	
1 — 8 2 — 2	
1 — 8 2 — 7	
1 — 9 2 — 2	
1 — 10 2 — 4	

Lammertz Needles: Schiffli needles.

Juki: Overlock Machines, Accessory Sewing machines.

The Merrow Machine Company:

The Merrow machine Model MG-3U lends its name to the finish of embroidered emblems. It is the stitch that actually goes around the edge of the fabric to form the border. Symetrical emblems can be overlocked around the edge making a clean border which will not fray. Each emblem is overlocked individually.

Rimoldi of America:

"Orion" overlock sewing machine for binding the edges of enbroidered emblems, available in 5 different models including flat and cylinder bed.

Saurer Textile Systems:

Saurer grinding machines for precision borer sharpening.

Saurer supplied single needle chain stitch machine for sewing spans.

Saurer "Perfecta" is an automatic applique cutting machine. When uncut goods is used for appliques, this method cuts the perimeters as if the piece was originally die-cut.

Saurer "Perfecta" SA 85 is a manual adjustable shearing device to cut floating threads while the goods is still spanned on the machine. The unit is attached to a vacuum to draw in the loose cut threads.

Saurer "Perfecta" HZ 78 with a universal cutting head has a wide range of feelers which can be turned to cut difficult edges.

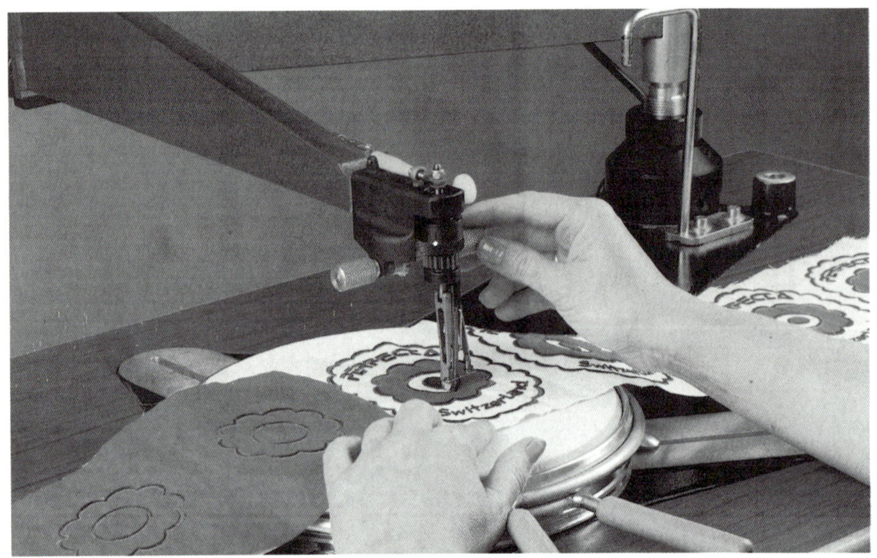

BACKING

Backing includes those materials which will be used on the front or the back of a spanned fabric. They are either spanned with the goods you wish to embroider or used on the back as a support for unstable fabric. Some fabrics like knits, when framed, may become distorted if not framed properly with a support fabric. Backing can be as simple as a paper hand towel or as sophisticated as another fabric. Some are "tear away", some must be cut and trimmed, some are removed with water or heat.

What determines the proper backing is the eventual use of the embroidery. Will the backing be noticeable? Will it hold the piece you want stitched securely for embroidery? Will it affect the use of the embroidery?

You have to make the decision.

Accessory Resource Corp.
Acme Thread & Supply
American International Machine
J. Dashew, Inc.
Data Stitch
Dolphin Cove
Felt Fabrics Co.
Fisher Textiles, Inc.
Freudenberg Telas Sin Tejer S.A.
5 T's Embroidery, Inc.
G.M.P. Sales Co.
Gunold + Stickma
Handler Textiles/HTC
Hersey Levinson Co., Inc.
Hirsch International
Kluger Co., Inc.
Macpherson Associates
Madeira USA
Opal Embroidery
Pantograms Mfg. Co.
Pellon Sales Corp.
Permess Americas, Inc.
QST Industries, Inc.
Reflective Images
Sommers, Inc.
Troy
Zim Chemical
ZSK Stickautomaten

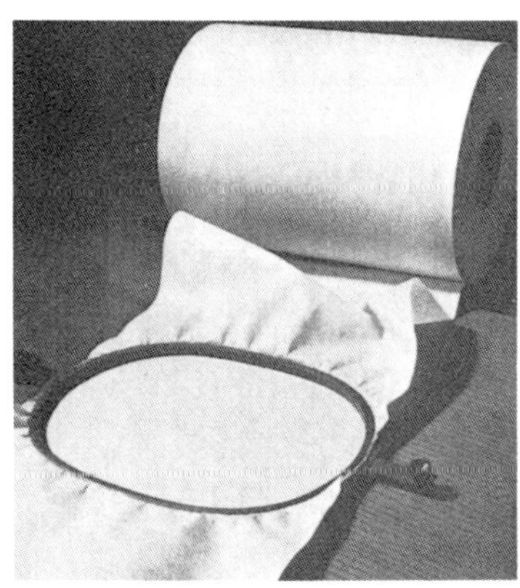

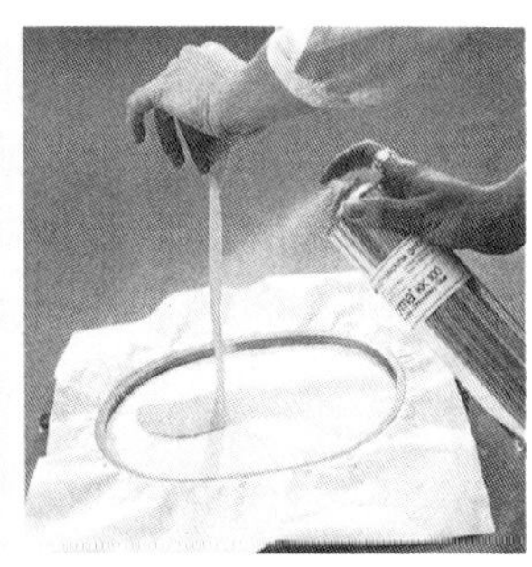

BLEACHING, DYING & AETZING

Schiffli bleaching, dying and aetzing require special bleachery services because of small runs and lengths of fabrics.

ABD
Fashion Textile Finishing Co.
Inter-state Dying & Finishing
Zenith Lace & Embroidery Corp.

BOBBIN WINDERS

Elder Service, Inc.

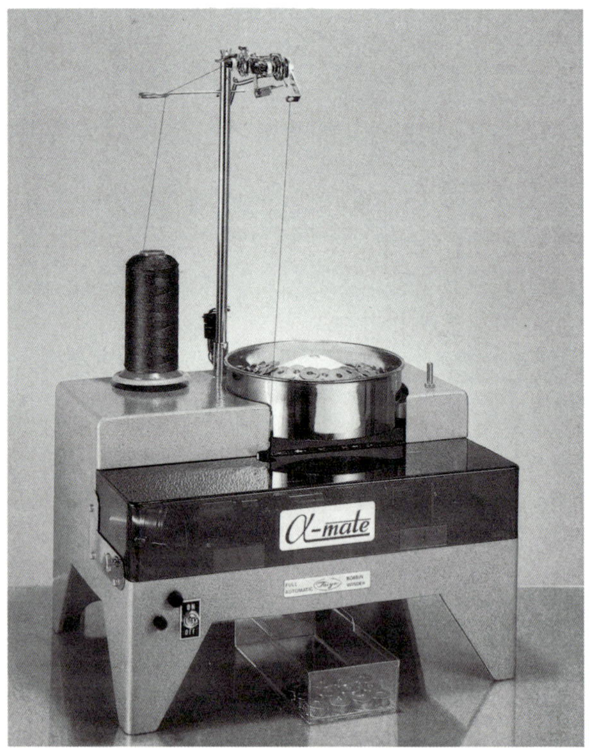

Automatic Bobbin Winder

Comerio Ercole
Gunold + Stickma
Happy/Kanematsu USA, Inc.
Hershey Levinson Co., Inc.
Hiraoka
Hirsch International
Macpherson Associates
Marco
Pfaff
Saurer Ltd.
Tajima
Ultramatic
ZSK Stickautomaten

DESIGNING AND PUNCHING SUPPLIES

Elder Service, Inc.
Gunold + Stickma
Happy/Kanematsu USA, Inc.
Hirsch International
Macpherson Associates
Perforated Pattern Co. Inc.: Perforating Machines

Pfaff
Saurer Ltd.: Optiskop 2000, enlarging machine, for projection of opaque or transparent originals.

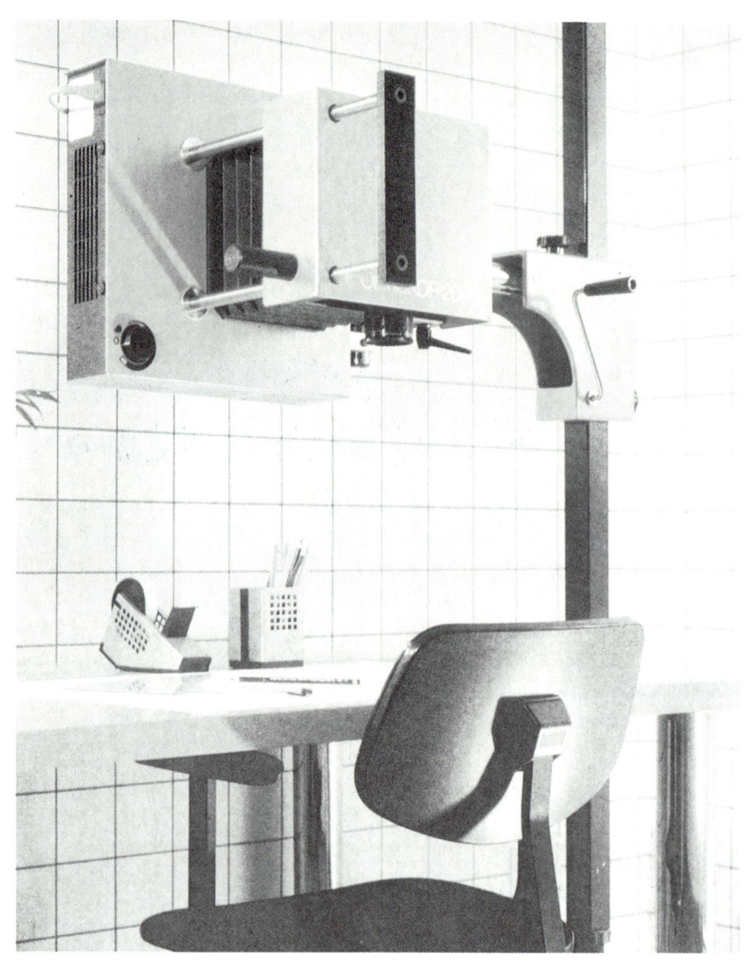

Optiskop Enlarging Machine

Ultramatic
United Numerical Controls
ZSK Stickautomaten

DECORATING EMBROIDERIES

Automatic heat sealing of rhinestones, sequins and other novelties add glitter to designs.

Elder Service, Inc.
C & C Metal Products Corp.
Fred Frankel & Sons, Inc.
Gunold + Stickma: Rhinestone Heat Sealing Machines
Hirsch International: Rhinestone Heat Sealing Machines
Macpherson Associates

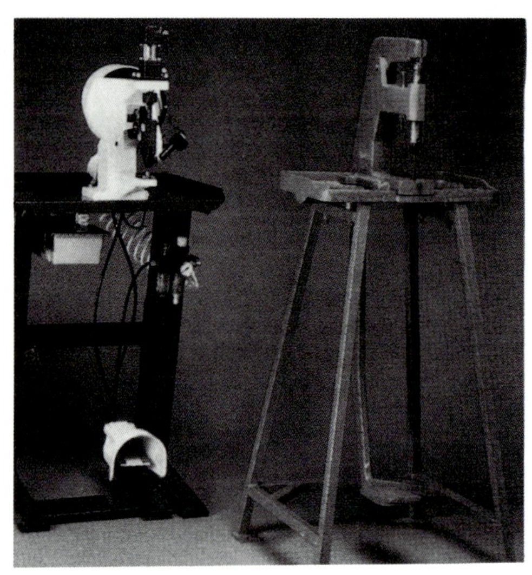

Sequin & Novelty Heat Seal Attachments

Merli Industries, Inc.: Rhinestones, Jewels, Cabochons

Saurer Ltd.:

"Posmatic" for attachment of iron-on precious stones of different sizes, and sequins in a multitude of colors. Excellent to embellish all kinds of fabrics.

Time and temperatures can be regulated. Production can be as high as 3500 stones per hour.

Sequin Heat Sealing Automat

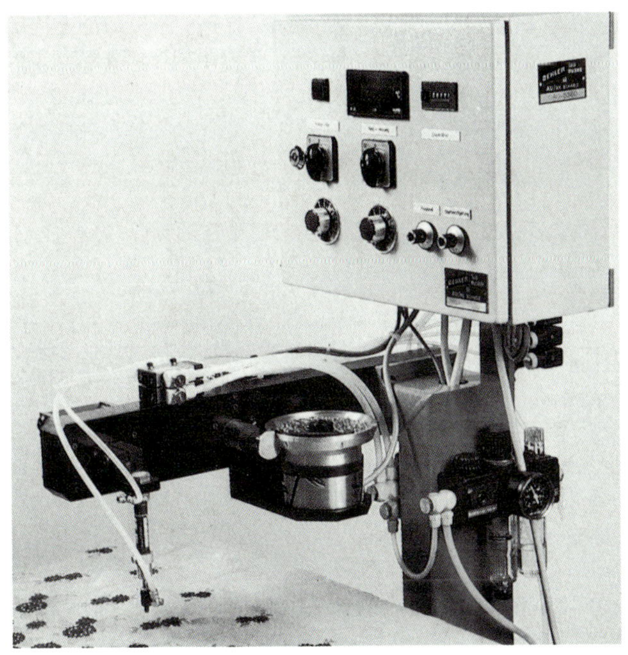

Posmatic Rhinestone Heat Attachments

DIES & CLICKING MACHINES

To cut a clean applique or an emblem, it is necessary that all cuts be exactly the same. This can only be accomplished by die cutting the finished goods with a steel die. For emblems, die cutting is usually an interim process, after an emblem is cut it is usually finished around the edge with an overlock stitch.

Dies allow appliques to be cut so precisely that a cam can be used to sew the item to a garment.

The die should be made after the goods is off the machine. With the thousands of penetrations of the needle, the tensions of the yarns and the tensions of the spanning, you will find that, technically, every emblem is a different size and shape.

We have perhaps 10 3″ round dies. Now, everyone knows a 3″ patch is 3″, in theory. Sometimes a 3″ round die does not fit a 3″ round patch, sometimes the lettering is too close to the cut edge, we then need a slightly larger circle. Sometimes the 3″ is not round, perhaps because the spanning was not tight enough around the whole perimeter, and sometimes there is too much goods showing between the embroidery and the edge.

Die Cutting machines are usually shoe clicking machines. Lighter, smaller and less expensive machines have recently been introduced to the market. Swing beam cutting machine with safety features to click each emblem individually is the only proven method of cutting symmetrical emblems.

However, there is no way at present to gang die cut; it has to be done piece by piece, since in stitching on goods there are many factors which can change the exact shape of an item. Be safe, and cut these items singly. Hand held "Perfecta" cutters also exist for Schiffli appliques.

Accurate Die Mfg., Inc.: Steel Rule Dies
A & G Rule & Die Inc.: Steel Rule Dies
Central Penn Sewing: Clickers
Cutters Exchange: Clickers
Dashew, J., Inc.: Clickers
Freeman Co.: Dies and Pads
Fremont Tool & Die Co.: Dies
Hershey Levinson Co., Inc.: Clickers
Hoffman Brothers: Clickers
Indusco/Southern Cutting Die: Dies
Keen Edge Steel Rule Die Mfg., Co.: Dies
National Die Steel & Machinery: Dies and Clickers

National Steel Rule Die: Dies
Ontario Die Co., Inc.: Dies
Perfect Steel Rule: Dies
Prima Die Co., Inc.: Dies
Professional: Dies
Progressive Service Die Co.: Dies
Rubenstein Bros.: Clickers
Schoen Machinery, USA: Clickers
Schwabe, Herman, Inc.: Clickers

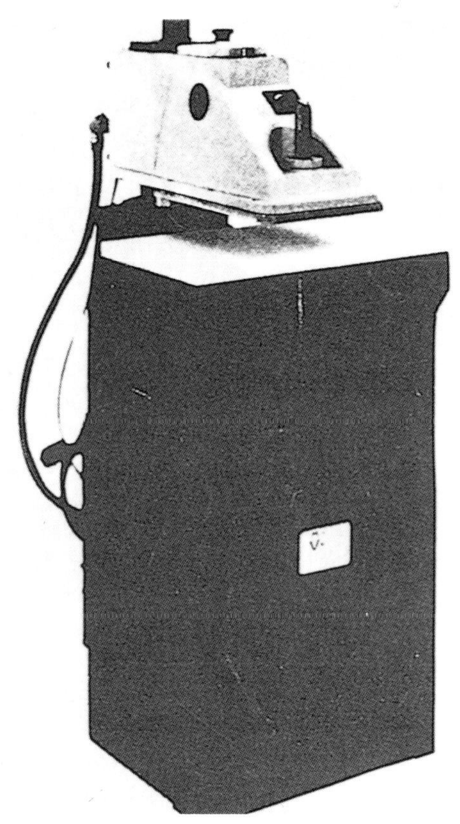

Sewing Machine Exchange, Inc.: Clickers
Sloan Machinery Co.: Clickers
Speedy Die., Inc.: Dies
USM Industrial Cutting Machinery: Clickers
Viking Products, Inc.: Clickers

EMBROIDERY REFERENCE ART - LIBRARIES

Belvedere Design Books: Textile design & Clip art.
Davidson Publishing Co., Inc.: Textile Directories
Design Inspiration Bookshop Inc.: International design books and magazines.
European Publishers Representatives Inc.: Foreign Publications and fashion magazines
Fashion Institute of Technology: Library
The New York Pret/Designers Network: New ideas
Overseas Publishers Representatives: International Fashion Magazines.
Shima Seiki U.S.A. Inc.: Computer Design Systems/color.
Textile Graphic Designs, Inc.: Computer Aided Design
Textile View/Trend Union: Magazine and Fashion Forecasting

FABRICS

The Schiffli machine is capable of embroidering most any fabric. The construction of the machine and its tensioning devices and adjustments for heavier and lighter goods are made possible by the long experience of the Schiffli industry.

This is a fashion industry, which means various styles have been popular over the 100 years of the machine's existence. This constant changing requires that the machine be very versatile and have the ability to stitch on all types of fabrics, including organzas, tricots, knits and wovens, tufted toweling, paper and light clear plastics and leather as well as fine hosiery. Yarns and needles are as important as the fabric. In combination he has a huge selection that makes most any fabric embroiderable.

Fabrics must be uniform in width and length as required by the particular machine. Some loss is expected in the spanning process since in no case can you stitch from edge to edge in width or in length.

Usually 21 yards of 60 inch goods will produce 20 yards by 56″ of embroidery in 2 10 yard pieces.

Multi-head requirements are similar to Schiffli, however, contractors are usually supplied with the fabric. Multi-head requirements would naturally be much smaller than for Schiffli.

Explanations of various fabrics are found in the Glossary.

A & S Textile Co., Inc.: *Chintz, Linen, Polyester/Sheer, Poly/Cottons, Rayon*
Absolutely Terry Co. Inc.: *Terry*
Acker & Jablow Textiles, Ltd.: *Nylon, Polyester, Taffeta, Satin*
Aetna Felt Corp.: *Fire Retardant Felt*
Apex Mills Corp.: *Nettings, scrims, heavy and light tricot fabrics.*
Arkwright Mills: *Twills, Flannels*
Avanti: *Cottons and Blends*
Avondale Mills, Inc.: *Cotton goods*
Balson Industries: *Spartan Tackle Twill*
Balson-Hercules Group: *Nylon, Quilting, Taffeta*
Bank-Miller Co., Inc.: *Plaids, Stripes, Flannels, Broadcloth, Twills*
Bendixen Textiles: *Rayon, Linen, Cotton*
Blank Textiles, Inc.: *Nylon & Polyesters*
Boverman Fabrics Inc.: *Rayon and rayon blends*
Brandeis Fabrics Corp.: *Poly/blends*
Burlington Denim: *Denim.*
Cahn, M.J., Co. Inc.: *Uniform Fabrics*
California International
Carabella Textile Co.: *Twills*
Central/Shippee, Inc.: *Wool and Wool/Viscose Felt*
Chantel Fabrics: *Viscose and cotton blends*
Charter Fabrics, Inc.: *Woven Fabrics/Synthetics*
Clarino America Corp.: *Suede and Leather fabrics*
Collins & Aikman: *Fashion Fabrics*
Cone Mills: *Corduroys, Denims, Flannels, Shirting Uniform Fabrics*
Creative Fabrics: *Twills, Poly/cottons, Rayon Challis*
Cristall: *Tackle Twill*
Dan River, Inc.: *Cotton goods*
Dismoda Ltda.: *Woven Fabrics*
Diversitex Inc.: *Camouflage, Twills*
Dupont de Nemours, E.I. & Co.: *Fire Retardant Fabrics*
Eastbank Trading Co.: *Camouflage, ducks, twills, poplins, nettings.*
Elder Service, Inc.: *Hiselon, Solvron and other special embroidery materials.*
European Textile Trading Corp.: *Poly, Viscose, Cotton*
Fabrica Textil Riopele, SA: *Cotton, Viscose Cotton*
Fairhaven Textile Corp.: *Luana Faille, Nylon, Polyester, Rayon*

Felt Fabrics Co.: *Backing Materials*
Fieldcrest Cannon: *Cotton Goods*
Filtex Int., Inc.: *Natural & Synthetic Blends*
Flock Products: *Cotton Suede*
A. Frank & Sons Inc.: *Twills, Satins*
Granitville Co.: *Cotton Goods*
Greenwood Mills: *Greige Goods*
Hamilton Adams Imports, Ltd.: *Linen*
Hartwill Textiles: *Chiffons, Metallics, Nettings, Taffeta, Tulles*
Huber Textiles, Inc.: *Acetate Satin, Nylon, Nylon Satin, Taffeta*
Imperial Laminators, Inc.
Itex, Inc.: *Greige goods, Flame retardant fabrics*
Jackson Mills: *Twills*
Kabat Textile Corp.: *Chiffon, Organza, Satin*
Kaldor, John: *Rayon, Polyester, Cotton, Linen*
Kaplan-Simon Co.: *Acetates, Nylon, Satin*
Karatex S.A.: *Greige goods, Terry*
Kaufman, Robert Co., Inc.: *Rayons, Blends, Bridal*
Kay-Pel Fabrics, Inc.: *Moirs, Satin, Taffeta, Twill, Satins*
Klopman Fabrics
Kunin, SK Felt Co., Inc.: *Poly felt.*
L. Z. Products: *Poly Crepe de Chine, Double Georgettes, Metallics*
La Lam, Inc.: *Lam, Quilting, Taffeta, Velvets*
Lamberto-Lanificio Lamberto SPA: *Cotton, Linen, Viscose*
Lanificio River: *Viscose, Printed novelties*
Libas, Ltd.: *Cotton, Silk*
Liba Fabrics Corp.: *Satins, Taffeta*
Liberty Fabrics, Inc.
Litwin Bros., Inc.: *Surplus fabrics*
Lucerne Textiles, Inc.: *Acetates, Polys, Nylons, Taffetas, Satins, Twills, and Moirs*
Mainzer Minton Co.: *Solid and Print Cottons*
Manufactura Textil Patagonica: *Cottons, Synthetics*
Manufacturas Textiles Ideal: *Cotton, Poly textile ribbons*
Majestic Mills, Inc.: *Corduroys*
Mandl, Joanna: *Cotton, Viscose, Acetate*
Mayfair Mills, Inc.: *Twills*
Milliken & Co.: *Cotton*
Miroglio: *Cotton, Rayon, Blends*
Model Fabrics: *Solvtex (desolveable fabrics)*
National Felt Co.: *Wool Felt*

Otten, Josef, Testilwerke: *Rayon, Linen, Cotton*
Picchi SPA: *Viscose linen, cotton Linen*
Robex/Tec International: *Rayon, Printed novelties*
Safety & Security Systems, Div. 3M: *"Scotchlite" Reflective Fabrics*
Saxon Textile Corp.: *Twills*
Schott International Inc.: *Twills*
Sequins International, Inc.: *Sequined fabrics*
Sequins U.S.A.: *Sequined fabrics*
S.F.T. Fashion Team S.R.L.: *Acetate, Viscose cotton*
Silk Ltd.: *Pure Silk Fabrics*
Silverman Products and Textiles: *Chiffon, Lam, Linen, Metallics, Organza, Satin, Taffeta, Velvet*
Spartan Mills: *Denim*
Spartex, Inc.: *Ducks, Drills, Twills, Poplins, Canvas.*
Spring Industries: *Cotton greige goods*
Stevens, JP & Co., Inc.: *Denim*
Strachman Associates: *Fake Fur*
Stutz-Horowitz: *Twills*
Stylecrest Fabrics, Ltd.: *Chiffon, Satin, Pure silk, Taffeta*
Supersil SA: *Greige Goods*
Tandler Fabrics, Inc.: *Printed cotton, Rayon, Linens*
Te-Ver: *Viscose and Cotton blends*
Texa Mill, SA: *Cotton blends*
Texfi Industries: *Twills, Taffeta*
Textil Manuel Goncalves, s.a.,: *Cottons, Blends*
Toscolaniera, S.P.A.: *Rayons and Blends*
Troy Corp.: *Fashion fabrics*
Ulster Weaving Co., Ltd.: *Linens*
Ultramatic Embroidery Machine Co.: *Premanufactured imitation chenille embroidery in yard goods form, ready to stitch into individual letters or custom designs.*
Ulster Weavers: *Pure Irish Linen*
Ultrasuede: *Ultrasuede (imitation suede)*
Universal Textile Brokers: *Batiste, Poplin, Greige goods*
Vandenfil S.A.I.A.: *Cottons and Blends*
Waldon Textiles: *Cottons & Blends, Printed Cottons*
Wala Fabrics, Inc.: *Corduroys*
Weisbrod-Zurrer AG Ltd.: *Natural & Synthetic Blends*
Wellington Custom Fabrics: *Felt*
West Point Pepperell: *Twills*
Yarnell Fabrics Corp.: *Cotton, Crepe, Rayon, Satins*

HEAT SEAL FILM

There are dozens of heat seal films. To choose the right one you have to know the goods to which you want to attach your embroidery. It is best to discuss the problems with your supplier. There is a nylon backing for caps and outerwear, polyester for other uses.

The best backing can withstand washing in industrial chemicals. The thickness of the backing is also important, usually there are 3 sizes: .003 for light weight goods, .005 for the average sealing and .007 for heavy duty sealing.

Banasch's, Inc.
Bemis Associates, Inc.
Cutters Exchange
Dashew, J.
Electro-Seal Corp.
Gunold + Stickma
High Tech Machinery
Hirsch International
Macpherson Associates
Rubenstein Bros. Co., Inc.
Sewing Machine Exchange
ZSK Stickautomaten

HEAT SEALING EQUIPMENT

Heat seal machines are made for flat pieces like Tee shirts, garment parts or anything that can easily be heated on a flat surface. There are automatics for industrial production and all are made in various sizes which should be decided upon before a purchase is made.

Curved bed machines are available for cap applications.

The settings are usually simple. The timing depends on the type of heat seal being used, the time required to melt the film sufficiently, and the amount of pressure, which should be based on time and use, again as suggested by your supplier.

It is necessary for the film to melt sufficiently to bond the two pieces of fabric. Too much heat will make the film run off the one surface through the second, and too little heat will not melt it enough to cause the bond. Therefore, the amount of heat is important and the bond should be checked when the items have cooled. Anytime you use a different type of fabric you should check the bond to see all is going well.

Heat can be applied from the top, from the bottom or from both sides simultaneously. The heat should be on the side from which you wish the flow to travel, usually the back of the item.

To heat seal at home it is necessary to set a home iron on the cotton setting, and press firmly for 15 seconds.

Test the success of the heat seal when the item has cooled.

AA World Class Embroidery

Astechnologies, Inc.
Electra Seal
High Tech Machinery

HIX Corp.
Insta Graphics Systems, Inc.

George Knight & Co.

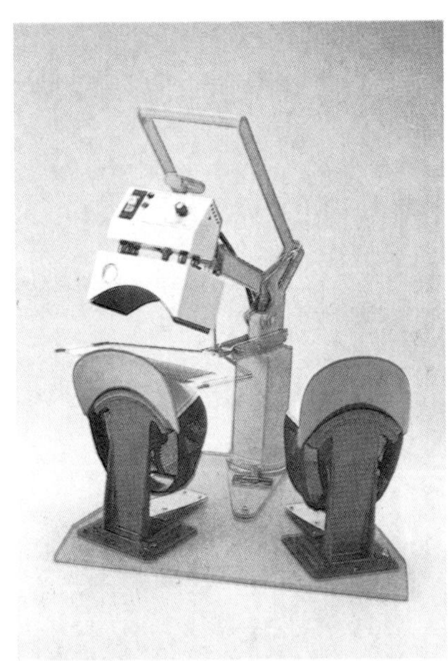

Pennsylvania Sewing Research Corp.

Sal-Bee Machine International
Sewing Machine Exchange
Speedy Die, Inc.
Stahls

MULTI-HEAD SUPPLIES

All manufacturers of Embroidery machines are also suppliers. Besides parts and services they also stock the backings, films, frames, and most accessories.

Accessory Resource Corp.: *Hoops, Threads and Multi-head Supplies*
Acme Design, Ltd.: *Multi-head Supplies*
Allied International, Inc.: *Embroidery Supplies*
American Intl. Machine: *Multi-head Supplies*
B & B Bonnaz, Inc.: *Sewing Machines*
B & G Liberman Co., Inc.: *Embroidery Supplies*
Beka-Gebr. Queck: *Needles*
Brother International: *Accessory Sewing Machines*
Central Monogramming: *Multi-head Supplies*
D.M.C. Corp.: *Multi-head Supplies*
J. Dashew, Inc.: *Embroiderers Supplies*
Data Stitch: *Multi-head Supplies*
Diamond Needle Corp.: *Needles*
Elder Service, Inc.: *Laser Cutters, Winders, Computer Accessories*

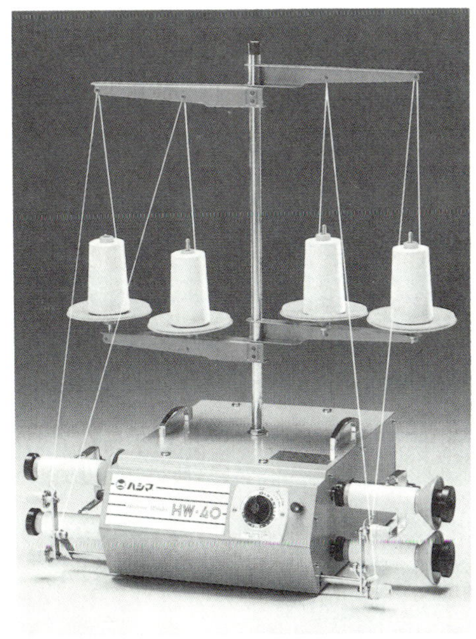

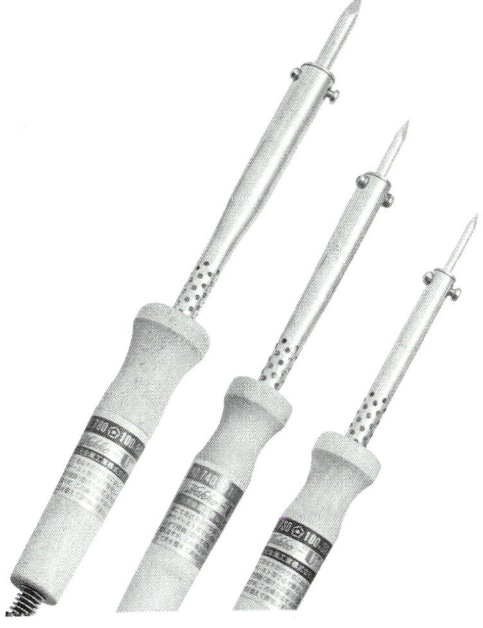

Embroiderers Choice: *Embroidery Supplies*
Embroidery Graphics: *Multi-head Supplies*
Fawn Industries: *Multi-head Supplies*
5 T's Embroidery: *Embroidery Supplies*
Flameproof Chemical Co.: *Flameproof sprays*
Franklin Embroidery: *Computer Supplies*
G.M.P. Sales Co.: *Multi-head Supplies*
Gunold + Stickma: *Computer, Fabric, Embroidery Accessories*
Happy/Kanematsu: *Multi-head Supplies*
Hershey Livenson Co.: *Multi-head Supplies*
Hirsch International: *Computer and Embroidery Supplies, Winding Machines*

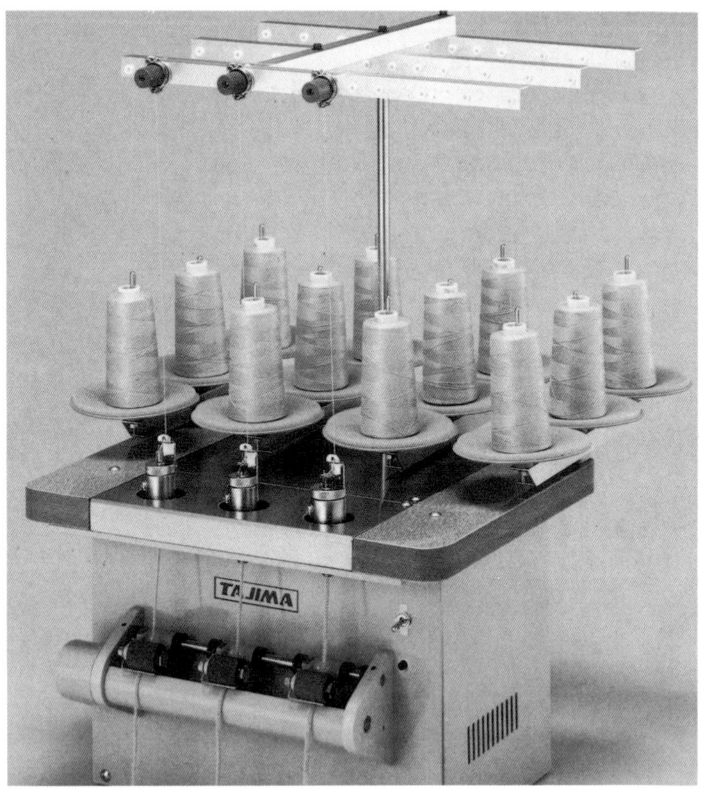

Holderby, C.H., Co.
Juki: *Accessory Sewing Machines*
Kluger Co.: *Multi-head Supplies*
M.E.T. Inc.: *Embroidery Supplies*
Macpherson Associates: *Computer and Embroidery Supplies*

Marco GmbH: *Embroidery Supplies*
Moritz Embroidery Works: *Q.D.T, Punching Supplies*
P & F Equipment Co., Inc.: *Framing Devices*

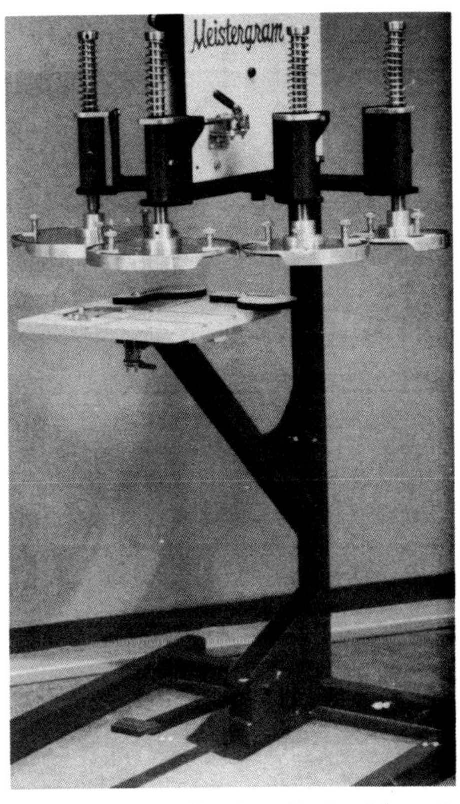

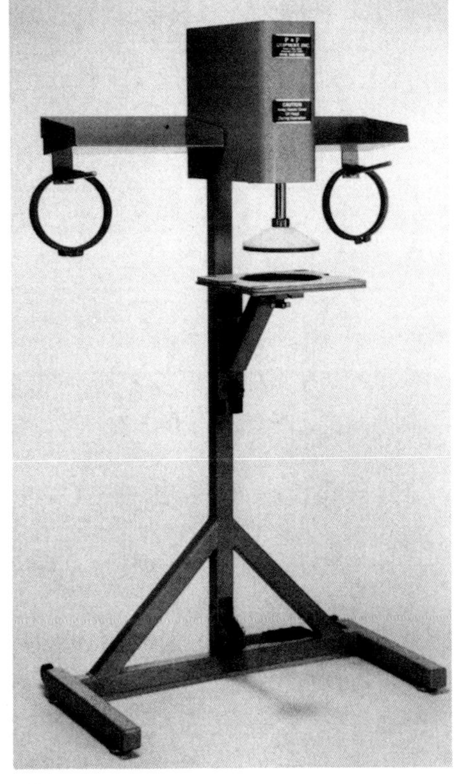

Pantograms Mfg. Co.: *Embroidery Supplies*
Perez Bros.: *Embroidery Supplies*
RNG Enterprises: *Hoops, Computer Supplies*
Rubenstein & Ziff: *Embroidery Supplies*
Rubenstein Bros.: *Sewing Machines and Embroidery Supplies*
Salus Textile Co.: *Multi-head Supplies*
Saurer Ltd: *Embroidery Supplies and Accessories.*
Schaftex, Inc.: *Multi-head Supplies*
Schmetz, Fred. Needle Corp.: *Embroidery Needles*
Sedeco Inc.: *Multi-head Supplies*
Sew Canada: *Multi-head Supplies*
Sewing Machine Exchange: *Embroidery Supplies*
Sewing Systems: *Embroidery Supplies*

Sunrise Turquoise, Inc.
Tajima America Corp.
Telepunch: *Computer and Embroidery Supplies*
TOSA Products, Inc.: *Hopping Systems*
3 A Thread and Supply: *Embroidery Supplies*
Troy Corp.: *Embroidery Supplies*
Ultramatic Embroidery Machines: *Bobbin Winders, Computer Supplies*
Western Numerical Control: *Embroidery Supplies*
ZSK Stickautomaten: *Computer Supplies*

SCHIFFLI PARTS AND SERVICES

Schiffli parts and services are supplied by the machine manufacturers, but local suppliers also exist in those countries with sizable Schiffli industries.

Comerio Ercole

This Plauen type machine's parts are supplied by Comerio Ercole directly from Italy as well as by Saurer and Schlesinger Industries in the USA.

Diamond Needle Corp.

Henry Embroiders Supplies

Hiraoka Shoji Co., Ltd.

This Plauen type machine service and parts can be obtained directly from the factory in Japan. In the USA service is available from Schlesinger Industries.

Moise, Lester L & Son, Machinist

Nielson, Henry Inc. Machinist

P & G Machinery Repair Corp.

Saurer Embroidery Service Center

Major service center for all Saurer machines. Introducing the new Direct Drive System for Plauen machines, an electronically controlled drive system which eliminates mechanical automats. Service and parts for Saurer and Plauen type machines

Schlesinger Industries, Inc.

Major service center for Plauen machines of all types.

Erection and parts for all ages of Plauen Schiffli machines. Borers sharpened, span cloths and frames made to order.

Weiss Manufacturing & Tool Co.

Manufacturers of springs and slides for shuttle boxes of Plauen and Saurer machines.

SWISS EMBROIDERED SAMPLES

Sample makers are always important to Schiffli stitchers throughout the world. Fine Swiss embroideries made in Switzerland are collected and envied by all Schiffli embroiderers. These samples offer new ideas and embroideries to be copied 'back home'.

Swiss embroidered Laces and yard goods samples and souvenirs are available from Peter Hilpertshauser AG.

SCHIFFLI COLOR CHANGE DEVICE

Comerio Ercole.

Comerio has offered a color change device on its machines for more than 10 years, and reports are always positive.

Hiraoka Shoji Co., Ltd.

Color change available, similar to the Comerio Ercole.

Laesser

The color change system provided by Laesser is of their own design.

Saurer Textile Machinery Corp.

Saurer had offered a color change system specifically for the Saurer machines. With the acquisition of the Zangs Company, Saurer now offers their Repeat and Color change for all Plauen and Saurer machines. One of the most widely tested and universally used systems.

VR ANTRIEBSTECHNIK AG

Agent Leonard La Verghetta, Inventor Stephen Markl.

Mechanical change work device for any Schiffli machine.

A new generation of hand operated change work developed by Stephan Markl of St. Gallen, Switzerland.

One of the unique features of this attachment is the savings of all existing color change punchings. Normally, with other change work systems, the older punchings are valueless. Repunching is expensive and time consuming.

The attachment can be either 2/4 or 4/4 system with a minimum down time of 6 to 7 days for installation.

Present needle bars, emery rollers, and electric watcher are removed. A new needle bar, made of aluminum with a sideward sliding movement, and new thread tension controls, consisting of individual rollers for each thread which will be twisted once around, are controlled by a simple air system requiring only 20 p.s.i.

The electric watcher is a state-of-the-art system with 8 positions. Each yarn position is changed by the turn of a knob at each end of the machine. The spool rack is modified to hold twice the normal number of spools.

A typical example of a 12/4 4 color change:

We thread 4 needles in 12/4 as follows, #1 red, #2 blue, #3 white, #4 yellow, all spools are on the machine, twisted and threaded into the needles.

The watcher sets the machine for the first needle (#1 red to stitch) all other threads are held in position and do not interfere with the stitching. When #1 stitching is complete, the watcher presses an air release button so the needle holder sliders can be retracted. The watcher uses a special flat bar measuring 25″ long x 1 1/2″ wide to retract all needles toward the edge of the needle bar. This action locks all the #1 threads and the watcher cuts the ends. Using the same bar, upsidedown, with 12/4 cutouts and placing it over the next color (#2), he proceeds to push out the next set of needles. The needles are relocked with the air switch and move the needle bar sideways to meet the same needle hole plate and shuttle that the #1 red vacated. This procedure is accomplished at the end of the machine with a handle to drive the needle bar sideways. The proper direction of the move is indicated at the end of the machine for each color.

At the same time, the turning of a knob activates the proper thread watcher for the new color, and now the machine is ready to stitch the next color. The average time for the complete changing of colors is approximately 6 minutes with one person attending.

There is great savings in down time and labor, and some stitchers have claimed up to 200% increased production.

With 2 color 4/4; 4 color 8/4; 6 colors 12/4 etc., you can plan for colors to remain on the machine at all times, saving continuous thread changes.

Machines are now operating in Germany, Austria, Japan, France, Italy and the U.S.A.

SCHOOLS AND TRAINING

In addition to those listed for expert training in all phases of Fashion and Embroidery Design and Production, the machine manufacturers also hold seminars in pattern making, machine maintenance, and production.

A. R. Technical Services

Affiliated Embroidery Services Co.:

Consultant for training and assistance for Multi-head operators. Working together with your supervisor they will help improve production and quickly spot areas that need attention and propose improvements. Proven machine operation and work flow documentation are available.

Auburn University: *Design and Fashion Courses*

Austrian Textile School: *Textiles & Embroidery Trades*

Banasch's Inc.

Berkeley School, The: *Fashion Design*

Chmara, Barbara: *Factory Training for Multi-head Operations*

Chmara, Greg: *Custom Wholesale, Factory Training for Multi-head Operations*

Colorado State University: *Fashion production and design.*
Embroidery Educational Services: *Multi-head technical services.*
Fashion Institute of Technology: *College offering courses in all phases of fashion design and production. Special workshop programs in all phases of textile and apparel design.*
Fawn Associates
Floriani International
Florida Intl. University: *Fashion Design*
Foremost Midwest
French Fashion Academy: *Fashion Design*
Gunold + Stickma: *offering a full week training at the Gunold Institute in Marietta, GA*
Harlem Institute of Fashion: *Fashion Design*
International Academy of Merchandising & Design
Iowa State University
Maison Sapho School of Design: *Fashion Design*
Mayer School of Fashion Design
New York/Phoenix, Art School
Opel Embroidery and Weaving Corp.
P & F Equipment Co.
Parsons School of Design
Philadelphia College of Textiles & Science
Pratt Institute, Art and Fashion Design
SCS USA
Sew Art
Sewing Machine Exchange
Southern Star Embroidery
Streamline Tech. Services: *Training in use of Multi-head machines of all types, marketing, machinery and sewing.*
Swiss Embroidery School

Traphagen School of Fashion
University of Missouri
University of Wisconsin-Stout
Vogue School of Fashion Design

STOCK TAPE DESIGN CATALOGS

Independent programmers are constantly making tapes for their customers, they have the equipment and ability to make any design. Therefore, if they have time they can punch 'fun' designs which they offer to the public, AND in this manner they may sell one design many times over. By collecting designs into catalogs the following companies offer them to the trade. Stock designs, sold over and over again, should cost much less than custom made designs.

Often, many designs required for custom orders are similar, such as school mascots. Many machine programs allow the stitcher to combine these designs with special lettering, thus affording the embroidery supplier the ability to customize designs at low cost.

AA World Class Embroidery: stocks finished patches and appliques.
Accessory Resource Corp.
Accu-Stitch Enterprises
Acme Design Ltd.
American Int'l Machine Corp.
B & G Lieberman Co.
Balboa Threadworks
C.E.C. Designs, Inc. (Meistergram)
Carco Embroidery Co.
Columbus Embroidery
Commercial Textil Arbitex, S.A.
Compupunch
Dakota Collectibles
Data Stitch, Inc.
Digitape Designs
Ellison's Embroidery
Embroidery Design Service
Embroidery Exchange, Inc.
Embroidery Graphics
Fine Designs
Five Star Embroidery
5 T's Embroidery, Inc.
Floriani Embroidery
Gunold + Stickma

The worlds largest collection of stock embroidery tapes is Gunold's. They were the first to make tapes for Multi-head machines in the 1930's and have offered stock designs continuously for many years.

Harry Jay Originals
Hirsch International
Hoosier Emb. Supply
J&S Embroidery
Kashmir Embroidery
Lamro, Inc.
Logo Link
M D C Programming
Macpherson & Associates
Macpherson Monogram
Madeira USA Ltd.
Melco West
Moritz Embroidery Works
National Emb. Co., The
Noonan ID Designs
Paragon Tape Punching
Paws Punching
Pfaff Embroidery USA
Punch Line
Rainbow Monograms
Sececa
Sew Canada
Sewing Machine Exchange
Southern Monograms
Spectrun Punching
Stitchmaster, Inc.
Stitchworks, Inc.
Studio 3D Ltd.
Sweat Pea Designs
Threadgraphics
Triple Stitch, Inc.
Troy Sunshade Co.
Turnco Designs
Ultramatic Embroidery
Zines, M.D.

SUPPLEMENTAL READING BOOKS, MAGAZINES & NEWSLETTERS

Accessory Resource Corp.
Apparel Industry Magazine — Monthly Textile Magazine
Apparel Technology — Supplement to WWD/DNR
Applique by Pauline Brown:
    Madeira Threads
The Art of Embroidery, Julia Barton:
    Madeira Threads
Bobbin Blenheim Media Corp. — Monthly Textile Magazine
The Business of Computerized Embroidery,
    Barbara J. Behm, Melco Industries, Inc., 1990
The Complete Encylopedia of Needlework,
    The de Dillmont Running Press 1972

D&D Distributing
Davidson Publishing, — Textile Directories
Denco Sales
Design Inspiration Bookshop, Inc. — Belvedere Design Books
Embroidery News — Quarterly Newsletter
  Schiffli Lace & Embroidery
  Manufacturers Ass'n
From Thought...To Thread,
  The Basics of Digitizing
  Fred & Wendy Griffiths, Opal Embroidery Co., Ltd.
Hirsch Headlines — Newsletter
Impressions Magazine — Monthly Imprinted Sportswear
Machine Embroidery, Gail Harker:
  Madeira Threads
The Madeira Book of Gold and Silver Embroidery
  Madeira Threads
The Madeira Book of Needlepoint Stitches
  Madeira Threads
The Madeira Book of Needlepoint Miniatures
  Madeira Threads
Madeira Newsletter — Newsletter
  Madeira Threads below
Majestech Corp.
The Melco Star — Quarterly Newsletter
  Melco Industries
Reich Supply Co.
Threads — A New Magazine
  Madeira Threads
Stitches Magazine — Monthly Embroidery Magazine
  Wiesner Publishing
Stumpwork Society — Monthly Newsletter
  Silvia Fishman
Textilforum — Monthly Textile Magazine
T.I.P. — Annual Resource Guide
Vital Link — Quarterly Newsletter
  Macpherson Monogram, Inc.
Women's Wear Daily — Daily Fashion Newspaper
  Fairchild Publications
Working with EDS/EPICOR
  Classic Embroidery & Screen Printing

THREADS AND YARNS

Embroidery yarn dealers have kept abreast of the needs of the individual stitchers. They have learned how to twist yarns that work well on Schiffli and Multi-head machines. The industry is very specialized because of the small amounts of various yarns and colors required, the special twist and the put-up. All of the major American yarn dealers are located in Northern New Jersey, in the U.S.A.

France, Germany, Japan and Taiwan are other major suppliers of embroidery yarns and threads.

Those stitchers who are part of a small industry within a country having no embroidery yarn manufacturers have to twist their own yarn or depend on imported yarns.

SCHIFFLI EMBROIDERY YARNS

Rayon: Most embroiderers use two-ply yarns in sizes from 75/2 to 300/3, the common sizes being 100/2 and 150/2. Each size has different twists due to the thickness of the thread. Each supplier stocks about 100 colors which can be purchased in small lots put up on Schiffli spools. The spool holds 60 to 120 grams (2 to 4 ounces). Minimum dyeing requires 4.5 kilograms for single colors. Stocks include two, three and four color varigated pastel colors and 3 tones of one color known as ombres. Fast dye (colorfast) represents ⅔ of all sales of rayon.

Cotton: Cotton yarns are usually domestic CPM (Comb Peeler Mercerized, Gassed). 100 colors are stocked, including black, white and natural. The twist (18s) is prepared in sizes from 8/2 to 60/2, the most popular being 20/2 and 40/2. The put-up is usually on tubes and all cotton is fast dyed. The yarn people are not limited to sizes, but stock what is popular in today's market. 100/2 cotton is rarely made or used, but in former years this size was popular, so the yarn dealers have to keep up with the demands of fashion.

Other yarns in continuous use are stocked. Polyester in many colors, beaded twist, and mylars, both supported and unsupported are among those in use. New yarns are constantly being developed.

Bobbins are usually 75/2 Spun Polyester or 75/2 SAK cotton. They are stocked in all required sizes. #5 is the smallest, #4 is common with prewar machines and the newer #7 and #9 are normal with the newer machines.

#2 bobbins for the oldest machines are still available on request. Special sizes and colors are made to order. Rubber bobbins for Matlessie are available.

Nylon bobbins supplied by Danfield Threads and Culver Textile are used to a great extent in the industry, especially in the manufacture of emblems. Nylon bobbins are stronger and contain much greater yardage for their weight requiring less down time for shuttle changes. It is extremely hard for a single dealer to supply all threads and yarns for the entire industry.

Burke Mills, Inc.: Schiffli yarns

Culver Textile Corp: Major supplier of all types of yarns to the Schiffli trade. Offers over 100 shades of 150/2 fast dyed rayon. Nylon bobbins are made and stocked for Schiffli machines.

Danfield Threads, Inc.: Nylon Bobbins

Filtex Inc.: Rayon, Polyester and Metallic Schiffli Threads

London Yarns: Schiffli rayon yarns.

Robison Anton Yarn Co.: Largest supplier of cotton, rayon and mylar threads and novelty yarns for the Schiffli machines. Comprehensive color card for 100/2, 150/2 rayons and 20/2, 40/2 cottons, merrowing yarns and bobbins.

MULTI-HEAD EMBROIDERY THREADS

Multi-head yarns are supplied by many thread manufacturers: American, European, and Asian, all available in the U.S.A. In the U.S. the #122 (European #40) is most commonly used. Minimum colors for special dyelots are 12 kilograms (25 lbs. or 100 king spools). Special yarn sizes are also available, such as #152, #153, #182 and #75. The twist in this ply is Z and put-up is on king spools.

Sizes available, yards on king spools, applications and European equivilants:

Size	Yds/King Spool	Europe Equiv.	Applications
# 75	3,000	#60	Very fine lettering
#122	5,500	#40	High speed monogramming
#152	3,250	#35	High speed coverage
#182	5,500	#30	High speed decorative st.
#153	2,100	#20	High speed heavy coverage

Another popular thread used on Multi-head machines is metallic. It is available in approximately 15 colors and is supplied on small king spools and large cones.

Metallic yarns contain real silver to enhance their running properties.

Mylar with cotton support is stocked but unsupported yarns are also available and are used extensively in Europe and Asia.

Heavier yarns that might be used with cord devices can be purchased from most any yarn dealer since they require no special preparation for embroidery.

Bobbins for Multi-head machines are the same as for sewing machines, usually 75/2 white cotton or 70/2 nylon, 75/2 spun polyester or single end nylon. Both are supplied on King spools for the embroiderer's bobbin preparation or in prewound form in boxes of 120 or 144 bobbins.

Ackermann-Goeggingen AG: 125 years of experience make Ackermann-Goeggingen one of the most important embroidery thread manufacturers in the world. The machine embroidery rayon is known as ISAFIL, 100% viscose rayon, and is stocked in 176 colors. The brand ISACORD is a polyester machine thread in 30 and 40 denier and stocked in 107 colors.

Well established German manufacturer of 100% polyester Multi-head embroidery threads, brand name "ISACORD".

ARC Accessory Resource Corp.: A major supplier of embroidery threads for Multi-head machines.

Allied Threads, Inc.: Multi-head threads.

California Shirt Sales: Multi-head threads.

Coats & Clark: Well known and long time American manufacturer of sewing threads, Multi-head threads trade named "TRUSEW" specializing in high speed polyester yarns.

Culver Textile Corp.: Featuring yarns and bobbins for Schiffli and Multi-head embroidery machines.

Danfield Threads Inc.: Nylon and polyester coreless bobbin threads; a complete line of knotless high-tenacity embroidery threads in 100s and 150s.

Filtex, Inc.: a major supplier of Multi-head threads.

5 T's Embroidery: Multi-head threads.

G.M.P. Sales Co.: Multi-head threads.

Gunold + Stickma: Multi-head threads.

Hershey Levinson Co.: Multi-head threads.

Hirsch International: Hi-Tex Multi-head threads.

IMRA-R.I.T. Inc.: a major supplier of Multi-head threads.

Kawaguchi Shoji Co., Ltd.: (Trading as Pearl Yacht) a well known Japanese manufacturer of thread and yarn including: cottons, rayons and metallic yarns.

Leff Bros.: Multi-head threads.

Macpherson Monogram, Inc.: Monogram threads.

Madeira:

German manufacturer of fine Multi-head threads.

Madeira #40 120/2 denier
Rayon available in 250 colors, 5500 yd cones and 1100 yd spools.
Sticku #30 180/2 denier
Heavier yarn, used for background fills on larger designs. Suggested for heavier fabrics and terry toweling. Rayon yarns available in 122 colors, 5500 yd cones and 714 yd spools.
Toledo #60 75/2 denier
Fine yarn for very fine embroideries. Excellent for Petti Point embroideries. Stocked in 60 colors, 550 meter snap spools.
Decor #12 600 denier (300/2)
Specially made for Merrowing and chain stitch machines. In 60 colors, 3300 yd cones.
Decor #6 1200 denier (300/4)
Double the thickness of #12 for chenille embroidery, in 41 colors, 1650 yd cones.

Tanne #50 85/2:
Finest Egyptian cotton for fine embroideries, on table cloths, bath and bed linens and handkerchiefs. Stocked in 176 colors 5,500 yd cones and 1265 yd spools.
Tanne #30 50/2
For heavier fabrics and terry cloth toweling. Stocked in 176 colors, 5500 yd cones and 714 yd spools.

Tanne #20 34/2
To give a hand embroidered look to designs on embroidery machines, best for chain stitches and chenille embroidery. See color cards for stocked colors, in 5500 yd cones and 495 yd spools.
Tanne #12 27/2 cord
Cording for embroidery machines, stocked in 44 solid colors and 16 multi-shades. 2750 yd cones and 385 yd spools.
Tanne #3 6/2 cord
Cording for embroidery machines, stocked in 67 solid colors and 16 multi-shades, 550 yd cones.
FS 7/2 #50 metallic fine thread.
Very thin thread for fine details. Perfect for high speed embroidery machines, 1100 yd spools.
FS 5/2 #40 metallic medium thread.
Stocked in 15 metallic colors and 5500 yd spools.
FS 4/2 #30 metallic heavy thread.
For high speed embroidery machines, stocked in 17 metallic colors and 5500 yd cones.
FS 2/2 #20 metallic thread.
Made of 80% rayon and 20% metallics, good for special effects, stocked in 450 yd spools.
Supertwist #30 metallic thread.
Available in 32 colors, heavy duty thread for sewing machines in 42 colors, 1100 yd spools and 5500 yd cones.
Supertwist #20 metallic thread.
For chain stitch embroidery and industrial sewing machines. Available in 12 colors, 3300 yd cones and 20 gram spools.
Neon #40 120/2 denier.
Polyester thread in vibrant fashion colors, fast dyed, stocked in 120 colors including 20 fluorescent colors. Stocked on 5500 yd cones and 1100 yd spools.
Burmilana #12 14 denier wool.
Wool-like embroidery thread, 70% acrylic and 30% wool. For chenille and chain stitch embroidery, in 76 colors, packed in 325 yd spools.
Burmilana #3 4 denier wool.
Heavy wool-like cord yarn. Available in 32 solid colors and 12 metallic effects. Stocked in 550 yd cones.
Bobbin threads 120/2 polyester.
Use where polyester and rayon threads are used. Available in black and white in 11000 yd cones.

Bobbin threads 100/2 cotton.
11000 yd cones, available in black and white.

Robison-Anton Textile Co.:
Major supplier of all types of yarns to the Schiffli trade. Bobbins, cotton, rayons, polyesters and metallics in all sizes. Merrow yarns.
Major supplier of Multi-head yarns to the Multi-head industry. Color cards available.
Multi-head embroidery yarns:

Color Super Strength Rayons in sizes	#75 in 14 colors.
Color card no. SSR-2	#122 in 204 colors.
	#152 in 204 colors
	#153 in 40 colors
	#182 in 14 colors.
Super Luster Cottons in sizes	#52 SAK in 64 colors
Color card for #52 SAK no. 52A	#20 S.L.in 50 colors

Color card for #20 & #00/3 70A #00/3 SAK in 32 colors Polyester in #00/2 in 78 colors.
Color card no. 65A

Soltex Thread Co.: Polyester Threads and Novelty Yarns.

Superior Thread & Yarn:
J. Metallics in 13 colors.
Color card no. 10C
Bobbin threads

Troy Corp.: Multi-head threads.

Yamazaki Thread Co., Ltd.: Trading as "Cupie" brand, a leading yarn manufacturer in Japan. Cotton, Rayon and metallic yarns.

Y L I Corp.: Major supplier of Multi-head embroidery threads.

TRADE SHOWS AND EXHIBITIONS

American Textile Machinery Int.	Annual, Greenville, SC Basic Textile Machinery
Bobbin Show, The	Annual, Atlanta

Bobina, La	Annual, Miami, Central/South American, Spanish Speaking.
Fashion Supplier Expo Jonathan Larkin	Annual, New York, NY
Imprinted Sportswear Shows Impressions Magazine	Long Beach, CA., Orlando, FL. 2 Annual shows, various cities
Incentive and Premium Industry Expo The Interface Group	Annual, Mid Western Expo
International Clothing Machine Fair Cologne Int'l Trade Fairs	Annual, Cologne, Germany
International Craft Show	Annual
International Textile Machinery Ass'n	Every 4 years in Europe
Interstoff	Semi-annual, Frankfurt, Germany
National Merchandise Show	New York, Annual
National Sporting Goods Ass'n	Chicago, Annual
New York Fabric Show American European Trade & Exhibition Center, Corp.	Semi-Annual, NY
Premium Incentive Show Thalheim Expositions, Inc.	Annual, New York and Chicago
Press Expo, The Wiesner Publications	Annual, various cities
SAAC, Specialty Adv., California	Annual, San Diego, CA
SAAGNY, Specialty Advertising, NY Regional Show	Annual, Kiamisha, NY
Speciality Advertising Ass'n Int.	Annual, Dallas 2 Summer Shows, various cities.
Stitchers Embroidery Conference, The	Annual, various cities
The Super Show	Annual, Atlanta
Trimming Show, National Knitwear & Sportswear Ass'n	Annual, New York City
Variety Merchandise Show	Annual

USED MACHINERY

Most of the machinery manufacturers can offer used embroidery machines of all types, mechanical and computerized. They often take older machines in trade for new equipment. Others who trade used machines are listed.

American Intl. Machine; Multi-head
Berowitz, Irving, Co., Inc.; Multi-head
Comerio Ercole; Schiffli
Commercial Textil Arbitex, S.A.; Multi-head
Elder Service; Schiffli and Multi-head
Elizabeth Sewing Machine; Multi-head
Fiedler, Robert, Enterprises; Multi-head
Floriani, Walter; Multi-head
Happy/Kanematsu; Multi-head
High Tech Machinery; Multi-head
Hiraoka; Schiffli
Hirsch International; Multi-head
Hoffman Bros.; Multi-head
Holderby, C.H.; Multi-head
Macpherson Associates; Multi-head
Marco GmbH; Multi-head
Markowitz, Steve, Nalbandian Realty; Schiffli Machines
Melco Industries; Multi-head
Roberts, ET5 & Cie; Multi-head
Rubenstein Bros.; Multi-head
Saurer; Multi-head and Schiffli
Schlesinger Industries; Schiffli
Sedeco; Multi-head
Sew Canada; Multi-head
Ted Thorsen; Multi-head
Ultramatic Embroidery Machine; Multi-head
ZSK Stickautomaten GmbH; Multi-head

INDEX OF ADDRESSES

AA World Class Corp.
151 Hobart St.
Hackensack, NJ 07601
Tel 201 489 0808
FAX 201 489 1909

ABD (Bleachery)
2011 85th Street
North Bergen, NJ 07047
Tel 201 861 6242

A & G Rule & Die, Inc.
38 West 21st Street
New York, NY 10010
Tel. 212 255 0532

A & R. Technical Services
52A New Main St.
Haverstraw, NY 10927
Tel. 914 429 1424

A & S Textile Co., Inc.
1365 38th St.
Brooklyn, NY 11218
Tel. 718 972 0166

AETEC
American European Trade
& Exhibition Ctr., Corp.
225 West 34th St., Suite 906
New York, NY 10122
Tel. 212 563 5350
FAX 212 736 0027

Absolute Terry Co., Inc.
110 West 40th St.
New York, NY 10019
Tel. 212 719 4830

Accessory Resource Group
471 E. 124th Ave.
Denver, CO 80241
Tel. 303 421 0420
FAX 303 451 5605

Accurate Die Mfg., Inc.
22 West 21st St.
New York, NY 10011
Tel. 212 242 0860

Accu-Stitch Ent., Inc.
4611 Military Rd.
Niagara Falls, NY 14305
Tel. 716 297 3310
FAX 716 297 3312

Accu-Stitch Ent., Inc.
5468 Dundas St. W, Suite 623
Toronto, Ontario,
Canada M9B 6E3
Tel. 416 626 1179
FAX 416 695 1573

Acker & Jablow Textiles, Ltd.
519 8th Ave.
New York, NY 10018
Tel. 212 563 5799
FAX 212 629 0048

Ackermann-Goeggingen AG
Fabrikstr. 11,
D8900 Augsburg 22, Germany
Tel. 0821 901 467
FAX 0821 901 401

Acme Design Ltd.
265 Princess St.
Winnipeg, Mtba., Canada
R3B OS2
Tel. 204 956 0052
FAX 204 957 5816

Acme Thread & Supply Co.
826 S Los Angeles St.
Los Angeles, CA 90014
Tel. 213 680 0860

Aetna Felt Corp.
2401 West Emaus Ave.
Allentown, PA 18103
Tel. 215 791 0900

Affiliated Emb. Services
1007 Crabtree Close
Woodstock, GA 30188
Tel. 404 442 5388

Aisin Seiki 10, LTV.
2.1 Asahi-Mach, Kariya City
Aichi 448 Japan
Tel. 0566 24 8647
FAX 0566 24 0168

Aldwick Textile (UK) Ltd.
Unit 2 Web Complex
Admin Rd., Knowsley
Industrial Pk, Liverpool, L33 7YB
Great Britain
Tel. 51 549 1783
FAX 51 549 2073

Allied International Inc.
64 Blakeslee Ave.
North Haven, CT 06473
Tel. 203 239 3597

Allied Threads, Inc.
99 Chabanel W.
Montreal, Quebec
Canada H2N 1C3
Tel. 514 382 4800
FAX 514 382 4699

All Steel Rule Dies Co., Inc.
12 Park Street
Ridgefield Park, NJ 07660
Tel. 201 641 4154

American Apparel Manufacturers Ass'n
2500 Wilson Blvd., Suite 301
Arlington, VA 22201
Tel. 703 524 1864
FAX 703 522 6741

American Int'l. Machine Co., Inc.
1700 Savage Court
Longwood, FL 32750
Tel. 407 331 8280

Apex Mills Corp.
PO Box 149
Inwood, NY 11696
Tel. 516 239 4400
FAX 516 239 4951

Apparel Industry Magazine
180 Allen Rd., Suite 300 N.
Atlanta, GA 30328
Tel. 404 252 8831
FAX 404 252 4436

Apparel Technology,
supplement to WWD/DNR
7 East 12th St.
New York, NY 10003
Tel. 212 741 6726
FAX 212 337 3426

Arkwright Mills
2 Hudson Place
Hoboken, NJ 07030
Tel. 201 656 7777
FAX 201 656 4912

Astechnologies, Inc.
PO Box 395
950 Sun Valley Dr.
Rosewell, GA 30077
Tel. 404 993 5100

Auburn University
Spidle Hall
Auburn University, AL 36849
Tel. 205 844 1329
FAX 205 587 7911

Avanti
990 Ave of the Americas
New York, NY 10018
Tel. 212 629 8800

Avondale Mills, Inc.
1438 Broadway
New York, NY 10018
Tel. 212 730 3000

B & B Bonnaz, Inc.
26 East 31st
New York, NY 10016
Tel. 212 679 2997

B & G Lieberman Co. Inc.
2420 Distribution St.
Charlotte, NC 28203
Tel. 704 376 0717
FAX 704 333 1676

Balboa Threadworks
204 Washington
Balboa, CA 92661
Tel. 714 675 8358

Balson Industries
38 West 32nd
New York, NY 10001
Tel. 212 736 3636

Balson-Hercules Group
30 Irving Place
New York, NY 10003
Tel. 212 475 2500
FAX 212 529 4649

Banaras House Ltd.
D 29 Connaught Circle
110 001New Delhi, India
Tel. 332 3657
FAX 331 0457

Banasch's Inc.
2810 Highland Ave.
Cincinnati, OH 45212
Tel. 513 781 2040
FAX 513 731 2090

Bank-Miller Co., Inc.
55 West 39th St.
New York, NY 10018
Tel. 212 869 3916
FAX 212 921 4614

Barudan Co., Ltd.
906 Josoiji
Ichinomiya City
Aichi-pref., Japan
Tel. 0586 76 1137
FAX 0586 77 1499

Behm Consulting
8118 Raleigh St.
Westminister, CO 80030
Tel. 303 427 6114

Beka-Gebr. Queck
PO Box 1229
D-5100 Aachen, Germany
Tel. 0241 47755
FAX 0241 22215

Belvedere Design Books
See Design Inspiration Bookshop, Inc.

Bemis Associates, Inc.
1 Bemis Way
Shirley, MA 01464
Tel. 508 425 6761
FAX 508 425 2278

Bendixen Textiles, A.H.
1440 Broadway, Suite 1651
New York, NY 10018
Tel. 212 221 5877
FAX 212 221 5973

Berkely School, The
3 East 43rd St.
New York, NY 10017
Tel. 800 446 5400

Berkowitz, Irving, Co., Inc.
33 West 26th St.
New York, NY 10010
Tel. 212 242 2050

Blank Textiles, Inc.
350 5th Ave.
New York, NY 10118
Tel. 212 239 8115
FAX 212 465 1029

Bobbin Blenheim Inc.
Bobina, La
PO Box 1986
Columbia, SC 29202
Tel. 803 771 7500
FAX 803 799 1461

Boverman Fabrics, Inc.
470 7th Ave.
New York, NY 10018
Tel. 212 736 7310
FAX 212 736 7441

Brandeis Fabrics Corp.
309 5th Ave #503
New York, NY 10016
Tel. 212 686 4747
FAX 212 889 5245

Brother Industries, Ltd.
Nogoya, Japan

Brothers Int.
8 Corporate Place
Piscataway, NJ 08855
Tel. 201 981 0300
FAX 201 981 0153

Burke Mills Inc.
Box 190
Valdese, NC 28690
Tel. 704 874 2661

Burlington Mills
1345 Ave. of the Americas
New York, NY 10019
Tel. 212 631 3000

C & C Metal Products Corp.
456 Nordhoff Pl.
Englewood, NJ 07631
Tel. 201 569 7300
FAX 201 569 4112

C.E.C. Design
PO Box 41006
Brecksville, OH 44141
Tel. 216 838 6200
FAX 216 838 6204

Cahn Co. Inc., M.J.
510 West 27th St.
New York, NY 10001
Tel. 212 563 7292
FAX 212 563 7299

California International
P O Box 861776
Los Angeles, CA 90012
Tel. 213 483 0292

California Shirt Sales
7307 Edgewater Dr.
Oakland, CA 94621
Tel. 415 430 0486

Cam Steel Rule Die
9 Romanelli Ave.
South Hackensack, NJ 07606
Tel. 201 488 4666
FAX 201 488 0201

Carabella,
29 West 36th St.
New York, NY 10018
Tel. 212 695 3500

Carco Embroidery Co.
11 Tech View Drive
Cincinnati, OH 45215
Tel. 513 563 6999
FAX 513 563 8672

Carlin Reports
5 rue les Cases
75007 Paris, France
Tel. 1 4551 1717
FAX 1 4551 9981

Casati, Carlo, AG Maschienenfabric
Industriestr 5
CH9434 AU/St Gallen, Switzerland
Tel. 071 71 55 40
FAX 071 71 56 24

Central Shippee, Inc.
45 Star Lake Rd.
Bloomingdale, NJ 07403
Tel. 201 838 1100
FAX 201 838 8273

Central Monogramming
4029 S.R. 98
Bucyrus, OH 44820
Tel. 419 562 3194

Central Penn Sewing
351 East 7th Street
Bloomsburg, PA 17815
Tel. 717 784 1312
FAX 717 784 3312

Chantal Fabrics
570 7th Ave.
New York, NY 10018
Tel. 212 354 6787
FAX 212 768 8141

Charter Fabrics, Inc.
1430 Broadway
New York, NY 10018
Tel. 212 391 8110

Chmara, Barbara
PO Box 42616
Tucson, AZ 85733
Tel. 602 327 1701

Chmara, Greg
Custom Wholesale Embroidery
424 North 5th Ave
Tucson, AZ 85705
Tel. 602 884 1120
FAX 602 882 4555

Clarino America Corp.
489 5th Ave.
New York, NY 10017
Tel. 212 972 6166
FAX 212 972 6172

Classic Embroidery
4184 Redwood Hwy.
San Rafael, CA 94903
Tel. 415 472 2648

Coats & Clark Inc.
#213, 1400 Lake Hearn Drive
Atlanta, GA 30319
Tel. 404 843 6700
FAX 404 843 6738

Collins & Aikman
210 Madison Ave.
New York, NY 10016
Tel. 212 578 1300

Cologne Int'l Trade Fairs
Messe und Asstellungs Ges. m.b.H
Postfach 210760
W 5000 Cologne 21
Germany
Tel. 114 92 218211
FAX 114 92 218 212574

Colorado State University
Dept.of Design, Merch.,
and Consumer Sciences
314 Gifford Bldg.
Fort Collins, CO 80523
Tel. 303 491 1629
FAX 303 491 7975

Columbus Embroidery
2330 Midway
Columbus, IN 47201
Tel. 812 376 8820
FAX 812 376 8061

Comerio Ercole S.p.A.
Via S. Pellico
21052 Busto Arsizio (VA), 3 Italy
Tel. 0331 635 473
FAX 0331 635 346

Commercial Textil Arbitex, S.A.
Numancia 187, ent. 2A
08034 Barcelona, Spain
Tel. 34 3 203 774
FAX 34 3 205 3561

Compupunch Inc.
4375 Beverly Blvd.
Los Angles, CA 90004
Tel. 213 666 6192
FAX 213 666 6195

Con-Cepts
20021-B Ballinger Way N.E.
Seattle, WA 98155
Tel. 206 365 7221

Cone Mills
1440 Broadway
New York, NY 10018
Tel. 212 391 1300

Convention Business Services, Inc.
2054 E. Desert Inn Rd., Suite C
Las Vegas, NV 89109
Tel. 800 338 5282

Corbett Systems,
3316 N.E. 73rd Ave.
Portland, OR 97213
Tel. 503 284 5750
FAX 503 472 7306

Crafted With Pride in U.S.A. Council
1045 Ave. of the Americas
New York, NY 10018
Tel. 212 819 4397
FAX 212 819 4493

Creative Fabrics
Div. Quick Service Textiles, Inc.
5 West 37th St.
New York, NY 10018
Tel. 212 764 1544
FAX 212 575 2352

Cristall, S.M.
775 Main Street
Buffalo, NY 14203
Tel. 716 852 6392
FAX 716 852 0346

Culver Textile Corp.
525 52nd St.
West New York, NJ 07093
Tel. 201 866 6200
FAX 201 349 8884

Cutters Exchange, Inc.
4500 Singer Rd.
Murfreesboro, TN 37133
Tel. 615 895 8070
FAX 615 895 3210

D & D Distributing
Portal Drive #114
Pine, AZ 85544
Tel. 800 289 9773
FAX 602 476 3828

DMC Corp.
Port Kearny Bldg #10
South Kearny, NJ 07032
Tel. 201 589 0606
FAX 201 589 8931

Dakota Collectibles
3520 Saratoga
Bismarck, ND 58501
Tel. 701 255 2409
FAX 701 255 7207

Dalco Athletic
P.O. Box 550220
Dallas, TX 75355
Tel. 214 494 1455
FAX 214 276 9608

Danfield Threads, Inc.
118-126 Colebrook River Rd.
Winsten, CT 06098
Tel. 203 379 0786
FAX 203 379 0789

Dan River, Inc.
111 West 40th St
New York, NY 10018
Tel. 212 554 5555

Dashew, J, Inc.
2709 Frederick Ave.
Baltimore, MD 21223
Tel. 301 233 1660
FAX 301 945 7245

Data-Stitch Inc.
4784 Hwy 377 South
Fort Worth, TX 76116
Tel. 817 244 0171
FAX 817 560 4221

Davidson Publishing Co., Inc.
PO Box 477
Ridgewood, NJ 07451
Tel. 201 445 3135
FAX 201 446 4397

Design Inspiration Bookshop, Inc.
488 7th Ave. #12C
New York, NY 10018
Tel. 212 736 1537
FAX 212 465 1134

Designs Today
208 Parkersburg Rd.
Savannah, GA 31406
Tel. 912 355 7904
FAX 912 352 8102

Diamond Needle Corp.
GPO Box 1355
New York, NY 10001
Tel. 212 929 2277

Digitape Designs Ltd.
1220 Ellesmere Rd., Unit 27
Scarborough, Ontario
Canada M1P 2X5
Tel. 416 297 6019
FAX 416 297 0508

Dismoda Ltda.
Zona Franca, Bloque E., 1erP.
Apartado Aero 29631
Barranquilla, Colombia
Tel. 316056 419332
FAX 5758 417667

Diversitex Inc.
PO Box 131
Caldwell, NJ 07006
Tel. 201 228 5262

Dolphin Cove
8700 Dayton Pike
Soddy Daisy, TN 37374
Tel. 615 332 9467
FAX 615 332 9910

Dupont de Nemours, E.I. & Co.
Laurel Run Building, Fibers Dept.
Wilmington, DE 19880
Tel. 302 999 3234
FAX 302 774 5304

E Z Hoop
1414 Henn-Hyde Rd.
Warren, OH 44484
Tel. 717 382 4855
FAX 717 382 4711

Eastbank Trading Co.
915 Hill Park
Macon, GA 31208
Tel. 912 745 4040
Fax 912 746 9626

Eileen Lavine Informations Services
4733 Bethesda
Bethesda, MD 20814
Tel. 301 656 2942
FAX 301 656 3179

Elder Service, Inc.
6-13 Ajihara-cho, Tennoji-ku
Osaka, Japan
Tel. 06 764 1300
FAX 06 764 6087

Electro-Seal Corp.
55 Wanaque Ave.
Pompton Lakes, NJ 07442
Tel. 201 835 6000
FAX 201 835 3106

Elizabeth Sewing Machine Co.
725 Spencer St.
Melbourne West
Victoria 3003 Australia
Tel. 61 3 329 5411
FAX 61 3 328 4260

Ellisons Embroidery & Design
PO Box 434
Franklin, TX 77856
Tel. 409 828 3380
FAX 409 828 3110

Embroidery Design Center
P.O. Box 790
Manchester, MO 63011

Embroidery Design Service
#116-110 Ruth Street East
Saskatoon, Sas., Canada S7J OP7
Tel. 306 956 8273
FAX 306 933 2585

Embroidery Educational Services
7062 Huntley Rd.
Columbus, OH 43229
Tel. 614 888 6028
FAX 614 888 4265

Embroidery Exchange, Inc.
1422 Channing St.
Los Angeles, CA 90021
Tel. 818 363 4134

Embroidery Graphics
406 W Mockingbird Ln.
Dallas, TX 75247
Tel. 214 630 0924
FAX 214 638 7613

Embroidery Punchers Alliance
c/o R. Schmidt
415 Henry Street
Fairview, NJ 07022

Embroidery Trade Ass'n
745 North Gilbert Rd
Suite 124-201
Gilbert, AZ 85234
Tel. 602 497 1274
FAX 602 892 6859

European Publishers Reps, Inc.
11 03 46th Ave.
Long Island City, NY 11101
Tel. 718 937 4604

European Textile Trading Corp.
1457 Broadway
New York, NY 10036
Tel. 212 354 0126
FAX 212 354 0128

Expocon
7 Cambridge Dr.
Trumbull, CT 06611
Tel. 203 374 1411
FAX 203 374 9667

Fabrica Textil Riopele, SA
Pausada De Saramagos
4760 Famalicao (VN)
Portugal
Tel. 52 921 002
FAX 52 921 170

Fairchild Publications
7 West 34th
New York, NY 10001
Tel. 212 630 3600

Fairhaven Textile Corp.
250 Belmont Ave.
Haledon, NJ 07508
Tel. 201 942 5200
FAX 201 942 6590

Fashion Institute of Technology
227 West 27th St.
New York, NY 10001
Tel. 212 760 7446
FAX 212 594 9413

Fashion Supplier Expo
100 Wells Ave.
Newton, MA 02159
Tel. 617 964 5100
FAX 617 964 0657

Fashion Textile Finishing Co.
280 River Road
Edgewater, NJ 07020
Tel 201 941 3636

Fawn Industries, Inc.
Hwy. 851, PO Box 230
New Park, PA 17352
Tel. 717 382 4855
FAX 717 382 4711

Felt Fabrics Co.
210 14th Street
Hoboken, NJ 07030
Tel. 201 420 8177
FAX 201 233 5116

Fiedler, Robert, Enterprises, Inc.
707 Gardens Dr. #203
Pompano Beach, FL 33069
Tel. 305 972 1739

Fieldcrest Cannon
60 West 40th St.
New York, NY 10018
Tel. 212 536 1200

Filtex International Inc.
247 West 38th St #10FL
New York, NY 10018
Tel. 212 354 0924
FAX 212 764 5738

Filtex, Inc.
500 Beaumont Ave.
Montreal, Canada
Tel. 514 274 3544
FAX 514 274 4138

Filtex, Inc.
982 Englewood Dr.
Willoghby, OH 44094
Tel. 216 951 2548

Fisher Textiles, Inc.
4812 Starcrest Dr.
Monroe, NC 28110
Tel. 704 289 1160
FAX 704 289 1136

Five Star Embroidery Tape Punching
3709 N. 84th St.
Milwaukee, WI 53222
Tel. 414 461 8273
FAX 414 466 8428

5 T's Embroidery Supply
165 Park Ave.
Brockport, NY 14420
Tel. 716 637 7945

Flameproof Chemical Co.
635 West 23rd St.
New York, NY 10011
Tel. 212 242 2265

Florida Intl. University
University Park
Miami, FL 33199
Tel. 305 348 2531
FAX 305 348 1940

Flock Industries
1157 Center St.
Easton, PA 18042
Tel. 215 559 5625
FAX 215 559 9528

Floriani Embroidery Ent., Inc.
Star Rt 1 Box 2800-83A
Tehachapi, CA 93561
Tel. 805 822 3234
FAX 805 822 8422

Foremost Midwest
1307 East Maple Rd.
Troy, MI 48083
Tel. 313 689 3850
FAX 313 689 4653

Frank, A, & Sons Inc.
1501 Guilford Ave.
Baltimore, MD 21202
Tel. 301 727 6260
FAX 301 685 2461

Frankel, Fred & Sons, Inc.
19 West 38th St.
New York, NY 10018
Tel. 212 840 0810
FAX 212 391 1214

Franklin Mills, Inc.
86 S Water St.
Franklin, IN 46131
Tel. 317 736 8299
FAX 317 736 5946

Freeman Co.
1369 Cox Ave.
Erlanger, KY 41018
Tel. 606 371 4433
FAX 606 525 0992

Fremont Tool & Die Co.
432 N. Wood St.
Fremont, OH 43420
Tel. 419 334 9709
FAX 419 334 3426

French Fashion Academy
462 Broadway
New York, NY 10013
Tel. 212 219 9313

Freudenberg Telas Sin Tejer S.A.
Av. Teziutlan Sur 83
Puebla, Mexico 72160
Tel. 5255 22 8086
FAX 22 49 3875

G.M.P. Sales Co., Inc.
49 Orchard Street
New York, NY 10002
Tel. 212 226 4340
FAX 212 431 8693

G N Telematic, Inc.
46 Manning Rd.
Billerica, MA 01821
Tel. 508 667 8644
FAX 508 667 8260

Gemini di G Roma & C s.a.s.
Via Friuli 10
Edif Quaternario 31029
San Vendemiana (TV) Italy
Tel. 0438 401 868

Genuth, S.
725 West 181 SAt St.
New York, NY 10033
Tel. 212 781 6138
FAX 212 928 0673

Gilardone & Son, Inc.
Virginville, PA 19564
Tel. 215 562 2229
FAX 215 683 6570

Ginsberg, William, Co.
242 West 38th St.
New York, NY 10018
Tel. 212 244 4539
FAX 212 921 2014

Granitville Company
43 West 42nd St.
New York, NY 10036
Tel. 212 869 8700

Greenwood Mills
111 West 40th
New York, NY 10016
Tel. 212 679 2997

Gunold + Stickma Of America, Inc.
1000 Cobb Place Blvd., #500
Kennesaw, GA 30144
Tel. 404 421 0300
FAX 404 421 0505

Gunold + Stickma
Main Office:
2140 Newmarket Pkwy.
Suite 112
Marietta, GA 30067
Tel. 404 955 7968
FAX 404 955 1028

Gunold + Stickma, N.E.
One John Street
Haledon, NJ 07508
Tel. 201 595 0029
FAX 201 595 7176

Gunold + Stickma
Central 86 Eisenhower Lane
Lombard, IL 60148
Tel. 708 691 1303
FAX 708 691 1349

Gunold + Stickma, West
1241 E Warner Ave.
Santa Ana, CA 92705
Tel. 714 751 0481
FAX 714 751 3911

Gunold + Stickma, East Canada
90 Clairport Crescent
Rexdale, Ontario
Canada M9W 6P4
Tel. 416 675 2010
FAX 416 675 2095

Gunold + Stickma, West Canada
114-8400 Main St
Vancouver, BC, Canada V5X 3L8
Tel. 604 325 3383
FAX 604 325 4168

Hamilton Adams Imports, Ltd.
104 West 40th St.
New York, NY 10018
Tel. 212 221 0800

Handler Textile
450 7th Ave.
New York, NY 10123
Tel. 212 695 0990
FAX 212 695 1496

Handler Textile/HTC
1717 Litton Drive
Stone Mountain, GA 30083
Tel. 800 666 3874
FAX 404 938 7018

Hanes Converting Co.
Industrial Hwy.
Southampton, PA 18966
Tel. 215 364 7980

Happy/Kanematsu Germany
AM Wehrhahn 41
4000 Dusseldorf 1, Germany
Tel.. 0211 363 419

Happy/Kanematsu Japan
9-5 Taito 2-Chome, Taito-ku
Tokyo 110, Japan
Tel. 03 834 079
FAX 03 835 8917

Happy/Kanematsu USA Inc. (Dist)
400 Cottontail Lane
Somerset, NJ 08823
Tel. 201 271 7379
FAX 201 271 7357

Harlem Institute of Fashion
157 W 126th St.
New York, NY 10027
Tel. 212 666 1320

Harry Jay Originals
8241 Brentwood Ct.
Arvada, CO. 80005
Tel. 303 422 3131
FAX 303 421 0723

Harwill Textiles
600 West Van Buren St.
Chicago, IL 60607
Tel. 312 707 8838

Headware Institute of America
1 West 64th St.
New York, NY 10023
Tel. 212 724 0888

Headway Trade Fairs, Ltd.
907 Great Eagle Center
23 Harbour Rd.
Hong Kong
Tel. 852 8335121
FAX 852 8345164

Henry Embroidery Supplies
7000 Bergenline Avenue
Guttenberg, NJ 07093
Tel. 201 867 2438

Heitzman Machine Works, Alfred
303 Park St.
Moonachie, NJ 07074
Tel. 201 489 8888
FAX 201 641 5554

Hersey Levinson Co.
300 N. Elizabeth St.
Chicago, IL 60607
Tel. 312 226 7100
FAX 312 266 6739

High Tech Machinery
982 Eaglewood Drive
Willoughby, OH 44094
Tel. 216 751 2548
FAX 216 951 4419

Hilpertshauser, Peter, AG
Embroidery Designer
Bleichestr 9
CH 9001 St. Gallen, Switzerland
Tel. 071 23 62 61
FAX 071 23 11 46

Hiraoka Shoji Co., Ltd.
No. 22-6 Ueno 5 Chome
Taito-ku
Tokyo, Japan

Hiraoka Kogyo Co., Ltd.
c/o Nissho Iwai America Corp.
1211 Avenue of the Americas
New York, NY 10036
Tel. 212 704 6757

Hirsch International Corp.
355 Marcus Blvd.
Hauppauge, NY 11788
Tel. 516 436 7100
FAX 516 436 7054

Hirsch Intl., Corp., KY
Box 331A, Rt 8
Melbourne, KY 41059
Tel. 606 781 6310
FAX 606 781 7010

Hirsch Intl., Corp., FL
3223 NW 10th Terrace, #602
Ft. Lauderdale, FL 33309
Tel. 305 568 9226
FAX 305 568 9229

Hirsch Intl., Corp., GA
1331 Citizens Pkwy., #102
Atlanta, GA 30260
Tel. 404 961 2602
FAX 404 961 2693

Hirsch Intl., Corp., Midwest
4060 Mayfield Rd.
Cleveland, OH 44121
Tel. 216 382 6662
FAX 216 382 8002

HIX Corp.
1201 7th Street
Pittsburg, KS 66712
Tel. 316 231 8568
FAX 316 231 1598

Hoffman Brothers
5290 N. Pearl St.
Rosemont, IL 60018
Tel. 708 671 1550
FAX 708 671 1320

Hoosier Embroidery Supply
2330 Midway
Columbus, IN 47201
Tel. 812 376 8879
FAX 812 376 8061

Huber Textiles, Inc.
Jim Cline Rd.
Fallston, NC 28042
Tel. 704 538 3132
FAX 704 538 7530

IMRA-R.I.T. Inc.
1751 Richardson St., #4131/4th Fl.
Montreal, Quebec, Canada
H3K 1G6
Tel. 514 931 4314
FAX 514 933 8647

Imperial Laminators Inc.
961 Elton Street
Brooklyn, NY 11208
Tel. 718 272 9500

Impressions
PO Box 801470
Dallas, TX 75380
Tel. 214 239 3060
FAX 214 788 1490

Indusco/Southern Cutting Die
3611 Keystone Ave.
Nashville, TN 37211
Tel. 615 833 0666
FAX 615 834 8722

Insta Graphics Systems
13925 East 166th St.
Cerritos, CA 90702
Tel. 213 404 3000
FAX 213 404 3000

Inter-Continental Computer
Products, Inc.
3575 NW 31 Ave.
Oakland Park, FL 33309
Tel. 800 940 2333

Interface Group, The
300 1st Ave.
Needham, MA 02194
Tel. 617 449 6600

International Academy of
Merchandising & Design, Ltd.
Main Concourse
Chicago Apparel Center
Chicago, IL 60654
Tel. 312 828 0202
FAX 312 828 9405

International Textiles (ITBD)
33 Bedford Place
London WC1B 5JXc
Great Britian
Tel. 71 637 2211
FAX 71 637 2248

International Textile Machinery Ass'n
Fachgemeinschaft Textilmaschinen
im VDMA
Lyoner Str 19 / PO Box 71 08 64
D 6000 Frankfurt/Main 71
Germany

International Trade Fair, Paris
Tel. 33 1 43 80 73 41

Inter-State Dying & Finishing Co.
35 8th Street
Passaic, NJ 07055
Tel. 201 473 8370

Interstoff
PO 970126
6000 Frankfort/Main 1, Germany

Iowa State University,
Textile & Clothing Dept.
140 LeBaron Hall
Ames, IA 50011
Tel. 515 294 2628
FAX 515 294 9449

Itex Inc.
9145 E. Kenyon Ave, Suite 201
Denver, CO 80237
Tel. 800 525 7058
FAX 303 770 1519

J & S Embroidery Punching
926 Washington Blvd.
Williamsport, PA 17701
Tel. 717 326 9515
FAX 717 327 5604

Jackson Mills
1441 Broadway
New York, NY 10018
Tel. 212 719 3330

Joanna Mandl, Inc.
110 West 40th St. #1804
New York, NY 10018
Tel. 212 977 1360

Juki America, Inc.
Torrence, CA 90505
Tel. 213 325 5811

Juki America, Inc.
Duluth, GA 30136
Tel. 404 623 1880

Juki America, Inc.
5 Haul Rd.
Wayne, NJ 07470
Tel. 201 633 7200
FAX 201 633 9629

Just Right Ind. Co., Ltd.
6F, No. 162, An Ho Road
Taipei, Taiwan, R.O.C.
Tel. 2 7051696
FAX 2 7006180

K-H Machine Works
4322 Grand Ave.
North Bergen, NJ 07047
Tel. 201 867 2338

Kabat Textile Corp.
215 West 40th St.
New York, NY 10018
Tel. 212 398 0011
FAX 212 719 9706

Kaldor, John
500 7th Ave
New York, NY 10018
Tel. 212 221 8270
FAX 212 921 1759

Kaplan-Simon Co.
115 Messina Drive
Braintree, MA 02184
Tel. 617 848 6500
FAX 617 848 6506

Karatex S.A.
Santiago del Estero 453
1075 Buenos Aires, Argentina
Tel. 1 30 0435
FAX 1 11 2088

Kashmir Embroidery Co.
154 E. 211th St.
Cleveland, OH 44123
Tel. 216 713 9002

Kaufman, Robert Co., Inc.
135 West 132nd St.
Los Angeles, CA 90061
Tel. 213 538 3482
FAX 213 538 9235

Kawaguchi Shoji Co.
(Pearl Yacht) Ltd.
Taito 1-Chome, 23-12 Taito-ku
Tokyo, Japan
Tel. 03 831 1030
FAX 03 835 1420

Kay-Pel Fabrics, Inc.
6001 Equitable Rd.
Kansas City, MO 64120
Tel. 816 241 1600

Keen Edge Steel Rule Die Mfg. Co.
49 West 27th St.
New York, NY 10001
Tel. 212 679 4418

Klopman Fabrics, Div. Burlington Ind.
1345 Ave. of the Americas
New York, NY 10018
Tel. 212 621 3401

Kluger Co., Inc.
900 East 29th St.
Los Angeles, CA 90011
Tel. 213 234 3400
FAX 213 234 6061

Knight, George, & Co., Inc.
54 Lincoln Street
Brockton, MA 02403
Tel. 508 588 0186
FAX 508 587 5108

Knitting Times
386 Park Ave South
New York, NY 10016
Tel. 212 683 7520
FAX 212 532 0766

Kunin, SK Felt Co., Inc.,
Brussels St.
Worcester, MA 01615
Tel. 508 755 1241

L.Z. Products
2126 West 21st Place
Chicago, IL 60608
Tel. 312 847 0572

Laesser, Franz AG
Hohenemserstr
CH 9444 Diepoldsau, Switzerland
Tel. 071 73 13 17
FAX 071 73 23 17

La Lame, Inc.
250 West 39th St.
New York, NY 10018
Tel. 212 921 9770
FAX 212 302 4359

Lammertz Needles, Dunlap Sales, Inc.
PO Box 751
Bradshaw Pike Extension
Hopkinsville, KY 42241
Tel. 800 626 9200
FAX 502 885 6210

Lamberto Lanificio Lamberto SPA
Via Boito, 24
50045 Montemurlo
Italy
Tel. 574 791731
Fax 574 680920

Lamro, Inc.
911 East Main St.
Mesa, AZ 85203
Tel. 602 844 2004
FAX 602 835 7984

Lanificio River
Via Pontalto 26, CP 793
50047 Prato (FI)
Italy
Tel. 0574 632491

Larkin Group, The
485 7th Ave.
New York, NY 10018
Tel. 212 594 0880
FAX 212 594 8556

Ledge Rock Designs
Route 9 Box 1176-1
Branson, MO 65616
Tel. 417 338 8732

Leff Bros.
2505 Texas Ave.
Houston, TX 77003
Tel. 713 223 4365
FAX 713 223 0339

Leonard LaVerghetta
2600 Outwater Lane,
Carlstadt, NJ 07072
Tel. 201 933 8270
FAX 201 460 1620

Letter Perfect, Inc.
1226 Prairie Drive
Racine, WI 53406
Tel. 414 886 1503

Liba Fabrics Corp.
132 West 36th St.
New York, NY 10018
Tel. 212 563 4991
FAX 212 268 5299

Libas, Ltd.
1333 South Hope
Los Angeles, CA 90015
Tel. 213 747 2406
FAX 213 747 4812

Liberty Fabrics, Inc.
295 5th Ave.
New York, NY 10016
Tel. 212 684 3100

Licensing Ind. Merchandisers Ass'n
350 5th Ave.
New York, NY 10118
Tel. 212 244 1962

License Watchdog
151 Hobart St.
Hackensack, NJ 07601
Tel. 201 489 0808
FAX 201 489 1909

Little, George, Mgmt.
Tel. 212 686 6070

Logo Link Canada Inc.
3773 19th Street, N.E.
Calgary, Canada T2E 6S8
Tel. 403 291 2952
FAX 403 291 2223

London Yarn Co.
596 56th St.
West New York, NJ 07093
Tel. 201 863 8171

Lucerne Textiles, Inc.
519 8th Ave.
New York, NY 10018
Tel. 212 563 7800
FAX 212 563 7937

MDC Programming
PO Box 67133
Phoenix, AZ 85082
Tel. 416 626 1290
FAX 416 626 5065

M.E.T. Inc.
248 N. Queen St.
Etobicoke, Ontario, Canada,
M93 4XI
Tel. 602 470 0434
FAX 602 892 3576

MnM Publishing Corp.
California Mart
110 East 9th St., Suite A-777
Los Angeles, CA 90079
Tel. 213 627 3737
FAX 213 623 5707

MacKay Publishing Corp.
309 5th Ave
New York, NY 10016
Tel. 212 679 6677

Macpherson Meistergram Inc., CA
3505 Cadillac Ave.
Costa Mesa, CA 92626
Tel. 714 241 8073

Macpherson Meistergram Inc., OH
9200 Market Place, Bldg. B
Broadview Heights, OH 44147
Tel. 216 838 6207

Macpherson & Assoc., TX
7916 East Elizabeth Lane
Fort Worth, TX 76116
Tel. 817 560 0390

Macpherson & Assoc., MO
10735 Ambassador Drive
Kansas City, MO 64153
Tel. 816 891 0551
FAX 816 891 2586

Macpherson Inc., MA
32 Carriage Way
Danvers, MA 01923
Tel. 508 774 7974

Macpherson Inc., NC
3517 W Wendover Ave.
Greensboro, NC 27407
Tel. 919 294 5165

Macpherson Inc., NJ
26 Chapin Rd., #E
Pine Brook, NJ 07058
Tel. 201 882 5312

Macpherson Monogram, Inc., NC
3517 W Wendover Ave.
Greensboro, NC 27407
Tel. 919 292 5153
FAX 919 855 0106

Macpherson, Geof., Canada, Inc.
2244 Drew Rd., #5
Mississauga, Ontario
Canada L5S 1B1
Tel. 416 671 4010
FAX 416 671 0945

Madeira South
4801 Executive Park Ct.
Bldg. 200 Suite 201
Jacksonville, FL 32256
Tel. 904 281 1999
FAX 904 281 9158

Madeira Thread (UK) Ltd.
Thirsk Industrial Pk.
York Rd., Thirsk
North Yorkshire YO7 3BX
Great Britain

Madeira U.S.A.
30 Bayside Ct
Laconia, NH 03246
Tel. 603 528 4264
FAX 603 281 9158

Madeira West
2727 N. Grove Ind. Drive
Suite 145
Fresno, CA 93727
Tel. 209 454 8173
FAX 209 454 1017

Mainzer Minton Fabrics Co.
48 West 38th St.
New York, NY 10018
Tel. 212 944 3630

Maison Sapho School of Design
312 West 38th
New York, NY 10018
Tel. 212 873 9183

Majestech Corp.
Route 100 Box 440
Somers, NY 10589
Tel. 914 232 7781
FAX 914 232 4004

Majestic Mills, Inc.
989 Ave. of the Americas
New York, NY 10018
Tel. 212 268 7755
FAX 212 268 6417

Manufactura Textil Patagonica S.A.
Av. R. Scalabrini Ortiz 764
Buenos Aires
Argentina
Tel. 773 1188/2760

Manufacturas Textiles Ideal
Km 2 Blvd. Aeropuerto Miguel Aleman
San Pedro Totoltepec
Mexico, D.F. Mexico

Marco Trading GmbH
Bargkoppelweg 56
D2000 Hamburg 73, Germany
Tel. 040 6 78 20 94
FAX 040 6 79 12 92

Mayer School of Fashion Design
70 West 36th St.
New York, NY 10018
Tel. 212 563 3636

Mayfair Mills, Inc.
2 Hudson Place
Hoboken, NJ 07030
Tel. 201 656 7777
FAX 201 656 4912

Meistergram
3517 W. Wendover Ave.
Greensboro, NC 27407
Tel. 800 888 4201

Melco Atlanta
8601 Dunwoody Place #500
Atlanta, GA 30350
Tel. 404 518 7727
FAX 404 518 7824

Melco Industries, Inc.
1575 West 124th Ave.
Denver, CO 80234
Tel. 303 457 1234
FAX 303 252 0508

Melco New York
675 Grand Ave.
Ridgefield, NJ 07657
Tel. 201 941 8080
FAX 201 941 8719

Melco South-AR
4000 McCain Blvd. #2034
North Littlerock, AR 72116
Tel. 501 771 0826

Melco Southwest
3627 E. Indian School Rd. #204A
Phoenix, AZ 85018
Tel. 602 956 9516
FAX 602 788 0085

Melco West
1516 S. Bundy, #201
West Los Angeles, CA 90025
Tel. 213 207 2990
FAX 213 207 6118

Melco West-Northern Terr.
2138 Hidden Valley Drive
Santa Rosa, CA 94010
Tel. 415 697 1953
FAX 415 697 2254

Melco/ZSK South
1700 Alma Drive #120
Plano, TX 75075
Tel. 214 422 0808
FAX 214 423 0259

Merli Industries, Inc.
7166 N.W. 12th St.
Miami, FL 33126
Tel. 305 592 8266
FAX 305 592 8566

Merrow Machine Co.
240 Day St.
Newington, CT 06111
Tel. 203 666 0109
FAX 203 666 7730

Micro Emb. Punch Systems
5005 Palisade Ave.
West New York, NJ 07093
Tel. 201 865 7947
FAX 201 617 7570

Milliken & Co.
1045 Ave of the Americas
New York, NY 10018
Tel. 212 819 4200

Miroglio
1430 Broadway
New York, NY 10018
Tel. 212 382 2020
FAX 212 383 2609

Model Fabrics, Inc.
180 Madison Ave.
New York, NY 10016
Tel. 212 532 5415

Moise, Lester L & Son
14 Chamberlain Avenue
Elmwood Park, NJ 07407
Tel. 201 945 4044

Moritz Embroidery Works, Inc.
Pocono Mt. Ind. Park
Route 940 Box 187
Mt. Pocono, PA 18344
Tel. 800 533 4183
FAX 717 839 9430

Morris, Norma, Design Products
110 West 40th St Rm 306
New York, NY 10018
Tel. 212 730 0758
FAX 212 691 1923

Nalbandian Realty
12 B1 - State Plaza Center
Old Tappan, NJ 07675
Tel. 201 666 0007

Narcisco Ferreira de Oliveira & Filhos
Largo Delfim Ferreira, Apt 3
4481 Vila do conde
Portugal
Tel. 52 631 021
FAX 52 632 881

National Association of Uniform
Manufacturers and Distributors
1156 Ave of the Americas
New York, NY 10036
Tel. 212 869 0670
FAX 212 575 2847

National Felt
160 5th Ave.
New York, NY 10010
Tel. 212 243 7729
FAX 212 243 5422

National Knitwear & Sportswear Ass'n
386 Park Ave.
New York, NY 10016
Tel. 212 683 7520

National Merchandise Show, Inc.
42 Bayview Ave.
Manhassett, NY 11030
Tel. 516 627 4000
FAX 516 365 5844

National Sporting Goods Ass'n
1699 Wall St.
Mount Prospect, IL 60056
Tel. 312 439 4000

National Steel Rule Die
17 West 17th St.
New York, NY 10011
Tel. 212 243 2680

National Supply Co., Inc.
549 West 13th Street
Apopka, FL 32703
Tel. 407 889 4874
FAX 407 889 0865

Nationwide Die Steel
& Machinery Inc.
1620 Hillcrest Dr.
Desoto, MO 63020
Tel. 314 586 7979
FAX 314 586 7980

New York Connection
516 5th Ave.
New York, NY 10036
Tel. 212 221 1050

New York Pret/Designers Network
225 West 34th St., #10FL
New York, NY 10122
Tel. 800 843 7738
FAX 212 736 0027

New York Textile Design Center
110 West 40th St., Suite 304
New York, NY 10018
Tel. 212 398 6607

Nielsen, Henry, Inc.
174 Lakeside Boulevard
Oakland, NJ 07436
Tel. 201 869 8173

Nomura (American) Corp.
60 East 42nd St.
New York, NY 10165
Tel. 212 867 6684
FAX 212 697 3202

Noonan I D Products
252 Churchill Lane
Ballwin, MO 63011
Tel. 314 394 7252

Ontario Die Co. of America
2735 20th St.
Port Huron, MI 48061
Tel. 519 576 8950
FAX 519 576 3670

Opal Embroidery Co., Ltd
#3, 4623 Manilla Rd., S.E.
Calgary, AB, Canada T2G 4B6
Tel. 403 287 0054
FAX 403 287 9456

Otten, Josef Textilwerke
A 6845 Hohenems
Austria
Tel. 5576 2304 314
FAX 5576 2139

Overseas Publishers Reps
47 West 34th Street
New York, NY 10018
Tel. 212 764 5695
FAX 212 465 8938

P & F Equipment Co.
Route 2, Box 310A
Stokesdale, NC 27357
Tel. 919 548 6598
FAX 919 548 6599

P & G Machinery Repair Corp.
140 Cedar Road
New Milford, NJ 07646
Tel. 201 943 5055

Palmetto Int'l Expositions
PO Box 5823
Greenville, SC 29606
Tel. 803 233 2562
FAX 803 233 0619

Pantograms
6807 S. Macdell Ave.
Tampa, FL 33611
Tel. 800 872 1555
FAX 813 831 0441

Paragon Tape Service
PO Box 580041
Orlando, FL 32858
Tel. 407 293 6806

Parsons School of Design
66 West 12th St.
New York, NY 10011
Tel. 212 741 5600

Paws Punching
523 W 24th St.
Norfolk, VA 23517
Tel. 804 627 9169

Pellon Sales Corp., MA
20 Industrial Drive
Cheimsford, MA 01824
Tel. 508 250 8323
FAX 508 256 1620

Pellon Sales Corp., NY
119 West 40th St.
New York, NY 10018
Tel. 212 391 6300

Pellon Sales Corp., PA
850 Henderson Blvd., Bldg. 10
Folcroft, PA 19032
Tel. 215 534 4515
FAX 215 534 0583

Pellon Sales Corp., TX
2120 Hutton Dr., #600
Carrollton, TX 75006
Tel. 214 241 1823
FAX 214 241 0829

Pellon Sales Midwest
2105 Atlantic St.
N Kansas City, MO 64116
Tel. 816 842 6420
FAX 816 472 6424

Pennsylvania Sewing Research Corp.
1321 E Drinker St.
Dunmore, PA 18512
Tel. 717 344 4000
FAX 717 343 0618

Perez Bros
Ave Escorial 719 Caparra Terr.
Rio Piedras, Puerto Rico 00920
Tel. 809 783 0200

Perfect Steel Rule Die Corp.
604 Union
Brooklyn, NY 11215
Tel 718 855 3970

Perforated Pattern Co., Inc.
351 West 35th St.
New York, NY 10001
Tel. 212 563 5278
FAX 212 967 5875

Permess Americas, Inc.
Orchard Mills
PO Box 186, Wilbraham Rd.
Monson, MA 01057
Tel. 413 267 5888

Peterson Steel Rule Die Co.
220 Gracie Place
Hackensack, NJ 07601
Tel. 201 343 5030

Pfaff Industriemaschinen GmbH
Kimplestr 280
D-4150 Krefeld 1, Germany
Tel. 0631 200-0
FAX 0631 17202

Pfaff/Schaftex Inc.
PO Box 1123
Taylors, SC 29687
Tel. 803 244 6045
FAX 803 268 6508

Philadelphia College of Textiles & Science
Schoolhouse Lane & Henry Ave.
Philadelphia, PA 19144
Tel. 215 951 2930
FAX 215 951 2615

Picchi SPA
via Marcella Tempesti 13, C.P. 241
50047 Prato (FI), Italy
Tel. 0574 4561
FAX 574 456260

Pratt Institute
295 Lafayette St.
New York, NY 10011
Tel. 212 925 8481

Press Magazine
5951 S. Middlefield Rd.
Littleton, CO 80123
Tel. 303 798 1274

Prima Die Co., Inc.
3546 East 15th St.
Los Angeles, CA 90023
Tel. 213 268 3434
FAX 213 268 6055

Professional
96 Spring St.
New York, NY 10012
Tel. 212 966 0955
FAX 212 431 7678

Progressive Service Die Co.
2720 Clark Ave.
St Louis, MO 63103
Tel. 314 531 4300
FAX 314 531 4401

Punch Line
6414 Rodeo Drive
Wichita, KS 67226
Tel. 316 744 1635
FAX 316 744 0013

QST Industries Inc.
5 West 37th Street
New York, NY 10018
Tel. 212 764 2828
FAX 212 575 2352

Quality Steel Rule Die Co., Inc.
325 Hudson St.
Hackensack, NJ 07601
Tel. 201 488 0034

R.N.G. Enterprises, Inc.
550 W. Cienega Ave #G
San Dimas, CA 91773
Tel. 714 599 0996
FAX 714 599 6279

Rainbow Monogram, Inc.
335 N.E. 59th Terrace
Miami, FL 33137
Tel. 305 757 1189
FAX 305 757 0553

Reflective Images
618-B Guilford College Rd.
Greensboro, NC 27409
Tel. 919 852 6448
FAX 919 855 6931

Rimoldi of America, Inc.
2001 N.W. 79th Ave
Miami, FL 33126
Tel. 305 477 9943
FAX 305 477 9950

Robex/Tec International
512 7th Ave, 2nd Floor
New York, NY 10018
Tel. 212 944 8928
FAX 212 944 8968

Robison Anton Textile Co.
175 Bergen Blvd.
Fairview, NJ 07022
Tel. 201 941 0500
FAX 201 941 8994

Rochelle Fabrics
526 7th St.
New York, NY 10018
Tel. 212 819 0590
FAX 212 819 1720

Rubenstein Bros. Co., Inc.
865 Hodge Street, St Laurent
Montreal, Quebec
Canada H4N 2B1
Tel. 514 747 2929
FAX 514 747 6677

Rubenstein Bros. (Ont) Ltd.
27 Kodiak Crescent
Downsview, Ontario
Canada M3J 3E5
Tel. 416 638 0638
FAX 416 638 5160

Rubenstein Bros. (West)
133 Market Ave. E.
Winnipeg, Manitoba
Canada R3B OP5
Tel. 204 943 5526
FAX 204 957 5880

SAAC, Specialty Adv. Ass'n of California
Box 2037
Simi Valley, CA 93062
Tel. 805 520 9322
FAX 805 520 9785

SAAGNY, Specialty Adv. Ass'n of Greater NY
SAAGNY Expo Office Suite 304
179 Allyn Street
Hartford, CT 06103
Tel. 203 246 6566
FAX 203 249 3631

SAAI Specialty Advertising Ass'n International
1404 Walnut Hill Lane
Irving , TX 75038
Tel. 214 580 0404

SCS USA
9631 Northeast Colfax
Portland, OR 97220
Tel. 503 252 1452

S.F.T. Fashion Team, S.R.L.
Via Vetreria 1 Bldg., Como 90
22070 Grandate (COMO)
Italy
Tel. 31 452 566
FAX 31 452 632

Safety and Security Systems, (Div.)
3M Center Bldg 225 4N 14
St. Paul, MN 55144
Tel. 800 328 7098

Sal-Bee Machinery International
419 Allen St.
Hackensack, NJ 07601
Tel. 201 487 7702
FAX 201 487 0753

Salus Textile Co.
3176 Pullman Street #108
Costa Mesa, CA 92626
Tel. 714 557 4138
FAX 714 557 8278

Sasson Brothers Emb., Corp.
312 Bergen Blvd.
Fairview, NJ 07022
Tel. 201 945 4009

Saurer, Adolph Limited
CH 9320 Arbon, Switzerland
Tel. 071 46 91 11
FAX 071 46 13 35

Saurer Corp., Textile Machinery
PO Box 27095
Greenville, SC 29616
Tel. 803 297 1500
FAX 803 297 9688

Saurer Embroidery Service Center
675 Grand Ave.
Ridgefield, NJ 07657
Tel. 201 941 8080
FAX 201 941 8719

Saxon Textile Corp.
89 Franklin St.
New York, NY 10013
Tel. 212 966 3680
FAX 212 966 9023

Schiffli Lace & Embr. Assoc. Inc.
8555 Tonnelle Ave.
North Bergen, NJ 07407
Tel. 201 868 7200

Schlaepfer, Jakob & Co., AG
11 Teufener Str.
CH 9001 St. Gallen, Switzerland
Tel. 071 20 11 40
FAX 071 22 14 18

Schlesinger Industries
1106 Edgewater Ave.
Ridgefield, NJ 07657
Tel. 201 943 5030
FAX 201 943 5015

Ferd. Schmetz Needle Corp.
PO Box 23438
Knoxville, TN 37922
Tel. 615 966 4050
FAX 615 966 4619

Schoen Machinery U.S.A.
901 N. Nicholas Blvd.
Elk Grove Village, IL 60007
Tel. 708 956 1900
FAX 708 956 7939

Schott International Inc.
1340 E. Archwood Ave.
Akron, OH 44306
Tel. 216 773 7851
FAX 216 773 7856

Schwabe, Herman, Inc.
147 Prince St.
Brooklyn, NY 11201
Tel. 718 237 1700

Sedeco, Inc.
1124 West Fuller Ave.
Fort Worth, TX 76115
Tel. 817 926 2221
FAX 817 927 8643

Semco/Saurer Textile Systems
Embroidery Machine Division
CH 9320 St. Gallen, Switzerland
FAX 071 46 1335

Sequins International Inc.
110 West 40th St.
New York, NY 10018
Tel. 212 221 3121
FAX 212 869 4319

Sequins U.S.A.
34-20 45th St.
Long Island City, NY 11101
Tel. 718 937 9090
FAX 718 361 7219

Sew Canada Industries, Inc.
66 Drumlin Circle, #5
Concord, Ontario, Canada L4K 3E9
Tel. 416 660 7470
FAX 416 669 6019

Sewing Machine Exchange
1840 S. Michigan Ave.
Chicago, IL 60616
Tel. 312 842 3700

Sewing Systems
100 W. Hoover #14
Mesa, AZ 85210
Tel. 800 628 7951
FAX 602 844 0778

Shamash & Son, S, Inc.
42 West 39th St., 12 Floor
New York, NY 10018
Tel. 212 840 3111
FAX 212 575 7891

Shima Seiki U.S.A., Inc.
22 Abeel Rd.
Cranbury, NJ 08512
Tel. 609 655 4788
FAX 609 655 3989

Shuttle Repair Service
70 West Columbia Ave.
Palisades Park, NJ 07650
Tel. 201 945 0740

Sieber, Hugo
Heldstr 26
CH 9443, Windau, Switzerland
Tel. 071 72 23 61
FAX 071 72 42 81

Silk Ltd.
350 North New Orleans
Chicago, IL 60654
Tel. 312 329 1678

Silverman Products and Textiles, Inc.
205 West 39th St.
New York, NY 10018
Tel. 212 944 8200
FAX 212 869 8881

Sloan Machine Co.
589 Essex St.
Lynn, MA 01902
Tel. 617 593 1887

Soltex Thread Co.
30 West 24th St.
New York, NY 10011
Tel. 212 243 2000

Sommers Inc.
PO Box 1910
High Point, NC 27261
Tel. 919 886 7111
FAX 919 886 7509

Southern Star Embroidery, Inc.
5040 Virginia Beach Blvd. #107
Virginia Beach, VA 23462
Tel. 804 552 0500

Sparten Mills
111 West 40th
New York, NY 10018
Tel. 212 764 0580

Spartex Inc.
PO Box 6365
Spartanburg, SC 29304
Tel. 803 585 7186
FAX 803 582 0837

Spectrum Punching
1800 S. Flower St.
Los Angeles, CA 90015
Tel. 213 746 4040
FAX 213 747 1028

Speedy Die., Inc.
151-15 W Industry Ct.
Deer Park, NY 11729
Tel. 516 586 1811
FAX 516 586 1816

Spinnerei und Webereien
Zell-Schonau AG
Postfach 1120
7863 Zell im Wiensental
Germany
Tel. 7625 12273
FAX 7625 12339

Springs Industries, Inc.
104 West 40th St
New York, NY 10018
Tel. 212 556 6000

Stahls
20600 Stephans Drive
St Clair Shores, MI 48080
Tel. 313 772 6161
FAX 313 772 6237

Stevens, J.P. & Co., Inc.
1185 Ave of the Americas
New York, NY 10036
Tel. 212 930 2000

Stitches Magazine
7009 S. Potomac
Englewood, CO 80112
Tel. 303 397 7600
FAX 303 397 7919

Stitchmaster, Inc.
6188 Gulliford College Rd.
Greensboro, NC 27409
Tel. 919 852 6448
FAX 919 855 6931

Strachman Associates, Inc.
151 West 40th St.
New York, NY 10018
Tel. 212 695 5688
FAX 212 695 6908

Streamline Technical Services
Tel. 817 261 4711

Stumpwork Society
Sylvia Fishman
PO Box 122
Bogota, NJ 07603

Stutz-Horowitz & Co.
42 West 39th St.
New York, NY 10018
Tel. 212 719 5555
FAX 212 302 6167

Stylecrest Fabrics, Ltd.
215 West 39th St.
New York, NY 10018
Tel. 212 354 0123
FAX 212 921 7679

Super Show, The
1450 NE 123rd St.
North Miami, FL 33161
Tel. 305 893 8771
FAX 305 893 8783

Superior Threads & Yarns
3065 Kalakaua Ave., #10
Honolulu, HI 96815
Tel. 808 923 3978
FAX 808 885 5655

Superior Threads & Yarns
PO Box 1213
Kamuela, HI 96743
Tel. 808 885 7049
FAX 808 885 3312

Supersil S.A.
Malabia St. 140
1414 Buenos Aires-Capital
Argentina
Tel. 854 0045/8
FAX 541 856 3074

Tajima America Corp.
550 Commerce Street
Franklin Lakes, NJ 07417
Tel. 201 405 1201
FAX 202 405 1205

Tajima Industries Ltd.
19-22 Shirakabe-3 chome
Higashi-ku, Nagoya 461 Japan
Tel. 052 932 3811
FAX 052 932 2457

Tajima East
620 Kinderkamack Rd
River Edge, NJ 07661
Tel. 800 869 9776

Tajima West
12401 Slauson Ave., Suite C
Whittier, CA 90606
Tel. 213 945 9526
FAX 213 945 8155

Tandler Textile, Inc.
104 West 40th St.
New York, NY 10018
Tel. 212 730 1212

Ted Thorsen Co. (Needle Trader)
Box 263
Wilkes Barre, PA 18703
Tel. 717 288 8426

Telepunch
4N-221-84 Court
Bloomingdale, IL 60108
Tel. 708 260 9195

Te-Ver
via Chiere 64
10020 Torino, Andezeno
Italy
Tel. 11 946 4253
FAX 11 946 4675

Texa Mill S.A.
Domingo Orue, 983 Surquillo
Lima 34, Peru
Tel. 14 410059
FAX 14 413987

Textile Graphic Designs, Inc.
350 5th Ave. #603
New York, NY 10018
Tel. 212 947 0270
FAX 212 639 1832

Textile Industries
1430 Broadway
New York, NY 10018
Tel. 212 930 7200
FAX 212 930 7213

Textilforum
Postfach 5944
D3000 Hanover 1, Germany

Textile View/Trend Union
90 Riverside Drive #9D
New York, NY 10024
Tel. 212 724 3835
FAX 212 724 3129

Thalheim Expositions, Inc.
42 Bayview Ave.
Manhassett, NY 11030
Tel. 516 627 4000
FAX 516 365 5844

Thread at Work
425 West Allen Ave., #109
San Dimas, CA 91773
Tel. 714 599 7666
FAX 714 599 3645

T.I.P.
PO Box 5161
New York, NY 10185
Tel. 212 289 0267

TMG Textil Maqnuel Goncalves, s.a.
S. Cosme do Vale, P.O.B. 14
4761 V.N.de Famalicao
Codex, Portugal
Tel. 52 72202
FAX 52 23460

TOSA Products, Inc.
1145 E. Main St.
Lakeland, FL 33801
Tel. 813 682 7254

Toscolaniera S.P.A.
Viale Labriola 231
50045 Montemtemurlo
Italy 574 721621

Traphagen School of Fashion
257 Park Ave. South
New York, NY 10017
Tel. 212 673 0300

Triple Stitch
6 New Haven Rd.
Prospect, CT 06712
Tel. 203 758 6303
FAX 203 758 3231

Troy Corp.
2701 North Normandy
Chicago, IL 60635
Tel. 312 227 2400
FAX 312 804 9600

Troy Sunshade Co.
607 Riffle Ave.
Greenville, OH 45531
Tel. 800 833 8769

Ulster Weaving Co., Ltd.
148 Madison Ave.
New York, NY 10016
Tel. 212 684 5534
FAX 212 689 0937

Ultramatic Embroidery Machine Co., Inc.
60 United Drive
North Haven, CT 06473
Tel. 203 234 7606
FAX 203 234 7562

Ultrasuede, Div. Springs Mills,
104 West 40th
New York, NY 10018
Tel. 212 556 6000

United Numerical Controls
1400 East 28th St.
Long Beach, CA 90806
Tel. 213 426 9386
FAX 212 426 0208

Universal Textile Brokers
108 West 39th St.
New York, NY 10018
Tel. 212 398 0505
FAX 212 764 5139

University of Missouri
137 Stanley Hall
Dept. of Textiles/Apparel Management
Columbia, MO 65211
Tel. 314 882 6634
FAX 314 882 5127

University of Wisconsin-Stout
Dept. of Apparel, Textile and Design
Menomonie, WI 54751
Tel. 715 232 2483
Fax 715 232 2588

Vandenfil S.A.I.A.
Santiago del Estro 315
RA-1075 Buenos Aires
Argentina
Tel. 1 38 1212
FAX 1 11 1205

Variety Merchandise Show, Inc.
98 Cuttermill Rd.
Great Neck, NY 11030
Tel. 516 627 4000
FAX 516 365 5844

Velcro USA, Inc.
406 Brown Ave.
Manchester, NH 03108
Tel. 603 669 4892
FAX 603 669 9271

Viking Products, Inc.
4600 Highlands Pkwy., Suite 1
Smyrna, GA 30082
Tel. 404 434 3366
FAX 404 434 3368

Vogue School of Fashion Design
462 Broadway
New York, NY 10013
Tel. 212 966 7250

VR Antriebstehnik AG
Achslenstr 13
CH 9016 St. Gallen
Switzerland
Tel. 071 35 20 60

Wala Fabrics, Inc.
450 7th Ave.
New York, NY 10123
Tel. 212 279 0111

Waldon Textiles
566 7th Ave.
New York, NY 10018
Tel. 212 221 8555
FAX 212 221 8558

Weisbrod-Zurrer AG Ltd.
Tel. 1 764 0366
FAX 1 764 1851

Weiss Mfg. & Tool Co.
520 66th St.
West New York, NJ 07093
Tel. 201 868 6865

Wellington Custom Fabrics
416 12th St, Suite 116
Columbus, GA 31901
Tel. 404 327 1891
FAX 404 327 8880

West Point Pepperell
2401-B 1st Street
Opelika, AL 36801
Tel. 404 645 7269

Western Numerical Control
6985 A3 Via Deloro
San Jose, CA 95119
Tel. 408 281 7575
FAX 408 365 1935

Wiesner Publishing
7009 S. Potomac
Englewood, CO 80112
Tel. 303 097 7600
FAX 303 397 7619

Wilcom Australia
16 Vine Street
Chippendale, Sydney
NSW 2008, Australia
Tel. 612 319 3866

Wilcom Japan, Inoue Bldg
3-12-6 Nihonbashi
Ningyo-cho Chua-ku
Tokyo 103 Japan
Tel. 03 669 9341

Wilcom USA Inc.
1701 Golf Road
Rolling Meadows, IL 60008
Tel. 708 806 0000
FAX 708 290 1111

Wilcom Europe
Postfach 1552
St George/Schw.
D7725, Germany
Tel. 49 7724 3030
FAX 49 7724 1060

Women's Wear Daily
Fairchild Pub.
7 East 12th St.
New York, NY 10003
Tel. 212 741 6726
FAX 212 337 3426

Yamzaki Thread Co., Ltd., (Cupie)
1-24-24 Tamatsukuri
Chuo-ku, Osaka 541, Japan

Yarnell Fabrics Corp.
48 West 37th St.
New York, NY 10018
Tel. 212 563 1270

YLI Corp.
482 N. Freedom Blvd.
Provo, Utah 84601
Tel. 800 854 1932
FAX 801 377 3900

Zenith Lace & Embroidery Corp.
312 Bergen Boulevard
Fairview, NJ 07022
Tel. 201 945 0590

Zines, MD
8121 Auburn Blvd.
Citrus Heights, CA 95610
Tel. 916 726 5553
FAX 916 726 2440

ZSK Stickmaschinen GmbH
Magdeburger Str. 38-40
D-4150 Krefeld-Bockum, Germany
Tel. 02151 444 0
FAX 02151 444 170

ZSK/USA California
2727 N. Grove Ind. Drive, #145
Fresno, CA 93727
Tel. 209 454 8173
FAX 209 454 1017

ZSK/USA Ltd.
42 Franklin St.
Laconia, NH 03246
Tel. 603 527 1205
FAX 603 524 0432

CHAPTER X

COPYRIGHTS AND TRADEMARKS

Copyright, in the simplest sense, is a system for protection of a person's creative rights in certain literary or artistic works which that person has created. Such rights are derived from Article 1. Section 8 Clause 8 of the United States Constitution, which empowers Congress to protect the writings of authors. From this foundation, Congress through the years has enacted various legislation to provide such protection. At the present time the basis for all matters of copyright is the 1976 "Copyright Act".

Under the copyright act, protection extends to "original works of authorship fixed in any tangible medium of expression now known or later developed from which there can be perceived, reproduced or otherwise communicated either directly or with the aid of a machine or device".

The Act sets forth seven general categories of works which are eligible for protection:

1. Literary works (defined as "works expressed in words or numbers, including books, manuscripts, periodicals and computer programs");
2. Musical works, including any accompanying words;
3. Dramatic works, including any accompanying music, stage plays, screen plays and television plays;
4. Pantomimes and choreographic works;

5. Pictorial, graphic and sculptured works, including fine arts, photographs, prints, maps, globes, technical drawings, logos, architectural blueprints, diagrams, statues and figures;
6. Motion pictures and other audiovisual works and
7. Sound recordings, including musical, spoken or other sounds (but not sounds accompanying motion pictures or other audiovisual works) regardless of the material nature of the objects (discs, tapes, compact discs or other phone records).

It is important to note that this list is not exclusive. However, copyright protection does not extend to the following:

1. Useful articles such as industrial products;
2. Creations that have not been fixed in a tangible form of expression, such as unwritten speeches;
3. Titles, names, short phrases, telegrams or slogans; passages;
4. Typographic facts, ornamentation, lettering, coloring, lists of ingredients or contents and blank forms;
5. Ideas, procedures, methods, systems, processes, concepts, principals or discoveries, regardless of the form in which described, explained, illustrated or embodied in such work;
6. Factual information;
7. Works consisting entirely of common information, such as height and weight charts, tape measures and rulers, lists taken from public documents or common sources; and
8. Works of the U.S. Government except for certain standard reference data prepared by the Secretary of Commerce and Copyrights which have been transferred to the Federal Government.

Both published and unpublished works are eligible for copyright protection.

The originality requirement of the Copyright Act is not a difficult standard to satisfy. Indeed, copyrights can be secured for works possessing a minimal amount of creative authorship and design. Thus, while a unique design created entirely from one's imagination would be eligible for protection, the total and exact reproduction of an oriental rug design in a fabric would not. However, because the number and variety of creations are virtually unlimited, it would be virtually impossible for the copyright office to determine whether a work submitted for registration is original or copied. Accordingly, the U.S. Copyright Office will register a work on the assumption that the work is original, unless the Copyright Office recognizes the work as not original. Thus, it is clear that the one who copies bears the burden of proving that the work which he copied was not original and that the copyright claimant improperly obtained registration of his claim of copyright. Establishing such a defense may prove very costly and time consuming, and therefore it is recommended that one seek legal advice from a licensed attorney who practices in the area of copyright law before embarking on a program of copying any work.

Of particular concern to those in the embroidery industry, is the issue of registering a copyright. From a legal perspective, it is not necessary to register a work with the copyright office in order for the work to be entitled to protection: a right to such protection arises at the moment a work is created (provided the substantive requirements discussed above are satisfied). From a practical standpoint, however, it is essential that one who creates a work secure registration with the copyright office. There are three primary reasons for registering a work. First and most importantly, a registration certificate from the copyright office entitles an author to the right to sue infringers in Federal Court. Because the Federal Judiciary possess exclusive jurisdiction over copyright matters, one seeking relief against infringers will be unable to bring suit unless that person possesses a registration certificate for the work in question. Second, a registration certificate establishes an important evidential presumption in an infringement suit in that a registration certificate is prima facie evidence of the validity of the copyright and the facts stated in the certificate when the work is registered within five years after the work is first published. This is a significant benefit to the creator because it shifts the burden to the alleged infringer to prove that the copyright is invalid. Finally, registration entitles a creator who wins an infringement action to statutory damages, which includes attorneys fees. A registration certificate entitles the work to the protection for the life of the author plus 50 years.

In order to register a work, one must complete an application form provided by the Copyright Office. A completed copyright application includes the application form, two copies of the work to be registered (one copy if the work is unpublished); and the registration fee.

Copyright forms may be obtained from the following:
Registrar of Copyrights
Library of Congress
Washington, DC 20559

Related to copyright registration is the question of copyright notice. Prior to March 1, 1989, the Copyright Act required that the copyrighted work bear a copyright notice which included:

1. The appropriate markings consisting of the words "Copyright" or "Copr" or the letter "C" enclosed in a circle.

2. The date of the first publication of the work.
3. The name of the copyright owner.

The notice requirement was eliminated upon U.S. adherence to the Berne Convention For the Protection of Library and Artistic Works. U.S. adherence to this international copyright convention was initiated on March 1, 1989, the effective date of the "Berne Implementation Act of 1988"

Accordingly, works published after March 1, 1989 do not require the use of the copyright notice. Such works are protected irrespective of notice. However, works first published before March 1, 1989 must still bear proper copyright notice in order to be fully protected.

For works which must bear notice, such notice must be placed on every work sold, placed on sale, or publicly distributed in any manner. Further, such notice must be permanently affixed to the work, and each copy or repeat of the work. Notice affixed by means of removable labels and hang tags is insufficient and therefore, such practice should be avoided.

The author, based on his experiences in dealing with licensed products, has found that it is at times difficult to satisfy the notice requirement on embroidered items. For example, in many instances, the use of different color threads to embroider the notice markings will distort the design of the overall piece of work. However, markings created using the same thread of the same color as the overall design may not be visible. In addition, lettering in embroidery is not legible if it is less than 3/16" in size. Further, if a label bearing the notice affixed to the back of the embroidery, and the embroidery is subsequently heat sealed or sewn to a garment or cap, the notice will become invisible.

Problems also arise if the notice is added to yard goods, particularly if the stitches required for the notice are more than that necessary for the design itself. Additionally, if the repeats are small and notice is required in each repeat, the design can be completely distorted or destroyed. This in turn raises the question as to whether notice is required on an allover fabric. If the repeats are 4/4 or 8/4 and notice would be required for each repeat, perhaps every one or two inches, the same with a vertical repeat of short length, the design could contain more stitches than the design itself and become a design of copyright notices. Factoring in the total length and width of the fabric it becomes extremely difficult to determine where the markings should be placed. Further, the pattern cutter laying out his fabric for cutting the goods into various parts so the garment can be constructed, would have no idea where the mark would be for each part. This raises the question of where the embroidered mark should be placed. In one length of embroidered fabric, say 10 yards, with different size parts: pants legs, sleeves, pockets, collars, cuffs etc., you can see that the mark would be difficult to place, not only to guarantee the mark shows on the parts, but the parts could also be cut in various sizes. It is clear how impractical such a copyright notice would be.

Copyright notices have been affixed to emblems and appliques where possible. In many instances copyright holders have granted permission to eliminate the marks altogether. In other cases, copyright holders have given instructions to stitch the notice if possible, even if such notice was not legible, with the intention that the embroidery could be enlarged enough to show that the stitches could indicate a copyright mark. This could also be proved from the original enlarged drawing. It also applies to Union bugs which must appear on some embroidered works.

Protection for these embroidered forms has been lax and the laws have not helped solve the problem. The author has never heard of a case that produced a fine, much less correct the problem or compensate the original designer.

TRADEMARKS

The term "Trademark" includes any word, name, symbol or device, or any combination adapted and used by a manufacturer or merchant capable to identify his goods or services or distinguish them from those manufactured or serviced by others.

Trademarks may be protected whether or not they are registered with the appropriate federal agency (which is the U.S. Patent and Trademark Office). Federal registration of a work protects the registrant with the following procedural and substantive legal advantages over non-registration:

1. Federal jurisdiction in infringement actions;
2. The recovery of profits, damages and costs and in certain circumstances, treble damages and attorneys fees;
3. Registration is prima facie evidence of the registrants' ownership and exclusive right to use the mark, as well as prima facie proof of the continual use of the mark, dating back to the original filing date of their application for registration;
4. Registration constitutes constructive notice to the world of a claim of ownership of the mark and eliminates a depose of good faith adaption of the mark by another party.
5. A registration may become incontestable as conclusive widening of the registrants' exclusive right to use the mark

6. Registration may be used to stop the importation into the U.S. of articles bearing an infringing mark through recordation with the U.S. Customs Service.

In filing a registration, it is necessary for the registrant to assert that the mark is in use in interstate or foreign commerce and to allege that to the best of your knowledge, no one else has a right to use that mark. Alternatively, a registrant can file an application to register a mark which has not yet been used in commerce, so long as the registrant possesses a bona fide intention to use the mark in commerce. In the latter case registration will not actually be granted until the registrant files a verified statement, together with samples, that the registrant has actually used the mark in interstate commerce.

The following marks may not be registered:

Marks which consist of immoral, deceptive or scandalous matter or disparage or falsely suggest a connection with persons, living or dead, institutions, beliefs or national symbols; marks which use the flag, coat of arms or insignia of the United States, a State, a municipality, or a foreign nation; marks which use the name, portrait or signature of a living individual without consent; a mark which is similar to an existing mark which is either registered or is a trade name which has been used and not abandoned in the U.S., so as likely to cause confusion; marks which can not be registered unless the applicant proves secondary meaning, i.e., marks which are descriptive of the goods, geographically descriptive or surnames. Further, there are many names and designs which have special protection by law including the 5 rings of the Olympics, the Red Cross, Boy Scouts of America, Girl Scouts and other special nonprofit organizations.

Registrations issued after Nov. 16, 1989 must be renewed every 10 years. Within the 5th year after registration, the mark owner must file an affidavit that the mark is still in use on the goods specified. Otherwise the registration will be automatically cancelled on the 6th anniversary of the registration date.

Notice of registration is indicated by the application of the mark "R" "Registered in the U.S. Patent Office," or "Reg. U.S. Part. Off." to the trademark. Failure to provide notice does not invalidate a registration; it simply means that profits and damages may not be recoverable by the registrant in an infringement action. Thus, the registrant may still bring an action for infringement of a trademark which lacks actual notice.

Accordingly, do not be fooled into believing that an embroidered patch without the notice of registration automatically allows you to copy the mark. Let it be the assumption in your design studio that all Trademarks known are registered, whether or not the registration notice (R) appears. For instance, the author used to manufacture many patches indirectly for "STP" and never made one with the registration notice thereon. Injunctions can be granted even though the statutory notice is not used. You must assume it applies to all marks. Theoretically, permission should always be requested from the company or person owning the mark. Any valid trademark may be enforced even though not registered.

Many trademarks owners require embroidered emblems or decals as reproductions of their trademarks. When a mark might be used to denote a service and is registered, then the mark is only used legally by those licensed by the owner of such mark.

The advertising advantages afforded through the use of embroidered emblems are immeasurable. In the last few years, owners of trademarks have discovered the value of licensing and now issue licenses to retail stores and garment manufacturers to use their marks, with or without a fee. For many years, however, embroidery manufacturers produced emblems for sale without permission. This practice was determined to be improper in the late 1970's in the Dallas Cap & Emblem case. In that case, the Supreme Court refused to review a decision made by the U.S. Court of Appeals for the 5th Circuit that a mark, even if not applied to a product may not be sold without the permission of the markholder.

Unfortunately, the method of requesting permission does not always work in practice. Emblem manufacturers receive hundreds of orders per week, sometimes directly from the trademarks owner, many times from intermediate sources, independent salesmen or advertising agencies. To obtain permission for each and every order is just not practical. Since very little is assumed to be in the public domain, everything must be assumed to be owned by the company or name on the patch.

Emblem manufacturers always have the question of obtaining copyright or trademark permission. However, because time is always a factor and orders are usually stitched for known parties, production commences without the required letter of permission. When permission is required, then someone within the company that holds those rights must be contacted. This can cause a real problem, putting together the buying agent with the legal department. Try sometime to contact, in a large company, the people who can authorize the manufacture of embroidered emblems when your supplier is an independent agent. It can be very, very difficult.

For the embroiderer to be protected, he or she must document the design as it is being formed, i.e., document the sketch, the enlargement, the punching and the sample. If you can prove originality, then it is not necessary to register the trademark. The premise being, you might have to prove originality, so be prepared to offer the documentation, whether you are being questioned or you wish to question someone else's right to the design.

A case in point is the design created by the author in 1977 which was not copyrighted or trademarked and has been stitched by just about every embroiderer in the world who makes emblems.

RULES FOR COPYING

The answer is simple: DON'T!

It is easier and safer to create a new design out of your own imagination, as it must be presumed to be unknown. Simple alteration of an existing design does not constitute the creation of a new design. The ultimate test for whether a design is new or merely a copy of a copyrighted design is an objective one: would the design appear to be different to the average person? It does not make a difference whether 5, 10, or more changes have been made to the design, the question is whether the "new" design represents, in any way, the original design, or in legal terms, whether the "new" design is "substantially similar" to the original.

A related test exists for the copying of trademarks; this test looks at whether the altered design could confuse a buyer into thinking the altered design is the same design or is representative of the same product or supportive of the same organization as the original. The question often arises with a name. For example, consider the hypothetical situation of an unlicensed person selling jackets with the name "Giants" embroidered across the back, near Giants stadium. In the strictest sense, there is no problem of selling a jacket with the name "Giants" embroidered on it, however, if the colors used are the same as those used by the NFL football team, the jacket is the same as or similar to an authorized "Giants" jacket, the lettering is the same style as that used in the authorized jacket and the jacket is being sold at the gathering place of New York Giant fans, this would clearly constitute trademark infringement. Changing one of these variables, such as the style of lettering would still constitute infringement. However, completely changing the colors, style of lettering, style of jacket and the place of sale would probably not result in a buyer being misled into believing the product is representative of a New York Giants jacket. (Just as long as the changes do not lead the buyer into thinking the jacket is representative of a San Francisco baseball product!)

In any event, it certainly does not pay to copy either copyrights or trademarks without written permission.

Experiences from life:

In the opinion of the author, there are U.S. Patents and copyrights that have been issued which are unfair or outright incorrect.

Appearing as an embroidery expert at a court case where the author held in his hand the proof that someone did not invent a particular method of stitching and finishing embroidery, only to have it discarded by the judge because the time of discovery was past, is a case in point. That was 10 years ago and as this is written in 1991 you will see advertisements claiming the same Patent, which involves laser (hot knife) cutting, where some of the background fabric is visible after an applique is laser cut, is really a patented process.

The author has seen stitch types copyrighted which appear in publications 10 years before the copyright date.

It is difficult to believe that curved lettering could be patented, when, as a pattern maker for 25 years prior to the date of the existing patent, we designed and punched hundreds of curved lettering emblems. Besides, in the early and middle 1970's software programs could not be patented. How then can curved lettering, programmed with a historically old mathematical formula be patented? It exists.

Unfortunately, if you don't agree with the patent or copyright, the only way to overturn the decision is to contest the owner's rights in court; that doesn't pay simply because of the time and legal costs to the challenger.

Who owns the design?

There are many judgments with reference to creation of the design, its use, and subsequent responsibility for those who reproduce and sell these designs commercially. It seems that art created while in the employ of a company will be adjudged the property of the employer.

An interesting situation occurred when a stitcher was ordering a tape for his customer. The art was created by the original customer, the stitcher sent the design to a punch center to have the tape made, then sold it to his customer. The tape center claimed they added their punch expertise to the cutting of the tape and therefore, it could not be sold. It was made for his customer to use, but not to sell his expertise. The author's opinion: as long as a monetary payment was made and accepted the tape belonged to the purchaser.

Some tape centers have created clubs and libraries and offer these to the public. Again, if you pay for the tape then it is yours. However, if restrictive covenants are part of the sale and you sign for the same, then they govern use of the tape. Example: you can use the tape for your own machine, for orders or for sampling but the tape can not be resold. Some even go so far as to say the rights to the design and therefore, the tape belong to the tape center forever and should the business be sold with the tapes as part of the sale, the tapes must be returned to the original seller or paid for again. It all comes back to the original contract you make with the tape center.

Designs and logos copied, no matter how long in use (and still in use) can be copyrighted and/or trademarked by the original owner and therefore can not arbitrarily be reproduced in any form by others without permission. This primarily applies to long established and well known names, such as colleges. The law is unclear in this respect; in some cases this is true in others not.

It is unfortunate that most of this enforcement only came to pass in the late '70s. Until that time the question of 99% of the existing copyrights did not come into question in the embroidery industry. Before then, you could embroider any copyright without legal entanglements. Unfortunately, very few enforced their rights of protection under the law. Because you were a manufacturer of a popular auto, the embroiderers helped by advertising it through the sale of embroidered patches on caps and clothing. New copyright laws brought new rules for protection, then everyone saw the profitability of licensing. Embroiderers lost a market. The name or logo added the same aura of perfection to the licensed product as the copyrighted name implied. Another source of profit was created.

Still the orders for emblems today, most of which represent someone's copyright, are produced daily. It would be utterly impossible to conduct a business in the manufacture of screened, woven or embroidered emblems if every name had to be checked for copyright infringement and proof of the copyright owner's permission were to be sought. Most orders do not originate with the copyright holder, many requisitions are directed through third parties, established companies such as advertising agencies, advertising specialty companies, or sales companies, who have conducted this type of business since advertising promotions came into existence.

LICENSING

Licensing is the method used to approve the sale of a copyrighted or trademarked college or corporate owned logo for a fee.

It also gives you the right to reproduce an art form for a supplier of the copyright holder. For instance, Walt Disney does not want anyone to make their embroideries without knowing who the manufacturer is, where it is made and that they have final approval of the finished stitching. This is required of their suppliers as well. They will approve a particular design for a particular order, it is not a general approval.

Without the proper permission of the NFL you can not produce their logos for any of the manufacturers who they have licensed.

These rules go beyond the normal process of embroidering for licensed manufacturers; most will allow the supplier to assign their orders to embroidery contractors.

However, from the embroiderer's standpoint, the author sees nothing wrong with the manufacture of licensed items for a supplier who has been licensed for a particular design or motif. If the work is shoddy, poor quality, cheapened or in any way not representative of the licensee, then he believes it is the responsibility of the supplier who placed the order and the stitcher.

Licensees are required to report regularly all sales of licensed emblems. All contracts are different, some require names and some require you sell only licensed suppliers.

Therefore, as an embroidery contractor you may have to deal with two different situations, first the copyright holder and secondly the license holder, who are not always the same organization.

Next comes U.S. Customs, in case you made the embroideries outside the U.S.A. It is easy for corporate copyright holders or licensees to inform customs to check that licensed products do not come in from foreign countries. When goods is entered into the Government computers they can easily pick up those items that have been entered illegally. U.S. Customs will then hold the goods until a letter from the copyright holder agrees to the import of their logo and information as to where the goods were made.

In 1989, the Ford and General Motor Corporations of automobile manufacturers in the U.S. decided to protect their logo copyrights, which they have every right to do, on the sale and manufacture of embroidered emblems. The embroidery industry has stitched them since the early 1950's. People like to wear a Chevy or Ford emblem because they are proud of the auto they drive. It seems shameful that they must now pay a royalty or cease their sale completely.

Ford has eliminated the use by anyone who would want to produce a Ford emblem for resale except for those that supply Ford directly, or for Ford products which they have authorized.

General Motors has allowed the sale of their logos in the form of embroidered patches, but after approval of your workmanship they require 15% royalty on the sales of these emblems.

DON'T HAVE A COW, MAN!
BART SIMPSON
I SAVED THE PRINCESS
TURTLES
LICENSED

EMBROIDERIES
U.S. MAIL
LA CHEMISE LACOSTE
LOTUS
ROTARY INTERNATIONAL
US SKI TEAM
GEORGETOWN UNIVERSITY
HOYAS
Chevy
Gators
FIGHTIN' IRISH
NOTRE DAME
NATIONAL BASKETBALL ASSOCIATION
NBA
FANTASTIC
SUPER BOWL
XXV
NFL
UNIVERSITY OF NOTRE DAME
ND
NATIONAL FOOTBALL LEAGUE
MEMBER CLUB
Detroit Red Wings
NEW YORK
KNICKS
KNICKERBOCKERS
LOUISVILLE
SINCE 1884
MOTOR
HARLEY-DAVIDSON
CYCLES
MILWAUKEE
BUCKS
NEW YORK
RANGERS
DETROIT
LIONS

IMPORTING

The explosion in information and delivery technology has made importing foreign made emblems and embroideries a profitable endeavor. If you could find the country that had the basic knowledge and inexpensive labor and the willingness of someone to establish embroidery manufacturing then you might have production that could prove profitable to the entrepreneur. But it doesn't last forever. Countries such as Japan, Korea, Hong Kong and Taiwan all had good days, their money increased in value, wages rose and soon the cost of the item made there was equal or higher to that made without the hassle of importing by having it produced in the U.S.A. The profits on most orders were lost because of custom duties and freight plus poor deliveries and misunderstood instructions.

There might be other countries in eastern Europe, Russia or Indonesia, that will be the next great exporters. Meanwhile, we have China which has a number of domestic Schiffli plants as well as established emblem manufacturing facilities set up by Americans (Lion Bros) by Japanese (Goda Embroidery) Hong Kong Chinese (Mock) and Taiwan (Mei Chaun-Oriental-Liberty). They have all felt the effects of the political upheaval and increased wages, shortages of power, telephone and Fax service, bad deliveries and many more traumas, the same problems that any developing country would undergo.

In China, people are easily trained and can operate equipment as well as anyone. Costs are still relatively low and therefore, profitable for those established businesses. An understanding partner is basic to operation in China, you have to know the system.

The goods are sold from the manufacturing country, at a low price, then rebilled for final export at a higher price, leaving most of the profits in the exporting country thus avoiding taxes in the U.S.A. The profits remain in foreign banks.

Establishing a foreign operation is a costly gamble and we're sure Tiananmen Square caused a rise in blood pressure for many of the participants.

The same situations can arise in any country that is not stable. Let the investor beware.

Costs drove many to buy overseas, as companies who use many embroidered items decided to buy at cheap import prices.

Importing is not in itself an answer to embroidery sales in the U.S.A. The cost of duties and freight are enough to take away small profits, The increasing costs of labor and the standard of living in all Asian countries are rising to the point where the difference from the U.S. costs are negligible or, may even be higher.

U.S. CUSTOMS

U.S. Customs is well organized today. For a time in the early '80s rules and regulations did not seem to be the same in various parts of the United States.

Some of the former rules in the early 1980's allowed packages with a value of less than $250.00 to be imported free of duty. At that time it was better to send 2 packages of $250.00 each rather than a $500 value. If a parcel had no invoices with it the box went through without duty.

There are always those who take advantage and we think the one that broke the camel's back occurred when some importer sent a hundred packages to various relatives and friends at a value of $250.00 each and naturally got caught.

PLAY THE GAME BY THE RULES

Business people abroad who need accurate information about customs matters can contact customs attaches at over 14 American embassies who have these specialists assigned to their posts.

The United States adapted the harmonized commodity description and coding system in January 1989. Therefore, tariff commodity descriptions of both imports and exports conform with those of its major trading partners.

There are about 120 ports of entry where goods can be imported, some at borders others at major international airports. At these points, imports can be cleared by custom officers for entry into the United States.

Entry of goods into the U.S.A. is simple if you follow the rules for importing. Special entry documents are filed with customs at the port of entry. Imported goods are not legally entered until after the shipment has arrived and duties have been paid, then delivery is authorized.

The entry papers must include:

1. The commercial invoice which includes:
   a. The port of entry.
   b. A detailed description of the merchandise, the name by which each item is known, the quantity included in the shipment, the marks, numbers and symbols by which the product is known in the country of exportation. The numbers and marks of the packages in which the merchandise is packed.

c. The quantities in weights and measure.
d. The value of each item in the currency of the transaction.
e. The currency of payment.
f. All charges, including freight, insurance, commission, and packaging.
g. Any rebates or commissions.
h. The country of origin.
i. All goods and services not mentioned in the production, such as art work or punched tapes.
j. The invoice and all parts are to be in English.
k. Each invoice shall state the merchandise which is in each individual package. (packing list)

2. Special requirements:
   a. Each class of merchandise requires a different invoice.
   b. Different suppliers may be assembled in one shipment with various invoices.
   c. Production assists would cover other costs such as punchings or fabric or yarn which might not be included in the invoice but might be supplied free or invoiced separately.
      Such costs are dutiable since they are part of the cost of production of embroidery.

U.S. and Canada free trade agreement (FTA)

The purpose of this agreement was to promote better relations between us and our neighbor, to foster production, employment, and formulate advantageous rules governing their trade.

The law took effect on September 28, 1988. It is important for us as embroiderers, since it is to remove all tariffs progressively within a 10 year period.

Drawbacks of 99% of duty and taxes are possible within 90 days only when goods were shipped without consent, damaged or do not meet sample specifications. Such merchandise can not be destroyed but must be reexported.

All merchandise must be marked with country of origin. If not marked properly at the time of importation, a marking duty of 10% can be assessed.

Trademarks and copyrights are not protected from importation.

U.S. Customs officers and Inspectors generally work well, they are performing an important job. They expect you to follow the rules for everyone's protection, don't try to pull the wool over their eyes. They know the cost of an item as well as you and the idea that your supplier can save you costs by falsifying invoices is only asking for trouble. After all, what percentage of your import costs are related to duties? Isn't it ridiculous to corrupt yourself to save pennies and end up with big costs in penalties?

Some of the stories of cost fixing to save duties are insane. A case in point is a long time friend of the author who was fined $250,000 by falsifying invoices and what did he save? Nothing! It cost him his business.

Before 1980 it was hard to receive an invoice from certain countries that was correct. It seemed then the exporters didn't know how to write an invoice for the true amount. All they added was a 'F' by the invoice number shipped with the package then mailed an actual invoice for payment. The penny savings were never justified.

The author imported from Japan in the '70s and never had these problems. There was a different morality. (Or was it government regulation?)

Today's duties for yard goods, emblems and appliques are minimal.

Duty for aetzed embroidery (chemically treated laces) is higher. This is rated as 100% embroidery with no visible ground. The rule for 100% embroidery (with visible ground) is still the same as for normal embroidery, i.e., the only time the 'no visible ground' rule applies is when some costs are involved that can not be seen. Added processes such as the aetzing process which adds value to the product in removing the base cloth, adds unseen value to the embroidery.

Brokers are employed to clear all merchandise, whether shipment is by the Postal Service or by airfreight, all invoices are fed into your Brokers computer which interfaces with the U.S. Customs data bank in Washington, D.C. Once they have all the information and record the receipt of the shipment the formal entry papers can be forwarded to customs for clearance. Then, according to the amount of work they have, the approval can arrive in a matter of hours for your broker to issue the pick up order.

There was some confusion about visa and quotas at times but neither are required for embroidered motifs, emblems etc., as of this writing, the author thinks the system works well.

NEW INTERPRETATIONS OF OLD RULES BY U.S. CUSTOMS

TRADEMARK PROTECTION 1990

Under section 42 of the Lanham Act and section 526 of the Tariff Act, the U.S. Customs Service has responsibility for preventing the importation of goods bearing marks which infringe federally registered marks that have been recorded with it.

Trademark recordation with Customs should be actively considered by all trademark owner's. Because it takes 2 or 3 months for the Customs Service to process the papers, trademark owners should not wait until they encounter a problem with the importation of infringing or counterfeit goods to file.

Recordation of a trademark does not automatically list that mark with the U.S. Customs service. In fact, Customs will not bar the importation of counterfeit merchandise from abroad unless the trademark owner's mark is recorded with them. This is a departure from previous practice in which Customs interpreted that it had the ability and obligation to stop counterfeit or infringing merchandise under the Trademark Act of 1984. This change was made necessary by the Counterfeits Act's failure to make specific provisions for seizures.

To record a federally-registered mark with U.S. Customs Service, the following information should be submitted on a corporate letterhead to:

U.S. Customs Service
1301 Constitution Ave., N.W.
Entry, Licensing and Restricted Merchandise Branch
Room 2417
Washington, DC 20229

Include the following:

1. Registered ownership of the trademark with proof that the registration was issued on the Principal Register.
2. A filing fee of $190.00 per class of goods.
3. Name and address of trademark owner.
4. Those abroad who have the right to use the trademark.
5. The countries approved by the trademark owner.
6. The name and address of those in the U.S. authorized to import such goods.
7. The name and phone number of someone who can be contacted by Customs if questions arise about its importation.

U.S. Customs Service may require you to show proof of your approval to produce a certain licensed embroidery outside the U.S.A. If you are a third party manufacturing for a sales organization, it may be necessary to show written proof from the trademark owner designating you as the manufacturer.

FLAMMABILITY

The Congress of the United States enacted a Consumer Products Safety Act (Public Law 92-573; 15 USC 2051) in 1972. The law confers numerous authorities on the Commission to help marshal the consumer, the business community and public agencies to reduce the risk of injury associated with consumer products. The law specifically prohibits a person from manufacturing for sale, offering for sale, distribution, or importing any item that might prove dangerous to the health and welfare of the public.

Rules have been made which apply to embroidered products. The most important are those that apply to flammable fabrics for infant and children's wear. This includes any hazardous substance which might be toxic by ingestion by children, is corrosive an irritant, combustible, generates pressure through heat or decomposition or by other means.

"Extremely flammable" means any item which has a flash point below -7 degrees C (20 degrees F). "Flammable" covers from -7 degrees C to 27 degrees C (20 degrees F to 80 degrees F). Combustible indicates temperatures from 27 degrees C to 65 degrees C (80 degrees F to 150 degrees F). A test you can conduct yourself will show if the item can be accepted. Try 5 separate samples measuring 8cm x 25cm (3" x 10"). Suspend them vertically in holders in a cabinet and expose them to a small gas flame along the bottom edge for 3 seconds.

The samples can not have a charred length more than 17.5cm (7"); no single specimen can have a charred length more than 25cm (10") or "full burn"; no single specimen can have flaming material on the bottom of the cabinet 10 seconds after the flame is removed. This is required for finished items after one washing and after 50 washings and dryings. Flame resistant does not mean flame proof. It will burn but is able to resist flames better than ordinary fabrics.

Effective July 29, 1972, the law required that all children's wearing apparel (such as nightgowns, pajamas, robes or any garments worn for sleeping) up to and including size 14, comply with the Flammability Act. It excludes diapers and underwear.

This does not include laces and embroideries of individual pieces less than 50cm (2″) in their longest dimension provided that such pieces do not cover more than a total of 130 square cm (20 square inches) of a garment. Continuous embroidered trims are therefore susceptible to the flammability rules if they are edges, borders or flounces. Every textile product sold to the consumer must carry a label giving fiber content and laundering instructions.

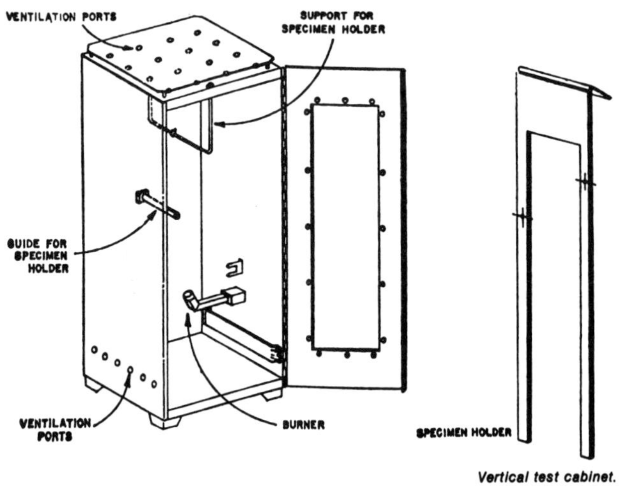

Vertical test cabinet.

CHAPTER XI

EMBROIDERY ASSOCIATIONS

EMBROIDERY TRADE ASSOCIATION

A new trade association formed for the purpose of education and the dissemination of information to operators of Multi-head machines in the U.S.A.

EMBROIDERY PUNCHERS ALLIANCE

Established association of Schiffli punchers, both mechanical and computerized in the New Jersey area.

THE JAPANESE EMBROIDERY ASSOCIATION

The history of Japanese embroidery dates back 1,200 years, to the time it was first imported from China. In the beginning it was used for Buddhist decorations and in the manufacture of the Kimono, the Japanese national costume. Embroidery is still widely employed in the manufacture of these items today.

Minoru Goda, President JEA

After the Meiji revolution, European culture and technology was widely introduced into Japan. At this time, machine embroidery was also introduced into Japan.

After the second World War, there was a vast growth in the Japanese textile industry. It was one of the main factors in the reconstruction of the devastated country. Embroidery was one of the industries which partook in, and benefited from, the tremendous growth. Textile goods, including embroidered laces, were being exported in very large quantities, and at the same time the home market was expanding considerably.

Manufacturers of Kimonos, especially in and around the Kyoto area of Japan, enjoyed a boom in their business.

At the same time, some of these previously very small companies expanded until they became quite major employers in their area with staffs of over 200.

However, fashion, the environment and life styles have changed and the Kimono has become a garment which is usually worn only on special occasions, rather than every day. Coupled with this general change in life style, we have had a continued strengthening in the Japanese economy which has resulted in a very stable, strong Yen. Wages increased, working hours gradually decreased, particularly in the Textile Industry. This, together with very strong competition from N.I.E.S. countries has gradually forced the Japanese textile trade balance into the red. This is a big swing when compared with the postwar years when Japanese textiles were a major source of foreign income for the Japanese economy.

The embroidery industry has not escaped the huge down turn in exports. It now has to create new items and ideas and suggest new usages in order to create and satisfy various needs. The embroidery industry must search for ways in which it can change and improve the character of our life, and add 'class' to the garments we wear and make the wearer feel good about wearing embroidered clothing.

The history of Multi-head embroidery in Japan only dates back about 40 years to 1950 when the first Multi-head embroidery machine was imported from West Germany. The first punching system followed about 2 or 3 years later. It was not until 1963 that the "ELENA" Company succeeded in producing the first, 100% Japanese-made Multi-head embroidery machine. Until this time, the Japanese Multi-head embroidery industry was totally reliant on imported machinery, and delivery time for these West German machines was extremely slow in many cases.

In 1969, the Eltac Company became the first company in the world to introduce the concept of an electronic controlled embroidery machine with an 8 channel tape replacing the 68mm jacquard card and to change the frame movement from a rack and gear system to an electronic motor control. In 1965 the Unitec Company obtained a patent for a Multi needle mechanism and proceeded in producing a viable "automatic color change" system. This system was employed by Barudan in their embroidery machinery. Since these systems were first created and put into practical use, great steps forward have been made by the Japanese embroidery machine makers and now Japanese machines have taken a dominant position in today's market, putting their German competitors in second place.

Because of the new developments made by the Japanese embroidery machine manufacturers, the Japanese embroiderers have benefited considerably because they have been the first to learn about and have access to the latest hardware and softwear. The survival of the Japanese embroiderers depends on their ability to keep up and utilize the latest developments, as well as on the management's ability to ensure that they supply the highest quality goods to the Japanese consumers, who are most probably the most critical in the world. The ability of Japanese management to utilize new equipment, to manage their companies very strictly and maintain high quality will affect embroidery worldwide in the future.

At present, according to the Japanese Embroidery Association, there are 2,145 embroidery companies in Japan.

However, there are about 4,500 embroidery companies listed in the telephone directory! There are an estimated 17,000 sets of Multi-head machines operating in Japan. The total number of employees in embroidery factories is about 23,000. This gives an average of only about 5 employees per company, showing that it is very much a cottage industry here in Japan. The annual turnover in the embroidery market is about 16,800,000,000 Yen. ($112,000,000) — and it is increasing every year. There is very little export of embroidery products from Japan now because of the strong value of the Yen and strong competition from abroad, so the Japanese manufacturers have changed their strategy and are concentrating on promotion of their goods in the local market.

50% of the embroidery market is in the production of apparel, and this percentage is gradually increasing. About 20% of the production is accounted for by emblems and appliques and 30% goes in the production of sundry items.

The embroidery of apparel goods is generally done on a sub-contract basis whereby the apparel makers themselves supply the actual base cloth to the embroiderers. The embroiderers only stitch the embroidery and charge for machine time. It is the Japanese embroiders' purpose to become equal partners with the apparel makers in the 21st century. We want to use our ideas to enable us to cope with the wide variety of items, small lot and short turn around production systems and to become an industry which suggests and innovates style rather than following the styles, trends and ideas of others.

Minoru Goda, *President*
The Japanese Embroidery Association

Minoru Goda, whom the author had the pleasure to meet for the first time in 1974 when he visited his Company in New Jersey, introduced us to Japanese quality embroidered appliques made by Multi-head machines and hot-knife cutting.

The Goda Company was the first to establish, in 1955, a punching center in Japan. Since that time, they have been at the forefront of new developments in embroidery techniques in Japan. They were the first in 1970 to perfect the art of hot knifing with heat seal film. Soon they also added Schiffli machines to their operation, stitching emblems and appliques.

They were the forerunners in automatic finishing applicable to various kinds of embroideries such as laces which did away with the aetzing process or the 'boil away' base materials. They have also developed a method of heat seal application which can be combined with 'non-aetz' finishing. The trade name is "Moko-Moko".

The future of the Japanese Embroidery industry has the cooperation of the Japanese Ministry of Trade and Industry (MITI) to design a new organization for the ordering and production of embroidery. This is known as Embroidery Factory 21, also known as the L.P.U. system; Linkage, Production and Unit system. In the past, embroiderers in Japan have tended to aim more at the export market where emphasis was placed on large production runs and stock items at low prices. Goda believes that more emphasis must now be placed on the local market. The L.P.U. system will enable very quick, efficient production of small orders of high quality goods to be processed. They will work with the original concept of the item to the delivery of the finished product to the customer.

SCHIFFLI LACE & EMBROIDERY ASSOCIATION (U.S.A.)

The Schiffli Lace and Embroidery Association (SLEMA) is an organization that speaks for, and acts in unison, in matters of common interest that affect the well-being of its member companies and the embroidery industry.

SLEMA's purpose is to promote and protect the interests and image of the suppliers of the embroidery industry. It facilitates the development, exchange, and dissemination of information beneficial to that industry.

Collectively, we speak with a more authoritative voice. SLEMA provides a vehicle for networking — sharing non-confidential information directly related to the businesses of the embroidery manufacturing industry. Members can save money by avoiding duplication of effort and achieving economies of scale.

The recent climate of doing business has not been easy. Surely it's better to have colleagues to fight at your side than to try fighting alone, or worse still hide away from the stark realities of business life.

SLEMA'S OBJECTIVES

1. To provide members with services of a kind not possible or affordable on an individual basis.
2. To provide a forum for the exchange of ideas and opportunities for members to discuss business relationships and undertake cooperative projects.
3. To promote and publicize innovations, progress and technology in the embroidery industry.
4. To gather and disseminate information and conduct educational programs to benefit its members and the embroidery industry.
5. To work for the embroidery industry through cooperation with other associations' government agencies and the media to achieve the association's goals and objectives.

A. If you are a member - resolve to become more actively involved.

B. If you are not a member - resolve to join today.

An interesting assistance program is practiced by the American Schiffli Ass'n known as the 'Yarn Exchange'.

SWISS EMBROIDERY ASSOCIATION

Verband Schweizerischer Stickeriei - Fabrikanten
9014 St. Gallen, SWITZERLAND

Officers:

Dr. Adrian Ruesch, St. Gallen	Central President
Erich Ruegg, Kirchberg	1st Vice President
Emil Bickel, Steinebrunn	2nd Vice President
	Section Pres., Thurgau
Max Altherr, Grabs	
Johannes Kuster, Diepoldsau	
Thomas Leemann, Lichtensteig	
Erich Schoenenberger, St. Gallen	
Fredy Weder, Diepoldsau	Section Pres. Rheintal
Paul Wigert, Bazenheid	Section President Wil-Gossau-Toggenburg

Section President Vorderland-Werdenberg:
Max Altherr, Speicher

Revisoren:	Willi Blank, Widnau Rene Kast, Wald Emil Schweizer, Kirchberg
Association Secretary:	Ida Wenger-Baumann, Gossau Waldmannstrasse 6 9014 St. Gallen Switzerland Tel. 071 27 22 33

MANUFACTURING ASSOCIATIONS IN THE U.S.A.

American Apparel Manufacturers Ass'n
American Textile Machinery International
International Textile Machinery Ass'n
Headware Institute of America
National Ass'n of Uniform Mfgs & Distributors
National Knitwear & Sportsware Ass'n
National Sporting Goods Ass'n
Crafted With Pride in the U.S.A. Council.

THE FUTURE

The future holds so much promise for embroidery that we have only scratched the surface of technology that will keep this art form in vogue for many years.

Here is an idea the author has for a machine that he had invested in back in 1968. Call it a fantasy, but he believes there is a great need for such an investment.

Many have tried, Zangs tried to build this as a small Multi-head in 1965, unsuccessfully. Barfuss and Pfaff went a step further with a huge investment and now Tajima, again with a Multi-head machine, are introducing a similar product.

All of those machines could not cover the basic need of the garment industry because they were trying to stitch embroideries with a sewing machine. Yes, in some instances, they have solved some of the problems and are able to serve some industries. But the fashion industry needs a machine which is more versatile and that is still best served by a special stitching of the Schiffli machine.

But the machine he proposes, already exists in the form of a Schiffli machine. The basic reason he chose Schiffli is that it can stitch on most any fabric. That is because of the great control of tensions it has, the "soft" stitch you can effect. It is a true embroidery machine, not a machine adapted to embroidery.

It is becoming ludicrous to continue building Schiffli machines longer and higher with horrendous spanning problems, and so expensive that the field of manufacturers has been severely restricted. It is like building larger and larger guns to shoot further and further when a rocket accomplishes the same with less cost, less weight and more power.

The technology to build what he proposes already exists in part, in the quilting machine, in the Meyer tricot machine and substantially in the existing Schiffli machine.

It would be a boon for the embroidery contractor, just as the Multi-head machine is for frame work and cut parts and finished garments.

The premise of the machine is simple. Just turn the goods around to work from a roll to a roll.

The simplest way to begin is to use the first 3 yards of an existing Schiffli machine, from the automat to the first leg, the same needle bar and tension controls. Stitching could be vertical or horizontal, whichever works best. The machine should run continuously, similar to the Meyer machine goods advancing system, with their hooked side bands. This type of spanning should be sufficient for embroidering piece goods. Automatic color change, thread cutting, scallop cutting and stripping (straight cutting) all included, will simplify the whole operation.

The author is not suggesting that all these parts automatically fit together, he is sure there is much engineering required or it would have happened a long time ago. Just look at the Multi-head machines. In the past 15 years they have permanently taken business and production away from the Schiffli industry. They have added automatic color change, thread trimmers, increased speeds, computerized work stations, etc.

This machine could also be competitive and less expensive. If the machine were able to embroider the widest goods made, for example 120″ tricot fabrics, how much less would it cost to operate? Perhaps more than a 21 yard Schiffli, but unending embroidered goods is an asset to the apparel industry.

The cost savings is in the new machine, 3 yards of machinery instead of 21 yards, 3 yards of needles and bobbins, instead of 42 yards, 3 yards of color change apparatus instead of 42 yards. The engineering of the 15 and 21 yard machines results in so much more machine cost, weight, sophisticated drives, space, etc., that the new machine now becomes an option for the small manufacturer.

The idea is to maintain the "soft stitch" only existing with the Schiffli machine and so essential to the project, and almost impossible to obtain with a Multi-head.

Machines would become available to small contractors just as the Multi-heads have. And give them credit, every Multi-head owner is a promoter of his wares, he advertises to manufacturers and the public, while Schiffli advertising and design are relatively stale in most cases.

This new "dream machine" of the author will cultivate a market for yard goods, put it back in the public eye and bring many new ideas to a field in the doldrums, which has been relying on antiquated design ideas.

Take it from there. . .

Vogtlabdischer Maschinen Fabric, Plauen, Germany

Then after writing this, the author was given some photos from the Voglandische Maschinen Fabric in Plauen, Germany which show that his "Dream Machine" had already been tried in the early 20th century. Instead of one section of the machine with one roll they already used the entire 10 yard machine in this instance, just think of its advantages! It is time to resurrect the ideas and bring them to fulfillment.

APPENDIX

GLOSSARY

ACETATE: A salt or ester of acetic acid of cellulose made into a synthetic filament, yarn, or fabric.

AETZ: The result of the aetzing process, imitation lace made on a Schiffli machine.

AETZING: The process of eliminating the base fabric to make Schiffli laces, leaving only the threads remaining.

ALLOVER: Continuous embroidery which covers all of the goods from selvage to selvage.

APPLIQUES: An embroidered motif, aetzed or cut which can be used as a separate embroidered figure.

AUFSATZ: The last stitch of a design before it repeats itself.

BACK APPLIQUE: A piece of goods used in the back of a design, where the front will be cut away to reveal the fabric in back.

BADGE: An insignia of identification.

BATISTE: A fine, sheer fabric made of cotton and of various fibers.

BLATT STITCH: Wide zig zag stitches laid close together, also known as a satin stitch.

BOBBIN: The back thread used in the shuttle to form the lock stitch.

BOBBIN CASE: The unit holding the bobbin thread of a sewing machine.

BONE: A hard bone or wood used to rub off penciled or charcoal design to fabric for samples, or for enlargements.

BONDING: The joining together of two fabrics permanently with a bonding agent. Heat sealing.

BORE: A sharp pointed instrument used to puncture goods, part of the embroidery machine.

BOUCLE: A yarn with loops producing a rough, nubby appearance on woven or knitted fabrics.

BROADCLOTH: Any fabric woven on a wide loom. A woolen or worsted dress goods fabric constructed in a plain twill weave, having a compact texture and lustrous finish. A closely woven dress goods fabric of cotton, rayon, silk, or mixture of these fibers, having a soft, mercerized finish and resembling poplin.

BUCKRAM: A woven net like fabric with starch used to stabilize fabric for stitching.

BULLION: A hand made emblem, made with brass or silver hollow like thread a product of India or Pakistan. The finished emblem.

BURN OUT LACES: See Aetzing.

CAMBRIC: A thin, plain cotton or linen fabric of fine close weave, usually white, with a high glaze.

CANVAS: A closely woven, heavy cloth of hemp, flax or cotton, used for tents, sails, post office bags, etc.

CARD: A paper tape to control the frame. Various sizes for Schiffli machines, 7 channel for Multi-head.

CARTOON: The enlargement.

CHAIN STITCH: A form of stitch in 3 movements, the automatic formation of the stitch made by a Cornely single head embroidery machine.

CHALLIS: A soft fabric of plain weave in wool, cotton or rayon, either in a solid color or, more often, a small print.

CHAMBRAY: A fine cloth of cotton, silk or linen, commonly of plain weave with colored warp and white weft.

CHENILLE: The chain stitch, forming a large loop on the back of the goods, usually made by the Cornely machine.

CHIFFON: A sheer light weight fabric in silk, nylon, or rayon in plain weave.

CHINTZ: A printed cotton fabric, used especially for draperies, a painted calico from India

COCKADE: an emblem.

CONDENSED FORMAT: The recording of only the points digitized which are later expanded to include all the stitches the machine will stitch in the format required.

CORDUROY: A cotton filling pile fabric with lengthwise cords or ridges

CORD-IN-LAY: A special apparatus to automatically lay on cord or ribbons on a Schiffli machine.

COUPE: One full width of goods either 10, 15 or 20 yards in length.

CREPE: A thin light fabric of cotton or silk or combination, with finely crinkled or ridged surface. Also a silk fabric, usually black, used for mourning veils or bands.

CREPE DE CHINE: A light soft thin silk or rayon fabric with minute irregularities of surface.

CREST: An embroidered motif like an emblem, an insignia or a Coat of Arms.

CRT: see monitor

DAMASK: A reversible fabric of linen, silk, cotton, or wool, woven with patterns.

DENSITY: Amount of stitches per given area.

DESIGNER: The creator of embroidered designs who originates the ideas. Also the enlarger.

DIGITIZER: Equipment on which one digitizes, person punching the pattern.

DISC: Unit inserted into computer containing punched embroidery design, 3.5 inch or 5.25 floppy disc.

DOBBY: Named after an attachment on a loom used in weaving small geometric or floral patterns.

DRILL: A strong, twilled cotton fabric with a diagonal weave similar to denim. Also known as Khaki when dyed that color.

DUCK: A heavy plain weave cotton fabric for tents and clothing.

EMBLEMS: An embroidered design usually worn on outer clothing.

EMERY ROLLER: The Schiffli roller on which the threads are twisted and part of the control of tensions.

ENLARGER: The draftsman or designer who draws the technical drawing for the puncher to follow.

ENLARGEMENT: The technical drawing usually 6 times larger than the original design, indicating the stitches to be digitized.

EPAULET: A badge of identification worn on the shoulder. Sometimes referred to as shoulder boards.

EXECUTION: The amount of stitches per inch.

EXAMINER: The inspector of the finished embroidery.

EXPANDED TAPE: An expanded tape which has every stitch of the design punched.

EYELET: A hole bored into a fabric with reinforced stitching around its edges.

FADENLEITER: Small and large cams of the Schiffli machines used to control the feed and tension of yarns.

FAILLE: A soft transversely ribbed fabric of silk, rayon or lightweight taffeta.

FELT: A nonwoven fabric of wool, fur or hair, matted together by heat, moisture, and great pressure. Melton is an example of felt.

FESTOON: A type of stitch. An apparatus to make reinforced edges on scallops, etc., for a strong cutting edge.

FLANNEL: A warm, soft napped fabric of rayon or cotton blends or cotton warp which resembles wool.

FLOAT: Those stitches made when the needle is disconnected, later removed by thread cutting.

FLOCKING: The decoration of a fabric with a design or lettering using an adhesive and powder through a stencil. Also known as suedene or imitation suede.

FOLLOWING: The directions drawn on the enlargement by the designer as a guide for the puncher's advancement and sequence in punching.

FORMAT: The tape holes of a punching, in a prearranged sequence to conform to the input requirements of a particular computer.

FRAME EMBROIDERY: cut parts or finished garments to be embroidered on a Schiffli machine.

FRAME BOY: A helper in a frame shop to help load and unload frames of a Schiffli machine.

FRENCH INCH: A measurement used for the spacing of needles on the Schiffli machine.

FUNCTIONS: Controls for all apparatus and attachments on the Schiffli machines, other than frame movements.

FUSING: See bonding.

GABARDINE: A firm woven fabric of worsted cotton or spun rayon with a twill weave.

GEFLECT: light or heavy stitching to fill in an area of a design with running stitches.

GEORGETTE: A sheer silk or rayon crepe of dull texture.

GREIGE GOODS: A woven cotton or poly-cotton goods in its natural state before dying or bleaching.

GUIPURE: A lace. (French)

HARDWARE: The computer equipment, monitor, keyboard, digitizer.

HERALDRY: The art and design history of crests.

HOOP: The frame used to hold a span of goods for embroidery on a Multi-head or sewing machines.

INSIGNIA: A design of identification, an emblem or patch.

JACQUARD: The inventor who first used a perforated stencil to control machine functions in the design of woven fabrics.

JERSEY: A knitted fabric of one or more mixtures of wool, cotton, or silks. A plain stitch knitted cloth in contrast to rib-knitted fabric.

JOBBER: See merchandiser.

JUMP STITCH: See float.

KNOCK OFF: The copying of an original design. The cheapening by removing of stitches and or design to produce a less expensive embroidered copy of a design.

LACE: The use of threads alone to produce a designed fabric.

LAME: An ornamental fabric in which metallic threads are woven with silk, wool, rayon or cotton.

LAWN: A thin sheer linen or cotton fabric, plain or printed. Pre-shrunk, crisp & crease resistant.

LINEN: A fabric woven from flax yarns. Often linens, clothing, bedding, etc., made of linen cloth or a more common substitute as cotton. Linen has a natural luster and is soil resistant.

LOCK STITCH: The use of two threads, intertwined to form a lock at close intervals. A stitch used to tie in an end before a jump stitch is made.

LOGO: A trademark or copyrighted design.

LOOM: The Schiffli loom on which the goods is framed to be embroidered.

LOOM RUN: The stitching of one complete pattern in one row on a Schiffli machine.

MACHINE OF GOODS: Two coupes. 20 yards on a 10 yard machine, 30 on 15 or 40 on a 21 yard machine in its full width.

MACRAME: A knotted cotton trimming usually in a geometrical pattern.

MEDALLIONS: see appliques, self contained finished designs.

MENDER: The skilled sewing machine operator who stitches embroidery to repair misses, broken needles or defective areas caused while the machine continued to operate.

MERCHANDISER: A sales organization that buys and sells embroidery, usually it has no embroidery equipment.

MERROW: A type of sewing machine that is used to stitch the overlock edge on emblems.

MICRO-PROCESSOR: Part of a computer to which memory and counting can be added. Computes and processes as required.

MOCCA: Spider web stitching over an eyelet.

MODEM: Unit to telegraphically send computer information from one computer to another.

MOHAIR: A fabric made from yarn of the fleece of the Angora goat.

MOIRE: Any fabric which shows a watery or wavelike appearance, sometimes pressed into the fabric.

MONITOR: The screen on which punching or stitching progress can be followed, stitch by stitch.

MOSS STITCH: Chenille type stitch.

MOTIF: An applique. A single embroidered design.

NEEDLE BAR: A part of the sewing machine to which a needle is attached and driven. The bar on which all the needles are attached on a Schiffli machine. Also known as a needle rack.

NEEDLE ROLLER: The function to connect and disconnect the operation of the needle rack.

OMBRE YARN: Yarn which has been dyed various shades of one color.

ORGANDY: A fine thin cotton fabric usually having a crisp finish, used for blouses and curtains.

ORGANZA: A sheer rayon, nylon, or silk fabric for evening dresses and trims.

OVERLOCK STITCH: See Merrow.

OVERSTITCHING: When the frame moves further than the pattern directs.

OXFORD: A rayon or cotton fabric in plain, twill, or basket weave constructed on a pattern of two fine yarns woven as one in the warp and one loosely twisted yarn woven in the weft.

PANTOGRAPH: An attachment on a Schiffli machine to direct the frame to form the design by hand. A mechanical design to enlarge or reduce a drawing.

PATCHES: Emblems of identification.

PATTERN: The design. card, punching, tape, disc. or enlargement.

PILE: A fabric with a surface of upright yarns, cut or looped, as corduroy, or terry towels.

PIQUE: A fabric of cotton, spun rayon woven lengthwise with raised cords.

PLATINE: The metal fingers which read the tape of mechanical embroidery machines.

PLISSE: A chemical treatment which causes fabric to crinkle.

POPLIN: A finely corded fabric of rayon, cotton, silk, or wool for dresses and draperies.

PRESSER: The fingers which hold the goods steady when the needle penetrates the goods to form the stitch.

PRODUCTION MAN: An employee of the merchandiser who places work with the contractors and oversees production. Common to the American Schiffli industry.

PROGRAMMER: The puncher who cuts tapes for embroidery machines. The one who punches tapes by computer.

PROGRAM TAPE: The computer punching.

PULL THROUGH: Pulling the loop of the first stitch on a Schiffli machine to the back of the goods when the shuttle is in the loop, by opening the shuttle rail, thus leaving no loose ends in the front of the goods at the start.

PUNCHER: The skilled programmer who makes the tapes for embroidery machines.

PUNCHING: The card, tape, program or jacquard that contains the punched directions for the machine to read.

RAM: Random Access Memory, computer chip maintaining memory.

REPEAT: The distance between needles. The point at which the design repeats itself.

RIBBAND: A ribbon or sash worn across the chest.

ROLLOVER: The point at which the goods is shifted (loosened and reset) vertically to continue stitching. Common on long goods Schiffli machines.

RUBBING BONE: see Bone.

SATIN: A closely woven fabric of rayon or silk with a smooth and glossy finish.

SATIN STITCH: A blatt stitch.

SATINET: A low quality cotton satin weave fabric containing cotton.

SCHLAG: The punching mechanism of the mechanical punch machine.

SCRAMBLED EGGS: The embroidery worn on the peak of a cap by high ranking officers of the Navy. Usually an oak leaf cluster.

SCREEN PRINTING: The art of printing design and color to a fabric through a screen.

SEERSUCKER: A plain woven cotton, rayon or linen fabric, traditionally striped cotton with alternate stripes crinkled in the weaving.

SELVAGE: The outer edges of piece goods, usually crimped in some manner to retard fraying.

SHIRTING: any shirt fabric, as broadcloth, or oxford.

SHUTTLE: The metal case holding the bobbin.

SHUTTLE BOX: The part of the Schiffli machine holding the shuttle.

SHUTTLE LATCH: The part of the sewing machine holding the bobbin case.

SHUTTLE RAIL: The rail upon which the shuttle boxes are mounted.

SHUTTLER: The watcher's assistant who helps in loading and unloading, roll overs and filling the shuttles.

SIDE BAND: Extra goods sewn to the selvages and ends of each coupe to allow closer stitching to the edges.

SIDE MOVEMENT: The distance the frame can move horizontally on a Schiffli machine, measured in quarters.

SIDE STICK: Adjustable bars with pins on each end of the Schiffli frame to hang or pin the ends of the goods being spanned.

SILK: The only natural fiber that comes in a filament form. It is woven in a shiny, soft, luxurious fabric.

SINKER: Same as a platine on a Schiffli machine, term used for Multi-head machines.

SIZING: The starching or stiffening of the fabric after stitching to firm the goods for overlocking or to deter fraying.

SKETCHER: The artist who creates embroidered ideas.

SOFTWARE: Computer programs.

SPAN: The prepared goods ready to load the Schiffli machine. It may contain many machines of goods.

SPAN CLOTH: Fabric attached permanently to the roller of the Schiffli machine with pins onto which the fabrics are attached.

SPANNING: The loading of the goods on the frame, placing it under tension preparatory for embroidery.

SPRING STITCH: See float.

STEIL: Small zig zag stitching, straight or curved with the stitches laying close together.

STITCH DOWN: A complete design which is stitched without jump stitches.

STITCH MASTER: The technical person in charge of stitching, responsible for maintenance of equipment, production and quality control.

STITCH OFF: Difficult stitches or too many in one area causing the front or back yarns to break.

STITCH RATE: Price paid for 1000 stitches.

STITCHER: The skilled operator of the pantograph machine. The contractor who manufactures embroidery.

STUMP: Threads that are not trimmed properly, leaving a small end of thread.

STUMP WORK: Embroidery filled with cotton etc., full three dimensional work with added wood, mirrors, semi-precious stones, usually hand made. An extension of trapunto.

STUPFEL: An attachment to clean out holes after boring.

SUEDE: A flocked or brushed cotton, imitating suede leather.

SUEDENE: same as suede.

SWAP AXIS: The reversing of the X and Y directions of the punched tape.

SWATCH: A piece of fabric, embroidery or yarn.

SWING: The frame movement caused by the punching.

TACKLE TWILL: A tight woven twill with a satin finish.

TAFFETA: A smooth crisp, lustrous fabric of acetate, nylon, rayon, or silk in plain weave. Any of various other fabrics of silk, wool, linen in use at other periods of history.

TAPE: punching in paper form.

THREAD CUTTING: The removal of floats, by hand or machine.

THROUGH MISS: A mistake in design or punching where a part of the design was left out.

TIE IN: See lock stitch.

TOURS: The travel stitches drawn and punched to pick up parts of the design and show a recommended following.

TULLE: A thin, fine net of acetate, nylon, rayon, or silk, for millinery, dress good or the embroidery of imitation laces.

VARIEGATED: The dying of yarns with 3 or more colors in one spool.

VELVET: A pile fabric of silk or nylon, etc., with a soft, deciduous covering of a growing antler. When the pile is more than ⅛″ in height the cloth is called plush.

VELVETEEN: A cotton fabric with a short pile, resembling velvet.

WATCHER: The operator of the Schiffli machine who sets the pattern, twists the yarns, maintains the shuttles, loads and unloads the machine, performs the roll overs and watches for thread and needle breakage. The machine operator.

WORSTED: Finely twisted yarn of thread spun from combed, staple wool fibers of the same length for weaving, or knitting. Wool cloth woven from such yarns, having a hard, smooth surface and no nap.

YARD RATE: Rates paid to stitchers per yard of finished embroidery. Used generally when labor cost is greater than stitching time.

ZARI BADGES: See Bullion emblems.

PHOTO CREDITS

Cover: Electronic Component:
Ultramatic
Dressing Component:
C. Schneider
Threads: *Robison Anton, Chenille Prod.*
Photo: *Alphons Endler*

Handloom Machine 19
Gaechter, Hohenems
Austrian Embroidery Ass'n

Shuttle 21
Saurer

Groebli's Single Needle Demonstration Model 22
Austrian Embroidery Ass'n

Lock Stitch 23
Drawing: Coleman Schneider

Alphonse H. Kursheedt 24
Swiss Embroidery Ass'n

Isaac Groebli 24
Swiss Embroidery Ass'n

J. Arnold Groebli 24
Swiss Embroidery Ass'n

Saurer Cam Disc Machine 25
Saentis Inc.

Handloom Stitcher and Spanners at Work 26
Herb Petermann

The Groebli Automat 27
C. Schneider
Comet Embroidery

Robert Zahn 28
Robert Reiner, Inc.

10 Yard Schiffli Plauen Pantograph Machine 29
Robert Reiner, Inc.

John Hewetson 32
Hewetson Embroidery Works

Kappel Schiffli Machine with Automat 33
Bowman Lace & Embroidery Trade

Saurer 2S55 15 yard Machines 41
Swiss Embroidery Ass'n

Barfuss Machine 42
Pfaff

Pfaff Continuous Length Schiffli Machine 43
Pfaff

Flow Chart, Continuous Embroidery, Pfaff Machine 43
Pfaff

The Flow of Yarn on the Schiffli Machine 47
Drawing: C. Schneider

Plauen Mechanical Automat 50
Comerio Ercole

Saurer Mechanical Automat 51
Saurer Ltd.

The End of the Mechanical Automat 52
Comerio Ercole

Computer Aided, Hydraulic Drive, Schiffli Automat 53
Comerio Ercole

Comerio Ercole 15 yard Schiffli Machine 55
Comerio Ercole

Comerio Ercole Futura 56
Photo: C. Schneider, Kalish, Poland.

Hydraulic Drive with Servo Motors 56
Photo: C. Schneider, Kalish, Poland.

3.5″ Disc, the New Punching 56
Comerio Ercole

Color Change Device 57
Photo: C. Schneider, Kalish, Poland.

Hiraoka Mechanical 15 Yard Schiffli 58
Hiraoka Kogyo

Hiraoka Computerized 15 Yard Schiffli 59
Hiraoka Kogyo

BIBLIOGRAPHY

Bowman's Lace & Embroidery Trade, 1st Edition, Bowman Publishing, 1920

Bowman's Lace & Embroidery Trade, 2nd Edition, Bowman Publishing 1920

Clark, W.A. Graham, Swiss Embroidery & Lace Industry. Washington, D.C., U.S. Gov't Printing Office 1908

The Complete Encyclopedia of Needlework. The deDillmont Running Press 1972

Consumer Product Safety Act. Washington, D.C. Consumer Product Safety Commission, 1972

Cuthbert, Norman, Lace Makers Society. Derry & Sons Ltd. 1960

Dictionary of Textile Terms
Dan River, Greenville, S.C.

Die Schiffi Machine, Germany, Herrenzuelis & Co. 1915

Grosvenor, Gilbert H., Insignia of the Armed Forces. Washington, D.C., National Geographic Magazine June 1943

Guide to Fabric Flammability, Washington, D.C., Consumer Product Safety Commission, 1976

Importing into the United States, Dept of the Treasury United States Customs Service, Washington, DC 1990

Jones, Mary Eiriven, A History of Western Embroidery Great Britain, Studies Vista, Ltd. 1969

Jopp, Keith, The Hewetson Story, 1958

Kellner's Official Statistics,
1919 Ludwig Kellner, Author and Publisher

Lawton, Clifford
The Lace & Embroidery Review, Switzerland

Lefebure, Ernst,
Embroidery and Lace, J.P. Lippincott Co. 1889

Lisi, Vgo J.
The Schiffli Embroidery Industry in the USA (Thesis) 1950

Moser, J., Industrie & Gerwerbe Museum, St. Gallen Switzerland 1898

Pallsor, Bury, A History of Lace, Sampson Law and Son, & Marston 1869

Risley, Christine, Machine Embroidery, Charles T. Branford Co., 1961

The Robert Reiner Importing Co., Weehawken, NJ Robert Reiner Inc., Publisher 1914

Schneider, Coleman, Machine Made Embroidery. Author & Publisher, Globe Litho, 1968

Embroidery: Schiffli & Multi-head, Author & Publisher, Qualigraphics, Inc. 1978

Schoener, Fritz, Stickerei. Leipzig, Fachbuchverlag 1963

Stitches Magazine, Weisner Publications, 1991

Stumpwork Society Chronicle, Sylvia Fishman, 1991

USTA Bulletin, Vol 45 No. 48 Copyright 1990

INDEX

T

U

V

ABOUT THE AUTHOR

Coleman "Coke" Schneider was born in Union City, N.J. He attended local schools and excelled in drafting which was to be an asset later in life.

Anticipating the draft during World War II, he applied and was accepted to the United States Merchant Marine Academy at Kings Point, NY.

Sailing as a cadet/midshipman in 1943, on his first ship, the Jeremiah O'Brien (which is now a National Monument located in San Francisco), he crossed the North Atlantic 8 times while studying a sea course. Back at the Academy in NY again, he graduated and sailed as third and second Mate on various ships, even gaining a NY Harbor 1st Class, unlimited tonnage Pilot license.

His first employment in 1945 was as a draftsman but with the lure of better pay he accepted a job as a learner watcher on a Groebli Schiffli frame machine.

After one year, he leased his employer's factory in 1947 and began contracting various embroidery stitching. The company was known as "C. Schneider Embroideries" and consisted of 4 10 yard Schiffli machines stitching cut parts such as lingerie, panties, half slips and blouses.

Embroidery was good for a time but reverted to depression days again in 1949/50. Having learned Groebli punching in a leased shop, he decided to go into the punching and designing business. His total instruction on Saurer and

Plauen lasted for 1 hour, but the process was similar to the Groebli. Designing was natural to him, part drafting, in which he was proficient, and part free hand, which came naturally. His father-in-law was a Swiss designer, therefore any design problems could be easily solved.

Building a design and punching business meant competition with long established studios. The youngest designer in the U.S. was 30 years older than he. Punchers were not considered proficient until they had at least 30 years experience.

The only thing he could offer besides hard work was service. The standard at the time was one week for a cartoon (enlarged drawing) and another for the punching, if the puncher liked you.

He would offer the service in one or two days, drawing the design in the evenings and punching long hours during the days. He tells of having a stitcher come into the office, crying that his machine was stopped and he badly needed the tape. Mr. Schneider told him to have a cup of coffee and return in an hour, and the tape was ready.

Soon, more than 22 designers and 7 punchers were employed, punching Plauen, Saurer, Groebli and Multi-head tapes. (He began punching for Gross machines in 1952). The company was known as "C. Schneider International". Business was good until the middle 60's when it once again went into a recession. Cutting tapes for many foreign accounts keep things going until 1970.

As business slowed in the 60's he became an agent for Zangs and Marco Multi-head embroidery machines in the U.S.A.

Mr. Schneider was continually asked questions about embroidery from those starting embroidery businesses in other countries. He thought he would put it all down in the form of a book and published his own writings in 1968.

Design awards were won in 1969 and 1970, Man of the Year followed in 1971 from the Schiffli Industry and in 1972 from the Embroidery Salesmen's Association.

His most famous original creation, widely used and copied design was the Captain patch worn by people all over the world.

Another record he set in the late 1970's was publication of a small CB bible, a book for CB operators which sold 200,000 copies.

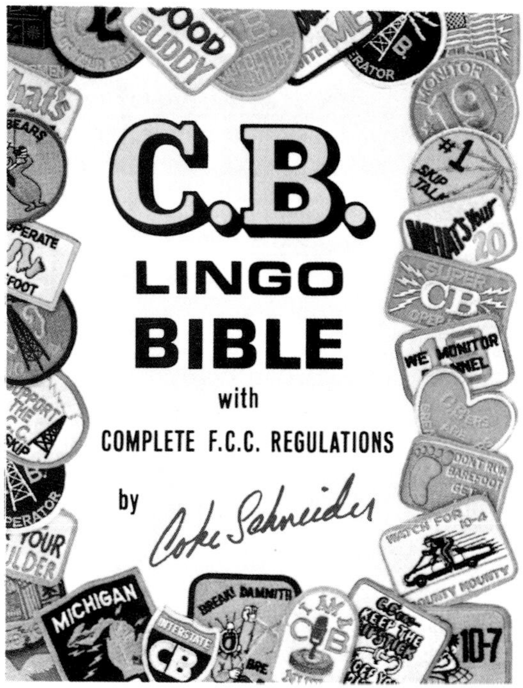

He started work on the first computer for punching tapes in 1967 (completed in 1976). He also sold the first 13 computer punch systems built for Schiffli and Multi-head machines in 1977.

For 3 years, he taught embroidery design at the Fashion Institute of Technology in New York.

He formed a new company known as The All American Emblem Company in 1968, and as President built it into the largest stock embroidery company in the U.S.

In 1976 he commissioned a film on Schiffli embroidery entitled "Stitches in Time" which was shown internationally. In 1978, he wrote his second book on embroidery; "Embroidery: Schiffli and Multi-head." 3000 copies were sold in 35 countries. More than 100 unfilled orders exist as of this writing.

In 1982 he sold his interest in the All American Co. and formed a new embroidery organization known as AA World Class Embroidery. This company's sales are based on service and quality and it is the leading embroidery custom and stock house in the U.S.A. He is C.E.O.

A new book was required since there was an explosion in embroidery technology in the 1980's. This new work is once again being published by the author.

This book represents another step in the life of a very prolific personality in the Embroidery Industry. His achievements include designing and punching (2 separate professions at the time), developing the first computerized punch system, receiving many awards for outstanding contributions to the industry, teaching, and writing and publishing of the first definitive work on embroidery, which became the world standard. He has gone on to write the second and third books, making up to date information available to the embroidery industry.

The reward is the knowledge gained daily, working in a rewarding industry that he loves.

He says, those who wish to gain similar rewards need only understand that hard work pays off and doing something you enjoy makes it so much easier.

There have been few disappointments in the many years of association with embroidery that haven't been overcome with success. Each day brings new problems to solve and each day is better than the last, he says.

The embroidery industry has only begun to use and appreciate the electronics that are available, and so much more will be developed and added in the future. His only hope is that all the hard work of the past, that opened the door to today's achievements is not forgotten. He feels there is so much artistic ability which is being usurped by computers, however, he hopes that too will become part of the programming, but will it be much fun to reproduce Rembrandt by computer? or is it even possible?

He says: "What's left for me? A little relaxation, time to go back to flying again, but never, ever retiring!"

SUPPLEMENT

The advancement in Embroidery technology has been so rapid that this book had to be updated 2 weeks after it was off the press. In order to bring the embroiderer up to date, for the balance of this year at least, this supplement was prepared and added to the book before distribution.

SUPPLEMENT CONTENTS

COMERIO ERCOLE: A new color change attachment was recently developed by the Comerio company which adds more needle and bobbin color and design changes through the use of their new Futura Computerized Machine controls.

The system allows selection of individual needles from all points of the needle bar to work in tandem or separately from one another, likewise the borers can be programmed in the same manner. The design possibilities are enormous. The parts can be easily programmed for 4/4 or a flick of the switch and they are 12/4 etc., meanwhile needles can be used in broken repeats of 2 needles 4/4, space 3 needles 4/4, 2 needles 8/4 or any combination. Each needle and border can be programmed individually.

SAURER TEXTILE SYSTEM: 2040 5 yard sampler was recently demonstrated at the ITMA Fair in Hanover, Germany where it was erected. The sampler stitched at 270 r.p.m. with small stitches in automatic color change mode. Larger models of the 2040 stitch at lower speeds; 10 yd. at 220; 15 yd. at 200 and 21 yd. at 180. Likewise the speed would be dependent on the pattern used, the larger the stitches the more reduction of speed is required.

MULTI-HEAD

BARUDAN: Has just introduced a single take up lever for each color and needle. The competitors felt they had an advantage because of the one take up lever used in the past, now they have to find another complaint, but there is none. The machine stitched well at the Bobbin Show and ITMA at 850 stitches per minute.

Model BEMS (without monitor) Standard Head

Heads	**Colors**	**Head Spacing**	**Continuous Border**	**S.P.M.**
8		380	320 x 3040	
10		380	320 x 3800	
10		480	320 x 4800	
12 (WF)		300	320 x 3600	
12	YF--5	380	320 x 3840	200-900
15	YS--7	320	320 x 4800	
17 (WF)		240	320 x 4080	
17		320	320 x 5440	
20 (WF)		240	320 x 4800	

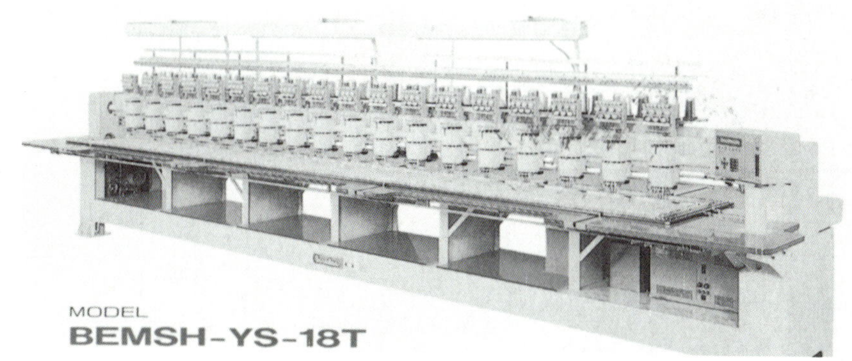

Model BEMSH (with monitor) Bridge Machine

Heads	Colors	Head Spacing	Continuous Border	S.P.M.
10		480	450 x 4800	
12 (WF)		300	450 x 3600	
12		400	450 x 4800	
15	YF--5	350	450 x 5250	
17 (WF)		240	450 x 4080	200-900
17	YS--7	300	450 x 5100	
18		300	450 x 5400	
20 (WF)		240	450 x 4800	

Measurements in mm

Orders will be received for the single take-up machines for all models in their current program.

HAPPY: Has added a cylinder head machine to their line, Model HMC, which is supplied in all sizes as Happy machines listed on page 99. Additionally, all stitching areas have been enlarged to 300 x 330mm. Automatic color change remains at 8. Recommended speeds are 300-700 spm.

Although cap devices are not supplied for this machine, those of other manufacturers are compatible.

GUNOLD+STICKMA: New Model GT 116 sample machine is built in one and two head models. It can be your next sample machine or ideal for monogramming. The machines are fully programmed for all phases of lettering with state-of-the-art computer technology. Five alphabets can be managed at one time and can be adjusted in 1mm increments for size, or radius, results can be adjusted via the monitor.

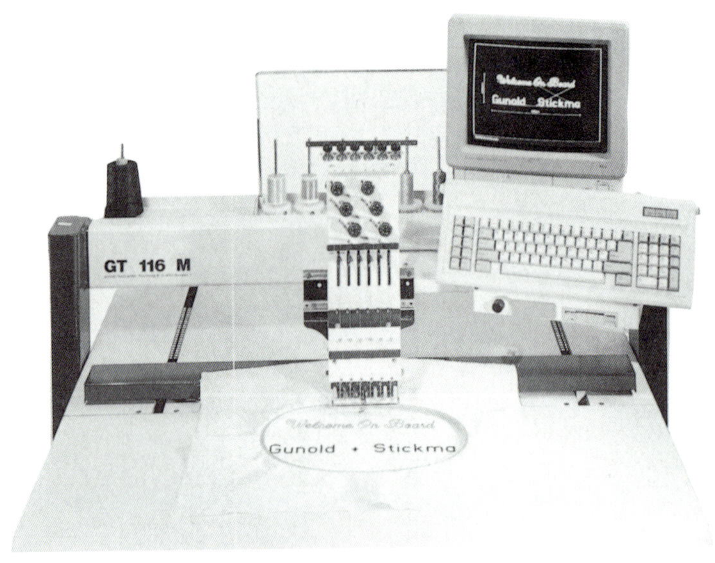

MARCO TRADING GmbH: Has developed a 12 color automatic color change known as the "Berlin". This new computerized Multi-head is being developed in the following sizes:

Model	Heads	Colors	Head Distance	Border
12-108	8	12	595	540 x 4760
12-110	10	12	463.5	540 x 4635
12-112	12	12	410	540 x 4920
12-114	14	12	347	540 x 4858
9-108	8	9	595	540 x 4760
9-110	10	9	463.5	540 x 4635
9-112	12	9	410	540 x 4950
9-114	14	9	347	540 x 4858
9-116	16	9	300.5	540 x 4808
9-118	18	9	265.5	540 x 4779
6-108	8	6	595	540 x 4760
6-110	10	6	463.5	540 x 4635
6-112	12	6	410	540 x 4920
6-114	14	6	347	540 x 4858
6-116	16	6	300.5	540 x 300.5
6-118	18	6	265.5	540 x 4779
6-120	20	6	237.5	540 x 4750

POINTEX: A small Italian company that supplies single head machines. Model BME M4 a single head machine for moss, chain stitches and braiding, tape attachment and other fancy stitching.

SAURER TEXTILE SYSTEMS: A new sewing head has been substituted for all previous Melco heads supplied by Tajima. A new chenille head has been substituted for the Model OS1. The quality of the chenille produced has vastly improved. It is indicative of Saurer to continue to improve the Melco line by improving quality, production and customer usage.

TAJIMA: Model TMLG-G112 Standard and Specialty embroideries for coiling using the special jumbo rotary hooks. Normal or coiling stitching available with various size yarns, ribbons, etc.

Model TMLG-100 and L00 include the zig-zag stitching for tacking all kinds of novelty yarns, ribbons, tapes, heavy cords etc. to form all kinds of designs, limited only by the designer's imagination. For 2 color stitching the TMLG-L00 joins 2 heads that work in sequence to form designs in two color without color changing or changing the novelty trims.

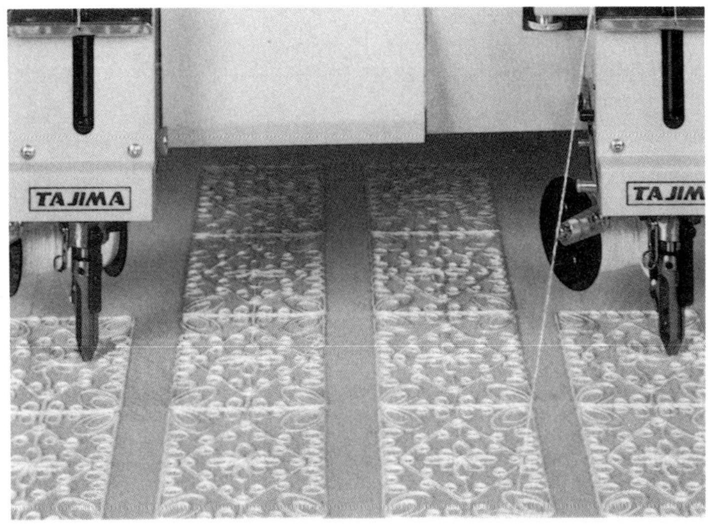

TMLG-100 Series

Heads	Emb. Space
6	680 x 550
8	680 x 500
10	680 x 400
12	680 x 345

TMLG-L00

Heads	Emb. Space
12	680 x 600
16	680 x 500
16	680 x 550

Measurements in mm

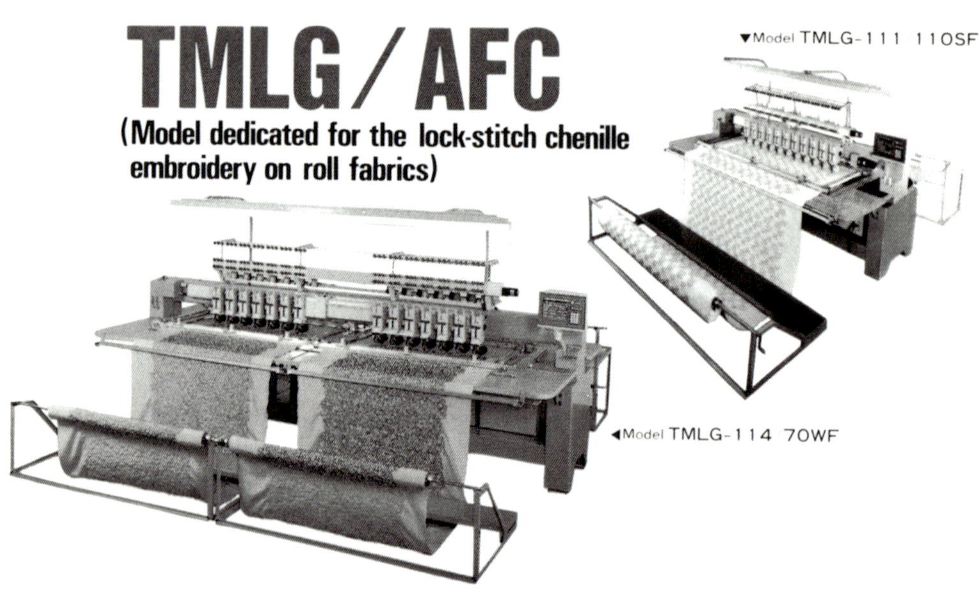

Model TMLG/AFC dedicated machine for lock stitch chenille for yard goods.

	Heads	Head Interval	Maximum Fabric Width
TMEG/AFC-100WF			
	24	135.4 mm	1524 mm (60″)
TMSEG/AFC-160SF			
	16	135.4 mm	2325 mm (92″)
Model TMLG/AFC-110SF			
	11	135.4 mm	1850 mm
Model TMLG/AFC-70WF			
	14	135.4 mm	1200 mm

ZSK STITCHTRONIC: Has recently introduced its 11 automatic color change machine along with a multitude of new advances in fashion attachments.

Model	Heads	Needles	Field Depth	Border Length
M 0807/0809/0811	8	7/9/11	500	3960
M 1007/1009/1011	10	7/9/11	500	4000
M 1207/1209	12	7/9	500	3960
L 1007/1009/1011	10	7/9/11	500	4800
L 1207/1209/1211	12	7/9/11	500	4800
L 1507/1509	15	7/9	500	4950
L 1807	18	7/9	500	4950
L 2007	20	7	500	4800
X 1207/1209/1211	12	7/9/11	500	6000
X 1507/1509/1511	15	7/9/11	500	6000
X 1807/1809	18	7/9	500	5940
X 2007/2009	20	7/9	500	6000
X 2607	26	7	500	6240

The new Model 'X' has an expanded embroidery field. All machines are equipped with thread monitor, automatic thread trimmers for upper and lower threads and modified take up lever for 'soft' embroidery.

Sequin Attachment

Monogram Embroidery

Cord/Loop Embroidery

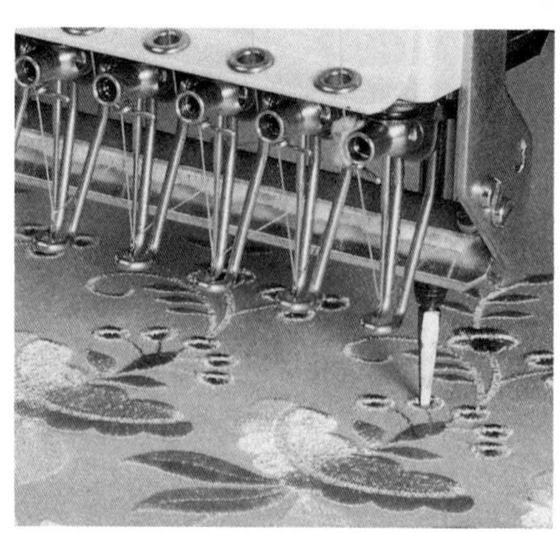

Boring Embroidery

Cord Embroidery

New Chain Stitch Machine Model, ZSK CS
CS 601-550, 6 heads 1 color Emb Field 3200 x 500
CS 801-400, 8 heads 1 color Emb Field 3200 x 500
Each head is independently controlled.
Program controlled thread tensioning.
Adjustable moss stitch loops.
Electronically adjustable coiling density.
Control unit with color monitor.

What is the advantage of building 12, 11 or 9 color automatic change embroidery machines? After all, how often will you have orders for 12 colors? However, once you thread up your most used colors it will seldom require more than one or two changes between orders.

Programming should always use the same sequence of colors so when one order is completed, you can follow with the next order in sequence. Set-up time is greatly reduced. The machines are set to run any sequence of colors, as an example: you could run the sequence 2 9 6 3 12 for the fixed colors you may need for an order, then go immediately with the next order to a different sequence, without threading.

COMPUTER EQUIPMENT

GEMINI: An Italian computer system for Schiffli machines which is IBM PC 386 or 486 capable, 16 Mob basic RAM + 6 Mob RAM for the graphic card with a Mitsubishi 19″ color monitor.

It is possible to connect with any peripheral unit: Digitizer, Drafting Machine, Tape Punch, Puncher, Plotter, Scanner, Color Printer, Modem, Color Scanner, Embroidery Machine.

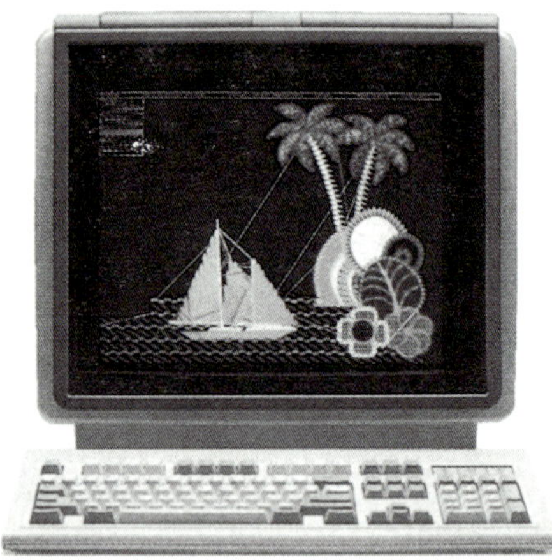

Software includes: Automatic shorting of stitches for curved lines for perfect density.

Shortened stitches.

Deletion of too short stitches in old programs.

Automatic addition or removal of underlay stitches.

Automatic stitch pull compensation according to parameters set depending on fabric employed.

Special fill by expansion: New method avoids fabric folds. Internal jagging to avoid cuts on delicate fabrics.

Including many special features for Schiffli embroidery of delicate fabrics. Fill stitches of wave, wave slant, arched, double arched, parallel, fills highlighting internal shapes, fills combining satin and fill stitch.

Automatic internal shading, possibility of creating personalized menu with all commands or sequenced commands.

Help key and menus in 5 languages.

Also included are the common programs of arching, reverse arching, rotation, enlarging, reduction, complete control and changes of densities.

Scanning has improved and becomes part of the Gemini punching system.

GUNOLD+STICKMA: Is now offering its proven Schiffli embroidery punch system which has had in-house testing and is now ready for installation. Conversion of Saurer and Plauen tapes are available.

PROEL: The Artista is a multi-head punch system with 286 or 386 computer IBM compatible with 16 MHz, 40 Mbytes hard disc utilizing a 3.5″ disc or tape. The menu has 49 selectable functions.

This unit is capable of creating all types of stitches, tacking, single and double satin stitches, special motifs, background fills, personal creations can be added to memory.

Editing, density control, size control, lettering and monograms in straight lines, curves, reverse curves, circles, unlimited reprocessing of any type embroideries generated by other computers. Conversion of all tapes to 3.5″ diskettes.

Menu in operator selectable languages.

SAURER TEXTILE SYSTEMS shows advances in programming that have been continuously added to their Semco Schiffli system and combined with Multi-head use, now offers a complete embroidery machine programming system for any machine. Their Melco system has been integrated partially into the Semco. Melco is still available for Multi-head. Demonstrated Scanner possibilities for the Saurer make their use ever more important for punching. The future here eliminates the enlarger altogether. The art is left to the artist, the programmer now becomes the sole creator of the pattern.

ZSK Schiffli punching system, capable of punching and storing 35,000 to 40,000 stitches per minute to a 3.5″ disc. Electropneumatic card puncher for Plauen and Saurer machines. Cards can be punched in their original format 600 stitches per minute for mechanical tape readers. Eight channel tape input is optional.

The new punch system 185HP332 offers expanded possibilities for parallel step stitch for shadow effects and curved step stitch fills, boll effects similar to French knots and dots, rosettes, etc. Step stitch lines for special effects. This HP computer can maximize output to 50,000 stitches per second.

The CSCII system/CSCII Punch expansion for compiling, processing and managing designs has a computer memory of 8 Mbytes with options of 96 Mbytes and 383 Mbytes for hard disc capacity. This allows multitasking with new software which includes:

Color graphics design data and backup.

Editing modifications and amendments.

New types of design processors for stitch and reference data.

Background multitasking for different modes, such as input/output on tape, disc, plotter, printer, etc.

Networking of 16 embroidery machines.

Modem transfer.

SUPPLIERS

MADIERA introduces a new dyed yarn that is affected by light, the name CHAMELEON tells it all. When exposed to sunlight the colors will change. Available in Blue, Pink, Purple and Turquoise.

LIOKUJI LMCE-109 is the newest automatic laser cutter designed for fast cutting of embroideries, borders, intricate shapes and interior shapes.

The Laser cutter with computer imaging will cut a series of emblems from one piece of goods even if each emblem is slightly different. The parameters are read independently. If there are slight differences in each emblem it will find the right line to cut upon so each is cut properly.

The process now works within 1/16″ of your desired size which is excellent for items being merrowed. Work is continuing to bring the cut closer to the actual embroidery as a hot knife would cut.

It saves the cost of cutting dies and set up of the cutting is easily learned.

Don't be fooled by the photo of the unit, it weighs more than 2000 lbs.; it measures 5′ x 4′ x 4′, and also included is a computer numerical control system. Sizes up to 20″ x 21½″ can be cut.

It is a big boost for the woven label industry at present.

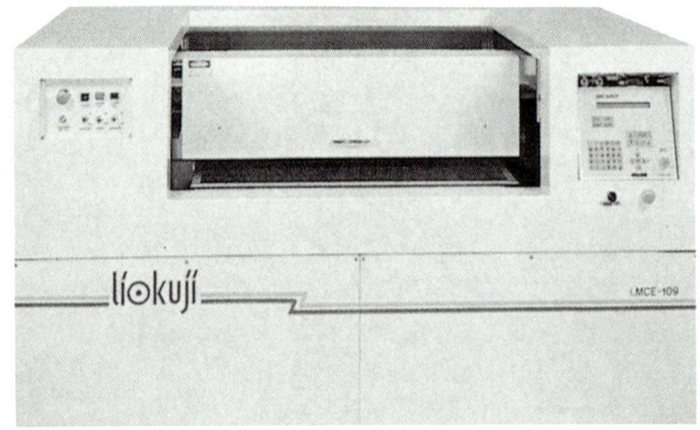

POINTEX is another advanced laser cutting machine whose principal size and abilities match the Liokuji laser machine. It is the wave of the future, and with refinements this is the way emblems, appliques and labels will be cut in the future.

ADDRESSES AND CHANGES

New Address:
Embroidery Educational Services Intl.
7996 Simfield Rd.
Dublin, OH 43017
Tel 614 889 4992
FAX 614 889 4992

P & W Technic Corp.
4F, 33 Chung Chen N Rd.
San Chung, Taipei, Taiwan
Tel 2 982 1920
FAX 2 984 9630

Pointex
Via Combattenti 15
24060 Credaro, Italy
Tel 035 989651
FAX 035 929171

Western Textile Products
Poly Twills
3400 Tree Court
St. Louis, MO 63122
Tel 314 225 9400
FAX 314 225 9854

New Address:
Saurer Textile Systems Charlotte
P. O. Box 668027
Charlotte, NC 28266
Tel 704 394 8111
FAX 704 394 9802

Tajima 9 Color Change

ZSK Cord & Metallic

Marco 12 Color Change

Happy Expanded Area

Barudan Embroidery on Print